CW01091579

Disaster Archipelago

Disaster Archipelago

Locating Vulnerability and Resilience in the Philippines

Edited by
Maria Carinnes P. Alejandria and Will Smith

LEXINGTON BOOKS
Lanham • Boulder • New York • London

Published by Lexington Books
An imprint of The Rowman & Littlefield Publishing Group, Inc.
4501 Forbes Boulevard, Suite 200, Lanham, Maryland 20706
www.rowman.com

6 Tinworth Street, London SE11 5AL, United Kingdom

Copyright © 2020 The Rowman & Littlefield Publishing Group, Inc.

All rights reserved. No part of this book may be reproduced in any form or by any
electronic or mechanical means, including information storage and retrieval systems,
without written permission from the publisher, except by a reviewer who may quote
passages in a review.

British Library Cataloguing in Publication Information Available

Library of Congress Cataloging-in-Publication Data

ISBN: 978-1-4985-6993-4 (cloth)
ISBN: 978-1-4985-6994-1 (electronic)

Names: Alejandria-Gonzalez, Maria Carinnes P., 1983- editor. | Smith, Will
    (Anthropologist), editor. | Piepiora, Zbigniew. At a glance.
Title: Disaster archipelago : locating vulnerability and resilience in the Philippines /
    edited by Maria Carinnes P. Alejandria-Gonzalez and Will Smith.
Description: Lanham : Lexington Books, 2019. | "This project is the result of discussions
    between anthropologists working on issues of environment and disaster in the
    Philippines at the American Association of Asian Studies annual conference in
    2017"—Introduction. | Includes bibliographical references and index. |
    Summary: "This interdisciplinary collection examines the complex nature of
    disaster—typhoons, floods, earthquakes, and drought—in the Philippines. The
    contributors analyze the challenges of the country's internal heterogeneity of
    language, ethnicity, and class and its effect on responses to natural disaster"—
    Provided by publisher.
Identifiers: LCCN 2019040003 (print) | LCCN 2019040004 (ebook) |
    ISBN 9781498569934 (cloth) | ISBN 9781498569941 (epub)
Subjects: LCSH: Natural disasters—Philippines—Management. | Natural disasters—
    Social aspects—Philippines. | Natural disasters—Philippines—Psychological
    aspects. | Disaster relief—Social aspects—Philippines. | Disaster relief—
    Philippines—Psychological aspects. | Resilience (Personality trait)—Philippines.
Classification: LCC HV555.P6 D57 2019(print) | LCC HV555.P6(ebook) |
    DDC 363.3409599—dc23
LC record available at https://lccn.loc.gov/2019040003
LC ebook record available at https://lccn.loc.gov/2019040004

Contents

Acknowledgments

This volume was produced in response to a panel organized around ethnographic approaches to disaster in the Philippines at the 2017 Association for Asian Studies annual conference in Toronto, Canada. Though the scope of the book has expanded considerably, the volume remains dedicated to the critical orientation of original panelists. As such, the editors would like thank the original contributors and our discussant, Noah Theriault, who have kindly extended their work into this volume. We also gratefully acknowledge the Philippine Studies Group for their sponsorship which made this panel possible.

We would like to acknowledge the financial assistance of the Alfred Deakin Institute at Deakin University and the Research Center for Social Sciences and Education at the University of Santo Tomas, which helped support the finalization of the volume. We would also like to recognize the linkage and promotion of this book through the Brown International Advanced Research Institute (BIARI) Philippines which was co-organized by Brown University and the Philippine Disaster Resilience Foundation through the leadership of Alfredo Ayala, Guillermo Luz, and Adam C. Levine.

The editors are grateful for the assistance of Michele O'Toole for her close reading of the volume's earlier drafts. Technical and editorial assistance were provided by Tisha De Vergara and Phamella Edralin for the proofing and indexing of the final drafts.

We are also indebted to the detailed and constructive commentary of two anonymous reviewers. We would also like to thank our endorsers Adam C. Levine, Vincenzo Bolletino, and Wolfram Dressler.

Introduction

Place, Politics, and Disaster in the Philippines

Will Smith

Images of calamity in the Philippines circulate globally as an important part of disaster discourses; witness, for example, internationally broadcasted video footage of flooded streets in the aftermath of powerful cyclones, colonial-era Spanish churches crumbled by earthquakes or the enduring connection between the Philippines and contemporary volcanic disaster such as the Mt Pinatubo eruption. Exploring Filipino experiences of disaster, a nation often considered one of the most vulnerable to environmental change by variety of global standards, should therefore be an important concern for disaster studies scholars. However, seeking out Filipino experiences of disaster confronts the challenge of internal heterogeneity and national contradictions of ethnicity, language, wealth, and class. The global circulation of disaster imagery, often mere snippets in news broadcasts or static images on a website, works to erase this variation. What, then, can be said of Filipino experiences of disaster? This book seeks to address this question by engaging the specificities of place amid diversity, and in doing so explores two broad but interrelating avenues of investigation: How can environmental extremity in the Philippines help us understand disasters? How can disasters help us understand the Philippines?

There is a wide body of international disaster literature that grapples with issues of place and disaster. Certain places and events have become the enduring locus of attention for disaster scholarship and have often come to constitute minor sub-fields in and of themselves: the droughts of the "African Sahel" (Glantz 1976; Franke and Chasin 1980); the vast "Asia-Pacific" (Sakai et al. 2014); the impact of Hurricane Katrina on New Orleans (SSRC 2006). In critical permutations of this scholarship, a focus on place does the work of considering diverse but malleable environmental processes in relation to contingent political and economic histories. This is very much the approach that frames this volume, but perhaps one area of departure is a consideration of the way that disasters occur, are produced and imagined in relation to *nation*, rather than region or city. As this introduction sketches out, there are few other countries where disaster is as deeply embedded in national identities and histories, routinized political practice and discourse or imagined within international regimes of aid and governance. Bringing nationhood implicitly and explicitly into conversation with disaster opens up a host of novel questions and problems that I tentatively point to below. To be clear, this is not an effort to formulate a general understanding of how disaster and nationhood work in relation to one another. There are no totalizing theories to be found. Instead, disasters in the Philippines reveal both the strains of a still-ongoing project of nation building and, at the same time, suggest a remarkable durability in the face of rapid environmental change.

This project is the result of discussions between anthropologists working on issues of environment and disaster in the Philippines at the American Association of Asian Studies annual conference in 2017. While the scope of the book has broadened beyond a solely ethnographic focus to include sociological, policy and practitioner perspectives, it remains grounded in an effort to illuminate the diversity of experiences with disaster in the Philippines—particularly among those who remain marginalized from dominant understandings of disasters and yet are often the most adversely impacted, such as the elderly, children, poorer communities, indigenous peoples and other ethnic minorities. This introduction provides a brief overview of the scope of disaster studies in the Philippines and points to avenues of further research that are tentatively examined in this volume.

MAKING MODERN DISASTERS: HISTORIES OF VULNERABILITY IN THE PHILIPPINES

Part of the story of disasters in the Philippines lies in ancient geological histories and global climatic patterns that were, until recently, considered largely outside the bounds of human control. In the literature surrounding disaster in the Philippines, there is a long list of oft-repeated and overlapping geophysical misfortunes that are used to describe the archipelago: much of the country is located on the geologically unstable "ring of fire" that encircles the pacific which, aside from an increased frequency of destructive tectonic activity, means that 30 percent of the population live within 30 km of a volcano. The eastern seaboard of Luzon, Mindanao, and much of the Visayan Islands lie exposed, unprotected by neighboring islands, to the cyclonic activity emanating from the Pacific Ocean. Southeast Asia more broadly is also subject to widely fluctuating rainfall patterns as a result of intra-decadal El Niño-Southern Oscillation dynamics that bring both drought and deluge.

The Philippine archipelago is therefore a place of environmental extremes where multiple hazards such as flooding, landslides, droughts, volcanic eruption, and storm surges occur with more frequency than much of the rest of the world, often in devastating intersection. However, as critical geographers and disaster scholars have effectively worked to establish for several decades, no disasters are entirely natural (Hewitt 1983; Theriault this volume): Why some are impacted by disasters, and others are not, is the product of long political-economic histories. Alongside these critical perspectives, a growing awareness of the profound impact humans have had on the environment as we enter the "Anthropocene" has confused the origins of phenomena previously considered solely environmental. Fires, drought, flooding, and even earthquakes are increasingly seen to be mediated by human-driven climate change or augmented by the failure of techno-science on increasingly grand scales, such as the Fukushima Daiichi disaster (Dalby 2017). The inability to untangle human and nonhuman agency increasingly and routinely renders the "naturalness" of "natural" disasters defunct. Analytically, this growing awareness points to the ways that disasters are situated in not only local experiences, but larger histories of colonialism and ongoing industrial environmental degradation that links consumers and producers in circuitous global flows (Hannigan 2012). These hybrid human-natural disasters are "slow" in that their histories are "incremental and accretive" with "calamitous repercussions played out across a range of temporal scales" (Nixon 2011, 2). These insights, however, do not provide a simpler framework with which to approach disaster and nation, and instead force scholars into ever more expanding frames of reference. The impact of disasters in the Philippines can only be understood through a complex bricolage of locally specific histories and global imperialism, such as the political economy of crony capitalism, recursive histories of resource depletion, the politics of patronage and the stark poverty and inequality that have tallied over time to structure daily experiences of risk and rupture for the urban and rural poor.

While the precolonial history of the Philippines is undeniably rich with accounts of disaster (Bankoff 2003; Warren 2018), the records of Spanish (1521–1898) and American colonial regimes (1898–1946) and their economic imperatives provide some poignant examples of the social production of disasters and their coproduction with social order. Extractive colonial economies, oriented toward the export of valuable agricultural commodities, shaped rural and urban livelihoods in ways that exacerbated food insecurity for rural peoples throughout the archipelago, but particularly in the densely populated areas of Luzon and the Visayas. For example, Spanish agricultural policies promoted the aggregation of land for cash commercial cash cropping, resulting in highly unequal distribution of land holdings between local Mestizo elite families and a large class of landless, bonded tenant households who were dependent on purchasing food rather than cultivating it themselves (Anderson 1988). While colonial society became increasingly dependent on irrigated rice production, rice farming was increasingly viewed as a commercially "impoverished" activity relative to the production of sugar, tobacco, and abaca (Doeppers 2016, 60–62). Bonded tenant farmers throughout both the Spanish and American period were encouraged to take up commodity cash cropping at the expense of securing their own subsistence needs. Given this manufactured precarity in food security, manifest in a high reliance on imported rice, the El Niño droughts of the nineteenth and early twentieth century had an understandably devastating impact on poorer rural and urban Filipinos, resulting in periodic famine and widespread food-related morbidity, particularly in areas most oriented toward commodity cropping (Davis 2001, 94–95; McLennan 1986).

In the postcolonial period (1946–), crony capitalism and resource depletion have been implicated in the production of disaster and sharpening of environmental extremes. Perhaps the most striking environmental transformation has been the deforestation of the archipelago during the twentieth century. Continuing from the colonial period, the harvesting of timber from Philippine forests was quickly industrialized in the decades following World War II in the service of economic elites and has had a profound impact on the archipelago's geomorphology. The degradation of the nation's forests has shaped experiences of disasters by removing environmental buffers against cyclonic and monsoonal rainfall. In Mindanao, for example, years of extractive forestry practices, enabled through close relations between Department of Environment and Natural Resources officials and developer-politicians during the Marcos dictatorship, has left much of the uplands denuded and prone to flash flooding and landslides (Bankoff 2003, 140–142). In surveying the devastating impact of a series of typhoons that passed through eastern Luzon in 2004, Gallaird (2015) similarly points to histories of legal and illegal logging since the 1970s and uneven agrarian economies that push landless farmers into denuded upland areas. The impacts of these overlapping political and environmental disasters fall, primarily, on the rural poor and indigenous peoples.

While the legacies of colonial and postcolonial extractivism continue to shape complex patterns of vulnerability, the depletion of forest resources and shifts in global demand for commodities have more recently opened up new intersections of development and the production of disaster. Mining, for example, has long been a feature of the Philippine government's economic strategies, but the sector has seen significant growth since pro-mining reforms of the 1990s. While the growth of mineral extraction has enriched compliant local governments and provided a measure of livelihood opportunity to the rural poor in closely adjacent areas, there are growing concerns that large-scale mining activities have a worrying impact on local hydrological cycles and may worsen already disastrous El Niño droughts for farming communities (Holden 2013). In 2018, for example, landslides resulting from Typhoon Ompong killed dozens of largely indigenous small-scale miners in areas of the Cordilleras disturbed by histories of corporate resource extraction (Beech 2018). The relatively recent prominence of mass urban poverty, linked to continuing histories of landlessness and violence in rural landscapes, also generates new forms of vulnerability and human suffering in the wake of environmental change. Newcomers to metropolitan Manila, Cebu, and other emerging urban centers are often relegated to the most precarious areas of residence, especially in the face of environmental hazards (Luna, this volume). Informal settlements, such as BASECO Compound in Manila, flood with ease, requiring regular and disruptive evacuations (Alejandria, this volume). Accelerating patterns of anthropogenic climate change add a new dimension to the study of disasters in the Philippines, exaggerating older threats such as drought and sea level rise.

LIVES OF CRISIS: EVERYDAY DISASTERS AND EVERYDAY KNOWLEDGE

While the environmental extremes that play out over the Philippine archipelago are considered exceptional by global standards, their frequency means that they are often a recurrent, if not routine, feature of the lives of Filipinos. Environmental hazards often also intersect with other domains of life already characterized by the language of crisis and uncertainty. Research by the Internal Displacement Monitoring Centre, for example, suggests that millions of people experience long-term displacement, largely as the result of tropical storms and storm water surges that force hundreds of thousands of people from their homes each year (IDMC 2019). Infrastructure failure, such as brownouts, are a persistent element of both urban and rural life, even in major metropolitan areas (Matejowsky 2009). Familial tragedy and health-related disaster, whether social or environmental in origin, is also a widespread dimension of daily life and common in discourses of poverty (Membrebe et al. this volume; Cajilig et al. this volume). Household livelihoods, especially in nominally "frontier" and "post-frontier" landscapes, are shifting and often ephemeral as diverse activities, such as fishing, vending, or handicraft production, can quickly rise and fall in a shifting kaleidoscope of opportunity (Eder 2006; Regoniel, this volume). Disaster, crisis, and uncertainty can therefore be understood as "everyday" in many respects (Webb, this volume), and a key emerging theme of Philippine disaster literature is concerned with the tension between extreme events and the "slow moving" and "quotidian" qualities of political and environmental calamity (Curato 2018; Delfin and Galliard 2012).

It is unsurprising then that not only are disasters and calamity the subject of special social and cultural elaboration, but are also often discussed as embedded in more fundamental aspects of national psyche and personhood (Bankoff 2001). What are deemed by some to be defining psycho-cultural traits of Filipino society are frequently tied to dealing with disasters, and in the aftermath of particularly devastating typhoons or earthquakes, it is common to find reference to the *bayanihan* spirit (often translated as "community spirit") or *lakas ng loob* ("internal strength"), and other traits that can explain the resilience and persistence of Filipino people in the face of adversity (Hilhorst et al. 2015). The widely studied *bahala na*—roughly "come what may"—attitude has likewise been interpreted as a tradition of fortitude and perseverance that has emerged from facing frequent disaster. Rather than simple fatalism, historian Greg Bankoff suggests that widespread expressions of *bahala na* throughout the archipelago are "equally an active calculation of the odds as it is a passive sense of acceptance of one's fate" (Bankoff 2003, 167). Narratives of disaster causality are, however, also bound up with critical reflection on more negatively defined national traits. A common self-critique of Philippine national character are perceptions of "crab mentalities"—or the widespread tendency to "pull down" successful peers. This attitude is routinely blamed for continuing under-development and unpreparedness for both environmental and economic disasters (Bulloch 2015).

DISASTER POLITICS: REPRESENTATIONS AND REALITIES, LOCAL AND GLOBAL

This brief sketch of historical and contemporary disaster experiences provides an overview of the ways in which human suffering resulting from environmental extremes is not purely the result of natural hazards but of "shifting patterns of power within the nation" (Bankoff 2003, 143). A review of Philippine environmental histories validates the truism that disasters are always political in nature, but the relationship between politics and disaster is also recursive. The symbolic and representational dramas of disaster and suffering are pervasive in the practice of politics itself (Mangada et al, this volume). The mobilization and circulation of imagery and discourses of victimhood, and the designation and allocation of blame and vulnerability are features of political discourse and interventions that link global donors to Filipino households.

The anticipation and aftermath of disasters are interwoven with the cycles of national political life in the Philippines. The impact of devastating events, particularly the aftermath of typhoons, often form a routine part of performative "dramas of nationhood" that play out on television screens, radio broadcasts, and other media throughout the archipelago (cf. Abu-Lughod 2008). Ong, for example, has examined the ways in which television broadcasters embody heroic narratives through media pilgrimages to impacted zones and, in doing so, mobilize nationalistic support for relief efforts (Ong 2015). In addition to media personalities, politicians also regularly tour the sites of disaster to be photographed assessing damage, distributing supplies, and broadly be seen fulfilling their obligations as patrons. For all of the suffering and rupture associated with disasters, this moral weight means post-disaster situations are also moments of redistribution as well as political and economic opportunity. In Vincanne Adams's ethnography of the aftermath of Hurricane Katrina in New Orleans, she describes the emergence of post-disaster relief: the "economy is based on the circulation of an affective surplus—the emotional responsiveness and ethical inducement to action generated by a recognition of ongoing need." While Adams pins this emergence in the United States on the rise of a neoliberal state concerned with privatizing disaster response, disaster capitalism in the Philippines has an older and messier lineage (Poteria 2015). The notion that needs must be powerfully and regularly performed is a central feature of long-standing practices of political patronage sustained on a grand scale through the rise of radio, television, and now social media (Pertierra 2018). In this national web, the aftermath of disasters are important sites where moral claims to resources are performed and contested. For example, emotive appeals to national pride and the ready release of "calamity" relief funds mean reconstruction efforts are fertile ground for redistributive politics, providing a space in which politicians may allocate disaster assistance to strengthen patronage ties or weaken rivalries by denying aid (Atkinson et al. 2014). These emotive politics are not limited to the wealthy or elite, and the moral weight of victimhood, poverty, and deprivation can be an important strategic resource for the poor in positioning oneself as *kawawa*, pitiful, which is a common means of eliciting sympathy to navigate personalized patron-client relations (cf. Cannell 1999; Fabyini 2013; see also Clarke and Sison 2003).

Beyond the media performances of individual politicians, institutionalized disaster governance is also an important field of contestation over representations and political economies that link local disasters to global development politics. Representations of human-environmental relationships in disaster management are particularly important. Specific renderings of communities as vulnerable or fragile entails the intervention into the lives of the rural and urban poor by government, civil society, and international aid organizations (Bankoff and Hilhorst 2009). Mirroring global experiences, neoliberal trends in the Philippines have seen the failure and explicit abdication of the state from its traditional responsibilities in many areas of disaster management—see, for example, the lawlessness following the devastation of Typhoon Yolanda in Tacloban. In this space, "Disaster Risk Reduction" has emerged internationally and in the Philippines as an important concept and framework through which humans and human-environmental relationships become the object of governance. Disaster management has therefore become a field of competition between state and nongovernmental civil society where different ways of understanding and managing risk, people, and environments play out. A lively and powerful civil society is seen as a defining feature of Philippine political life, and nongovernmental actors have an active role in securing and distributing resources in the aftermath of disasters and risk management planning, often by challenging dominant notions of development or existing policy agendas (Luna 2001; Allen 2006). Through such interventions, local aspirations and notions of risk mingle with the demands of powerful donors and international civil society and represent an important site of cross-scalar contestation oriented around the need to control disaster (Alindogan this volume).

Beyond the internal struggles of nationhood, rendering certain people and groups as vulnerable also "does something" in the world of global environmental politics (Bankoff 2001). Indeed, in focusing in the previous section on the historical and structural issues of power in the production of disaster experiences, it is an easy and perhaps dangerous conceptual misstep to naturalize the vulnerability of marginal peoples and communities. The discursive construction of people as vulnerable, and as helpless, opens communities to governmental intervention (Bankoff 2001; Grove 2014). Yet, at the same time, portraying disaster-prone people as perfectly adaptable to change is similarly problematic. For example, ideas of resilience, rooted in concepts from the ecological sciences, are an increasingly important part of disaster discourses within the Philippines, especially in the context of growing threats from climate change. However, while resilience may be an important way of emphasizing the power of communities, critical perspectives on resilience language in disaster policy have cautioned how international depictions of smiling residents of Manila in the face of floods may defer critiques of structural inequalities and histories of political violence (Tanyag 2018).

INSIGHTS FROM THE PHILIPPINES: FUTURE DIRECTIONS AND EMERGING PERSPECTIVES

Beyond offering insights into Philippine experiences of nationhood and political dynamics of marginalization and resource delegation, experiences with disaster in the Philippines also provide challenges to wider scholarly conceptions of disaster. Rather than drawing on comparative perspectives to produce a more refined definition of disaster or definitely pin down slippery terms through which disaster is understood and managed, "definitional consensus may be less important than stirring discussions in which conflicts may not be totally resolved, but important issues will be clarified, new perspectives and problem areas developed" (Oliver-Smith 1999, 19). Experiences of disaster in the Philippines are a rich resource for reflecting on seemingly stable and binding definitions of concepts that are key to disaster management such as risk, resilience, and vulnerability. As such, contributors to this volume are not focused on alignment with singular definitions, but reflect the multiplicity of ways that these concepts can be deployed by both academics and Filipinos beset by disaster. How meaningful is the notion of disaster, defined as an extraordinary social or environmental extreme, when everyday life is defined by such events? How might we revise notions of resilience in reference to the rural and urban poor's lived experiences of precarity that extend far beyond environmental uncertainty?

One important frontier of disaster scholarship links postcolonial analysis to issues of representation. In the Philippines, scholarly exploration of disasters often lean heavily on simplified reductions of people and place that have informed writing about the archipelago since the American colonial period. Ileto's (2001) scathing appraisal of American scholarship on Philippine history refers to an essentialized vision of Filipino culture defined by subservient masses blindly enthralled to a patron class of *cacique* bosses. These representations, he suggests, have their origin in colonial discourses that were deployed against arguments for self-rule. Disaster studies, which often point in a general fashion to agrarian political economies or corruption as the ultimate cause of disasters, run the risk of reproducing such essentializing representations. There is a need, therefore, for more nuanced explanations of disaster causality without recourse to tired neocolonial tropes, perhaps within a more rigorously organized postcolonial disaster studies. The challenge moving forward is to develop more sophisticated theoretical approaches that can accommodate the tightly interwoven and recursive nature of politics and disaster. There is a need, therefore, to embed experiences of disaster within colonial histories of representation and policy. Emerging studies of disaster by Filipino scholars have readily engaged this complexity (e.g., Curato and Ong 2015), but there remains considerable work in using place-based studies to contribute to and move beyond the well-established political-economic approaches which identify "unnatural disasters" or seek out the "root causes" of vulnerability (Ribot 2014).

The heterogeneity of the Philippines, where extreme environmental conditions unfold against enormous ethnic and geographic variation, is another key challenge that is yet to be fully taken up by disaster scholarship. Despite the increasing pace and scale of academic explorations of disaster in the

Philippines, scholarly discussions have focused, primarily, on the experiences of the lowland, Hispanicized majority in ways that are often homogenizing and do not account for regional specificity (cf. Manalo et al. 2015). Few accounts examine the experiences of indigenous peoples, whose cosmological priors, political-economic histories, and experiences of marginality often differ starkly from Christianized lowlanders (Hilhorst et al. 2015; Webb, this volume; Smith, this volume). Lowland populations, too, are not homogeneous, and impacts of disasters vary across lived experiences of gender, age, and region (Alejandria; Ancheta et al.; Riosa et al., all this volume). Regional variation is poorly accounted for in disaster scholarship that often considers the implications of environmental change for "the nation," figured through the prism of highly visible catastrophic experiences. Issues of internal heterogeneity also hint at as-yet unresolved issues of voice and representation that play out in a complex postcolonial context where indigenous peoples and ethnic minorities find themselves studied and represented, largely, by other Filipinos.

These are perennial concerns that warrant further attention, but recent research continues to raise increasingly varied intersections between society and disaster, and tentatively suggests the ways in which disaster impacts all aspects of national social and political life. How, for example, does disaster figure into long-running Muslim insurgencies and ethnic conflict in Mindanao (Bamford 2015; Walch 2018; Eastrin 2018)? In a country with a prominent "third gender" widely understood to be vulnerable to everyday forms of violence, how can disaster be understood beyond the binary of male-female (Gaillaird et al. 2017)? How does environmental calamity mediate new forms of political violence and the populist "drug war" that largely impacts the urban poor (McCoy 2017; Curato 2018)?

STRUCTURE OF THE BOOK: ASSEMBLAGES OF AID, KNOWLEDGE, AND RESILIENCE

This book engages with these diverse avenues of inquiry and approaches, and the specificity of place, in understanding disasters in the Philippines. In the first section, the authors focus on the diverse politics of governing, managing, and knowing disaster events in the Philippines. In providing a broad overview of the impact and scale of disaster events, Piepiora et al. suggest that the Philippine Disaster Management System, first established in 2010, has been dominated by recommendations from the United Nations Office for the Coordination of Humanitarian Affairs, and that greater operational distinction between seaside and inland areas can provide more effective and locally specific disaster risk reduction. Alindogan's chapter explores the role of donor expectations, particularly global trends regarding aid evaluation, in shaping disaster management systems in the Philippines which are increasingly designed for their ability to "manifest effectiveness." Through a focus on the post-Haiyan (Yolanda) relief program enacted by Save the Children, Riosa et al. focus on the ways in which children are constructed and targeted by aid agencies as discrete entities in development assistance. The chapter by Mangada et al. explores the complexity of accountability in the context of persistent patronage networks which shape post-disaster distribution of relief goods directly following Haiyan.

Grounded in an ethnographic sensibility, the second section pivots to focus on the grounded forms of knowledge and experiences of everyday disasters across a diversity of places and histories in the Philippines. The chapter by Cajilig et al. is concerned with problems with what was seen as the "irrational" tendency of poorer houses to stay put, rather than evacuate, prior to the impact of Haiyan by emphasizing the cultural and political constraints that shape decision making prior to disaster events. The two subsequent chapters by Alejandria and Ancheta et al. consider the perceptions of older residents and children, respectively, in the BASECO Compound in Manila. While both chapters emphasize the vulnerability of life and livelihood in the BASECO Compound to environmental change and point to the role of the state in exacerbating economic and environmental uncertainty, the authors also argue for the agency of residents who leverage flood conditions to secure resources and have developed complex coping mechanisms. The final two chapters in this section are concerned with the experiences of the archipelago's indigenous peoples. While there is a body of literature surrounding the ability of ethnic minority groups in the Philippines to navigate environmental change, indigenous peoples are often treated in isolation rather than as part of a broader projects of nation-building and resource management that shapes their understanding and responses to disasters. Smith's chapter, focused on indigenous experiences of extreme El Niño drought in southern Palawan, brings to the fore culturally mediated understandings of hunger among indigenous households to complicate policy responses to food insecurity. Webb's chapter explores indigenous Tagbanua understandings of environmental change, risk, and temporality on Palawan Island. By linking seemingly disparate events together, such as honey production, the rise in tourist activity, and the Mt Pinatubo eruption, Tagbanua accounts provide the basis for reevaluating definitions widely accepted within the disaster studies literature.

The final section is focused on locating practices of resilience and adaptation amid the structural political-economic constraints that the rural and urban poor face. Membrebe et al., focus their attention on the fisher folk of Manila Bay who face a series of compounding environmental and political pressures on their marine-based livelihoods. While they argue that local-level "micro-governance" and the sensitivity of residents to ecosystems are important reasons for community resilience, the authors also suggest that there are unexplored intersections between chronic health conditions (e.g., hypertension) and vulnerability to typhoons and flooding. The chapter by Regoniel et al concerns the residents of the archipelago's many fishing communities, where long-standing threats from cyclonic storms and tidal surges are being exacerbated by anthropogenic climate change. Rather than considering the role of external interventions, the authors demonstrate the locally generated adaptive capability of "highly vulnerable" populations in Honda Bay, Palawan Island. Finally, Luna's chapter focusing on the aftermath of the 2013 Bohol earthquake explores the resilience of urban dwellers who make their lives and livelihoods in post-earthquake landscapes.

REFERENCES

Abu-Lughod, L. (2008). *Dramas of Nationhood: The Politics of Television in Egypt.* University of Chicago Press, Chicago.

Adams, V. (2013). *Markets of Sorrow, Labors of Faith: New Orleans in the Wake of Katrina.* Duke University Press, Durham.

Allen, K. M. (2006). Community-based disaster preparedness and climate adaptation: Local capacity-building in the Philippines. *Disasters*, 30(1), 81–101.

Anderson, B. (1988). Cacique democracy and the Philippines: Origins and dreams. *New Left Review*, 169, 3–31.

Atkinson, J., Hicken, A., & Ravanilla, N. (2014). Pork & Typhoons: The influence of political connections on disaster response. University of Michigan—Manuscript.

Bamforth, Tom. 2015. "Social Impact of Typhoon Bopha on Indigenous Communities, Livelihoods, and Conflict in Mindanao." *Disaster's Impact on Livelihood and Cultural Survival.* https://doi.org/10.1201/b18233-19.

Bankoff, G. (2003). *Cultures of Disaster; Society and Natural Hazard in the Philippines.* Routledge Curzon, London.

Bankoff, G., & Hilhorst, D. (2009). The politics of risk in the Philippines: Comparing state and NGO perceptions of disaster management. *Disasters*, 33(4), 686–704.

Beech, H. (2018). Philippine Miners Trapped in Typhoon: Drawn by Gold, Drowned in Mud. *The New York Times*, September 17. Available at: https://www.nytimes.com/2018/09/17/world/asia/philippines-landslide-typhoon-mangkhut.html

Bulloch, H. (2015). Ambivalent moralities of cooperation and corruption: Local explanations for (under) development on a Philippine island. *The Australian Journal of Anthropology*. Forthcoming.

Cannell, F. (1999). *Power and Intimacy in the Christian Philippines.* Cambridge University Press, Cambridge.

Clarke, G., & Sison, M. (2003). Voices from the top of the pile: Elite perceptions of poverty and the poor in the Philippines. *Development and Change*, 34(2), 215–242.

Curato, N. (2018). Beyond the spectacle: slow-moving disasters in post-Haiyan Philippines. *Critical Asian Studies*, 50(1), 58–66.

Curato, N., & Ong, J. C. (2015). Introduction to the special issue: Disasters can lift veils: Five issues for sociological disaster studies. *Philippine Sociological Review*, 63, 1–26.

Dalby, S. (2017). Anthropocene formations: Environmental security, geopolitics and disaster. *Theory, Culture & Society*, 34(2–3), 233–252.

Davis, M. (2001). *Late Victorian Holocausts: El Niño, Famines, and the Making of the Third World*. Verso, New York.

Delfin, Jr, F. G., & Gaillard, J. C. (2008). Extreme versus quotidian: Addressing temporal dichotomies in Philippine disaster management. *Public Administration and Development: The International Journal of Management Research and Practice*, 28(3), 190–199.

Doeppers, D. F. (2016). *Feeding Manila in Peace and War, 1850–1945*. University of Wisconsin Press, Madison.

Eder, J. F. (2006). Land use and economic change in the post-frontier upland Philippines. *Land Degradation & Development*, 17(2), 149–158.

Fabinyi, M. (2013). *Fishing for Fairness: Poverty, Morality and Marine Resource Regulation in the Philippines*. ANU Press, Canberra.

Franke, R. W., & Chasin, B. H. (1980). *Seeds of Famine: Ecological Destruction and the Development Dilemma in the West African Sahel*. Rowman and Allanheid, Totowa.

Gaillard, J. (2015). *People's Response to Disasters in the Philippines: Vulnerability, Capacities, and Resilience*. Springer.

Gaillard, J. C., Sanz, K., Balgos, B. C., Dalisay, S. N. M., Gorman-Murray, A., Smith, F., & Toelupe, V. A. (2017). Beyond men and women: A critical perspective on gender and disaster. *Disasters*, 41(3), 429–447.

Glantz, M. H. (1976). *The Politics of Natural Disaster: The Case of the Sahel Drought*. Praeger, New York.

Grove, K. (2014). Biopolitics and adaptation: Governing socio-ecological contingency through climate change and disaster studies. *Geography Compass*, 8(3), 198–210.

Hannigan, J. (2012). *Disasters Without Borders: The International Politics of Natural Disasters*. Polity Press, Cambridge.

Hewitt, K. ed. (1983). *Interpretations of Calamity from the Viewpoint of Human Ecology*. Allen and Unwin, Boston.

Hilhorst, D., Baart, J., van der Haar, G., & Leeftink, F. M. (2015). Is disaster "normal" for indigenous people? Indigenous knowledge and coping practices. *Disaster Prevention and Management*, 24(4), 506–522.

Holden, W. N. (2013). Neoliberal mining amid El Niño induced drought in the Philippines. *Journal of Geography and Geology*, 5(1), 58.

IDMC. (2019). *Country Profile: Philippines*. Internal Displacement Monitoring Centre. Available at: http://www.internal-displacement.org/countries/philippines

Joshua, Eastin. (2018). Hell and high water: Precipitation shocks and conflict violence in the Philippines. *Political Geography*, 63, 116–134.

Luna, E. M. (2001). Disaster mitigation and preparedness: The case of NGOs in the Philippines. *Disasters*, 25(3), 216–226.

Matejowsky, T. (2009). When the lights go out: Understanding natural hazard and merchant "Brownout" behavior in the provincial philippines. In Jones, E. C. & A. D. Murphy (eds.) *The Political Economy of Hazards and Disasters*, pp.179–200. Rowman Altamira.

McCoy, A. W. (2017). Philippine populism: Local violence and global context in the rise of a Filipino strongman. *Surveillance & Society*, 15(3/4), 514.

Nixon, R. (2011). *Slow Violence and the Environmentalism of the Poor*. Harvard University Press, Cambridge.

Oliver-Smith, A. (1999). What is a disaster? Anthropological perspectives on a persistent question. In Hoffman, S. & A. Oliver-Smith (eds.) *The Angry Earth: Disaster in Anthropological Perspective*, pp. 18–34. Routledge NY.

Ong, J. C. (2015). The television of intervention: Mediating patron-client ties in the Philippines. In Tay, J., Iwabuchi, K. & Turner, G. (eds.) *Television Histories of Asia*. Routledge, London & New York.

Pertierra, A. C. (2018). Televisual experiences of poverty and abundance: Entertainment television in the Philippines. *The Australian Journal of Anthropology*, 29(1), 3–18.

Porteria, A. (2015). Making Money Out of People's Misery: Has Disaster Capitalism Taken Over Post-Haiyan Philippines? *Philippine Sociological Review*, 63, 179-206. Retrieved from http://www.jstor.org/stable/24717192.

Quilo, Q., Mabini, M., Tamiroy, M., Mendoza, M., Ponce, S., & Viloria, L. (2015). Indigenous knowledge and practices: Approach to understanding disaster. *Philippine Sociological Review*, 63, 105–129.

Sakai, M., Jurriëns, E., Zhang, J., & Thornton, A. (2014). *Disaster Relief in the Asia Pacific: Agency and Resilience*. Routledge, London.

Solway, J. S. (1994). Drought as a revelatory crisis: An exploration of shifting entitlements and hierarchies in the Kalahari, Botswana. *Development and Change*, 25(3), 471–495.

SSRC. (2006). *Understanding Katrina: Perspectives from the Social Sciences*. Social Sciences Research Council, Brooklyn. Available at: http://understandingkatrina. ssrc.org/

Tanyag, M. (2018). Resilience, female altruism, and bodily autonomy: Disaster-induced displacement in post-Haiyan Philippines. *Signs: Journal of Women in Culture and Society*, 43(3), 563–585.

Walch, C. (2018). Weakened by the storm: Rebel group recruitment in the wake of natural disasters in the Philippines. *Journal of Peace Research*, 55(3), 336–350.

Warren, J. F. (2018). Typhoons and droughts: Food shortages and famine in the Philippines since the seventeenth century. *International Review of Environmental History*, 4(2), 27–44.

Chapter 1

At a Glance

Disaster in the Philippines and the Philippine Disaster Management System

Zbigniew Piepora, Oliver Belarga,
and Anthony Alindogan

INTRODUCTION

In 2016, the World Risk Index listed the Philippines as the third most disaster-prone country in the world. This high-risk ranking is reflected in the high number of natural disaster events registered under the Philippines in the global Emergency Events Database (EM-DAT). Based on historical data available from 1946–2016, the Philippines experienced a total of 606 natural disasters. Collectively, these disasters caused damage to the country costing $26.1 billion. Over the seventy-year period, 208.8 million individuals have been affected, including an estimated 212,000 injured and 6.1 million home-less[1]. In order to counteract the effects on humans and the environment, it is essential to have an understanding of the occurrence of natural disasters in the Philippines.

The Philippine government, from its pre-Commonwealth days up to the present, has developed a scheme to mitigate the effects of disasters, both nat-ural and human-induced. The Philippine disaster management system origi-nated in 1941, when President Manuel L. Quezon created Executive Order (EO) No. 335, establishing the National Emergency Commission and imple-menting measures to control and coordinate civilian participation to meet serious crises[2]. Consequently, the Provincial Emergency Committee was cre-ated, in charge of the supervision and control over the Municipal Emergency Committees and City Emergency Committees. In 1954, the National Civil Defense Administration (NCDA) was established through Republic Act (RA)

1190, which also created national and local civil defense councils[3]. Thereafter, in 1968, the National Civil Defense Administration was designated as the national coordinator to oversee and implement Executive Order 159[4] and reports on the degree of preparedness of all government offices to the Office of the President. In 1970, President Ferdinand Marcos implemented a Disaster and Calamities Plan prepared by an Inter-Departmental Planning Group on Disasters and Calamities. Two years later, in 1972, the Office of Civil Defense was established by Letter of Instruction 19 (OCD, 2015). The Office of Civil Defense was mandated to coordinate national-level activities and functions of the national government, private institutions, and civic organizations. Finally, in 1978, through Presidential Decree 1566, the National Disaster Coordinating Council was established as the highest policy-making body and the focal organization for disaster management in the country (NDCC, 2007). The law also provided for the establishment of regional, provincial, city, municipal, and barangay disaster coordinating councils.

In 2009, the Congress enacted the Climate Change Act of 2009 and in 2010, Republic Act 10121 or the Philippine Disaster Risk Reduction and Management (PDRRM) Act[5]. These twin laws on Disaster Risk Reduction and Management have common goals and objectives: 1) to increase the resilience of vulnerable communities and the country against natural disasters and 2) to reduce damage and loss of lives and properties due to disasters. In particular, Republic Act 10121 provides for the development of policies and plans and the implementation of actions and measures pertaining to all aspects of Disaster Risk Reduction and Management, including good governance, risk assessment and early warning, knowledge building and awareness raising, reducing underlying risk factors, and improving preparedness for effective response and early recovery. The law acknowledges that there is a need to "adopt a disaster risk reduction and management approach that is holistic, comprehensive, integrated, and proactive in lessening the socioeconomic and environmental impacts of disasters including climate change, and promote the involvement and participation of all sectors and all stakeholders concerned, at all levels, especially the local community."

The aims of this study are (1) to identify the hazards and types of disasters that affected the Philippines, (2) to explore key issues affecting the disaster management system during a natural disaster, and (3) to illustrate the two different types of provinces in relation to disaster management in the Philippines. The result of this study will contribute to the overall understanding of the Philippine disaster history, its disaster management system, and key factors affecting that system. In addition, we also explore the different types of disasters experienced by provinces in the Philippines to make a contribution to developing appropriate and effective local disaster management plans.

METHODOLOGY

The methodology used in this study comprises three steps. Step 1 is conducting a review of disasters occurring in the Philippines, particularly on the impact and type of disasters the country has experienced. As mentioned above, historical disaster data from 1946 to 2016 obtained from the EM-DAT database was utilized in the study.

EM-DAT is managed by the Centre for Research on Epidemiology of Disasters (CRED) and collects data from various sources such as nongovernment organizations, the United Nations, and governmental sources. Each disaster is entered as a disaster event. One main disaster type is identified per event which is called the primary disaster. A primary disaster may be linked to another disaster. For example, an earthquake may generate a landslide. In such cases, the consequence of the primary disaster is regarded as an associated disaster. Only primary disasters were analyzed in generating the Philippine historical disaster data from 1946 to 2016.

As part of this overview, the current Philippine disaster management system is also discussed. This data serves as a platform for Step 2.

Step 2 consists of a situation analysis of disaster risk reduction in the Philippines. For this case, Typhoon Haiyan (Yolanda) was selected. Data for the situation analysis was sourced from various references.

Much progress has been made on disaster risk reduction (DRR) since the national agency was established, thanks to the combined efforts of the government, the communities, and the working group's members; however, significant gaps remain for the Philippines to become a disaster-resilient nation. The NDCC itself has evolved since it was established and the context in which it operates has changed dramatically, shaping new opportunities and threats for DRR work and calling for a re-alignment of the NDCC's engagement strategy. Recognizing the momentum created by the reform process and the importance of positioning itself strategically, this situational analysis has the objective of providing a comprehensive picture of the upcoming opportunities and challenges for DRR in the Philippines. This descriptive situational analysis is designed as a planning tool which reviews the current capacity and scope and provides recommendations on future strategic directions in view of the changing context of the Philippines.

The situation analysis is one of the most frequently used methods in strategic management and has a wide-ranging use. The analysis reviews the combination of internal and external factors leading to four categories (Gierszewska & Romanowska as cited in Goranczewski and Puciato, 2010): external positive—opportunities; external negative—threats; internal positive—strengths; and internal negative—weaknesses. This situation analysis will not focus on weight and ranking but on subjective analysis of identified factors that will provide a better perspective other than the listing of internal and external factors. This permits a better comparison between identified factors and improves the utilization of the available data. Analysis was developed through a combination of literature review and in-depth discussions.

Step 3 is a geographic analysis of disasters occurring at the local administrative level. The geographic analysis focuses on identifying neutral and seaside provinces. This provides an important perspective on the type of disaster an area can expect and prepare for. Geographic areas in the Philippines are categorized according to provincial administrative units. The researchers in this study noted that the provincial administrative units are the closest geographic classification to the European Union's LAU1 (Local Administrative Unit 1)[6]. Analyzing the Philippine geography according to provincial administrative units will allow comparison with other existing or future European study of the same nature.

THE OCCURRENCE OF NATURAL
DISASTERS IN THE PHILIPPINES

The analysis of seventy years of Philippine historical data shows that more than half (56.27%) of the disasters experienced by the Philippines were storms. As can be seen in figure 1, flooding was the second most common type of disaster event (24.26%). This is followed by earthquakes and volcanic activity (9.08%) and mass movements and landslides (5.45%). The succeeding discussions in this book will focus on these three most common disasters experienced by the Philippines.

A storm is defined as a violent disturbance of the atmosphere with strong wind, heavy rain, snow, or hail (McDonald, 2003). Storms are classified as meteorological disasters. Tropical and winter storms above the West Pacific are called typhoons. The occurrence of storms is attributed to the location of the Philippines close to the equator. The Philippines fall under the Northwest Pacific tropical cyclone basin, which covers most of East and South East Asia. The Northwest Pacific Basin had an annual average of sixteen typhoons during the 1968–1989 period (National Oceanic and Atmospheric Administration, 2014). Between 1946 and 2016, the Philippines experienced 341 storms which caused $21.4 billion worth of damages and affected 162.3 million people, including 70,800 people injured and 5.4 million homeless. The most destructive storm during the examined period was Super Typhoon Haiyan.

A flood can be defined as the height, or stage, of water above a given point, such as banks of a river channel (Alexander, 1993). Floods are considered hydrological disasters and are started by several factors, such as abundant rainfalls lasting for days, thunderclouds, short-lived natural dams created by landslides (Abbot, 2009) or by coastal storm surges. Floods can also be riverine or flash flooding attributed to the tropical rainforest climate of the Philippines. Occasionally, floods can be accompanied by landslides (moderate to rapid soil movements). During 1946–2016, a total of 147 floods were identified in the database. These floods caused $3.8 billion in damage and affected 31.8 million people, including approximately 1,000 individuals injured and 592,000 displaced. A total of 3,635 individual mortalities were attributed to floods (Centre for Research on the Epidemiology of Disasters 2017)[7].

An earthquake is defined as a rapid movement of a section of the Earth's crust along a geological fault and associated ground shaking. Earthquakes are often accompanied by mass movements (any type of downslope movement of earth materials). Earthquakes, volcanic activities (volcanic eruptions of lava, ash, hot vapor, gas, and pyroclastic material), and landslides can trigger a tsunami (a series of waves with long wavelengths when traveling across the deep ocean). Earthquake events are mainly attributed to the location of the Philippines along the Pacific Ring of Fire. This is a major area in the basin of the Pacific Ocean where a large number of earthquakes and volcanic eruptions occur. During 1946–2016, a total of twenty-nine earthquakes, twenty-six volcanic activities, thirty landslides and three mass movements collectively caused damage worth $616.5 million. These disasters also affected an estimated 6.1 million people, including 14,800 people injured and more than 27,000 homeless. A total of 12.7 thousand mortalities were attributed to these disaster events.

Overall, a total of 606 natural disasters occurred in the Philippines in the seventy-one years between 1945 and 2016. Of these, 69,711 individuals were killed, 211,870 were injured, and a total of 202,505,988 individuals were affected by natural disasters. In addition, a total of 6,123,573 individuals lost their homes. The total damage cost of these disasters is estimated to be at $26,188,570,000 (Centre for Research on the Epidemiology of Disasters, 2017).

The Philippine Disaster Management System

The Philippines is a medium developed country with a Human Development Index of 0.682 (UNDP, 2017). It is divided into eighteen regions (rehiyons), which are administrative divisions that do not possess separate local governments[8]. Regions serve primarily to organize the provinces (lalawigan) of the Philippines for administrative purposes, excluding the National Capital Region, which consists of seventeen cities.

The Philippines has eighty-one provinces (lalawigan) with an elected legislature (the Sangguniang Panlalawigan) and presided over by an elected governor. Provinces are the primary political and administrative divisions of the country. Each province consists of component cities and municipalities. The administrative unit in each city and municipality further devolves into smaller units known as barangays. It is worth noting that some cities are independent from the province in which they are geographically located[9].

The Philippines Disaster Management System functions to minimize disaster risk and to address the impacts of disasters in the country. The legislation upon which the system operates is Republic Act 10121 or the Philippine Disaster Risk Reduction and Management Act of 2010[10]. The Act forms the basis for core elements of the country's disaster management system, such as (1) the formation of the National Disaster Risk Reduction and Management Council and its regional and local counterparts; (2) development of a national framework on disaster management; and (3) creation of a long-term National Disaster Risk Reduction and Management Plan. The Philippine National Disaster Risk Reduction and Management Plan specifically covers four thematic areas: (a) disaster prevention and mitigation; (b) disaster preparedness; (c) disaster response; and (d) disaster rehabilitation and recovery (Global Disaster Preparedness Center, 2017).

The National Disaster Risk Reduction and Management Council is empowered to perform policy making, coordination, integration, and supervisory functions, as well as monitor the preparation, implementation, and evaluation of the National Disaster Risk Reduction and Management Plan to ensure the protection and welfare of the people in times of disaster. RA 10121 or the Philippine Disaster Risk Reduction and Management Act of 2010 expanded the membership of the previous National Disaster Coordinating Council from nineteen to forty-four members. The former National Disaster Coordinating Council, as chaired by the Secretary of National Defense, was composed of Cabinet Secretaries and Heads of Agencies with major contributions to disaster response. The new law transformed the National Disaster Coordinating Council into the National Disaster Risk Reduction and Management Council, which is still headed by the Department of National Defense (DND) but with four vice chairpersons, namely, the Secretary of the Department of Science and Technology (DOST) for disaster prevention and mitigation; the Secretary of the Department of the Interior and Local Government (DILG) for disaster preparedness; the Secretary of the Department of Social Welfare and Development (DSWD) for disaster response; and the Director General of the National Economic and Development Authority (NEDA) for disaster rehabilitation and recovery. Aside from government agencies, the Council's membership now includes financial institutions, local government leagues, the private sector, and civil society organizations which reflect the "Whole of Society" approach on disaster risk reduction (Office for the Coordination of Humanitarian Affairs, 2015).

At times of large-scale disasters, the Philippine disaster management system operates in a cluster system based on the recommendations of United

Nations Office for the Coordination of Humanitarian Affairs. The National Disaster Risk Reduction and Management Council acts as the lead agency for the overall disaster response while other governmental agencies typically act as cluster leads, along with United Nations agencies or nongovernmental organizations as co-leads. For example, the Department of Education chairs the education cluster along with United Nations International Children's Emergency Fund or Save the Children as co-leads (National Disaster Disk Reduction and Management Council, 2013).

The level of coordination between the National, Regional, Municipal, and Barangay Disaster Risk Reduction Management Councils can be described as procedural. If a barangay was affected by a natural calamity or a human-induced disaster, involvement in the disaster response is often limited to the Barangay Disaster Risk Reduction and Management Council or the Barangay Development Council. That is, it is a barangay-level response. If two or more barangays of the municipality/city were affected, then the response is often at the municipal/city-level and the Municipal/City Disaster Risk Reduction Councils takes action. If two or more municipalities/cities of the province are affected, then the response is led by the Provincial Disaster Risk Reduction and Management Council. If two or more provinces of the region were affected, then the Regional Disaster Risk Reduction and Management Council leads the response. Lastly, if two or more regions of the country are affected, the response is often managed at the national level and the National Disaster Risk Reduction and Management Council takes the lead.[11]

During a disaster, the National Disaster Risk Reduction and Management Council and Cluster Leads coordinate with Regional and Local Disaster Management Councils in the affected area to plan and implement disaster response programs. All local and international humanitarian organizations are encouraged to attend cluster meetings to share information and coordinate activities to improve the efficiency of the disaster response.

The National Disaster Risk Reduction and Management Plan (DRRMP) for 2011–2028 frames how Disaster Risk Reduction and Management contributes to sustainable development. The plan fulfills the requirement of the Philippine Disaster Risk Reduction and Management Act of 2010 and provides details on programs and projects to be pursued, timelines to be met, identifies the responsible lead agencies and groups, as well as the resources needed for implementation. Likewise, it stipulates the Disaster Risk Reduction and Management approaches and strategies to be applied to manage identified hazards and risks. It also identifies the roles of agencies, their responsibilities and lines of authority at all government levels. The DRRMP provides the vertical and horizontal coordination mechanism in pre-disaster and post-disaster activities. Significantly, it includes a system for monitoring and evaluation of programs implementing the plan and it tasks the Office of the Civil Defense to do the same (though this is rarely done). Disaster Risk Reduction and Management

Plans have been formulated and targets have been set but actual accomplishments have yet to be monitored. Except for policy development activities, many local government units have no reports on communities, teams, and managers trained on disaster preparedness and response, and no information on the training institutions that were established for Disaster Risk Reduction and Management. Although Republic Act 10121 requires the preparation of a Disaster Management Plan, many local government units have not complied with this requirement. On the other hand, the local government units that prepare a Disaster Management Plan do so not to give an account on local practices, but instead to comply with government rules because if they fail to submit such a plan they will not be able to access their disaster funds. In the validation made by the audit teams, local government units in four regions were reported to have either not been able to prepare their Local Disaster Risk Reduction and Management Fund Investment Plan or there is no evidence to show that the plan was considered by the Local Disaster Risk Reduction and Management Council, as required under Republic Act 10121. In one local government unit, the Local Disaster Risk Reduction and Management Fund was utilized without an approved Fund Investment Plan.

In terms of strengthening disaster preparedness for an effective response, the collection, compilation, and dissemination of relevant knowledge and information on hazards, vulnerabilities, actual losses, and capacities is essential. The majority of local government units appear to lack such information, especially in the case of low-income class local government units (LGUs), where the human resources and technical complement of disaster preparedness remain deficient in terms of a systematic approach. The National Disaster Risk Reduction and Management Plan outlines the activities aimed at strengthening the capacity of the national government and the LGUs together with partner stakeholders, to build disaster-resilient communities, institutionalize disaster risk reduction, and enhance disaster preparedness and response capabilities at all levels. "Republic Act 10121 and other laws passed by the government have provided solid plans, but there have been significant question marks about its implementation, in terms of funding and consistency in approach" (NDDRMC, 2013).

THE SITUATION ANALYSIS FOR SUPER TYPHOON HAIYAN (YOLANDA) (STEP 2)

The most devastating disaster that occurred in the Philippines was the Super Typhoon Haiyan (known locally as Yolanda). The disaster led to 6,300 mortalities, affected 16 million individuals and caused an estimated $2 billion in damage. Most of the deaths caused by the Super Typhoon Haiyan occurred in the province of Leyte, in the local government areas of Palo, Tacloban, and Tanauan (total 4,870) (Office for the Coordination of Humanitarian Affairs, 2013). Northern Leyte (also called Leyte) is situated in the Eastern Visayas region of the Philippines. The province unites three-quarters of the island of Leyte. The island is encircled by large bodies of water with the Camotes Sea to the west, the Philippine Sea to the east, the Samar Sea to the north, and the Mindanao Sea to the south of the island. The province of Northern Leyte has a land area of 5,712.8 km^2 and a population of 1,724,679. It consists of forty-three local government units, each managed by a municipal or city mayor. The entire province is directed by the Provincial Government of Leyte. Recent natural disasters that occurred in the province of Northern Leyte include landslides, flash flooding, strong typhoon winds, and storm surges, but the destruction caused by Super Typhoon Haiyan led the United Nations to designate the disaster as L3, the highest level of emergency.

During the aftermath of Super Typhoon Haiyan, a total of fourteen United Nations organizations and thirty-nine nongovernmental and international nongovernment organizations were involved in the recovery and early rehabilitation. Following the United Nations cluster system, the Typhoon Haiyan Strategic Response Plan outlined actions across a range of clusters (focus areas) that included camp coordination, health, and livelihood, among others. These clusters may be led by a local government department, an intergovernmental organization (e.g., United Nations) or an NGO (Commission on Audit, 2015).

As can be seen, a government agency acted as the lead agency for a disaster response cluster while a United Nations agency or nongovernmental organizations functioned as co-leaders. For instance, in the case of the Typhoon Haiyan disaster response, the Philippine Department of Health took the lead agency role while the World Health Organization was designated as the co-leader for the health cluster. Various organizations took part in the response as cluster members. The health response plan aimed at four main strategies, specifically (1) addressing immediate healthcare needs, such as maternal, neonatal, and trauma care; (2) strengthening surveillance capability; (3) establishing primary and secondary health care functions along with tertiary referral system; and (4) coordinating internally with health services and other clusters. Member organizations within the health cluster coordinated throughout the response to contribute to the achievement of these goals.

The Department of Health prepositioned PHP 350.9 million (approximately $7.2 million) worth of assorted drugs, cot beds, medical supplies, medicines, and other essential materials. The Department of Social Welfare and Development prepositioned PHP 178.383 million (approximately $3.7 million) worth of goods or 89,260 food packs. It coordinated with several local government units in the preemptive evacuation of their constituents to identified evacuation centers. The Department of Social Welfare and Development started repacking operations in the National Relief Operations Center in Pasay. Approximately 4,500 armed forces of the Philippines troops from various units in Samar and Leyte were positioned on red alert. Three C-130 Air Force cargo planes and thirty-two military helicopters and airplanes were placed on standby, along with twenty navy ships. In Leyte and the whole of Region VIII, more than 6,453 policemen and support units were placed on red alert, with five trucks and six watercraft available for their eventual use. Some 1,022 fire trucks of the Bureau of Fire Protection and local governments had been put on heightened alert. Twenty-two rubber boats and thirty-six ambulances were on standby (Economic Research Institute for ASEAN and East Asia, 2012).

It can be inferred that the response—that includes enormous citizen participatory audit and governmental audit of disaster response programs—is considered the strength of the Typhoon Haiyan disaster response activities in general. The National Disaster Risk Reduction and Management Council, through the DILG, had directed all mayors and governors in the Bicol Region, the Eastern and Western Visayas, and Region IV-B to activate their local disaster risk reduction and management councils, monitor the situation in their areas of responsibility, make the necessary precautionary measures and warn their communities through the local media, especially local radio stations, about the imminent danger posed by the typhoon. The National Disaster Risk Reduction and Management Council emphasized proactive actions, that is, evacuation instead of rescue operations, and its ultimate aim of zero casualties (Dela Cruz and Suerte-Cortez, 2015). It conditions disaster preparation and early evacuation.

It can also be analyzed that the programs associated to disaster preparedness, response and recovery are connected to the funds sleeping in government bank accounts (corruption); location of the Philippines in the area vulnerable to natural disasters (geographical location of country); high level of population density especially in Metro Manila area (Dela Cruz R and Suerte-Cortez, 2015). The government and relief organizations need money before they can commence operations and effectively respond to those in need. However, aid flows in only during times of disaster. While the law has amply provided for much-needed resources, it is concerning that calamity funds remain underutilized, both at the level of selected national and local government units. It implies the slow utilization of funds. Most agency officials are too afraid to violate the law or at the least incur the possibility of a certain transaction being disallowed. Many of the conditions created by the aftermath of a typhoon are unexpected and therefore awaiting a new set of guidance. The bureaucratic structure and reliance on written guides minimizes opportunities for an immediate response. The majority of relief goods are perishable, the conditions of the victims, and the limitations where agents of the government operate, significantly increase the difficulty of responding to a serious calamity such as Typhoon Yolanda. While there is an increasing need for the government to spend its resources, which are readily available, the reluctance of state actors to deploy funds when there are no rules or because they insist on following long-standing procedures as if there are no emergencies causes a lack of guidance in logistics management, especially in procurement, and has consequences for disaster survivors.

Due to the highly inequitable distribution of physical assets, especially land, and the varied economic activities (mining, plantation agriculture, etc.), income inequality is particularly high in most of the Visayas as well as in Mindanao. The Autonomous Region in Muslim Mindanao ARMM is a notable exception. Manila dominates the Philippine economy, generating a little over one-third of the country's gross domestic product in recent years. By far the largest of the three major island groupings, Luzon in aggregate contributes almost two-thirds of the national economy. Consequently, different levels of development can be observed in various areas of Philippines (Dela Cruz and Suerte-Cortez, 2015).

As of August 19, 2014, the Department of Interior and Local Government (DILG) portal has recorded a total of 71,010,446,819.82 Philippine Pesos or $1,626,032,076.66 of foreign aid pledges. Of this amount, 44.2 billion Philippine Pesos or $1 billion are cash pledges, while 26.9 billion Philippine Pesos or almost $615 million are non-cash pledges (Dela Cruz and Suerte-Cortez, 2015).

Moreover, there are existing economic disadvantages among the affected population and the increase in prices of commodities due to increased demand in the post-disaster period. First, coconut growing and copra production are important sources of economic activity in rural areas, with 1.7 million people in Region VIII engaged directly (e.g., farm owners, workers and traders) or indirectly (e.g. transport and logistics). Sixty percent of small-scale coconut farmers live in poverty, are often land-poor, and are at high risk of indebtedness if they receive no livelihood support (International Press Foundation, 2015). Secondly, the extent of damage created by the super typhoon resulted in a very high demand for basic relief goods like noodles and consequent artificial price increases (Dela Cruz and Suerte-Cortez, 2015).

Systems for disaster preparedness and response already exist in the country and were utilized during the disaster. The country was also able to launch its response program by capitalizing on available resources from international partners. The primary challenges were related to financial and logistical systems and procedures for disaster response, while other problems were related to the overall economic fragility of the local populations affected by the disaster.

This situation analysis illustrates that the Philippines should invest more in disaster management and improve on its ability to utilize existing resources, particularly existing funds, procurement, and logistics. Disaster management systems should also be sensitive to the different levels of development across the various geographical region of the country.

THE CLASSIFICATION AND SPECIFICATION OF ADMINISTRATIVE-SPATIAL UNITS ACCORDING TO NATURAL DISASTERS (STEP 3)

Prior to this study, the European Observation Network, Territorial Development and Cohesion conducted research concerning the spatial effects and management of natural and technological hazards. It was comparable but executed on a sub-regional level and was focused on the European Union (Piepiora, Belarga, Alindogan et al, 2016). Similar research has been conducted in the Philippines using data from the Office of Civil Defense, the National Disaster Coordinating Center, and the Department of National Defense. Results were presented in the Compendium of Philippine Environment Statistics 2004. The list of disaster-prone areas as of December 2000 and 2002 by the type of disaster takes account of the provinces vulnerable to droughts, earthquakes, floods, typhoons, and volcanic eruptions. The National Disaster Risk Reduction and Management Plan 2011–2028 consists of the prone maps according to disaster types, but without distinguishing the provinces. The Philippine Atmospheric, Geophysical and Astronomical Services Administration recognized provinces but only for the purpose of recognizing four types of climate. Provinces were not distinguished according to the types of natural disasters endured.

It is useful to compare the Philippines with the area of the European Union because they are situated over a similar area (approximately 300,000 km²). The administrative unit in the Philippines which is nearest to the European Local Administrative Unit 1 is the province administrative unit. For instance, in comparison with Poland, Philippine provincial administrative units have considerably more people than Polish ones. This is due to two main reasons. First, the Philippines has less provinces, districts, high urbanized cities, and independent component cities than Poland leading to larger provincial administrative regions. Second, the Philippine overall population density is higher than Poland (2.5 times more) (Piepiora, 2012).

Geographic analysis of the Philippines shows that provincial administrative units can be distinguished according to two types: neutral and seaside. Neutral provinces are vulnerable to effects of earthquakes, mass movements, volcanic activity, extreme temperatures, fog, storms[12], floods (excluding coastal floods, ice jam floods, and glacial lake outbursts), droughts, wild-fires, landslides[13], epidemics, insect infestations, animal accidents, impacts, and space weather events. In the case of volcanic activity, we consider also indirect effects. For example, engines of airplanes when in the space over the Philippines are vulnerable to volcanic dust after eruptions. Seaside provinces are vulnerable to the effects of storm surges, coastal floods, as well as the other disasters that can affect neutral provinces.

The neutral provinces and cities with rights of provinces (high urbanized cities and independent component cities) and the seaside provinces and cities with rights of provinces are shown in figure 1.1.

Overall, it can be observed that majority of provinces in the Philippines are seaside provinces that are prone to coastal flooding and storm surges. This should be taken into consideration in national preparedness planning, training of disaster risk reduction and management staff, the purchase of disaster equipment, and other forms of capacity building. The created map can add better context to planning, risk reduction, and disaster management. Recognizing the difference between types of disasters experienced by provinces in the Philippines and their vulnerabilities would further contribute to more sensitive and tailored disaster programs.

CONCLUSION

In times of disaster, impacts and losses can be substantially reduced if authorities, individuals, and communities in disaster-prone areas are well prepared, ready to act, and equipped with the knowledge and capacity for effective disaster management. Disaster preparedness is described as the knowledge and capacities developed by governments, professional response and recovery organizations, communities, and individuals to effectively anticipate, respond to, and recover from the impacts of likely, imminent, or current hazard events or conditions.

Based on the situational analysis, it conveys a paradigm shift from reactive to proactive Disaster Risk Reduction and Management wherein men and women have increased their awareness and understanding on Disaster Risk Reduction and Management with the intention to increase people's resilience and decrease their vulnerabilities as contained in the national framework. While it cannot be denied that there have been significant innovations in the area of disaster preparedness and considerable funds spent for the said phase, its various elements are continuously being challenged. Community participation and decentralization is ensured through the delegation of authority and resources to local levels, but existing financial constraints continue to affect the capacity of certain local government units for effective disaster

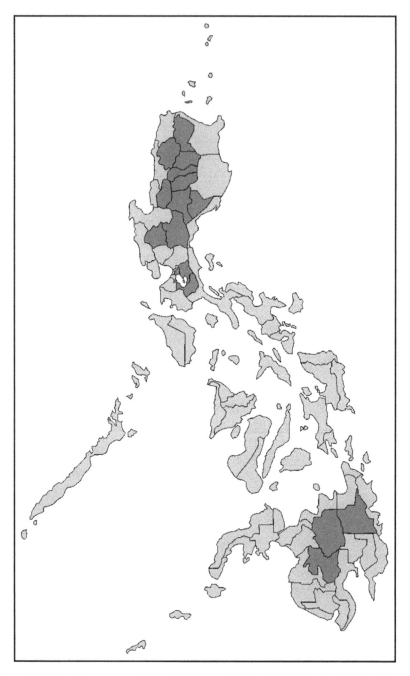

Figure 1.1 The Occurrence of Specific Forms of Natural Disasters in the Structure of Provinces in the Philippines.

preparedness and response. While the law encourages local government units' investment in disaster risk management, the current system, however, places local government units in poorer and island provinces (usually disaster-prone) at a disadvantage as they have lower revenues and thus, have fewer available funds. The situation is further aggravated by the fact that since the calamity fund is based on estimated revenues, there is no financial backup as poor local government units cannot collect the estimated revenues which are the bases of the budget. To strengthen the local government units' disaster preparedness for effective response at all levels, relevant knowledge and information on hazards, vulnerabilities, actual losses, and capacities must be collected, compiled, and disseminated. However, this is rarely implemented in the majority of local government units, especially among low-income class municipalities. The majority of the local government units have little capacity to establish databases which are useful in both disaster preparedness and response. The political will to implement existing laws on Disaster Risk Reduction and Management such as the Building Code and land use and zoning ordinances is another factor to consider. Mainstreaming disaster mitigation and preparedness in the local government unit development plan still remains a huge challenge. The human resource and technical complement of disaster preparedness remains inadequate in terms of a systematic approach.

The following conclusions can be drawn from this study. First, the Philippines is the third-most disaster-prone country in the world. In the past seventy years, storms accounted for more than half of the disaster events recorded. Flooding, which can also be attributed to storms, comes second. The most destructive storm among the disasters analyzed was Super Typhoon Haiyan. It caused 6,300 mortalities, affected 16.1 million people, and led to damages to the tune of $2 billion in damages.

Second, to address the effects of natural disasters in the Philippine, the Philippine Disaster Risk Reduction and Management Act was enacted. The Philippine disaster management system operates during a disaster in a cluster system. Moreover, our situation analysis highlights the need to further invest in disaster management and improve its ability to utilize existing resources, particularly in utilization of existing funds, procurement, and logistics. Disaster management systems should also be sensitive to the different levels of development across the various geographical regions of the country.

Last, our analysis of the disasters occurring in the country allowed the authors to generate a map distinguishing the two types of provinces in the Philippines, neutral and seaside. This map can add greater context to planning, risk reduction, and the management of disasters. Recognizing the difference between the types of disasters experienced by the provinces and their vulnerabilities would further contribute to more sensitive and tailored disaster programs in the Philippines.

NOTES

1. Centre for Research on the Epidemiology of Disasters (2017) EM-DAT Database.
2. Executive Order No. 335 s. 1941.Creating a Civilian Emergency Administration, Defining Its Powers and Duties and Providing for the Coordination and Control of Civilian Organizations for the Protection of the Civil Population in Extraordinary and Emergency Conditions.
3. Republic Act 1190. An Act to Provide for the Civil Defense in Time of War or Other National Emergency, Creating a National Civil Defense Administration, and for Other Purposes.
4. Executive Order No 159 s. 1969. Requiring All Departments, Bureaus, Offices, Agencies, Instrumentalities and Political Subdivisions of the Government, Including Corporations Owned or Controlled by the Government, The Armed Forces, Government Hospitals, and Public Educational Institutions, to Establish their Respective Disaster Control Organization. The Order required the establishment of a disaster control organization by all government offices including departments, bureaus, offices, agencies, instrumentalities and political subdivisions of government, including all corporations owned and/or controlled by government.
5. Republic Act No. 9729—An Act Mainstreaming Climate Change into Government Policy Formulations, Establishing the Framework Strategy and Program on Climate Change, Creating for this Purpose the Climate Change Commission, and for Other Purposes; Republic Act No. 10121: An Act Strengthening the Philippine Disaster Risk Reduction and Management System, Providing for the National Disaster Risk Reduction and Management Framework and Institutionalizing the National Disaster Risk Reduction and Management Plan, Appropriating Funds Therefor and For Other Purposes
6. Eurostat Local Administrative Units (LAU) is the classification being used in Europe for geographical representations.
7. The EM-DAT Database shows all the data on other related mortalities.
8. This excludes the Autonomous Region in Muslim Mindanao.
9. Republic Act No. 7160—An Act Providing for a Local Government Code of 1991.
10. Republic Act No. 10121: An Act Strengthening the Philippine Disaster Risk Reduction and Management System, Providing for the National Disaster Risk Reduction and Management Framework and Institutionalizing the National Disaster Risk Reduction and Management Plan, Appropriating Funds Therefor and For Other Purposes; 24.National Disaster Risk Reduction and Management Council (2011) National Disaster Risk Reduction and Management Plan 2011—2028.
11. Republic Act No. 10121: An Act Strengthening the Philippine Disaster Risk Reduction and Management System, and Providing for the National Disaster Risk Reduction and Management Framework and Institutionalizing the National Disaster Risk Reduction and Management Plan, Appropriating Funds Therefore and for Other Purposes.
12. Excluding storm surges, winter storms/blizzards, cold waves, severe winter conditions—snow/ice and frost/freeze.
13. Excluding snow avalanches.

REFERENCES

Abbott PL. (2009). *Natural Disasters*. San Diego: San Diego State University Press.

Alexander D. (1993). *Natural Disasters*. Berlin: Springer.

Balisacan A, Hill H, and Piza S. (2006). *An Overview: The Philippines and Regional Development*. Retrieved from https://www.adb.org/sites/default/files/publicatio n/159365/adbi-dynamic-regional-dev.pdf.

Centre for Research on the Epidemiology of Disasters. (2017). *EM-DAT Database*. Retrieved from http://www.emdat.be/database.

Commission on Audit. (2015). *Special Report on Haiyan*. Retrieved from https://do cs.unocha.org/sites/dms/CAP/SRP_2013-2014_Philippines_Typhoon_Haiyan.pdf, 24.05.2017.

Dela Cruz R. and Suerte-Cortez J. (2015). *Citizen Participatory Audit: An Approach for Accountability in the Philippines*. Retrieved from https://wpqr4.adb.org/ LotusQuickr/cop-mfdr/PageLibrary482571AE005630C2.nsf/0/9B4859AD13D1C 26348257F1800270FE2/$file/05%20Session%202_Asia_Vivien%2BRosa.pdf.

Economic Research Institute for ASEAN and East Asia. (2012). *Impacts of Natural Disasters on Agriculture, Food Security and Natural Resources and Environment in the Philippines*. Retrieved from http://www.eria.org/Chapter_15.pdf.

Eurostat. (2017). *Local Administrative Units (LAU)*. Retrieved from *in Extraordinary and Emergency Conditions*.

Global Disaster Preparedness Center. (2017) *Philippines*. Retrieved from http://www .preparecenter.org/countries/philippines.

Goranczewski, B., & Puciato, D. (2010). *SWOT Analysis in the Formulation of Tourism Development Strategies for Destinations*. Tourism, Vol. 20, Issue 2: 45-53. https://doi.org/10.2478/v10106-010-0008-7.

Integrated Research on Disaster Risk. (2014). *Peril Classification and Hazard Glossary*. Retrieved from http://www.irdrinternational.org/2014/03/28/irdr-peril-class ification-and-hazard-glossary/, 23.11.2015.

International Press Foundation. (2015). *Corruption in Disaster Recovery: Disturbing Tales from the Philippines and Haiti*. Retrieved from http://the-ipf.com/2015/1 1/27/corruption-in-ines-and-haiti.

McDonald R. (2003). *Introduction to Natural and Man-made Disasters and Their Effects on Buildings*. Linacre House, Oxford: Elsevier.

National Disaster Coordinating Council. (2007). *History of Disaster Management in the Philippines*. Retrieved from http://www2.wpro.who.int/internet/files/ eha/tookit_health_cluster/History%20of%20Disaster%20Management%20in%20 the%20Philippines%20NDCC%202005.pdf.

National Disaster Disk Reduction and Management Council. (2013). *Final Report Re Effects of Typhoon Haiyan*. Retrieved from http://ndrrmc.gov.ph/attachmen ts/article/1329/FINAL_REPORT_re_Effects_of_Typhoon_YOLANDA_%28HAI YAN%29_06-09NOV2013.pdf.

National Disaster Risk Reduction and Management Council. (2011). *National Disaster Risk Reduction and Management Plan 2011–2028*. Retrieved from http://www .ndrrmc.gov.ph/attachments/article/41/NDRRM_Plan_2011-2028.pdf.

National Oceanic and Atmospheric Administration. (2014). *Frequently Asked Questions*. Retrieved from http://www.aoml.noaa.gov/hrd/tcfaq/F1.html.

Office for the Coordination of Humanitarian Affairs. (2015). *Philippine Humanitarian Coordination Infrastructure*. Retrieved from http://www.unocha.org/what-we-do/coordination-tools/cluster-coordination, 23.11.2015.

Office for the Coordination of Humanitarian Affairs. (2013). *Typhoon Haiyan Strategic Response Plan*. Retrieved from https://docs.unocha.org/sites/dms/CAP/SR P_2013-2014_Philippines_Typhoon_Haiyan.pdf.

Office for the Coordination of Humanitarian Affairs. (2014). *Typhoon Haiyan Sitrep Number 34*. Retrieved from http://reliefweb.int/sites/reliefweb.int/files/resources/OCHAPhilippinesTyphoonHaiyanSitrepNo.34.28Jan2014.pdf.

Office of Civil Defense. (2015). *OCD Operation Manual for Response*. Retrieved from http://ocd.gov.ph/attachments/article/144/OCD_Operation_Manual_for_Res ponse.pdf.

Philippine Statistical Authority. (2017) *Philippine Standard Geographic Code*. Retrieved from http://nap.psa.gov.ph/activestats/psgc/listprov.asp.

Piepiora Z. (2012). *Ekonomiczne aspekty lokalnej polityki przeciwdziałania skutkom katastrof naturalnych. (Economic aspects of the local natural disasters policy)*. Warsaw: Kowary Publishing.

Piepiora Z. (2013). *The Occurrence of Natural Disasters in South East Asia and the International Cooperation in the Field of Preventing Their Negative Consequences*. Retrieved from https://www.ceeol.com/search/journal-detail?id=1136.

Piepiora Z, Belarga O, Alindogan MA, et al. (2016). *The Philippine Disaster Management System During Large-Scale Disasters*. Retrieved from http://www.sgem .org/sgemlib/spip.php?article8707.

Presidential Decree No. 1566. Strengthening the Philippine Disaster Control, Capability and Establishing the National Program on Community Disaster Preparedness.

Republic Act 1190. An Act to Provide for the Civil Defense in Time of War or Other National Emergency, Creating a National Civil Defense Administration, and for Other Purposes.

Republic Act No. 7160. An Act Providing for a Local Government Code of 1991.

Republic Act No. 9729. An Act Mainstreaming Climate Change Into Government Policy Formulations, Establishing the Framework Strategy and Program on Climate Change, Creating for this Purpose the Climate Change Commission, and for Other Purposes.

Republic Act No. 10121. An Act Strengthening the Philippine Disaster Risk Reduction and Management System, providing for the National Disaster Risk Reduction and Management Framework and Institutionalizing the National Disaster Risk Reduction and Management Plan, Appropriating Funds Therefor and for Other Purposes.

Schmidt-Thome P. (2006). *The Spatial Effects and Management of Natural and Technological Hazards in Europe—ESPON 1.3.1*. Retrieved from https://www.esp on.eu/programme/projects/espon-2006/thematic-projects/spatial-effects-natural-an d-technological-hazards.

Tupper A, Carnc S, Deveya J, et al. (2004). *An Evaluation of Volcanic Cloud Detection Techniques During Recent Significant Eruptions in the Western 'Ring of Fire'*. Retrieved from http://www.sciencedirect.com/science/article/pii/S00344 25704000562, 27.04.2016.

United Nations Development Program. (2017). *Human Development Index and Its Components*. Retrieved from http://hdr.undp.org/en/composite/HDI, 24.05.2017.

United Nations University and University of Stuttgart. (2016). *Work Risk Report*. Retrieved from https://www.google.com.au/url?sa=t&rct=j&q=&esrc=s&sour ce=web&cd=1&cad=rja&uact=8&ved=0ahUKEwilv9P21NrWAhUINpQKHcg8 A7gQFggmMAA&url=http%3A%2F%2Fweltrisikobericht.de%2Fwp-conte nt%2Fuploads%2F2016%2F08%2FWorldRiskReport2016.pdf&usg=AOvVa w1EoUrfSnsPF-TXe268oUp7.

Chapter 2

Aid Effectiveness and the Role of Evaluation in the Design and Implementation of Disaster-Oriented Programs in the Philippines

Anthony Alindogan

INTRODUCTION

The Philippines has been one of the countries in the world most heavily affected by disasters. Based on Philippine historical disaster data, the United Nations Office for Disaster Risk Reduction (2014) estimates an average annual loss of $1.2 billion from flooding and earthquakes alone. Globally, the Philippines ranks third among countries with the highest risk of disasters (United Nations University and University of Stuttgart, 2016) a position that it has held for several consecutive years.

Fortunately for the country, it has not faced the catastrophes alone. For instance, during Super Typhoon Haiyan, which caused an estimated $2 billion of damage and 6,300 lost lives (National Disaster risk Reduction and Management Council, 2013), the country received a total of $386 million of foreign aid from various countries (Foreign Transparency Hub, 2017). International aid workers and experts also came to the country to help with reconstruction and rehabilitation after the disaster. The current disaster risk reduction and management capability of the Philippines was not built by a single entity alone. It is the product of multiple sectors, local, international, public, and private, collaborating to improve the country's resilience and capability to respond to the threats of disaster.

Like any other investment in any sector of society, disaster-oriented programs need to show results in order to attract support and financing. Program stakeholders have a responsibility to ensure that resources are appropriately and effectively spent according to the needs of the disaster-affected population.

In line with this, recipients of funding for disaster-oriented programs such as government agencies, intergovernmental organizations, and nongovernmental organizations have to be accountable to their donors, beneficiaries, and other stakeholders and show that resources were spent efficiently.

Aid is not free; it comes with conditions. These conditions ensure that the funding is well spent and does not cause detriment (for example, as an avenue of corruption). Most importantly, these conditions ensure that the funding is properly allocated to the right programs that genuinely improve the lives of the people affected by disasters.

There is great demand to measure impact and identify results of disaster-oriented programs in the Philippines. Despite the Philippines being a leading regional actor in disaster risk management and response, recent research by Alcanya et al. (2016) reveals that there is no single study that compares the impacts and results of different disaster resilience and preparedness programs in the Philippines. Being able to generate data on these can rationalize and support further investment of resources on disaster-oriented programs. Investing in and strengthening evaluation systems can help fill the gap and address this challenge.

EFFECTIVENESS OF AID

Improving the lives of the disaster-affected population is not only about the amount of resources spent on disaster-oriented programs. It also concerns *how* these resources are spent. Disaster-oriented programs do not always produce the same level of results for similar amount of funding. Thus, organizations often seek ways to facilitate more effective aid delivery and to produce improved results for disaster-affected communities.

In 2005, through the Paris Agreement on Aid Effectiveness, there was an international recognition that aid needs to be more effective (Organisation for Economic Cooperation and Development, 2005a). The declaration was guided by five key principles which include (1) ownership, (2) alignment, (3) harmonization, (4) managing for results, and (5) mutual accountability (Organisation for Economic Cooperation and Development, n.d.).

The *Ownership* principle encourages countries to set their own strategies, improve their institutions, and tackle corruption. The *Alignment* principle requires countries and organizations to develop complementary and aligned strategies and to use existing local systems. The *Harmonization* principle recommends that countries and organizations coordinate their actions, simplify their procedures, and share information to avoid duplication of programs. The *Managing for results* principle requires countries and donors to focus on producing and measuring the results of programs. Lastly, the *Mutual accountability* principle emphasizes that donors and developing countries should be accountable for development results. These principles will be discussed in detail in the succeeding section of this chapter.

The Philippines is one of the participating countries in the Paris Declaration. The declaration involved agreement to 56 Partnership Commitments, all related to improving the effectiveness of aid. As each country's context may differ from one another, it was recognized that these commitments need to be interpreted in the light of the situation of each participating country. This allowed a certain degree of flexibility in the implementation of the declaration's commitments.

The principles mentioned above are expected to be implemented both in the development setting and in disaster-oriented programs. The Paris Declaration encourages agencies and organizations to adapt and apply these principles to differing country situations such as during complex scenarios like disasters. In the Philippines, compliance with the Paris Declaration commitments was steered by an inter-agency committee called the Philippine Harmonization Committee.

Principle 1—Ownership

Under the Ownership principle, participating countries are expected to exercise overall leadership in implementing programs while donor countries are expected to respect partner country leadership and help strengthen their capacity to exercise it. In addition, government agencies are expected to take the lead role in coordinating aid at all levels. This complements the current cluster coordination approach used in disaster response and rehabilitation. In the cluster approach, organizations working in a disaster response are grouped into different sectors of humanitarian action such as shelter, health, livelihood, etc. (United Nations Office for the Coordination of Humanitarian Affairs, 2012). Lessons from previous international disaster responses demonstrate that sectors can benefit from having clearly mandated lead agencies. Government agencies along with other organizations act as a lead and co-lead to coordinate all actions being taken in the sector. For example, in the Philippines the Department of Education acts as the lead coordinating agency for the education cluster of a disaster response, with another intergovernmental or nongovernmental organization acting as a co-lead. The cluster approach has been endorsed as a key approach to disaster management in the Philippines through the National Disaster Coordinating Council Circular No. 5 series of 2007.

Principle 2—Alignment

The Alignment principle minimizes fragmentation of aid efforts by encouraging government agencies and donor countries to work within a single aid or development framework. International organizations working in the Philippines are encouraged to use the country's own institutions and systems and work toward a common goal. This allows partnership development between government agencies and other organizations. In addition, it can facilitate concentration of resources to address a common problem leading to better results.

Principle 3—Harmonization

The Harmonization principle takes a pragmatic approach to the division of labor between government agencies and other organizations. Under this principle, government agencies commit to providing clear views on donors' comparative advantages and on how complementation can be achieved. There are organizations that specialize in specific sectors and it will be within every organization's collective agenda to maximize such expertise. In addition, the principle advocates for organizations to reform procedures and strengthen incentives for complementation and collaboration.

Principle 4—Managing for Results

This principle aims to establish results-oriented reporting and assessment frameworks that monitor progress toward desired results. Donor countries working in the Philippines are encouraged to align their monitoring and evaluation systems with existing systems being used in the country. Moreover, organizations are encouraged to work together in a participatory approach to strengthen the capacity and demand for results-based management.

Principle 5—Mutual Accountability

Under this principle, government agencies and donor countries commit to enhance mutual accountability and transparency in the use of aid resources. This will be done by involving aid partners in designing and evaluating aid programs and by jointly monitoring progress regarding agreed commitments on aid effectiveness.

By taking action to implement these principles, countries and organizations can address issues that influence the effectiveness of aid. These principles were embedded within governments and donor countries and were monitored at the international level through indicators of progress (Organisation for Economic Cooperation and Development, 2005b). The Global Partnership for Effective Development Co-operation currently tracks the global implementation of these principles. Country-level tracking of aid effectiveness is also conducted by some organizations. For example, in 2008 Australia's

Department of Foreign Affairs and Trade released an evaluation of their implementation of the Paris Declaration (Australia Department of Foreign Affairs and Trade, 2008). In the report they concluded that Australia made a reasonable start in implementing their commitment to the declaration, but improvements needed to continue.

In 2011, the Organization for Economic Co-operation and Development released a report regarding the implementation of the Paris Declaration in the Philippines. The report concluded that, overall, the Paris Declaration has contributed positively to aid effectiveness, particularly in reducing the fragmentation of aid efforts. However, as with Australia, more work needs to be done to fully implement the commitments in the declaration. The report highlighted friction and resistance within agencies regarding the changes the declaration entail. The report also mentioned the need for the Philippine government to broaden and intensify dialogue with the Congress and civil society organizations to achieve a more meaningful country ownership of the declaration. Despite the challenges, the Paris Declaration on Aid Effectiveness remains an important foundation in advocating for effective aid programs and in ensuring that aid efforts are aligned, generate results, and are accountable to the communities that it serves.

EVALUATION'S ROLE IN AID EFFECTIVENESS

A key method in determining aid effectiveness is through program evaluations. Program evaluation is defined as the systematic judgment of the worth of program and the production of knowledge to assist decision making about it (Owen, 2006). Typically, evaluations derive conclusions, highlight relevant findings affecting program implementation, and provide recommendations to improve the current or future similar programs. Despite its important role in disaster management, program evaluation is often overlooked. Much of the literature recommends conducting regular evaluations across the life cycle of a program to allow the program to be flexible and adaptive to the needs of target communities. However, in practice, evaluation is rarely done regularly and often only occurs toward the end of the program, driven by the funders' reporting requirements.

Evaluations of disaster-oriented programs usually focus on the outcomes and impacts of interventions in disaster-affected communities. Evaluation can be conducted internally or externally through an independent consultant, or could be a mix of both. Both internal and external evaluators carry their own set of advantages and disadvantages. For example, internal evaluators typically know more about the program and can develop better rapport with program staff, leading to more transparent and honest feedback. They are also more effective in continuously advocating for the utilization of evaluation findings. On the downside, internal evaluators may be perceived as biased toward the program that they are evaluating compared to an external evaluator, who is seen to be more independent.

From the previous discussions it can be seen that evaluation serves as the main mechanism to determine which programs are effective. Among the principles of aid effectiveness mentioned earlier, integral and most related to the practice of evaluation is the *Managing for results* principle. An effective aid program is one that leads to results that positively impact the lives of disaster-affected communities. At the core of an effective aid program is its ability to measure and demonstrate results. Disaster-oriented programs cannot afford to simply assume that good will come out of their actions. Programs need to confirm this and allot specific resources in measuring the outcomes and impacts of their interventions. Key to this principle is for countries and organizations to have transparent and timely evaluation frameworks.

Managing for results also relates to implementing aid in a way that actions are focused on working toward desired results and in ensuring that available information to support decision making is utilized. Information generated from evaluations should be gathered and taken into consideration not only when designing programs but also when making modifications during the program implementation phase. Knowing which programs are successful and able to achieve desired results can contribute to improving collective knowledge about which types of disaster programs are effective, how to improve the implementation of disaster-oriented programs, and in determining which programs are cost-effective.

WHY EVALUATION MATTERS—THE UNINTENDED NEGATIVE CONSEQUENCES OF AID

Each disaster-affected community is complex. Each has its own culture, political situation, and dynamic relationships with different stakeholders. At the same time, the impact of disasters also vary in terms of degree of damage, type of damage caused, and the timing of disasters. Due to these varying complex factors, designing disaster-oriented programs can be very challenging. What works in one community may not work in another. It is a reality that programs and program staff make mistakes. Thus, it is essential to be able to learn from mistakes and to be able to address them adequately in order to move forward. It is vital for disaster-oriented programs to develop a learning culture that is critical and that seeks to know the full impact of their actions.

If no performance assessment or evaluation of disaster-oriented programs is undertaken, negative unintended results could remain undiscovered. For example, in military conflict areas (such as in some provinces in Mindanao) program beneficiaries can be targeted for receiving aid. A report published by the Australian government (Commonwealth of Australia, 2012) regarding the effectiveness of aid in the Philippines highlights that inadvertently distributing more resources in one local group can cause resentment in excluded groups. This can put aid effectiveness at risk and harm donor reputation, which leads to difficulties working with the same community in the future. Research has shown that aid can influence local electoral processes in Philippine municipalities (Cruz and Schneider, 2012). These unintended results of aid provision may be wide-ranging and can counteract its positive effects. The possibility of having an unintended negative result also strengthens the argument that organizations implementing disaster-oriented programs would derive benefits from conducting an evaluation and measuring the effects of their actions.

Internationally, much has been learned regarding the unintended negative impacts of aid. For example, the immediate disposal of bodies after the Haiti earthquake led to long-term mental health problems for remaining family members (Jobe, 2010). The rapid disposal of bodies deprived the family of the knowledge of their loved ones' circumstances. This occurred despite the lack of evidence that cadavers pose an immediate public health risk. A study by Campos-Outcalt (as cited in Jobe, 2010) highlighted that epidemics that occur in a post-disaster period are generally respiratory and gastrointestinal disease related to poor living conditions. The United Nations also mentioned that peacekeepers deployed after the Haiti earthquake played a role in the initial outbreak of cholera that killed thousands of Haitians (The New York Times, 2016). The first victims of the cholera outbreak lived near a base of United Nations peacekeepers from Nepal where a cholera outbreak was underway. Waste from the base leaked to a nearby river further spreading the disease.

The large sudden influx of funding occurring after disasters also may have an unintended negative consequence. A large amount of aid can lead to almost instantaneous growth in all sectors which may cause inflationary and cultural disruptions (Kopinak, 2013). These disruptions can occur when hundreds of aid workers arrive in a community to work, contribute to the local community, and create a false economy. The creation of a false economy can be disastrous when donor money is reduced or withdrawn. This highlights the complexity of disaster management and the need to carefully plan interventions in order to avoid the negative unintended consequences of aid.

The examples highlighted above were mentioned not to discredit aid, but to highlight the importance of providing aid the right way. Conducting evaluations and learning from their findings can contribute in designing effective disaster-oriented programs and in allowing program implementers to address and minimize any possible negative unintended consequences of their programs.

EVALUATION IN THE PHILIPPINES

Evaluation has been included in Philippine national policy since 1987. Specifically, Executive Order 230 mandated the National Economic Development Authority (NEDA) to monitor and evaluate the implementation of the Philippine Development Plan. Across the years there have been changes and improvements in the policy context that supported the practice of evaluation in the country. Executive Order 376, issued during 1989, decentralized the practice of evaluation in government agencies and established the Regional Project Monitoring and Evaluation System. In 1999, NEDA Board Resolution No. 3 required the reporting of program outcomes and impact of agencies implementing development programs. In 2011, Administrative Order No. 25 created a nationwide performance framework to evaluate the Executive Branch of the government. However, most of these policies are tailored toward development programs

In 2015, NEDA and the Department of Budget and Management released Joint Memorandum Circular No. 2015-01 which led to the Philippine National Evaluation Policy Framework. The framework highlighted three main objectives. The first was to support evidence-based decision making. The second was to ensure program improvement through learnings and feedback obtained from the evaluation. The last was to ensure accountability to the people of the Philippines, funders, and other program stakeholders. The circular covered all government agencies which received funding from the government. It made evaluation universal and further increased demand for it. The circular also covered evaluation standards such as evaluation competencies, ethics, and best practices in evaluation. These standards remain relevant to the practice of evaluation in the Philippines today and are principally aligned with internationally recognized standards. For example, the evaluation criteria mentioned in the circular dictates that, at a minimum, evaluations shall address questions covering relevance, effectiveness, efficiency, and sustainability. This is aligned with the Organization for Economic Cooperation and Development Assistance Committee evaluation criteria (OECD, 2006).

Another provision in the circular is for the creation of neutral evaluation units within each government agency. Evaluators require independence to minimize biases and to be able to provide honest reporting regarding program impact. In countries like Australia, evaluation of aid programs is supported by an external body independent of the Department of Foreign Affairs and Trade. This strengthens credibility and ensures the independence of evaluation reports. To be properly executed, evaluation requires technical knowledge and skill. Having specialized evaluation units within government agencies to support the practice of evaluation can help improve the quality of evaluation reports.

IMPLICATION OF THE PARIS DECLARATION FOR THE PRACTICE OF EVALUATION AND THE DELIVERY OF DISASTER-ORIENTED PROGRAMS IN THE PHILIPPINES

Policy

The Philippine Disaster Risk Reduction and Management Act 2010 stipulates that the Philippines will adhere to and adopt universal norms and standards of humanitarian assistance and incorporate internationally accepted principles of disaster risk management. This includes the Paris Declaration on Aid Effectiveness.

The *Managing for Results* principle of the declaration requires disaster-oriented programs in the Philippines to have transparent and measurable assessment frameworks to gauge progress and show results. This commitment was specifically expressed in Section 9 of the Philippine Disaster Risk Reduction and Management Act where the Office of Civil Defense was required to

> review and evaluate the Local Disaster Risk Reduction and Management Plans to facilitate the integration of disaster risk reduction measures into the local Comprehensive Development Plan and Comprehensive Land Use Plan.

The Philippine National Disaster Risk Reduction and Management Plan 2011–2028 specifically outlines the monitoring and evaluation structure for the Philippine disaster setting.

The Philippines also has an active role in designing the Sendai Framework Monitor. This framework will establish a reporting mechanism to assist countries in measuring their progress in the implementation of the Sendai Framework for Disaster Risk Reduction 2015–2030, which the Philippines has adopted (National Economic and Development Authority, 2017). The Sendai Framework establishes global targets for disaster risk reduction. National targets and indicators are expected to be drafted and aligned to established global targets and indicators. Some of these targets relate to reducing disaster mortality, reducing the number of people affected by disasters, reducing the economic loss from disasters among others (United Nations General Assembly, 2016). Having specific targets and measurable indicators of success will drive further investments in improving data systems and in using it to evaluate the effectiveness of disaster-oriented programs.

Likewise, foreign government agencies funding or implementing disaster-oriented programs in the Philippines have policies to support the practice of evaluation. For example, Australian Aid, the Australian government agency for delivering aid, tracks its progress in implementing the Paris Declaration and emphasizes the need for better data quality for performance reporting (Department of Foreign Affairs and Trade, 2010).

Throughout the years, nongovernmental organizations (NGOs) working on disaster-oriented programs have been increasing their focus on evaluation. Multiple international guidelines have incorporated evaluation within their frameworks. For example, the Sphere Project (2011) initiated by various NGOs and the International Red Cross and Red Crescent Movement incorporated evaluation through the Core Standard 5: Performance Transparency and Learning. Evaluation has also long been expressed in the Red Cross Code of Conduct in Disaster Relief. Under the "Code of Conduct 9: We hold ourselves accountable to both those we seek to assist and those from whom we accept resources," it was specified that the organization "recognize the need to report on activities both from a financial perspective and the perspective of effectiveness." Such high-level policy implications of the Paris Declaration on Aid Effectiveness, particularly the emphasis on program evaluation, serve as the foundation for further changes seen in disaster-oriented programs at the operational level.

Operational Effects

In order to fulfil the policy commitments in the Philippine Disaster Risk Reduction and Management Act as well as in the National Disaster Risk Reduction and Management Plan, operational actions to support evaluation practice were employed. These includes the adoption of results-based programming, the development of a standard monitoring and evaluation template for disaster management, the use of specific indicators and target commitments, and the utilization and sharing of learnings from evaluation reports.

The adoption of "results-based programming" in the disaster risk reduction and management system required a shift on program planning, implementation, and reporting. Results-based programming involves planning in a way that ensures that the sum of interventions (actions) is sufficient to achieve the desired results and managing programs in a way that ensures the adequacy of financial and human resources to support the achievement of desired results (United Nations Children's Fund, 2003).

The Office of Civil Defense (OCD) developed a standard monitoring and evaluation template for disaster management. In addition, the OCD Operation Manual for Disaster Response (2015) emphasized that disaster response clusters will conduct post-response operation evaluations to document lessons learned and best practices observed. These evaluation reports will also be used by the National Disaster Risk Reduction and Management Council (NDRRMC) for policy improvement and organizational development.

There was also an emphasis on identifying specific indicators and target commitments across the various levels of disaster planning. These local-level targets are to be operationalized respective to local plans. These indicators will also be aligned to NDRRMP thematic areas. The NDRRMP thematic areas include (1) disaster prevention and mitigation, (2) disaster preparedness, (3) disaster response, and (4) disaster rehabilitation and recovery.

Lastly, there was an emphasis that learnings should be captured from implementing local plans and the lessons should be shared with stakeholders through evaluation reports.

The Philippine disaster management system followed a bottom-up evaluation structure.

For nongovernmental organizations, the increasing emphasis on evaluation prompted the creation of organizational units and positions which specialize in performing program evaluations. One role example is Monitoring and Evaluation Officer, whose responsibility is to establish and maintain a program's reporting and evaluation system. In some organizations, this position has a broader scope and includes a facilitating team or organizational learning as well as ensuring accountability to disaster-affected communities. Accountability includes transparency about program actions, funding sources, and program duration. It also encourages community involvement in disaster programming to be as feasible and practical as possible. There is acknowledgment of the value of community engagement, particularly in disaster risk reduction. Local people are acknowledged to be the main actors and instigators in reducing disaster risks (Asian Disaster Preparedness Center, 2008). People living in disaster-affected communities know the culture and context of their situations better than a program staff member, who may often be seen as an outsider. Overall, engaging community members can improve program design and implementation, making disaster-oriented programs better tailored to the communities that they intend to serve.

Establishing an effective monitoring and evaluation system early in the aftermath of a disaster has also been one of the priorities in present-day disaster response. This allows organizations to be more sensitive to the needs of disaster-affected communities and be responsive to the constantly changing disaster environment. Establishing an adequate monitoring system to support or complement the data collected during evaluations is essential to ensure evaluability of programs. Doing evaluability assessments early in the program cycle can help guarantee that conducting an evaluation for the program will be possible. Disaster-oriented programs need to allot specific and adequate resources to ensure that a responsive monitoring and evaluation system exists throughout the whole program cycle.

THE ROLE OF EVALUATION IN PROGRAM DESIGN AND IMPLEMENTATION

Given the complex and diverse nature of disasters, designing an effective and appropriate disaster-oriented program with no drastic negative unintended consequences is a prevailing challenge to organizations working with disaster-affected communities. The nature of disasters and their impacts are highly dynamic. It can be influenced by the political, societal, and developmental characteristics of the affected community, which can vary significantly between locations. It is because of these factors that the practice of evaluation holds an important role in implementing disaster-oriented programs. Evaluation influences the design and implementation of these programs by providing a practical on-the-ground perspective on which programs were generating desired results and what factors influenced program success or failure. Contrary to disaster research, evaluation of disaster-oriented programs has certain elements that allows it to be more appealing for designing and implementing programs. Some of these elements are discussed below.

Evaluation of disaster-oriented programs typically examines a program's (a) relevance/appropriateness, (b) efficiency, (c) effectiveness, (d) impact, and (e) sustainability. Reviewing these program aspects provides a consistent set of information that allows comparison between programs. Aside from the criteria stated above, other information collected during an evaluation typically relates directly to program implementation. This enables the generated information to be attuned to program designers and implementers.

There is a strong culture of beneficiary participation in the evaluation of disaster-oriented programs. This model serves two purposes; (1) to provide beneficiary perspectives relating to the effectiveness, impact, efficiency, etc., of the program and (2) to act as a means of demonstrating accountability to disaster-affected communities by providing them with a means to have their voices heard. Emphasis on stakeholder participation among all the actors in a disaster-oriented program fosters ownership of the evaluation. This increases the likelihood of the evaluation to be utilized and eventually influence how future similar programs are designed and implemented.

Aside from the main function of evaluation in providing relevant field data to influence program design and implementation, the act of evaluating serves several other purposes. First, evaluation planning would require stakeholders to commit to specific program outcomes. This contributes to propel program implementation, giving program staff a specific focus area in which to invest their efforts. Second, the act of evaluating is a manifestation of accountability. This is done by giving an opportunity to program beneficiaries to express their perspectives about the program, and by objectively analyzing the outcomes and impacts of the program to the communities that it serves. A strong culture of accountability drives quality improvement. Lastly, a positive evaluation of disaster-oriented programs can be a source of motivation for program staff and a means to celebrate accomplishments. Successful programs are often duplicated and scaled-up, and secure financial backing.

CURRENT TRENDS AND THE FUTURE
OF DISASTER EVALUATION

How disaster-oriented programs are evaluated continues to change over time as perspectives and priorities of program stakeholders evolve. Currently, the ability to be responsive and the capacity to show effectiveness are priorities in disaster program evaluation. These priorities are reflected in current evaluation methodologies that dominate the area, such as impact evaluations and real-time evaluations.

Impact evaluation is perhaps one of the long-standing evaluation methodologies for disaster-oriented programs. It focuses on the program's contribution in achieving higher level objectives (Austrian Development Cooperation, 2009). In impact evaluation, positive or negative long-term effects of a program are measured using an appropriate research design (e.g., pre- and post-testing, intervention and control group comparisons, etc.). Impact evaluations typically require a significant amount of planning and resources to conduct. There are multiple guidelines available in conducting impact evaluations. For example, a discussion paper of the Australian Office of Aid Effectiveness (Department of Foreign Affairs and Trade, 2012) highlighted a set of minimum standards in conducting impact evaluations and determining the appropriate time for when an impact evaluation should be undertaken. Those standards will not be discussed in this chapter. However, it is relevant to note that there are situations when conducting an impact evaluation is not appropriate and other evaluation methods should be chosen instead. There is a significant demand for programs to show impact but given the time-limited nature of disaster programs, impacts may take time to develop and the evaluation may not be able to immediately measure it. This may inaccurately lead to programs being evaluated as ineffective.

Real-time evaluation is a short and continuous process of evaluating a disaster-oriented program with an emphasis on immediate lesson learning rather than impact or accountability (Herson and Mitchell, 2006). It may sometimes be restricted to using some of the evaluation criteria discussed previously. This type of evaluation focuses on generating quick and timely reports to allow a program to make adjustments early on rather than waiting for the results of typical evaluations. Most organizations find real-time evaluations more appropriate for a disaster-oriented program, as program decisions made during a disaster response tend to be time-sensitive, especially during the early phases.

As organizations increasingly compete for limited aid resources, different methodologies emerge in disaster program evaluation. Some organizations are now focusing on their ability to show the "value" of their programs in financial terms. These "Value-for-Money" evaluations include methodologies such as the Social Return of Investment, which allows monetization of the social benefits and its direct comparison with program costs (Better Evaluation, 2017). Such a method allows organizations to show that the resources are allocated to the most cost-efficient and effective programs. Methods used for value-for-money evaluations are often limited by the assumptions used to monetize social benefits of disaster-oriented programs. Stakeholders need to agree on these limitations for the evaluation to be accepted and used.

Big data also presents opportunities to improve disaster evaluation. Big data can be loosely defined as large volumes of both structured and unstructured data which may come from social media and digital search engines, among other sources. It has already been used in assessing the impact of disasters in the past, such as during the Tohoku Earthquake in Japan, and Hurricane Sandy in the United States of America (Japan Science and Technology Agency and National Science Foundation, 2014). During Typhoon Haiyan there were attempts to use big data in similar ways. The MicroMappers website analyzes online data from tweets and uploaded photos and then displays the information to satellite maps (National Geographic, 2013). Organizations working in disaster-affected areas can use this information in their planning. Though typically used for assessments, big data analysis can complement current evaluation methods by providing a more reflective on-the-ground perspective of the impacts of disaster-oriented programs.

CHALLENGES TO EVALUATION AND EVALUATION UTILIZATION IN DISASTER-ORIENTED PROGRAMS

In the preceding sections of this chapter, I highlighted the critical role of evaluation in designing and implementing disaster-oriented programs. But despite the high-level commitments and organizational pressures to commit to evaluation, conducting an evaluation and utilizing evaluation findings can still be a challenge for individuals and organizations working with disaster-affected communities.

The absence of an organizational culture that promotes the use of evaluations in decision making can be a significant barrier for the practice of evaluation. Evaluation is a valuable source of information, but organizations and decision makers need to be familiar with when and how to use it (The World Bank—Independent Evaluation Group, 2011). The Philippine National Evaluation Policy Framework tried to address this challenge by requiring government agencies to ensure that an appropriate management response and follow-up will be conducted regarding evaluation findings and recommendations. The framework also emphasized that results of evaluations ought to be incorporated in planning and budgeting processes and the subsequent design of similar projects.

A review conducted by the World Bank regarding natural disaster response programs highlighted the need for stronger monitoring and evaluation systems which have a clear results focus. The review also mentioned that opportunities where meaningful evaluation could have taken place were missed. A similar finding in the Philippines complements this. A review performed by the Philippine Commission on Audit (2014a) during Typhoon Haiyan pointed out the challenges in reporting the compliance of local Disaster Risk Reduction and Management offices. The report concluded that the lack of information on what was delivered and the absence of feedback from disaster-affected communities made measuring the effectiveness of government response difficult. Developing an organizational culture which supports evaluation and sees it as a priority can help in preventing program staff to neglect important reporting tasks, especially when faced with a post-disaster environment that requires a lot of attention.

The complexity and dynamic nature of disasters may also influence how information flows in a disaster-oriented program. Challenges to information flow can affect the quality of evaluation generated to support program implementation. There can be multiple factors affecting information flow in a disaster setting (Altay and Labonte, 2014). These include low prioritization of data collection, unreliability of information, and even unwillingness of actors to cooperate. Clarifying data expectations, focusing on collecting relevant information, and cultivating good relationships with program implementers were some of the solutions recommended to address these challenges.

Technical capacity to conduct an evaluation is an area that requires significant investment. While technical knowledge and skill to conduct evaluations may be present at national and regional levels, local Disaster Risk Reduction and Management units may not have the same capacity to properly conduct a local-level evaluation. This is a key concern given the devolved structure of the Philippine disaster risk reduction and management system and the important role that local-level institutions play in disaster management. An assessment of disaster risk reduction and management at the local level conducted by the Philippine Commission on Audit (2014b) highlighted the need to improve local-level monitoring and evaluation. This cannot be done without investments in developing local technical capacity to conduct evaluations.

Timeliness of evaluations is a key factor that heavily influences the utilization of evaluations in disaster programming. Disaster-oriented programs work in a fast-paced environment. At the same time, decisions may need to be made within short time periods during which evaluation may not have been completed. Real-time evaluations are a solution to the need for fast reliable field data to support decision making.

A large number of evaluations may be commissioned, especially during high-profile disasters. There is often a missed opportunity to synthesize findings from these evaluations to make the information from them more usable to stakeholders and decision makers. Conducting meta-evaluations may help in creating a coherent set of information and recommendations to improve overall program implementation. Meta-evaluation is defined as the "meta-analysis and other forms of systematic synthesis of evaluations providing the information resources for a continuous improvement of evaluation practice" (Active Learning for Accountability and Performance in Humanitarian Action, 2003). Meta-evaluations of disaster-oriented programs may focus on synthesizing lessons learned and good practices from different agencies working with disaster-affected communities. This can be a valuable source of information to improve disaster management operations and policy.

LEARNINGS FROM EVALUATIONS:
THE CASE OF TYPHOON HAIYAN

Typhoon Haiyan was one of the most destructive disasters in the history of the Philippines. It affected the lives of millions of Filipinos and caused significant economic loss. At the same time, the disaster's high profile meant that it received a lot of media attention, which facilitated the influx of disaster recovery resources. A significant number of disaster-oriented programs were implemented by different organizations post-Typhoon Haiyan. This section examines some of the relevant learnings generated from evaluations of these programs.

Multiple evaluations made throughout the different stages of disaster response during Typhoon Haiyan provided valuable lessons that can be applied to other disaster-oriented programs. RTEs conducted by the United Nations Children's Fund (2014) within the first four months after the disaster highlighted key lessons learned early in the disaster response. They include a requirement for improved coordination between the different sectors working on the disaster, better metrics for performance management, and the need to develop a wider partner base in the Philippines and rely less on international NGO partners. As highlighted earlier, there are many sectors involved in implementing disaster-oriented programs. Local, international, public, and private sectors collaborate to help disaster-affected communities. Typically, high-profile disasters attract a wide variety of organizations implementing different types of disaster programs, and this necessitates a coordination mechanism to ensure that efforts are aligned toward a common goal.

In addition, it is important that local organizations and government agencies are empowered and have the capacity to provide greater contributions at times of disasters. Strengthening local capacity and making local agencies and institutions less reliant upon international support contributes to the sustainability of disaster-oriented programs.

Another relevant finding from UNICEF's evaluation was an emphasis on better accountability mechanisms. One recommendation was to improve communications with the disaster-affected communities, particularly being clear and transparent on what can be expected from them. Another recommendation was improving clarity of feedback and complaint mechanisms, which are valuable sources of information that evaluation researchers can use in advocating for program changes.

An evaluation conducted by Oxfam (2016) more than six months after the disaster showed how their program transitioned from an emergency response to a longer-term approach. It required the organization to focus on ensuring sustainability, retaining capacity, and maintaining good governance. Disaster-oriented programs are dynamic and need to be sensitive to the changing conditions of the communities they are working with. Timely evaluations can provide organizations with needed support to make such transitions effective.

There were significant lessons learned by the different government agencies during the implementation of disaster-oriented programs following Typhoon Haiyan. Some of these lessons were outlined in a special report written by the Philippine Commission on Audit (2014c) on the disaster. One finding from the report was the availability of funds to support local Disaster Risk Reduction and Management units to respond effectively. However, these funds were underutilized due to program staff being apprehensive in using the budget because of administrative accountability controls. The report described decision makers as "trapped in a struggle between implementing controls and accountability mechanisms and the demand for rapid response and recovery assistance." This is a significant lesson that can have a strong impact on national and local capacity to respond to disasters. The report recommended several actions to address this challenge, such as reviewing disaster work programs, revisiting existing relief operation systems, and adopting measures to ensure smooth flow.

Evaluations contain large amounts of information that can support programs throughout their life cycle. During Typhoon Haiyan, significant resources were allotted to evaluation and this yielded valuable information which was used in implementing disaster-oriented programs. These evaluations are also expected to contribute to organizational learning with important lessons adopted into organizational policies. Given the large amount of resources allotted to post-Typhoon Haiyan programs and evaluations, an independent meta-evaluation of the impacts and learning from these programs would be a valuable exercise to conduct. To the best of the author's knowledge, no such meta-evaluation has been carried out.

CONCLUSION

Assessing aid effectiveness is important in ensuring that disaster programs lead to genuine positive change for disaster-affected communities. Despite good intentions, the provision of aid can lead to unintended negative consequences for disaster-affected communities. This can lead to reputational harm for organizations, making it more difficult to work with the same community in the case of future disasters. Evaluation provides a mechanism to gauge whether disaster-oriented programs are effective or not. In the Philippines, the Philippine National Evaluation Framework requires all government-funded agencies to conduct evaluations of their programs Evaluation of disaster-oriented programs was also embedded in the national policy through the Philippine Disaster Risk Reduction and Management Act. At the same time, international agreements such as the Paris Declaration on Aid Effectiveness support the practice of evaluation and its use in decision making globally. Evaluation plays a unique and major role in the design and implementation of disaster-oriented programs. It provides valuable on-the-ground data tailored to the needs of both funders and program implementers. The data that it generates can influence the type and characteristics of programs that are funded and implemented. Evaluation contributes in driving the implementation of programs by allowing organizations to focus efforts in achieving specific and measurable objectives. In addition, evaluation is an important way of demonstrating accountability to stakeholders and a means to celebrate successes. Evaluation has been heavily embedded within disaster-oriented programs both in policy and within its operations. Despite this, challenges exist and evaluation is continuously evolving to address the demand of disaster-oriented programs and its users.

REFERENCES

Active Learning Network for Accountability and Performance in Humanitarian Action. (2003). Review of Humanitarian Action. Retrieved from www.alnap.org/material/75.aspx

Administrative Order No. 25—Creating an Inter-Agency Taskforce on the Harmonization of National Government Performance Monitoring, Information and Reporting Systems 2011.

Alcanya, T., Bolletino, V., Dy, P., et al. (2016). Resilience and Disaster Trends in the Philippines: Opportunities for National and Local Capacity Building. Retrieved from http://currents.plos.org/disasters/article/resilience-and-disaster-trends-in-the-philippines-opportunities-for-national-and-local-capacity-building/

Altay, N. & Labonte, M. (2014). Challenges in humanitarian information management and exchange: evidence from Haiti.

Asian Disaster Preparedness Center. (2008). Monitoring and Reporting Progress on Community-based Disaster Risk Management in the Philippines. Retrieved from http://www.adpc.net/v2007/Programs/CBDRM/INFORMATION%20RESOURCE%20CENTER/CBDRM%20Publications/2008/final_crphilippineshires_23nov.pdf

Australia Department of Foreign Affairs and Trade. (2008). Evaluation of the Implementation of the Paris Declaration: Case study of Australia. Retrieved from http://dfat.gov.au/aid/how-we-measure-performance/ode/Documents/evaluation-of-the-implementation-of-the-paris-declaration-case-study-australia-jan-2008.pdf

Austrian Development Cooperation. (2009). Guidelines for Project and Programme Evaluations. Retrieved from https://www.oecd.org/development/evaluation/dcdndep/47069197.pdf

Better Evaluation. (2017). Value for Money. Retrieved from https://www.betterevaluation.org/evaluation-options/value_for_money

Commission on Audit. (2014a). Disaster Management Practices in the Philippines: An Assessment. Retrieved from https://coa.gov.ph/phocadownloadpap/userupload/DRRM/Disaster_Management_Practices_in%20the%20Philippines-An_Assessment.pdf

Commission on Audit. (2014b). Assessment of Disaster Risk Reduction and Management at the Local Level. Retrieved from https://www.coa.gov.ph/phocadownloadpap/userupload/DRRM/Assessment_of_DRRM_at_the_Local_Level.pdf

Commission on Audit. (2014c). Report on the Audit of Typhoon Yolanda Relief Operations. Retrieved at https://www.coa.gov.ph/disaster_audit/doc/Yolanda.pdf

Commonwealth of Australia. (2012). Australian Aid in the Philippines Mid-term Evaluation of the Australia-Philippines Development Assistance Strategy 2007–11. Retrieved from https://www.oecd.org/countries/philippines/50024746.pdf

Cruz, C. & Schneider, C. (2012). (Unintended) Electoral Effects of Foreign Aid. Retrieved from http://wp.peio.me/wp-content/uploads/2014/04/Conf6_Cruz-Schneider-25.09.2012.pdf

Department of Foreign Affairs and Trade. (2010). Australia Update for the Evaluation of the Implementation of the Paris Declaration Phase 2. Retrieved from http://dfa

t.gov.au/aid/how-we-measure-performance/ode/Documents/australia-update-eval
uation-of-implementation-paris-declaration-phase-2-dec-2010.PDF

Department of Foreign Affairs and Trade. (2012). Impact Evaluation—A Discussion
Paper for AusAID Practitioners. Retrieved from https://dfat.gov.au/aid/how-we
-measure-performance/ode/Documents/impact-evaluation-discussion-paper.pdf

Department of Interior and Local Government. (2012). Primer: The National Disaster
Risk Reduction and Management Plan 2011—2028. Retrieved at http://www.dilg
.gov.ph/PDF_File/reports_resources/DILG-Resources-2012116-ab6ce90b0d.pdf

Executive Order No. 230—Reorganizing the National Economic and Development
Authority 1987.

Executive Order No. 376—Establishing the Regional Project Monitoring and
Evaluation System, Setting Forth Its Objectives, Defining Its Scope and Cover-
age, Requiring the Formulation of a Manual of Operations and For Other Similar
Purposes 1989.

Foreign Aid Transparency Hub. (n.d.) Retrieved from http://www.gov.ph/faith/

Herson, M. & Mitchell, J. (2006). Real-Time Evaluation: Where Does Its Value Lie?
Retrieved from http://odihpn.org/magazine/real-time-evaluation-where-does-its-va
lue-lie/

International Red Cross and Red Crescent. (n.d). Code of Conduct for the International Red Cross and Red Crescent Movement and NGOs in Disaster Relief.
Retrieved from https://www.icrc.org/eng/assets/files/publications/icrc-002-1067.
pdf

Japan Science and Technology Agency & National Science Foundation. (2014). Big
Data and Disaster Management A Report from the JST/NSF Workshop. Retrieved
from https://grait-dm.gatech.edu/wp-content/uploads/2014/03/BigDataAndDisas
ter-v34.pdf

Jobe, K. (2010). Disaster relief in post-earthquake Haiti: Unintended consequences
of humanitarian volunteerism. *Travel Medicine and Infectious Disease Journal*, 9,
1–5.

Kopinak, J. (2013). Humanitarian Aid: Are Effectiveness and Sustainability Impossible Dreams? Retrieved from https://sites.tufts.edu/jha/archives/1935

National Disaster Coordinating Council. (2007). Circular No. 05 Series of 2007—
Institutionalization of the Cluster Approach in the Philippine Disaster Manage-
ment System, Designation of Cluster Leads and Their Terms of Reference at the
National, Regional and Provincial Level.

National Disaster Disk Reduction and Management Council. (2013). Final Report
Re Effects of Typhoon Haiyan. Retrieved from http://ndrrmc.gov.ph/attachmen
ts/article/1329/FINAL_REPORT_re_Effects_of_Typhoon_YOLANDA_%28HAI
YAN%29_06-09NOV2013.pdf

National Disaster Risk Reduction and Management Council. (2011). National Disaster Risk Reduction and Management Plan 2011—2028. Retrieved from http://www
.ndrrmc.gov.ph/attachments/article/41/NDRRM_Plan_2011-2028.pdf

National Economic and Development Authority and Department of Budget and Management. (2015). Joint Memorandum Circular No. 2015-01 National Evaluation
Policy Framework of the Philippines. Retrieved from http://www.neda.gov.ph/wp

-content/uploads/2015/07/NEDA-DBM%20Joint%20Memorandum%20Circular
%20No.%202015-01%20-%20National%20Evaluation%20Policy%20Framework
%20of%20the%20Philippines.pdf

National Economic and Development Authority. (2017). PH Leads Discussions on the Sendai Framework Monitoring Prototype. Retrieved from http://www.neda .gov.ph/2017/06/05/ph-leads-discussion-on-the-sendai-framework-monitoring-p rototype/

National Geographic. (2013). Scanning Social Media to Improve Typhoon Haiyan Relief Efforts. Retrieved from http://news.nationalgeographic.com/news/2013/ 11/131108-typhoon-haiyan-philippines-crisis-mapping/

Office of Civil Defense (2015) OCD Operation Manual for Response. Retrieved from http://ocd.gov.ph/attachments/article/144/OCD_Operation_Manual_for_Res ponse.pdf

Organization for Economic Cooperation and Development. (2005a). Paris Declara-tion on Aid Effectiveness and Accra Agenda for Action. Retrieved from http:// www.oecd.org/dac/effectiveness/34428351.pdf

Organization for Economic Cooperation and Development. (2005b). Procedure for Additional Endorsement of the Paris Declaration on Aid Effectiveness. Retrieved from http://www.oecd.org/dac/effectiveness/36083092.pdf

Organization for Economic Cooperation and Development. (2006). DAC Evaluation Quality Standards. Retrieved from http://siteresources.worldbank.org/EXTGL OREGPARPROG/Resources/DACEvaluationQualityStandards.pdf

Organization for Economic Cooperation and Development. (2011). Second-Phase Country Level Evaluation of the Implementation of the Paris Declaration in the Philippines. Retrieved from http://www.oecd.org/countries/philippines/47670364 .pdf

Organization for Economic Cooperation and Development. (n.d). The Paris Declara-tion on Aid Effectiveness: Five Principles for Smart Aid. Retrieved from http:// www.oecd.org/development/effectiveness/45827300.pdf

Owen, J. (2006). *Program Evaluation Forms and Approaches* (3rd ed.). Crows Nest, NSW: Allen & Unwin.

Oxfam GB. (2016). Humanitarian Quality Assurance—Philippines: Evaluation of Oxfam's Humanitarian Response to Typhoon Haiyan. Retrieved from http://pol icy-practice.oxfam.org.uk/publications/humanitarian-quality-assurance-philippine s-evaluation-of-oxfams-humanitarian-re-592986

Republic Act 10121: Philippine Disaster Risk Reduction and Management Act 2010.

The New York Times. (2016). U.N. Admits Role in Cholera Epidemic in Haiti. Retrieved from https://www.nytimes.com/2016/08/18/world/americas/united-nat ions-haiti-cholera.html

The Sphere Project. (2011). The Sphere Project: Humanitarian Charter and Minimum Standards in Humanitarian Response. Retrieved from http://www.ifrc.org/PageF iles/95530/The-Sphere-Project-Handbook-20111.pdf

The World Bank—Independent Evaluation Group. (2011). Natural Disaster Response Lessons from Evaluations of the World Bank and Others. Retrieved from https://ie g.worldbankgroup.org/Data/reports/eval_brief_nat_disaster_response.pdf

UNICEF. (2014). Real-time Evaluation of UNICEF's Humanitarian Response to Typhoon Haiyan in the Philippines. Retrieved from https://www.unicef.org/evaldat abase/files/UNICEF_Philippines_Haiyan_RTE_FINAL_REPORT.pdf

United Nations Children's Fund. (2003). Understanding Results Based Programme Planning and Management. Retrieved from https://www.unicef.org/evaluation/f iles/RBM_Guide_20September2003.pdf

United Nations General Assembly. (2016). Report of the Open-Ended Intergovern-mental Expert Working Group on Indicators and Terminology Relating to Disaster Risk Reduction. Retrieved from http://www.preventionweb.net/files/50683_oiew greportenglish.pdf

United Nations Office for Disaster Risk Reduction. (2014). Basic Country Statistics and Indicators—Philippines. Retrieved from http://www.preventionweb.net/countr ies/phl/data/

United Nations Office for the Coordination of Humanitarian Affairs. (2012). OCHA Message: The Cluster Approach. Retrieved from https://www.unocha.org/sites/u nocha/files/dms/Documents/120320_OOM-ClusterApproach_eng.pdf

United Nations University & University of Stuttgart. (2016). World Risk Report. Retrieved from https://collections.unu.edu/eserv/UNU:5763/WorldRiskReport20 16_small_meta.pdf.

Chapter 3

Children in Post-Disaster Conditions

The Case of Humanitarian Intervention of Save the Children in Post-Typhoon Haiyan in Leyte, Philippines

Liezl Riosa, Fernanda Claudio, and M. Adil Khan

INTRODUCTION

The effects of disasters linger long after their appearance and always entail differential impacts within communities. Vulnerability analyses invariably highlight the higher risks of harm experienced by children in a post-disaster situation, and yet these risks are often overlooked, especially in aid interventions that can be formulaic and not sensitive to concerns prioritized by communities and local government leaders who may highlight specific vulnerabilities within their populations. Disaster responses are often devoid of a child's perspective and, for these reasons, we interrogate the role of international nongovernmental organizations (INGOs) in addressing the needs of children in post-disaster situation. We examine the work of Save the Children in the aftermath of Typhoon Haiyan in Leyte, Philippines, by reviewing programs and activities conducted by Save the Children, focusing first on the organization's priorities and programs, and second, on how it addressed relief, recovery, and rehabilitation of children. We assessed Save the Children's processes and outcomes against the UN Children's Charter to examine the appropriateness and effectiveness of these initiatives, including from the perspectives of children and adult residents (surviving parents and family), as well as other stakeholders.[1]

TYPHOON HAIYAN AND DISASTER RESPONSE

On November 8, 2013, Haiyan (locally known as Yolanda), the most powerful cyclone ever to make landfall in recorded history, struck the Central Philippines. A Category 5 typhoon on the Saffir-Simpson hurricane scale, Haiyan carried maximum sustained winds of 315 kilometers per hour (kph) with gusts of 379 kph (Lagmay et al., 2015). It swept through 171 cities and municipalities in 14 provinces of the country, destroying a million homes and affecting 13.5 million of the Philippines' 105 million residents: 1,061 people missing, 29,000 injured, 7.5 million displaced (Lagmay et al., 2015; Salazar, 2015), and approximately 10,000 deceased (Brown, 2013). Economic loss amounted to approximately $10 billion, making the natural disaster's impact greater than the 2010 Haiti earthquake in terms of damaged homes (95,000 shelters) and the 2004 Indian Ocean tsunami in terms of population affected (roughly 2.3 million) (Salazar, 2015).

Haiyan caused enormous damage and upheaval in the Philippines. It generated storm surges in many islands. The highest inundation, measuring 7 meters, occurred in Tacloban City, Leyte Province (Takagi & Esteban, 2015). Leyte Province was the area hardest hit by Haiyan and its coastal communities proved to have weak defenses against the typhoon (Lum & Margesson, 2014; Lagmay et al., 2015; Takagi & Esteban, 2015). Leyte is in the Eastern Visayas Region of the country, which is ranked third among seventeen regions in terms of poverty (31.9 percent of families) (Santos, 2013). Leyte incurred the highest number of Haiyan-related casualties at 5,073 individuals (Lum & Margesson, 2014). Between 66 and 90 percent of Leyte's structures were severely damaged or destroyed, including airports and medical facilities (Lum & Margesson, 2014).

Of the 13.2 million people affected by Haiyan (Lum & Margesson, 2014), children accounted for 4,000 of 6,300 of total deaths and 1.7 million of the 4.4 million displaced (Branigan, 2013). In total, the typhoon affected 5.9 million children with numbers of orphans remaining uncertain (United Nations International Children's Emergency Fund [UNICEF], 2014). Thirty-two percent of *barangays* (villages, the smallest Philippine political unit) in the hardest-hit areas reported cases of unaccompanied children, their caregivers (parents, grandparents, or senior relatives who were looking after the children) having died (Castro, 2014). In the aftermath, affected children displayed behavioral changes, including "fear of the wind and rain; uncontrollable crying and screaming and unwillingness to go to school" (Castro, 2014, p. 7). They endured lack of food and shelter as well as unsanitary facilities (Castro, 2014). Orphaned or unaccompanied children became particularly vulnerable to exploitation and trafficking (Branigan, 2013).

Many orphaned children were sheltered by grandparents and other relatives, proof of strong family ties which are central to Philippine society (Win, 2014). As one grandmother who became her grandson's carer stated, "It is Filipino custom to take in your kin if their parents passed away. I know of many who have done the same," (Win, 2014). Aid workers observed that living with relatives aided normalcy in children's daily lives but placed increased pressure on carers who already had their own families to look after (Win, 2014).

In response to Haiyan, as in previous large-scale disasters in the country, the Philippine government took the lead in addressing post-disaster needs but relied heavily on international support to boost its immediate response, rehabilitation, and recovery measures. The government created a national taskforce to facilitate rapid transition from relief to rehabilitation in typhoon-stricken areas (Salazar, 2015). It launched a four-year "reconstruction assistance plan" costing $8 billion in housing, education, agriculture, re-establishment of livelihood, disaster and protection to be rolled out in short-term interventions through 2014, and longer-term solutions through 2017 (Lum & Margesson, 2014, p. 218). Concurrently, international agencies immediately sent humanitarian assistance to the Philippines (Lum & Margesson, 2014, p. 218).

The United Nations, international nongovernmental organizations, private voluntary agencies, and bilateral and multilateral donors were the primary humanitarian responders in the Haiyan crisis because many of these agencies had preexisting development projects in the Philippines (Lum & Margesson, 2014, p. 221). NGOs such as Save the Children and World Vision that traditionally promote the rights and welfare of children in the Philippines were well-placed to provide a humanitarian response to children and "complement the (country's) reconstruction plan and fill gaps identified by the government or through inter-agency assessments" (Lum & Margesson, 2014, p. 221).

World Vision provided emergency relief across the Philippines immediately after Haiyan. In early 2014, the organization progressed from the relief phase to the recovery phase, employing a multisector approach that would address needs related to health including water, sanitation and hygiene, and community infrastructure (World Vision, 2015). World Vision then scaled up its response to the rehabilitation phase in early 2015, focusing on livelihood provision. At almost the same time, World Vision launched Hope for Tacloban's Children, a project designed to provide a "safer space to live, learn and play" (World Vision, 2015) for children living in the most impoverished parts of Tacloban City.

Save the Children was also among the first responders after Haiyan. Its activities included distribution of food and water, provision of mobile clinics, provision of housing materials and hygiene-related items, and repairing of health, school, and water facilities (Save the Children, 2014). In 2014, Save the Children transitioned to rehabilitation work by providing cash transfers, community grants, and skills development training to help recover livelihoods and local economies (Save the Children, 2014). The organization assisted victims in many Haiyan-affected areas, but prioritized critical need areas, including Leyte Province. This study critically examines Save the Children's work in aid of children after typhoon Haiyan against internationally agreed frameworks of assistance relevant to children in disaster, more specifically, in aspects relating to engagement of children and other key stakeholders in needs assessment, in interventions relevant to health and nutrition, water, sanitation and hygiene, and child protection and livelihood.

METHODS

This study employed qualitative research methods which are interpretive and "respect multiple meanings of human affairs" (Stake, 2010, p. 15), specifically addressing contexts, and individual and organizational perspectives to contribute to understandings of current or "emerging concepts that may help explain human social behaviour" (Yin, 2011, p. 8). We investigated child-centered disaster response and rehabilitation management in Leyte Province through an examination of secondary data and in-depth interviews. The secondary data consisted of published reports by Save the Children regarding their post-Haiyan programs. An internet search was conducted for reports related to the response to Haiyan which yielded a number of documents by aid agencies and the Philippine government. Ten semi-structured interviews were conducted online with nine residents of Leyte, and a child rights expert from the Philippines' House of Representatives. Purposive sampling and snowball-sampling were used to recruit Leyte-based respondents (Morgan, 2008). Initially two Leyte-based respondents were approached, who nominated a further seven individuals. All respondents were aged over eighteen years. The child rights expert was selected based on specific expertise and availability. Interviews were conducted in Tagalog and English. The questionnaire addressed children's vulnerabilities before and after Haiyan and the role of Save the Children in the humanitarian response and post-disaster recovery. Interview responses were thematically analyzed by the lead author for salient themes and reviewed by the coauthors. The results of the document analysis, namely the identification of child-focused disaster response frameworks, were compared to the results of the thematic analysis of interviews.

KEY CONCEPTS AND ANALYTICAL FRAMEWORK

This section proposes an analytical framework to understand and review the work of Save the Children, including its successes and difficulties in addressing children's needs post-Haiyan in Leyte. We review definitions and concepts relating to disaster, disaster vulnerability, children's disaster vulnerability, and humanitarian aid, and address their applicability in this context to build upon our framework.

Definitions of disaster vary, but can be summed up as any destructive event taking place anywhere in the world, affecting large populations and resulting in deaths, injuries, and damage to livelihoods, property, infrastructure, and the environment (International Federation of Red Cross and Red Crescent Societies (IFRC, no date); Wisner & Adams, 2002; Kreps, 1984; Lynch et al., 2010; Mohamed, 2007; Rutherford & Boer, 1983; Silverman & La Greca, 2002; Trivedi, 2013). Disasters are typically classified as either natural or man-made (IFRC; Lynch et al., 2010; Mohamed, 2007; Silverman & La Greca, 2002; United Nations Development Programme [UNDP], 2004; Wisner & Adams, 2002). Often referred to as "acts of God," natural disasters are cataclysmic activities, including typhoons (Lynch et al., 2010, p. 10; Mohamed, 2007, pp. 707–708). Man-made disasters comprise technological or industrial failure, terrorism, and complex humanitarian emergencies (such as international wars and genocides) (Lynch et al, 2010; Mohamed, 2007; Silverman & La Greca, 2002; Trivedi, 2013). Often natural and man-made disasters converge, becoming hybrid disasters (Mohamed, 2007, p. 705; Wisner & Adams, 2002, p. 10) and the effects of natural disaster on a community depend on preexisting social, economic, political, infrastructural, and environmental conditions that affect vulnerability.

Disaster vulnerability results from "social, political, environmental, and economic conditions" within the areas of impact (Bolin, 2007, p. 14). Disasters result from combinations of physical and social occurrences (Quarantelli, 1990). Similarly, vulnerability results from cumulative processes corresponding to "historical, political, economic, environmental and demographic factors" (Bolin, 2007, p. 124), causing inequitable resource distribution. Inequities manifest in inefficient government programs, environmental injustice, rapid urbanization, maldistributive economies, and political struggles, among others (Peet & Watts, 2004). These conditions create environmental risks linked to both geography and the built environment which are experienced through unstable livelihoods, meager incomes, legal and political discrimination, and inadequate social protections offered by governments (Bolin & Stanford, 1999; Cannon, 1994, as cited in Bolin, 2007, p. 124). In all of these circumstances, children's agency is diminished, highlighting the importance of child-focused response approaches that account for their needs across the whole of program cycles, from needs assessments to aid delivery.

Colonial legacies also influence present-day disaster vulnerability and anthropological studies analyze this phenomenon in relation to poverty, underdevelopment, and environmental decay (Johnston, 1994; Oliver-Smith, 1986; Peluso & Watts, 2001). The severity of the 1970 earthquake in Peru resulted from a colonial legacy of land-use patterns and government policies that disenfranchised First Peoples and small agriculturalists (Oliver-Smith, 1986). For these reasons, developing countries are generally most vulnerable to disasters (Alcantara-Ayala, 2002; Drabo & Mbaye, 2014; and Strobl, 2012). Between 1970 and 2002, 77 percent of all natural disasters worldwide[2] occurred in the developing parts of the world (Strobl, 2012, p. 130). When disaster strikes, conditions of poverty, including "malnutrition, homelessness or poor housing, and destitution" intensify vulnerability in developing countries (Wisner & Adams, 2002, p. 13). Factors that explain discrepancies in impact include social class and "occupation, caste, ethnicity, gender, disability and health status, age and immigration status" (Wisner et al., 2004, p. 11). Additionally, "political, economic and spatial processes of marginalization" also account for differential impact of disaster (Wisner et al., 2004, as cited in Bolin, 2007, p. 123). In short, "vulnerability is the characteristics of a person or group and their situation that influences their capacity to anticipate, cope with, resist, and recover from the impact of a natural hazard" (Wisner et al., 2004, p. 11).

Children, women, the elderly, and individuals with illnesses and disability are most vulnerable to disasters (Australian Red Cross, 2016; Lynch et al., 2010, p. 14; Rothstein, 2013, p. 602; WHO, 2016). Infants and young children in particular are physically defenseless to violent disasters "due to their partial or total dependence on adults" (Peek, 2008, p. 3). Older children and adolescents are vulnerable to injuries or deaths but more likely to develop "behavioral, psychological and emotional issues in the aftermath of disaster" (Peek, 2008, p. 3). Children comprise the greatest number of casualties during disasters (Rothstein, 2013, p. 602). In 2012, the United Nations estimated that the global numbers of children affected by disasters stood at 66 million (Nikku, 2012). Approximately 20,000 children were orphaned by the 2004 tsunami and almost 40 percent were under five years of age (Carballo et al., 2006, as cited in Ager et. al., 2010, p. 1271). Over 5,000 children were separated from parents or caretakers during the Sichuan earthquake in 2008 (Ager et al., 2010, p. 1271). In sub-Saharan Africa, over 12 million children have lost their parents to AIDS (UNICEF & UNAIDS, 2004). Disasters compromise children's general well-being and developmental growth (Ager, Stark, Akesson & Boothby, 2010, p. 1271; Silverman & La Greca, 2002). Separation from or loss of parents due to disasters is related to depression in children, which could be aggravated by trauma linked to disaster experience, leading to severe anxiety and post-traumatic stress disorder (Silverman & La Greca, 2002, p. 20; Stark et al., 2012, p. 229). Clearly, the scale of the impact of disaster on children is enormous and requires attention.

Research has shown that psychological and behavioral conditions after disasters are worsened by children's post-disaster circumstances (Lynch et al., 2010; Rothstein, 2013; Wisner & Adams, 2002). Children are exposed to risks inherent in evacuation centers such as food and water shortages, inadequate hygiene, and disease outbreaks (i.e., influenza; diarrhoea, malaria, measles, and respiratory tract infections) (Lynch et al., 2010, p. 15; Wisner & Adams, 2002, p. 46). Disaster-affected children, especially those displaced, separated, or having lost caretakers, are vulnerable to gender-based violence, exploitation, rape, prostitution, trafficking, and soldiering (ARC, 2016; Lynch et al., 2010, p. 14; Nikku, 2012). These perilous situations force children to stop attending school and compromise children's rights to "survival, protection, and development" as sanctioned by the Convention on the Rights of the Child (CRC) (Kunder, 1998, p. 2). In post-tsunami Aceh, for example, children suffered domestic violence, dropped out of school, and engaged in hazardous labor (Stark, Bancroft, Sustikarini and Meliala, 2012, p. 231). Mothers also forced young girls into early marriage as an economic strategy, thereby rendering them vulnerable to domestic violence (Stark et. al, p.232).

In inequitable societies, disruptions disproportionately affect children. In these contexts, conditions of powerlessness and risk often "lead to a sense of hopelessness and inability to think that the future will be better" (Lynch et al., 2010, p. 9), often expressed in failure to return to school or commencing early employment. Disasters often exacerbate risks and prejudice inherent in the preexisting conditions within communities. Prior to the 2004 tsunami, about three million children were engaged in labor, almost half of those aged between thirteen and eighteen years did not attend school, and approximately 2.5 million were abused or exploited (Stark et al., 2012, p. 229). Additionally, about a third of the 80,000–100,000 sexually exploited female Indonesians were below eighteen years (Indonesian Ministry of National Development Planning, 2012, as cited in Stark et al., 2012, p. 229). These hardships occurred in contexts of social disruption wrought by the three-decade-long political struggle between the Indonesian government and the Free Aceh Movement, which curtailed social and economic security. (Stark et al., 2012, p. 22). Similarly, Gupta and Agrawal (2010, p. 1997) described pre-earthquake Haiti as hostile for children because of chronic poverty, poor infrastructure, and an inadequate health system that compromised their health and safety and increased their vulnerability to disaster (Gupta & Agrawal, 2010, p. 1997). Despite the fact that it ratified the UN CRC in 1994, Haiti recorded high mortality among infants, children under five years of age, and mothers (UNICEF, 2010, as cited in Gupta & Agrawal, 2010, p. 1997). Additionally, only half of primary school-aged children attended school (Gupta & Agrawal, 2010, p. 1997).

Children are unquestionably the most vulnerable sector of society in disasters. Not only do they suffer disproportionately in terms of health and security, the impact of disasters can have severe and life-long effects on health, schooling and employment outcomes, and vulnerability to violence. Considering the young demographic profile of most developing countries, including the Philippines, and children's specific vulnerabilities and needs, it is unsurprising that many aid agencies increasingly target their work toward the care and well-being of children.

HUMANITARIAN AID: INGO POST-DISASTER WORK

When disaster strikes in developing countries, INGOs, along with official donors, often step in to provide or complement local capacities, often because of their access to relevant technical and logistical resources (Lynch et al., 2010, p. 20). Some INGOs specialize in humanitarian response, while others, whose primary focus is development, and whose presence in-country preexists disasters, often re-calibrate and re-allocate their resources to response and recovery (Lynch et al., 2010, p. 20). Many developing countries have disaster response policies, but, as outlined in the Sendai Framework for Disaster Risk Reduction 2015–2030 of the UN International Strategy for Disaster Reduction, disaster response and recovery is a "shared responsibility" among state and nongovernment stakeholders (UNISDR, 2015, p. 23). This framework, adopted at the Third UN World Conference on Disaster Risk Reduction in Japan in 2015, presents a structure with which natural or man-made hazards are expected to be addressed . The agreement stipulates that non-state stakeholders, such as INGOs, should strengthen disaster preparedness and disaster response.

The UN identifies three phases of disaster intervention: search and rescue efforts, rapid needs assessments, first aid, shelters, and humanitarian aid; rehabilitation encompassing basic services such as restoration of transport; and, recovery characterized by reconstruction of infrastructure and restoration of livelihoods (UN-Spider, 2016). Specifically, the Sendai Framework emphasizes that rehabilitation and recovery work must be carried out as partnerships between state and non-state actors to promote "building back better" (UN, 2015, p. 14), a concept that refers to the restoration of communities to promote improved resilience to future disasters (Mulligan & Nadarajah, 2011). The framework endorses disaster risk management that accounts for vulnerability, specific features of hazard, and community capacity, while also promoting disaster risk governance at various scales that maximizes "collaboration and partnership" (UN, 2015, p. 17). Children are an integral part of the future shape of any community, and any efforts to promote resilience would logically account for their needs and vulnerabilities.

In line with the CRC, humanitarian organizations are well-placed to advocate for children through their child-focused post-disaster programs (Ager et al., 2011). While the CRC provides a framework to address children's needs, these are often neglected during disasters, for example, their right to: "good quality healthcare, clean water, nutritious food, and a clean environment" (Article 24); a living standard that supports their physical and mental needs (Article 27); access to education (Article 28); ability to "relax, play and to join in a wide range of leisure activities" (Article 31); and, special assistance to address injustice (Article 39) (United Nations International Children's Emergency Fund—UNICEF, 2006). The CRC also emphasizes that wealthier countries should assist poorer ones in protecting these rights and that child-oriented organizations should contribute to achieving these aims (UNICEF, 2006). To maximize children's welfare in disasters requires partnerships among all stakeholders across all phases of the program cycle.

In 2011, the Children's Charter for Disaster Risk Reduction was launched at the UNISDR Global Platform for DRR. The Charter was designed to address children's specific needs in disasters and was the result of efforts by INGOs like Save the Children, World Vision, and Plan International, in partnership with UNICEF, who engaged over 600 children from twenty-one disaster-prone countries in Africa, Asia, and Latin America to create the document (Bild & Ibrahim, 2013). The Charter comprised the following DRR priorities for children:

1. Schools must be safe and education must not be interrupted;
2. Child protection must be a priority before, during, and after a disaster;
3. Children have the right to participate and to access the information they need;
4. Community infrastructure must be safe, and relief and reconstruction must help reduce future risk; and
5. Disaster Risk Reduction must reach the most vulnerable.

(Bild & Ibrahim, 2013, p. 17)

In sum, the 2011 Children's Charter for Disaster Risk Reduction, which was launched by the UNRISD, has highlighted among other things the issues of children's interrupted education, their safety and security, and their right to information as priority concerns of post-disaster recovery and rehabilitation.

Figure 3.1   Disaster, Children's Vulnerabilities, and Humanitarian Aid: An Analytical Framework.

CHILDREN'S VULNERABILITY AND HUMANITARIAN AID POST-DISASTER: AN ANALYTICAL FRAMEWORK

Based on three key parameters of the Children's Charter—education, safety and security, and right to information—we propose an analytical framework to better understand the place and vulnerability of children in disaster response, and specifically in post-disaster Leyte, Philippines. In addition to analysis of the Charter, our framework also derives from a document analysis we conducted to assess the effectiveness of Save the Children's response, which we then analyzed in terms of interview responses related to the appropriateness and effectiveness of the organization's programs in Leyte. We then compared Save the Children initiatives to the Children's Charter for DRR.

Save the Children's humanitarian aid post-Haiyan in Leyte

We examine Save the Children's Haiyan response in addressing children's vulnerabilities and priorities post-Haiyan in Leyte at three levels: (i) Immediate response; and (ii) Recovery; and, (iii) Overall results as compared to international standards (figure 3.1).

First Response: Key Issues Faced by Children

Children's needs in disaster situations are almost universal. Our interview results and Save the Children's reports clearly identified children's emergency needs as food, shelter, water, clothing, and medical care. The agreement in these views is unsurprising because first response has been extensively studied and documented. In Leyte, the response to Haiyan required partnership between government and international agencies using their complementary resources to provide aid. According to our respondents, when disaster struck, local communities became first responders because Leyte, surrounded by water, became almost inaccessible by land and air due to heavily damaged transport infrastructure. Local residents attended to the deceased and provided victims with first aid. Although Save the Children claimed to be among the first responders, the immediate response came from communities, Philippine agencies, and local government units. INGO aid arrived a few days later. Respondents reported that their ability to withstand the effects of Haiyan were due to the combined efforts of community, governments, and INGOs, including Save the Children.

Three weeks after Haiyan struck, Save the Children conducted a consultation among 124 children from a total of six provinces, including Leyte, using an assessment tool developed in collaboration with other child-focused INGOs and UNICEF. The small sample size was to be expected, given that the typhoon was Category 5 and created much disruption. Save the Children's attempts at conducting a participatory survey were in line with Chambers' argument that relevant information can be generated when communities are given the opportunities to participate in development processes (1997, cited in Kumar, 2002). Children augmented the organization's response by voicing their immediate needs and suggesting ways by which these needs could be addressed and, thus, providing data which enabled Save the Children to identify vulnerabilities. Respondents corroborated Save the Children's reports with regard to immediate response. Both sources stated that the INGO had rehabilitated school and hospital facilities; conducted sexual and reproductive health awareness campaigns; and provided the most vulnerable victims with shelter, reconstruction assistance, latrine repair materials, and back-to-school supplies. Respondents expressed gratitude to Save the Children, stating that such efforts benefited both the children and adult victims.

Recovery

While reports of Save the Children's first response were positive, their recovery efforts met with mixed reviews by respondents. In terms of the organization's livelihood assistance, some respondents were disappointed stating that the programs did not work and that they remained under pressure to provide for their children in circumstances of diminished income. They emphasized that providing for children in the context of devastated livelihoods was extremely stressful. Save the Children was reportedly more successful in providing for children's psychosocial needs, including therapy for trauma and protection against abuse and exploitation. Save the Children conducted counseling and created child-friendly spaces where children and youth could play and socialize. Both respondents and Save the Children's reports stated that these measures helped many victims to regain a sense of normalcy in their everyday lives. In terms of promoting child protection, Save the Children's efforts proved very successful because their proposed bill to recognize children's specific needs in disasters was enacted into law by the Philippine parliament. Some respondents believed that this law, which also ensures the increased participation of children in DRR planning and needs assessments, is Save the Children's major contribution because it is clearly sustainable. Gauging the impact and efficacy of this law's implementation would require a long-term study.

Despite Save the Children's initiatives in addressing the immediate and recovery needs of children, the need to treat ongoing trauma, as various respondents observed, was not addressed. Respondents censured the discontinuity of sociocultural events co-planned by Save the Children and local youth, highlighting the point that rehabilitation and recovery cannot be adequately covered by INGOs alone and must be done in a participatory way, addressing local needs, resources, and timelines. While respondents agreed that Save the Children's immediate response was both extensive and beneficial to children, they believed recovery efforts could be improved through better livelihood programs, longer-term psychosocial support, and programs for disaster prevention, mitigation, and recovery.

SAVE THE CHILDREN'S INITIATIVES AND AGREED INTERNATIONAL BENCHMARKS

Overall, respondents reported that Save the Children response programs in the wake of Haiyan were valuable because they addressed immediate and short-term needs. However, the programs fell short in terms of "recovery." We also explored whether these initiatives met with the Children's Charter for DRR, a document developed with the participation of children from disaster-prone developing countries, including the Philippines. The Children's Charter for DRR mandates all interested stakeholders to respond to five priorities listed earlier in this chapter. We review Save the Children's performance in this regard below.

Education: Charter 1

The first Charter requirement is safeguarding continuity of education. Based on both Save the Children's reports and interview responses, the organization contributed to restoring education by rebuilding or repairing schools. Six months after Haiyan, Save the Children was able to create more than 100 temporary learning spaces and repair damaged schools as part of its Back to Learning Campaign (Save the Children, 2014, p.7). The organization also distributed school supplies and bags to students, and teacher kits and recreational materials to educators. While children's education was interrupted, efforts were made to return them to schools as soon as safety permitted.

Protection: Charter 2

The second Charter stipulation is the prioritization of children's protection throughout all phases of disaster. According to a respondent who worked for an NGO, Save the Children campaigned for children's rights by encouraging beneficiaries of government financial assistance "to invest more in their children's well-being and to not compromise such during situations of stress, emergencies and hardships." The respondent added that, through its Project Charge (Child Rights Governance), Save the Children supported the government's DRR programs and rehabilitation efforts by monitoring its child-centered agenda, bolstering "service delivery coordination systems," and "facilitating children's participation in the rehabilitation/DRR processes."

Save the Children's successful promotion of a children's needs bill into law passed by the Philippine parliament was one crucial step in the prioritization of children during disasters. One respondent, a child's rights expert from the Philippine's House of Representatives, reported that Save the Children had actively partnered with the government at the policy-making level by co-drafting the Republic Act 10821 entitled "Children's Emergency Relief and Protection Act." The law seeks to "improve the care and protection of children affected by disasters," increases institutions' accountability to children, and disseminates best practices in disaster response, among others (Save the Children, 2017). This law mandates a comprehensive emergency response and recovery for children; a strict monitoring mechanism against child trafficking and other forms of violence against children after disasters; and a systematic participation of children in DRR planning and post-disaster needs assessment. It also warrants less disruption of education by limiting the use of schools as evacuation sites; prescribes an enhanced family tracing process for separated children; and requires provision of child-centered response training for rescuers and community and school leaders (Save the Children, 2017).

Save the Children's integration of DRR components in its livelihood, education, and reconstruction programs contributes to the minimization of future disaster risks for children. Additionally, Save the Children's prioritization of the most impacted areas, primarily Leyte Province, resulted in quick response to the neediest children. In practical terms, our study found that Save the Children adequately fulfilled the Children's Charter on DRR in terms of protection.

Children's Right to Participate: Charter 3

The third Charter requirement is that children have the right to participate in aspects of disaster response that affect them and to access information they need. Three weeks into the response to Haiyan, Save the Children, together with World Vision, Plan International and UNICEF, conducted consultations among 124 children from six affected areas from Leyte and Panay Island (Finnegan, 2015, p. 8). The assessment tool for consultation was developed by these agencies, "with reference to their own child participatory assessment" procedures, which were patterned after best practice. Save the Children aimed for a representative group of children to be included in the consultation, including the most vulnerable "who are still out of school, working children, and boys and girls with disabilities" (Finnegan, 2015, p.8). Facilitators informed parents and caretakers about the purpose of and the processes involved in the consultation and secured signed consent forms for the children's participation.

Save the Children used the Cyclone Yolanda framework of assistance to assess children's needs. According to results reported in the publication *After Yolanda: What Children Think, Need and Recommend* (Finnegan, 2013), two different age groups of children (7–12 and 13–17 years, respectively) were asked to provide recommendations with regard to disaster response. While some results varied, both groups emphasized two important interventions: restoration of education and income to their families.

Respondents between the ages of thirteen and seventeen years made very practical recommendations which they perceived would aid their parents and other individuals in need, as well as enhance social relationships. Their views suggested an understanding of the challenges faced by adults in recovering from disaster. Specifically, they asked for aid for livelihoods for their communities such as the provision of chainsaws to help adults cut coconut lumber to rebuild houses, reconstruction materials, restoration of variety stores, provision of seeds for coconut and other crops, new skills training for livelihoods, immediate income for family, and recovery of fishing boats. They were concerned with disruption and suggested that the community could use assistance in rebuilding a functional barangay organization to maintain security for local populations. Individuals in this age group also asked for livelihood aid for older children while they waited to resume school in January 2014, after the typhoon. School was a particular worry, with the children asking for supplies such as books, backpacks, pens, and notebooks, as well as maintenance of school and community gardens. This group was also concerned with vulnerability and asked for medicine for the sick, stated that friends should share feelings about the disaster for mutual support, and asked for a place where children could meet each other as they had before the typhoon. Interestingly, they also asked for food for Christmas, a holiday that is an annual highlight for children around the world.

Younger respondents, between the ages of seven and twelve years, expressed similar concerns, in more personal and experience-near terms. Their comments spoke to a desire to restore the order of their world as it had existed before the disaster. They also worried about continued schooling and asked for books, notebooks, pens, school bags, and slippers, and for schools to be repaired. They were concerned for their parents and asked for jobs and more food for families. However, their focus was very much on their own needs and that of their peers: they asked for mosquito nets to protect children from dengue; medicine for children who had coughs and colds; restoration of electricity to their communities; additional water pumps in the community so that children would not need to travel far from home to fetch water; removal of debris; and better security so that children would not be afraid of criminals.

We found that most children's views of their own and their communities' needs resonated with adult perceptions. Save the Children demonstrated strong commitment to ensuring children's participation in their DRR needs assessment. In response to the findings of their participatory assessments, Save the Children actively promoted passing of the Republic Act 10821 (Children's Emergency Relief and Protection Act of 2016), which is a ground-breaking law enshrining children's involvement in future planning of post-disaster responses in the Philippines

LESSONS LEARNED

Our aim in this study was to investigate whether the enshrinement of a Children's Charter for Disaster Response would enhance and appropriately target disaster responses to children's needs. We described specific vulnerabilities of children in disaster as related to immediate needs for food, shelter, medical attention, and social protection. We highlighted the long-term effects of neglecting these needs in terms of negative impacts on health and future education, and vulnerability to sexual and labor exploitation (Stark, Bancroft, Sustikarini and Meliala, 2012). We noted that children with disabilities are doubly vulnerable in disasters (Australian Red Cross, 2016; Lynch et al., 2010; Rothstein, 2013; WHO, 2016). We argued for adoption of participatory methods inclusive of children in assessments to understand their specific viewpoints and gauge their needs.

We found that Save the Children's response and relief work proved greatly beneficial to Haiyan-affected children on several fronts. First, by addressing basic and immediate needs, the organization eased the process of recovery. Second, inclusion of children's participation in needs assessments and planning for recovery interventions, promoted children's agency contributing to self-worth and resilience after disaster. Child-inclusive participatory approaches also contributed to addressing educational, psychosocial, disability-related and other needs and tailoring subsequent responses appropriately. Third, Save the Children's recovery programs enabled children to resume school, recover psychologically, feel safer, and regain a sense of normalcy. Fourth, its advocacy work, resulted in legislation that mainstreamed children's rights and strengthened institutions' accountability to children during disasters, and placed children as the top priority of both government and nongovernment stakeholders during disasters

In terms of needs assessment, immediate response, and advocacy, Save the Children was found to have performed well in Leyte, perhaps demonstrating that its strengths lie primarily in relief and immediate recovery of children in post-disaster contexts. However, in terms of its contribution to rehabilitation and resettlement, especially interventions relating to safe infrastructure and risk reduction, Save the Children took on a supporting role to government-led reconstruction, which started with comprehensive planning in the medium-term. The government also initiated a post-disaster needs assessment prioritizing recovery and reconstruction needs wherein it engaged local communities, CSOs, and NGOs (National Economic and Development Authority [NEDA], 2015, p.8). The assessment revealed policy issues to be addressed to build safer infrastructure that reduces disaster risks which includes expedient review of the national building code and strict implementation of building standards (NEDA, 2015, p.9).

To help reduce risk for many communities in Leyte, Save the Children established child-friendly spaces to provide immediate psychosocial support for children through provision of safe spaces for play, recreation, and socializing with other children, thereby facilitating a return to normalcy and aiding the building of resilience. Structured play through the child-friendly spaces helped children to progress past the immediate disruption caused by disaster because they were "not bored anymore" and could already "play without worrying about the debris" (Save the Children, 2015, p.8). However, some respondents said that some children still suffered from trauma as a result of Haiyan. Untreated trauma prevents children from returning to their normal functioning and may lead to more complex psychological conditions.

Save the Children was able to minimize immediate risks for children by distributing housing materials and conducting carpentry training so that community members could build more durable shelters. Save the Children also built latrines and promoted proper water, sanitation, and hygiene practices. They conducted medical consultations through mobile health units in many parts of Leyte. While the immediate response was perceived to be effective, respondents reported that livelihood programs did not meet needs and expectations.

Without viable livelihoods, parents and/or primary caretakers could not ensure that children's needs were met. In these instances, children become vulnerable to poor development, including abandoning school and entering into child labor. Respondents felt strongly that Save the Children should consider revitalizing its livelihood programs. With regard to the fifth aspect of the Charter, that disaster risk reduction should reach the most vulnerable, respondents suggested that Save the Children should revive social events co-planned with local youth to contribute to better psychosocial recovery and youth mental health. They also suggested that Save the Children contribute to community planning preparedness for disasters.

Three key lessons were learned from this study: First, children have voice and agency. They observe their environment, are able to articulate their experiences, empathize with members of their community, express worry for their parents, and focus very clearly on practicalities and social needs. Neglecting to include children and their participation in disaster policy and implementation would entail a serious missed opportunity to tailor and refine responses to disasters and to understand the long-term needs for reconstruction and rehabilitation especially those that are relevant to children. Secondly, reconstruction needs to be future oriented and must focus on education, trauma redress, and social reproduction. It is important to keep in mind that disasters become part of a child's learning experience and are incorporated into their autobiographical accounts which can be colored by memories of great suffering and disruption, or great community-building and resilience. It is in the power of governments and agencies to determine that experience. Thirdly, participatory disaster response must show results in terms of policy and practice, if not codification in law. While the Philippine law, Republic Act 10821 (Children's Emergency Relief and Protection Act) has not been evaluated in terms of its impact, it is a significant step in the right direction in a disaster-prone country and an example for others to follow.

CONCLUSION

Disasters often result in death, injury, and structural, environmental, and socioeconomic damage. Disasters disproportionately affect developing countries, and their children most of all. The Philippines is highly disaster-prone because it is in the Pacific Ring of Fire. It experiences some twenty typhoons each year. On November 8, 2013, the Philippines experienced the strongest typhoon ever recorded, Typhoon Haiyan. Our study has demonstrated that while NGO interventions are very good at addressing the immediate needs of children in disaster, they are less prepared or equipped to deal with long-term effects of disaster such as trauma recovery. However, our study found that Save the Children was fully aware of its and the government's shortcomings, and thus co-drafted and lobbied strongly for a bill that comprehensively deals with issues of children in disaster until its enactment into a law.

In sum, with climate change challenges looming large and occurrences of natural disasters of various types and intensities becoming more frequent, we believe that, by focusing on the issues of children in disaster, who are the worst casualties and sufferers, and also by focusing on NGO interventions that specifically addressed the issues of post-disaster recovery of children, we may have succeeded in highlighting the challenges, articulating the issues and bringing out the institutional, legal, and social interventions that are key to addressing the sufferings and concerns of children in disaster. This study also highlighted that every institution, from national to local and from governmental to nongovernmental, has a role to play in recovery and thus must cooperate to find solutions to children's experiences and needs in disasters. The case of Leyte also demonstrated the power of advocacy in institutionalizing children's disaster rights within the legal system of a disaster-prone country such as the Philippines. In short, lessons learned from this study are plausibly applicable to all countries, but especially developing countries that frequently experience disasters where children are most susceptible and suffer the most.

NOTES

1. Ethical clearance was granted by The University of Queensland's Human Ethics Review Panel. Confidentiality of participants was ensured through all phases of the study and data were stored in a password-protected medium. Consent was obtained by filling out a Consent Form sent electronically to each interview participant.

2. The number of natural disasters that occurred during that period totaled 6,436 (Strobl, 2012, p. 130).

REFERENCES

Ager, A., Blake, C., Stark, L., & Daniel, T. (2011). Child protection assessment in humanitarian emergencies: Case studies from Georgia, Gaza, Haiti and Yemen. *Child Abuse & Neglect, 35*(12), 1045–1052.

Ager, A., Stark, L., Akesson, B., & Boothby, N. (2010). Defining Best Practice in Care and Protection of Children in Crisis-Affected Settings: A Delphi Study. *Child Development, 81*(4), 1271–1286.

Alcantara-Ayala, I. (2002). Geomorphology, natural hazards, vulnerability and prevention of natural disasters in developing countries. *Geomorphology (Amsterdam), 47*(2–4), 107–124.

Assembly, U. G. (2015). United Nations Office for Disaster Risk Reduction (UNISDR).The Sendai Framework for Disaster Risk Reduction 2015–2030.

Australian Red Cross. (2016). How to protect children in a disaster response. Retrieved from http://www.redcross.org.au/child-protection-emergencies.aspx

Barlow, C. (2010). *Interviews.* SAGE Publications.

Benson, C. (1997). *The impact of natural disasters in the Philippines.* London: Overseas Development Institute.

Bild, E., & Ibrahim, M. (2013). Towards the resilient future children want: A review of progress in achieving the Children's Charter for Disaster Risk Reduction. *World Vision Milton Keynes.* http://www.preventionweb.net/files/globalplatform/519dd 2cbc89bbTowards_the_resilient_future_2013_lowres. pdf .

Bolin, B. (2007). Race, class, ethnicity, and disaster vulnerability. In Rodriguez, Havidan, Quarantelli, Enrico, Dynes, Russell (Eds.), *Handbook of Disaster Research* (pp. 113–129). Springer: New York.

Bolin, R. C., & Stanford, L. (1999). Constructing vulnerability in the first world: The Northridge earthquake in Southern California, 1994. In A. Oliver-Smith & S. Hoffman (Eds.), *The Angry Earth: Disasters in Anthropological Perspective* (pp. 89–112). New York: Routledge.

Branigan, T. (2013). *Typhoon Haiyan: Children in Disaster Zone are Vulnerable, Unicef Warns.* Retrieved from https://www.theguardian.com/world/2013/nov/20/typhoon-haiyan-children-vulnerable-unicef

Brown, L. D., & Moore, M. H. (2001). Accountability, strategy, and international nongovernmental organizations. *Nonprofit and Voluntary Sector Quarterly, 30*(3), 569–587.

Brown, S. (2013). *The Philippines Is the Most Storm-Exposed Country on Earth.* Retrieved from http://world.time.com/2013/11/11/the-philippines-is-the-most-storm-exposed-country-on-earth/

Castro, L. (2014). *Assessing Vulnerabilities of Women and Children Exposed to Disaster: The Philippine Experience.* Retrieved from http://unstats.un.org/unsd/gender/Mexico_Nov2014/Session%207%20Philippines%20ppt.pdf

Chan, J. C., & Kepert, J. D. (2010). *Global Perspectives on Tropical Cyclones: From Science to Mitigation* (Vol. 4). World Scientific.

Cinco, T. A., de Guzman, R. G., Ortiz, A. M. D., Delfino, R. J. P., Lasco, R. D., Hilario, F. D., Ares, E. D. (2016). Observed trends and impacts of tropical cyclones in the Philippines. *International Journal of Climatology, 36,* 4638–4650. https://doi.org/10.1002/joc.4659.

Davis, M. (2005). *Planet of Slums.* London: Verso.

De Leon, E. G., & Pittock, J. (2017). Integrating climate change adaptation and climate-related disaster risk-reduction policy in developing countries: A case study in the Philippines. *Climate and Development, 9,* 471–478. https://doi.org/10.1080/17565529.2016.1174659.

Drabo, A., & Mbaye, L. M. (2015). Natural disasters, migration and education: an empirical analysis in developing countries. *Environment and Development Economics, 20,* 767–796. https://doi.org/10.1017/s1355770x14000606.

Duque, R. L., Grecia, A., & Ching, P. E. (2013). Development of a national occupational therapy disaster preparedness and response plan: the Philippine experience. *World Federation of Occupational Therapists Bulletin, 68,* 26–30. https://doi.org/10.1179/otb.2013.68.1.008

Evangeliou, N., Hamburger, T., Talerko, N., Zibtsev, S., Bondar, Y., Stohl, A., Møller, A. P. (2016). Reconstructing the Chernobyl Nuclear Power Plant (CNPP) accident 30 years after. A unique database of air concentration and deposition measurements over Europe. *Environmental Pollution, 216,* 408–418.

Finnegan, L. (2013). *After Yolanda: What Children Think, Need and Recommend.* Retrieved from http://www.unicef.org/philippines/After_Yolanda.pdf

George, A. L., & A. Bennett. 2005. *Case Studies and Theory Development in the Social Sciences.* Cambridge, MA: MIT Press.

Gerring, J. (2004). What is a case study and what is it good for? *American Political Science Review, 98*(2), 341–354.

Gupta, J., & Agrawal, A. (2010). Chronic aftershocks of an earthquake on the wellbeing of children in Haiti: Violence, psychosocial health and slavery. (Analysis) (Report).*CMAJ: Canadian Medical Association Journal, 182*(18), 1997.

Hancock, P., & Skinner, B. (2000). *Oxford Companion to the Earth*/Editors, Paul L. Hancock and Brian J. Skinner; associate editor, David L. Dineley; subject editors, Alastair G. Dawson, K. Vala Ragnarsdottir, Iain S. Stewart. Oxford: Oxford University Press.

Hewitt. (1983). *Interpretations of Calamity from the Viewpoint of Human Ecology.* Boston; London: Allen & Unwin.

International Federation of Red Cross and Red Crescent Societies. (n.d.). *What Is a Disaster?* Retrieved from http://www.ifrc.org/en/what-we-do/disaster-managem ent/about-disasters/what-is-a-disaster/

Johnston, B. (1994). *Who Pays the Price? The Sociocultural Context of the Environmental Crisis.* Washington, DC: Island Press.

Kreps, G. (1984). Sociological Inquiry and Disaster Research. *Annual Review of Sociology, 10*(11), 309–330.

Kumar, S. (2002). *Methods for Community Participation: A Complete Guide for Practitioners.* London: ITDG.

Lagmay, A. M. F., Agaton, R. P., Bahala, M. A. C., Briones, J. B. L. T., Cabacaba, K. M. C., Caro, C. V. C., ... & Mungcal, M. T. F. (2015). Devastating storm surges of Typhoon Haiyan. *International Journal of Disaster Risk Reduction, 11,* 1–12.

Lang, C., & Ryder, J. (2016). The effect of tropical cyclones on climate change engagement. *Climatic Change, 135*(3), 625–638.

Lapadat, J. (2010). Thematic analysis. In A. J. Mills, G. Durepos & E. Wiebe (Eds.), *Encyclopedia of Case Study Research* (pp. 926–927). Thousand Oaks, CA: SAGE Publications Ltd. doi: 10.4135/9781412957397.n342

Lasco, R. D., Pulhin, F. B., Jaranilla-Sanchez, P. A., Delfino, R. J. P., Gerpacio, R., & Garcia, K. (2009). Mainstreaming adaptation in developing countries: The case of the Philippines. *Climate and Development, 1*(2), 130–146.

Lasco, R. D., Pulhin, F. B., Jaranilla-Sanchez, P. A., Delfino, R. J. P., Gerpacio, R., & Garcia, K. (2009). Mainstreaming adaptation in developing countries: The case of the Philippines. *Climate and Development, 1*(2), 130–146.

Lum, T., & Margesson, R. (2014). Typhoon Haiyan (Yolanda): US and international response to Philippines disaster. *Current Politics and Economics of South, Southeastern, and Central Asia, 23*(2), 209.

Lynch, J., Wathen, J., Tham, E., Mahar, P., & Berman, S. (2010). Disasters and their effects on children. *Advances in Pediatrics*, *57*(1), 7–31.

Mohamed Shaluf, I. (2007). Disaster types. *Disaster Prevention and Management: An International Journal*, *16*(5), 704–717.

Morgan, D. (2008). Snowball sampling. In L. M. Given (Ed.), *The SAGE Encyclopedia of Qualitative Research Methods* (pp. 816–816). Thousand Oaks, CA: SAGE Publications Ltd. doi: 10.4135/9781412963909.n425

Mulligan, M., & Nadarajah, Y. (2012). Rebuilding community in the wake of disaster: lessons from the recovery from the 2004 tsunami in Sri Lanka and India. *Community Development Journal*, *47*, 353–368. https://doi.org/10.1093/cdj/bsr025.

National Economic and Development Authority. (2014). *Yolanda Comprehensive Rehabilitation and Recovery Plan*. Retrieved from http://yolanda.neda.gov.ph/wp-content/uploads/2015/11/Yolanda-CRRP.pdf

National Geographic. (2016). *Ring of Fire*. Retrieved from http://nationalgeographic.org/encyclopedia/ring-fire/

Nikku, B. R. (2013). Children's rights in disasters: Concerns for social work–insights from South Asia and possible lessons for Africa. *International Social Work*, *56*(1), 51–66.

Nodalo, T. (2013). *Typhoon Yolanda: Looking Back, Moving Forward*. Retrieved from http://cnnphilippines.com/regional/2015/11/08/super-typhoon-yolanda-looking-back-moving-forward.html

Offia Ibem, E. (2011). Challenges of disaster vulnerability reduction in Lagos Megacity Area, Nigeria. *Disaster Prevention and Management: An International Journal*, *20*(1), 27–40.

Oliver-Smith, A. (1986). *The Martyred City: Death and Rebirth in the Peruvian Andes*. Albuquerque: University of New Mexico Press.

Patt, A. G., Tadross, M., Nussbaumer, P., Asante, K., Metzger, M., Rafael, J., & Brundrit, G. (2010). Estimating least-developed countries' vulnerability to climate-related extreme events over the next 50 years. *Proceedings of the National Academy of Sciences*, *107*(4), 1333–1337.

Peek, L. (2008). Children and disasters: Understanding vulnerability, developing capacities, and promoting resilience—An introduction. *Children Youth and Environments*, *18*(1), 1–29.

Peet, R., & Watts, M. (2004). *Liberation Ecologies: Environment, Development, Social Movements* (2nd ed.). London; New York: Routledge.

Peluso, N., & Watts, M. (2001). *Violent Environments*. Ithaca, NY: Cornell University Press.

Quarantelli, E. L. (1991). Disaster prevention and mitigation in Lada. In Kreimer, Alcira; Munasinghe, Mohan (Eds.), *Managing natural disasters and the environment : selected materials from the Colloquium on the Environment and Natural Disaster Management*. Washington, DC: World Bank.

Rothstein, D. (2013). Pediatric care in disasters. *Pediatrics, 132*(4), 602–605.

Rutherford, W. H., & De Boer, J. (1983). The definition and classification of disasters. *Inquiry 15* (1), 10–12.

Salazar, L. C. (2015). Typhoon Yolanda: The Politics of Disaster Response and Management. *Southeast Asian Affairs*, *2015*(1), 277–301.

Santos, R. (2013, November 10). Fast Facts: Eastern Visayas. *Rappler*. Retrieved from http://www.rappler.com/newsbreak/iq/43341-fact-file-eastern-visayas

Save the Children. (2014a). *Are We There Yet?* Retrieved from http://www.savethech ildren.org.ph/__data/assets/pdf_file/0009/59049/One-Year-On_Childrens-view-on-Yoland-recovery_Nov-2014.pdf

Save the Children. (2014b). *Six Months After Typhoon Haiyan: Save the Children Restoring Hope for Children and Families in the Philippines*. Retrieved from http://www.savethechildren.org/atf/cf/%7B9def2ebe-10ae-432c-9bd0-df91d2eba7 4a%7D/TYPHOON%20HAIYAN_SIX-MONTH%20REPORT_MAY%2020 14%20(2).PDF

Save the Children. (2015). *Typhoon Haiyan Response Two Years on*. Retrieved from https://resourcecentre.savethechildren.net/node/9546/pdf/phl-cn2-13-typhoon _haiyan_2yearson8nov15.pdf

Save the Children. (2017). *Children's Emergency Relief and Protection Act – Save the Children Philippines*. Retrieved from http://www.savethechildren.org.ph/childr ens-emergency-relief-and-protection-act

Silverman, W. K., & La Greca, A. M. (2002). *Children Experiencing Disasters: Definitions, Reactions, and Predictors of Outcomes*. American Psychological Association.

Stake, R., & Ebooks Corporation. (2010). *Qualitative Research: Studying How Things Work*. New York: Guilford Press.

Stark, L., Bancroft, C., Cholid, S., Sustikarini, A., & Meliala, A. (2012). A qualitative study of community-based child protection mechanisms in Aceh, Indonesia. *Vulnerable Children and Youth Studies, 7*(3), 228–236.

Stewart, D., & Kamins, M. (1993). *Secondary Research* (2nd ed., Secondary Research). SAGE Publications.

Strobl, E. (2010). The economic growth impact of natural disasters in developing countries: Evidence from hurricane strikes in the Central American and Caribbean regions. *Journal of Development Economics, 97*(1), 130–141.

Takagi, H., & Esteban, M. (2016). Statistics of tropical cyclone landfalls in the Philippines: unusual characteristics of 2013 Typhoon Haiyan. *Natural Hazards, 80*(1), 211–222.

Tellis, W. M. (1997). Application of a case study methodology. *The Qualitative Report, 3*(3), 1–19.

Terry, J. (2007). *Tropical Cyclones*. New York, NY: Springer New York.

Trivedi, J. (2013). *Disaster, Definition of* (pp. 264–266). SAGE Publications.

UN Spider (2016). *Emergency and Disaster Management | UN-SPIDER Knowledge Portal*. [online] Retrieved from http://www.un-spider.org/risks-and-disasters/ emergency-and-disaster-management

UNICEF, & UNAIDS, U. (2004). Children on the brink 2004: A joint report of new orphan estimates and a framework for action. *Population, Health and Nutrition Project for USAID*, Washington, DC, 2.

UNICEF. (2006). A simplified version of the United Nations Convention on the rights of the child.

Wahlstrom, M., & Guha-Sapir, D. (2015). *The Human Cost of Weather-Related Disasters 1995–2015*. Geneva, Switzerland: UNISDR, CRED.

Weinkle, J., Maue, R., & Pielke, R. (2012). Historical Global Tropical Cyclone Land-falls*. *Journal of Climate, 25*(13), 4729–4735.

Win, T. (2014, November 15). Philippines' typhoon orphans struggle with trauma a year on. *Reuters*. Retrieved from http://www.reuters.com/article/us- philippine s-haiyan-orphans-idUSKBN0IP1WC20141105

Wisner, B. (2004). *At Risk Natural Hazards, People's Vulnerability and Disasters/ Ben Wisner...[et al.]* (2nd ed.). London: Taylor & Francis.

Wisner, B., & Adams, J. (2002). *Environmental Health in Emergencies and Disasters: A Practical Guide*. World Health Organization.

Wisner, B., Blaikie, P., Cannon, T., & Davis, I. (2004). *At Risk: Natural Hazards, People's Vulnerability and Disasters*. Routledge.

World Bank. (2016). *Unprepared for a Risky Future*. Retrieved from http://www .worldbank.org/en/news/press-release/2016/05/16/unprepared-for-a-risky-future

World Health Organisation (2006). *Health Effects of the Chernobyl Accident: An Overview*. Retrieved from http://www.who.int/ionizing_radiation/chernobyl/ backgrounder/en/#1

World Meteorological Organisation. (n.d.). *Tropical cyclone naming*. Retrieved from http://www.wmo.int/pages/prog/www/tcp/Storm-naming.html

World Vision. (2015). *Two Years on: Typhoon Haiyan Response*. Retrieved from http: //www.wvi.org/sites/default/files/24%20month%20external%20report_FINAL.pdf

Yin, R., & Ebooks Corporation. (2011). *Qualitative Research from Start to Finish/ Robert K. Yin*. New York: Guilford Press.

Chapter 4

Post-Disaster Accountability in the Haiyan Shelter Response

Who had the Greater Say?

Ladylyn L. Mangada and Irma R. Tan

INTRODUCTION

On November 8, 2013, Super Typhoon Haiyan (ST Haiyan), locally known as Yolanda, slammed into the Visayas region of the Philippines. Making its landfall in the province of Eastern Samar, the storm had sustained wind speeds of 315 kilometers per hour (195 mph) with gusts of up to 380 kilometers per hour (235 mph). At the time, it was the strongest storm ever recorded at landfall, as measured by wind speed (Evans, 2014). The storm left over 6,300 casualties, 28,000 injured, and affected more than 16 million individuals (Guha-Sapir et al., 2016). Over 4 million people were displaced from their homes, more than 1.1 million homes were damaged or destroyed, and the economic impact was estimated at over $12.9 billion (National Disaster Risk Reduction and Management Council, 2014). In Eastern Samar, a total of 7,699 houses were partially damaged while 33,972 houses were completely damaged (Shelter Cluster, 2014).

In this chapter, we attempt to understand the issue of emergency shelter provision on the ground and from the perspective of accountability. Using the national and local laws and policies that govern shelter provision, we examine how the local government of Guiuan and its key actors responded to the devastating effect of Haiyan and which local offices manifested, facilitated, or advanced accountability. Moreover, we ask whether the people of Guiuan were able to demand for resilient houses to reduce their vulnerability to natural hazards. We investigate in this chapter the local accountability deficit in the shelter responses in the aftermath of ST Haiyan. Data for this chapter came from a desk review and extensive field work. A three-person research team undertook the data collection during a four-week period in August–September 2015. Key informants were identified through a combination of the authors' professional and personal networks. Primary qualitative data were collected through key informant interviews with individuals involved with shelter provision, such as municipal officials, humanitarian organizations, and national government agency officials. Focus group discussions (FGDs) were conducted among survivors in transitional shelters, bunkhouse occupants, and those living in the islands and other high-risk areas. All informants were provided with a letter prior to the interviews and conduct of the FGD and were orally requested to give their "consent" during the conduct of the interviews/FGDs to indicate their understanding of the research and giving their permission. The researchers also attended open public meetings in Guiuan and Tacloban city. Initial findings were presented to the different stakeholders in Guiuan.

Guiuan is a second-class municipality located at the southernmost tip of the Province of Eastern Samar. It is the second-largest town and the most populous in the province. The 2010 Census registered Guiuan as having a population of 47,037. The municipality has sixty barangays, twenty-two of which are coastal, twenty of which are island barangays, and eighteen of which are inland (Bawagan, 2015). In Guiuan, appointments to political positions in government offices are perceived to be based on one's connection or friendly relations with the ruling elite. There is hardly any political party that exists because electoral competition is between political candidates (Mangada, 2015). There is a dearth of organized groups in the area that engage local decision makers and mobilize community action to social change.

Known as the town where ST Haiyan made its first landfall, Guiuan is exposed to a number of natural hazards. These include floods, heavy storms, droughts, earthquakes, and typhoons. Being predominantly an agricultural-based economy, the municipality and its population are vulnerable to the frequent occurrences of typhoon, drought, and food insecurity. Weather-related disasters are the most common form of disasters in Guiuan.

Mayor Super Ales, former vice governor of the province, at the time of the study in 2014 is serving his first term as the local chief executive. He succeeded his eldest sister Anli Ales who served as municipal mayor for nine years. His elder brother, Matthew Ales is the current president of the Association of Barangay Captains and thus sits in the Sangguniang Bayan, the local legislative body.

Post-Yolanda Context

Eighteen months after Typhoon Haiyan struck the Philippines, the hardest-hit areas of Eastern Visayas had yet to recover fully from the impact of the typhoon. Every year, the typhoon season poses a great risk to the fragile recovery situation of the region. In Guiuan, the people identified as being the most vulnerable were 4,541 families living in bunkhouses or makeshift shelters along coastal areas, and those in the island barangays. Also at risk of flooding and being struck by strong winds were those living in bunkhouses which comprised more than 1,000 families when at maximum capacity.

Moreover, families that had already been transferred to transitional shelters but had returned to unsafe areas where they had easier access to earning a livelihood became an additional caseload. The resettled families in the Cogon resettlement site and those who were to be resettled in Tagpuro complained of the distance between the resettlement site and their source of income and the resulting transportation cost. They held concerns about the safety and security of their property, including fishing boats and gear. At that point, they no longer felt that the coastal barangays were unsafe for dwelling.

As a second-class municipality, Guiuan did not have sufficient funds to relocate and construct robust dwelling units for the Haiyan-affected families and individuals. Moreover, the magnitude and complexity of the effects of ST Haiyan demanded a collaborative response from different groups and institutions. One of the measures taken by the local government of Guiuan, through its mayor, was to pressure the National Housing Authority (NHA) to provide housing to the survivors. The NHA provided housing units and the LGU met the land requirements. In all three of the identified resettlement sites, Cogon, Sapao, and Tagpuro, it was the local government of Guiuan that purchased the land to ensure the immediate relocation of those still living in unsafe areas. For instance, Cogon, the first relocation site of the survivors, was purchased by the local government unit because of its availability, cost, and safety of location.

Aside from government efforts, some humanitarian organizations filled in the gaps by providing both temporary and permanent shelters. The temporary shelter provider was the International Organization for Migration. It resettled 133 families from the tent city. On the island of Manicani, Good Shepherd (a church-based organization), provided semi-permanent shelter to families regardless of whether or not the lot owned was located within the No Build Zone. Nickel Asia, a private mining company, provided transitional shelters to families, but without considering the location of the lots where the shelters were to be built. Habitat for Humanity provided housing units to inhabitants of Victory Island, a high-risk area. Other temporary shelter providers were International Organization for Migration and Catholic Relief Services. They provided transitional houses to families that owned lots outside the No Build Zone.

Some international and local groups provided permanent housing. Cordaid-Build Change distributed permanent housing units to families who lived in the No Build Zone areas but who owned lots outside the No Build Zone where they could build their permanent shelters. Philippine Misereor Partners Inc., through TAO Pilipinas, also provided permanent housing to families in their own lots outside high-risk areas.

The Municipal Planning and Development officer advised in an interview that a year after ST Haiyan, the National Housing Authority commenced the construction of 254 housing units to resettle families from bunkhouses and those still living in high-risk areas such as Barangays 6, 7, and Hollywood. In 2015, only fifty-four units have been completed.

Another issue was the community perception that housing beneficiaries were selected based on political consideration. This was due to an absence of guidelines for the assignment of beneficiaries for the permanent shelter initiated by NHA-LGU. This lack of information caused confusion, speculation, and misinformation among the affected households in the high-risk areas of Barangays 6, 7, and 8. According to the mayor and the municipal social welfare development officer, priority was to be given to families with elderly, children, persons with disability, and those who had large families. Yet, these selection criteria were not formally noted and communicated to the affected families and barangays. On the other hand, response organizations like Cordaid-Build Change, PMPI (Tao, Good Shepherd), and Nickel Asia had established clear guidelines for beneficiary selection. However, these too were not clearly communicated to the beneficiaries, or to the local government. In contrast, those resettled in Cogon had to fulfill only one criterion: they had to have come from the tent city. Beneficiary selection and prioritization never arose as an issue.

Despite the assistance of the humanitarian organizations, nongovernment organizations, and the national government, many are still without appropriate shelter, making them more vulnerable to hazards and exposed to protection risks. Although many households have been able to repair their homes, many of these structures will not be able to withstand heavy rains or major storms. There were still around 200 households that have yet been transferred to the resettlement sites. In St. Genevieve Village, for example, the first permanent shelter resettlement site progress has been slow. The lot was purchased by the local government in January 2014 and the National Housing Authority administered the bidding in April of the same year. It was later discovered that the area was prone to liquefaction. After more than a year, only fifty housing units had been completed. The community is dissatisfied with its low completion rate. Local government officials claim that the reason for the delay is the inability of the contractor to comply with provision of documents, such as the site development plan and the environmental certificate clearance from government agencies. Hence, the contractor could not collect payment from the National Housing Authority. Despite this, the contractor was approved to commence the construction after an incomplete document submission. Meanwhile, the survivors had been waiting for a lengthy period to transfer to the resettlement area. In the following sections we examine further who is responsible for the housing situation and how the elected politicians responded to public pressure to provide shelter.

THE LEGAL BASIS OF THE SHELTER RESPONSE

In the Philippines, the legal and institutional basis for accountability in shelter response is provided by the Philippine Disaster Risk Reduction Management Act (RA 10121), Reconstruction Assistance on Yolanda (RAY, 2013), and the Comprehensive Rehabilitation and Recovery Plan.

Passed in 2010, RA 10121, acknowledges:

[the] need to adopt a disaster risk reduction and management approach that is holistic, comprehensive, integrated and proactive in lessening the socioeconomic and environmental impacts of disasters, including climate change, and promote the involvement and participation of all sectors and all stakeholders concerned, at all levels, especially the local community.

It provides a strong legal and an institutional basis for disaster risk reduction and management in the Philippines and gives a boost to policy development planning, and implementation of actions and measures pertaining to all aspects of disaster risk reduction and management. This includes good governance, risk assessment and early warning, knowledge-building and awareness raising, reducing underlying risk factors and improving preparedness for effective response and early recovery. The Act supports the establishment of the Disaster Risk Reduction and Management Office and Disaster Risk Reduction Management Council as the lead bodies in protecting citizens and communities before, during, and after natural disasters (NDRRM Plan, 2011–2028).

The government's strategic plan, Reconstruction Assistance on Yolanda, or RAY (2013), which supports the implementation of recovery efforts, states that it shall be the responsibility of the local government to ensure that a disaster response is tailored to local conditions. The plan promotes community participation, ownership, and sustainability. It also emphasizes transparency and accountability.

By virtue of Memorandum Order No. 62, the president appointed the presidential assistant for rehabilitation and recovery (PARR) on December 6, 2013, to unify the efforts of government and other agencies involved in the rehabilitation and recovery of Yolanda-affected areas. To facilitate the presidential assistant's role as overall manager and coordinator of rehabilitation, recovery, and reconstruction efforts of government departments, agencies, and instrumentalities in affected areas, he established five clusters at the national level, in addition to engaging provincial governors and city mayors. The five clusters and the governors and mayors have supported the formulation of plans and programs to form integrated short-, medium-, and long-term programs of the Comprehensive Rehabilitation and Recovery Plan (CRRP) for the president's approval.

The CRRP provides projects, programs, and activities to meet the needs as identified in the post-disaster needs assessment. The CRRP is complemented and supplemented by rehabilitation and recovery plans prepared at provincial and city levels. The CRRP provides details of implementation modalities and establishes guidance for implementing national departments and agencies. Significant rehabilitation and recovery efforts come from the nongovernment sector for projects focused on four key areas: education, health, housing, and livelihood. These entities can engage in the recovery efforts as donors, sector sponsors, and/or development sponsors.

The CRRP, like the Philippine Development Plan (PDP), is structured on the basis of costed plans, projects, and activities. There are two levels of planning to facilitate coordination with other nationally and locally funded programs. At the national level, each department and agency has coordinated the rehabilitation and recovery PPAs with existing programs funded under the national budget. At the provincial level, the recovery PPAs have been coordinated with the extant PPAs under the PDP; relief and recovery PPAs funded by nongovernment entities and the private sector; and PPAs funded from their local revenue base. Coordination of the PPAs is achieved by identifying common PPAs between the cluster plans and the provincial plans through a detailed province-by-province analysis.

The cluster arrangement enables the PARR to exercise oversight of participating national government agencies regarding the implementation of their plans and programs, as well as submit implementation status reports as required by the president. The CRRP includes a results framework and performance indicators. The plan also details the monitoring and evaluation processes and the information database that the Office of the PARR will maintain.

The sections of the CRRP concerning local government rehabilitation and recovery plans and resettlement cluster, specifies the following: The local government units used their respective local disaster risk reduction and management plans as the guiding framework for rehabilitation and recovery, aimed at incorporating disaster resiliency in support of inclusive growth and sustainable development. Different strategies were employed by the LGUs in preparing their rehabilitation and recovery plans. Some of the LGUs such as the provinces of Cebu and Samar, and the city of Tacloban created task forces to coordinate, manage, and implement the rehabilitation and recovery process. For the others, existing LGU offices, such as the provincial risk reduction and management office, were maximized. Furthermore, to identify key interventions in their PPAs, the LGUs ensured a consultative approach by encouraging stakeholders to participate and contribute in the planning process.

To ensure that the local government rehabilitation and recovery plans are included in the plan, convergence between the LRRP and CRRP is needed. To achieve this, the provincial governments presented their plans to the clusters. After discussion, review, and vetting, the local recovery and rehabilitation plans were endorsed by the cluster heads for the final approval of the president.

The provincial government, being the highest local governing body, took the lead in consolidating the LRRPs by facilitating, collating, reviewing, and approving/endorsing the Yolanda CRRP. The resettlement cluster is headed by the HUDCC. In the event an office does not exist in the region, the National Housing Authority becomes the lead national government agency. The specific activities required to implement the projects under the resettlement program are: identification of sites for resettlement; 2) validation of land status and clearance from geo-hazards; 3) reparation of site development plans; 4) securing of government permits; 5) site development (road and drainage construction, electricity distribution network, water reticulation, sewerage system, etc.); 6) construction of housing units; 7) social preparation and selection/prioritization of beneficiaries; and 8) relocation of family beneficiaries.

The National Housing Authority, as the administering arm of the cluster, will implement the resettlement projects. To ensure a participatory approach in resettlement project implementation, Local Inter-Agency Committees will be established in each city or municipality. These committees will serve as the policy making and coordinating bodies to ensure harmonized and efficient implementation of the various programs and activities related to the development of resettlement projects and relocation of affected families. The LIAC will be chaired by the local chief executive and co-chaired by Housing and Urban Development and Coordinating Council. Members of the LIAC will include representatives from NGAs, including the Department of Social Welfare and Development, the Department of Environment and Natural Resources, the Department of Public Works and Highways, and the Presidential Commission for the Urban Poor, as well as LGUs, particularly the Municipal Planning and Development Office, Municipal Social Welfare and Development Office, Municipal Engineering Office, and Municipal Assessors Office. Whenever applicable, Provincial Inter-Agency Committees may also be established at the provincial level to oversee the resettlement efforts in the province.

THE ACTORS OF ACCOUNTABILITY IN GUIUAN

Accountability in this context involves the obligation of public officials to explain their actions or inactions and to be held answerable for the consequences of such (Haque, 1994; Salleh and Iqbal, 1995). The condition is essential in democratic governance because power is not normally exercised directly by citizens but through their elected representatives, and, by extension, the bureaucrats that the representatives appoint to perform particular tasks of government (Cabo, 2015). In times of eventful conditions such as the devastation of Super Typhoon Haiyan, one may ask if citizens and public officials came together to discuss, argue, dialogue, negotiate, and partner with each other to address housing issues.

One Act and one office under the local chief executive were used as the bases for action in responding to the shelter needs of the Haiyan-affected survivors: (1) the Guiuan Rehabilitation and Recovery Plan and its implementing arm the Guiuan Rehabilitation, Recovery and Sustainable Development Group, and (2) the Municipal Housing development Board and Housing Unit.

The Guiuan Recovery and Rehabilitation Plan and the Guiuan Rehabilitation and Recovery Sustainable Development Group

A month after Super Typhoon Haiyan, the national government ordered LGUs in the affected areas to produce a Recovery and Rehabilitation Plan. This "technology of recovery" guides the central government and the LGU in finding the path of effecting recovery and in identifying the desired goals after a disaster given certain conditions. This guidance document also assists government and nongovernment entities with funding the repairs of damaged infrastructure and utilities as well as the rehabilitation of communities and individuals.

To expedite the recovery process and to provide direction and order to the Guiuanons after ST Haiyan, Mayor Super Ales created a core group, the Guiuan Rehabilitation and Recovery Sustainable Development Group (GRRSDG), through EO No. 21 series of 2013, to facilitate the formulation of the Guiuan Recovery and Rehabilitation Plan (GRRP). In Philippine public administration and politics, the executive is accountable for the subordinates he or she has selected, whether or not the executive has knowledge of the person's actions.

The GRRSDG was composed of United Nations Development Program representative Ms. Rara Onon, Secretary to the Sanggunian Bayan Ito Ades, Municipal Local Government Operations Officer Ric Laba, and Municipal Planning Development Officer Eni Eceo. In April 2014, Goliath, a volunteer who was later hired by UN-Habitat, joined the group. The core group expanded the membership to include key department heads. Outside the local government, citizen groups were selected on the basis of "active involvement in the community" The Guiuan Rehabilitation and Recovery Plan had four sectors: economic, environment, infrastructure, and social and shelter. The social and shelter sector was led by the Municipal Social Welfare and Development Officer/Municipal Health officer. Its members included the police, the Municipal Nutrition Action Office, and the Office of the Senior Citizens Association. Representatives from the Department of Education, the United Nation Commission on Human Rights, the International Organization for Migration, the United Nations Children's Fund, and the Federation of Barangay Senior Citizens Association were also listed as members. Nonetheless, the poor, homeless, and displaced survivors of Haiyan were excluded. Discussions for recovery were made through the different charrettes. However, key informants claimed it was UN Habitat, Goliath, a licensed urban planner, who was leading the way. It was also Goliath who presented the output to the different audiences: the Sangguniang Bayan, the Municipal Development Council, and the local citizens who were assembled at the town plaza. Local bureaucrats, especially the core group, regularly referred to Goliath due to the technical nature of the GRRP.

Mayor Super Ales appointed Ito Ades, the Sanggunian Bayan secretary, as the overall point person because, in his words, "He is the only one who can speak and understand English well." Informants maintained that members of the different sectors gathered the data and statistics and these were handed over to Ades for processing and validation. The UN Habitat organization facilitated the charrettes and consolidated the information. However, in the immediate aftermath of the disaster, everyone was rushing to meet the requirements of the donors and national government and citizen consultation was overlooked. One may question whether the ideas, views, and experiences of those affected were integrated and institutionalized and whether the people were co-producers of the Guiuan Rehabilitation and Recovery Plan. It is a principle of recovery for the planning process to be conducted at the local level with the active participation of the affected community (Easthope, 2014). There must also be a strong reliance on local capacities and expertise.

In July 2014, the Guiuan Rehabilitation and Recovery Plan was first drafted. Ades maintained that it had been reproduced and distributed to department heads and Sangguniang Bayan members to review. However, the office in charge of reproducing and disseminating these copies collapsed. Ades did not know whether the draft plan had reached the local officials.

The plan was presented to the barangay captains, members of the Sangguniang Bayan, and to the people assembled in the town plaza. In all these dissemination activities, there were no copies of the GRRP distributed for the audience to read and study. The sole documentation relied upon was Goliath's PowerPoint presentation. Inquiry and discussion were limited. During the presentation to the Sangguniang Bayan, some of its members went in and out of the session hall during the course of the presentation. One of the participants who had been in attendance at the town plaza meeting recalled, "The PowerPoint presentation was colorful but we did not really bother with its content since it was almost 12:00 noon. We were hungry and the heat of the sun was unbearable." One may ask whether the plan was thoroughly explained to the lawmakers, barangay captains, and the community members, and whether the plan was understood and agreed upon by the people. Their inclusion (or not) would affect the level of co-ownership of the Guiuan Recovery and Rehabilitation Plan (GRRP).

After acquiring the approval of the Sangguniang Bayan and sending a copy to the provincial government, the mayor formally created the Guiuan Recovery and Rehabilitation and Sustainable Development Group (GRRSDG), led by Ades. This was also the same time the Comprehensive Recovery and Rehabilitation Plan (CRRP) was approved by the president of the Philippines. The GRRSDG was to oversee the implementation of the GRRP. According to Ades, the mayor assigned him in charge of monitoring the accomplishments of the Guiuan Rehabilitation and Recovery Plan. However, he has not yet carried out any monitoring initiative due to the absence of a monitoring instrument. Responsibilities related to planning, implementing and monitoring are best divided among different levels of management (Chalmers, 1997). The GRRSDG, as the organizational structure to implement the GRRP, was poorly informed about the CRRP. In this case, while the national government possesses the powers to create policies and plans, their adoption and implementation resides with local government units.

The mayor continued to make decisions on matters related to the purchase of lots for resettlement. Decisions were based on availability, costs, and safety. However, the GRRP clearly indicates that decision making is a shared task of the mayor, the Sangguniang Bayan, and UN Habitat. But the vice mayor and the members of the Sangguniang Bayan were not aware of the land purchases and the negotiations the mayor had been undertaking.

During a meeting presided over by the mayor, survivors residing in Cogon were informed that the cost of a lot would be PHP 50 per month, payable in five years. But they were not informed of their tenurial rights and the decision of the mayor to obtain funds for the permanent housing materials from the Core Shelter Program of the Department of Social Welfare and Development (DSWD). Some officers of the Marig-on Homeowners Association inadvertently learned about the misappropriation of funds from the Core Shelter Program when they went to the Municipal Hall for other concerns. The mayor was traveling to Manila to submit the proposal to the office of DSWD Secretary Corazon "Dinky" Soliman. On the other hand, the Marig-on Homeowners did not have an opportunity to collaborate with the government to craft disaster mitigation and development plans, or to become owners of the plans and programs and become real stakeholders. Their ability to influence the priorities of the local government was nonexistent.

A barangay official, "Tarzan," in an interview held on August 10, 2015, recalled that immediately after Haiyan's wrath, he went to the Eastern Samar State University campus to look after his constituents who had evacuated. He had taken with him tents for distribution but was denied of his right to lead as a local official and ordered by the Municipal Social Welfare and Development (MSWD) not to get inside the campus. Another barangay official, "Sally," in the NBZ area, said, "The staff and personnel of MSWD are *maisog* (unfriendly, stern). They do not really welcome barangay officials in their office. They would ignore our inquiries." A woman leader, "Tancia," of the Marig-on Homeowners Association (interview held on September 1, 2015) also shared this perception regarding the unwelcoming attitude of the staff and personnel of MSWD.

Municipal Urban Development and Housing Board/Local Housing Unit

Sixteen months after Super Typhoon Haiyan, the Sangguniang Bayan approved ordinance No. 09, creating the Municipal Urban Development and Housing Board,

> that will oversee not only the implementation of different housing programs in specific barangays, the poor and the other bona fide residents of the municipality who are homeless, but also to act as [a] one stop shop for the processing of public concerns regarding shelter and shall be responsible in taking changes and shall be tasked in the formulation of policies relative to shelter and different housing programs of the municipality.

> (Ordinance no. 09 series of 2015)

Locally known as the Housing Board, local government officials thought that this office would eventually attend to the housing concerns of those displaced and homeless due to Haiyan.

The Housing Board comprises sixteen members with at least three places for nongovernment organizations involved in shelter and housing. It is headed by the municipal mayor and meets every month, or as the need arises. The Marig-on Homeowners Association president represents the residents of the transitional shelter on the Board. However, we question whether one voice is sufficient to articulate the people's strategic interests, and mobilize pressure to align government decisions for the benefit of the poor population at risk. We also query whether that person may be in a position to be overpowered by the governing elites.

In 2015, the Housing Unit was headed by Mr. Morris Ara. He also serves as the executive secretary of the mayor. His office has yet to draft a Shelter Plan. Ara initially believed that task to be the responsibility of the National Housing Authority. He admitted, "Am new in my post. I lack training" (interview held on August 23, 2015).

Since its establishment, the Housing Board convened to discuss the tenurial rights of the settlers in the transitional shelters and the monthly fees to be collected in the NHA-LGU initiated permanent housing, St Genevieve Village, and the two other sites in Sapao. The plan was that St. Genevieve Village would accommodate 281 families and the Sapao sites would have more than 500 units. The former, as projected, has 100 completed units, while the latter is still in the site development stage.

Because the Housing Board and the Housing Unit are each still in the infancy stage of their development, and a Shelter Plan has not yet been written, the local chief executive is assisted by the municipal assessor, municipal engineer, and the Municipal Planning and Development coordinator in the identification and acquisition of resettlement sites. As to the selection and prioritization of the beneficiaries, the mayor and the MSWD made some initial "guidelines" which confused the people. However, the task relating to the selection and prioritization of the beneficiaries is lodged under the Local Inter-Agency Committee (LIAC). Furthermore, the mayor's office wrote to the Resettlement Cluster requesting that the Municipal Urban and Development Housing Board and the Local Housing Unit be converted into the Local Inter-agency Committee. However, this request has not been acted upon.

The agenda setting and strategy building for shelter provision were prompted by the call of the national government and humanitarian organizations. The GRRP would not have been initiated if there were no external pressure. The local chief executive disregarded the homeless and displaced local citizens in the social and shelter sector of the GRRP formulation. Furthermore, he did not involve the other co-decision makers in the GRRP—the Sangguniang Bayan and UN Habitat. Also, the mayor has not been compliant with national directives to assemble and make functional the LIAC. Instead, he pressed for the formulation of the Municipal Urban and Development Housing Board. There was no public awareness that the mayor erred. Hence, the conduct of the public information drive for the GRRP was inappropriate since it lacked the authenticity and sincerity to inform and educate community members to enable them to learn and adapt to post-disaster life.

The Agents of the Will of the People:
Sangguniang Bayan (Local Legislature)

Following the enactment of the Local Government Code of 1991, the municipalities and their component cities are the second-smallest local government units. There is thus a perceived proximity to their constituents. Mirroring the structure of the national government, local government units have executive, legislative, and judicial branches. The Supreme Court supervises local courts, while the local government units take charge of their executive and legislative branches.

The mayor is the chief executive of the city/municipality. He/she is tasked with the general supervision and control over all activities of the municipal or city government. Among the tasks assigned to the mayor are: formulation of the executive-legislative agenda, preparation of plans and budgets, appointment and oversight of personnel, representing the units, signing contracts and carrying out emergency measures in times of disasters. As chief executive, the mayor is assigned to enforce laws and ordinances, implement approved policies, programs, projects, and services of the municipality, and ensure the delivery of the services and facilities. The vice mayor, on the other hand, serves as the presiding officer of the Sangguniang Panlungsod (city council) or Sangguniang Bayan (town council). The vice mayor appoints the officials of the council and signs warrants drawn on the treasury for all expenditures appropriated for the operation of the city/town.

The Sangguniang Panlungsod or Sangguniang Bayan is the legislative branch of the city or municipality. It is composed of the vice mayor, the president of the municipal or city chapter of the league of barangays, the president of the federation of the youth council, regular sanggunian members (councilors) and sectoral representatives. Their tasks include the approval of ordinances and resolutions relating to peace and order, fines, penalties, appropriation, salaries, and finances of the city/municipal government. They are likewise responsible for the generation and use of resources and revenues and budgets, the granting of franchises and issuance of permits, and regulation of the use of land, buildings, and structures.

The Sangguniang Bayan represents the people. One of its functions is the writing of laws or ordinances. The Sangguniang Bayan, as a political institution, speaks for the people, advocates for its interests, and obtains compensation for grievances. It can criticize the executive branch and debate on big or small issues which are connected to lawmaking.

In Guiuan, the Sangguniang Bayan profile and composition has an interesting and important effect upon its mandate and operation. It is dominated by the mayor's party members, with only two of them coming from the opposition. The elected representatives are perceived to lack the necessary expertise to understand and solve complex community challenges. The Sangguniang Bayan members from the opposition maintain that even before Super Typhoon Haiyan, the chamber's legislative agenda came from the executive. They rarely engage in debates or interchanges during meetings. Items agreed in the executive-legislative agenda are no longer subject to debate. Resolutions coming from constituents which require legislative action, such as the mining issue in Homonhon Island, were delayed for several months by the committee. It is common knowledge within the community that the Ales leadership is supportive of the mining operations in the municipality.

In an interview with Vice Mayor Aspin on August 19, 2015, he said, "We are a cooperative office. We formulate ordinances and resolutions as needed by the Mayor." The vice mayor is proud to have steered the passage of the Guiuan Recovery and Rehabilitation Plan, the creation of the Housing Board and Housing Unit, and the full authority given to the mayor to enter into contracts with humanitarian agencies. However, the Sangguniang Bayan has not asked the local chief executive to apprise them of his transactions with the National Housing Authority, the humanitarian groups and development organizations vis-a-vis the housing provision in the municipality. The Sangguniang Bayan as a body has to exercise its oversight function on the missing but very important development guide, the Municipal Disaster Risk Reduction Management Plan and the Comprehensive Land Use Plan. Almost two years after ST Haiyan, a municipal DRRM Plan had not yet been officially prepared. As such, local government Disaster Risk Reduction policies, strategies, and implementation plans are unclear or nonexistent, this despite the fact that the designated DRRM officer has been in his post for the past ten years. Since the local government has yet to produce a Comprehensive Development Plan, it is possible for anyone to build a house anywhere.

After ST Haiyan, interviewed informants (August 20, 2015) of the Sangguniang Bayan claimed to have individually visited the different affected villages. But this was contradicted by the survivors in the aforementioned areas. According to the Sangguniang Bayan members, their "visits cum conversations" with the villagers centered on *kumustahan* or exchange of pleasantries. The survivors expressed their needs and the Sangguniang Bayan members observed the situation as well. There was no apparent conscious effort nor urgency to process the grievances of the survivors through formal government channels and structures.

As to the enactment of the GRRP in 2014 and the creation of the Housing Board/Unit in March 2015, the only significant participation of the Sangguniang Bayan was its favorable endorsement. Alternatives were unexplored and information was not validated. When asked whether each SB member was given a copy of the Rehabilitation and Recovery Plan to peruse and query during the presentation, the informants responded negatively. In other words, they simply accepted or were "satisfice" (Simon, 1978) with the information on which to base the approval. Only one Sangguniang Bayan member-informant saw the GRRP during the fieldwork for this study.

Sixteenth months after ST Haiyan, the Sanggunian Bayan approved the creation of the Municipal Urban Housing and Development Board (MUDHB) and the Housing Unit. The key people in the Office of the Mayor who pushed for this ordinance thought that the office would be able to resolve the lingering issues on housing and resettlement and at the same time be compliant with the Urban Development Housing Act passed in 1992, which compels all local government units to plan for affordable housing (Art X Sec 39, UDHA). However, the Yolanda Comprehensive Rehabilitation and Recovery Plan mandated the creation of a Local Inter-Agency Committee. The Sangguniang Bayan fell short in fully investigating the appropriate body that could respond to housing issues such as beneficiary selection, tenurial rights, and other processes. No one clarified whether the creation of the MUDHB would result in better shelter outcomes, or if there were better ways to address the municipality's shelter needs and concerns. This raises the question of whether the MUDHB and the Housing Unit would be able respond to the cause of the delay in the completion of the housing units.

The members of the Sangguniang Bayan need to demonstrate the organization's capacity to improve, reject, and offer initiatives and alternatives to the local chief executive so that the housing program is biased toward the safety and the preferences of the people. The lack of coordination and collaboration between offices contributed to disaster response failure (Gotham and Campanella, 2011; Kapucu et al., 2010; Shadrina, 2012). The failure to adequately respond was aggravated by the fact that there are few local citizens or groups monitoring the Sangguniang Bayan's performance, which limits the effectiveness of post-disaster performance (Pelling, 2011).

Moreover, the conduct of the weekly legislative session does not encourage interested citizens to listen. The session hall is a very small room with limited space. Members of the Sangguniang Bayan "respond" to individual voter need, considering solicitations for medicines, tournaments, and the like. The citizen-voter judges the Sanggunian Bayan member on his or her ability to "help, share or give" but not on his contribution in the session hall. Political leaders are not elected based on performance and competence. Citizens do not have the ability to elicit accountability through their vote. Electoral victory is achieved not through performance but through the effective use of money, favors, networks, or coercion (Aruguay, 2005).

The other reality in Philippine politics is that in terms of adopting new policies, the most challenging component is the commitment of the local chief executive, heads of the different departments and aligned legislative leaders because they are the decision makers in the local government. Therefore, a strategic and forward-looking Sangguniang Bayan is needed to protect citizen-survivors from vulnerability to future disasters (Hilhorst, 2003).

Citizen-Survivor Voice: The Marig-on Homeowners Association/Bunkhouse and High-Risk area Occupants

The Marig-on Homeowners Association (MHA) was formed in 2015 and is still working on its registration requirements with the Department of Labor and Employment. The members of the Association were residents of Barangay 6 who lost their homes to ST Haiyan and therefore had to seek shelter at the tent city which was erected at Eastern Samar State University. They were later transferred to the transitional shelter site in Baranagay Cogon. Members of the MHA heard about the GRRP. They said it was about having a "better Guiuan and *madig-on nga mga balay* (sturdy houses)."

According to the members and officials of the MHA, while survivors were at the tent city, the Office of the Mayor and some of the department heads and humanitarian organizations visited to instruct them about their transfer to the transitional shelter. The survivors' opinions or preferences regarding shelter provision were, however, not solicited. Also, they were too busy looking for food and queuing for humanitarian aid and were not able to demand from service providers because "life in the tent was difficult and so we did not care much about the place and type of shelter that would be given to us. We just wanted to get out of the Tent City" (Minerva, September 2, 2015). They could not express their preferences, demands, views, or disapproval. Moreover, there were no alternatives presented to them.

On the contrary, the bunkhouse occupants and those living near the coast revealed that municipal-level politicians have not visited them. They possessed minimal knowledge about the plan of the local government or who was obliged to respond to their plight. They did not have an opportunity to express their demands.

The members of the MHA and bunkhouse dwellers shared that they could not persuade the elected leaders to explain to them what is meant by Build Back Better or No Build Zone, and when and where they would be relocated. People who lack access to food, water, and education cannot exercise their other rights actively and meaningfully, such as participating in the political process (Co et al., 2007). The exercise of accountability is a serious challenge because it does not exist in the consciousness of the people. The values of transparency, participation, and accountability are still vague to the poor and homeless. The government has molded them into passive recipients of dispensed benefits Keister, 2013). In a patron-client environment (Sidel, 1999), venues for political participation are not widely disseminated to the people. Popular forces such as nongovernment organizations and people's organizations are disorganized and cannot compel local officials to implement people-centered programs. Brillantes (2002) points out that if there are independent nongovernment organizations and people's organizations that operate in the area they are uncomfortable dealing with the local government. This is to avoid political influence and control from the local chief executive and the local government.

At the local level, Guiuan survivors, particularly those in the bunkhouse, expressed that "the current administration does not appreciate views contrary to theirs" (Sam, September 1, 2015). These residents have renamed the local radio program "Radyo Natin" (Our Radio) to "Radyo Nira" (Their Radio). The radio station is owned by a politically powerful family so critical comments aimed at administration are not given attention. Where local communities are informed and able to participate in and shape local planning processes, they can hold their local bodies to account and this can be the beginning of a transformative social and political change (Archer, 2014).

When the Marig-on Homeowners Association (MHA) and bunkhouse residents were asked if they had a wish list to be transmitted to the appropriate office(s), both mentioned the following: potable water connection, electricity, a larger lot area (20 sq. m x 60 sq. m), permission to make improvements on their temporary shelters, a chapel, a health center, a *talipapa* (wet market), a titled house and lot, a sturdy house with a comfort room (bathroom), and most importantly, opportunity to have a livelihood. The homeless and those still living in risk areas commented that the shelter units built by the National Housing Authority (NHA) were small. They also mentioned that, if need be, they were willing to render sweat equity for a house they would eventually own.

Due to their marginal status in the community, the affected sector lacks the capacity to control or sanction their elected leaders for the dismal handling of the shelter provision. They are unaware that, as citizens, it is their right to participate in decisions on matters which may impact them. In fact, they hardly know which office is responsible for their shelter concerns. It is likely that the shelter beneficiaries, like any rural poor, will never feel they have the authority to challenge the wealthy and the powerful. In a post-disaster situation, the homeless and the displaced may not be interested in participating in political processes because they have other significant priorities, such as securing food and other necessities for survival.

CONCLUSIONS

After Super Typhoon Haiyan, the deficit in post-disaster accountability did not exist not because of the absence of laws or policies but because of government bodies and leaders who were not citizen/end-user–focused. Hence, they failed to deliver shelter to the typhoon survivors. The Office of the Mayor and the local legislative body shared little information and failed to consult the affected sectors on their shelter requirements. Given the strong particularistic bond or ties in the municipality, and the laws that barely sanction public officials for non-compliance with the law, it was difficult to develop accountability. At the minimum, local officials needed to relay to the people details of their activities and explain their actions to the public.[1] The homeless never demanded reasons for the latter's action or from the local government unit. Perhaps, the abnormal conditions caused by the magnitude of Super Typhoon Haiyan, plus the entrenched patron-client system and the people's lack of capacity in disciplining their leaders insulated the powerful from accountability mechanisms. At the very least, local government bodies demonstrated weak compliance with national mandates. Moreover, the local bureaucracy was not prepared for the effective inclusion of stakeholders in its post-disaster activities.

Local officials must comply and work within the rule of law. The centrality of the law in public administration must be upheld and practiced to enable them to respond in a clear and timely manner. The law should also be the basis for interaction within and outside the local government. Moreover, local officials must always be alert for laws or policy issuances that impact their communities and constituency. Ignorance of these laws could lead to an unresponsive or dysfunctional local government organization. The local chief executive and the Sanggunian Bayan are the chief implementers of the laws of the land in their political jurisdiction. With the unique political relationship of the executive and legislative branches in Guiuan, locating the accountability deficit was not difficult.

To elaborate, the municipal mayor and the Sanggunian Bayan are answerable to the people of Guiuan for the absence of the Disaster Risk Reduction and Management Plan, the unfinished Recovery and Rehabilitation Plan, Local Shelter Plan, Comprehensive Land Use Plan, and the unassembled Local Inter-agency Committee. Both the executive and legislative branches have exhibited low answerability to the people. The municipal mayor is responsible for purchasing resettlement lots which have been declared hazardous by the Department of Environment and Natural Resources. This has adversely affected the timely delivery of the housing units in St. Genevieve Village. The mayor is ultimately responsible for the safety and welfare of the future occupants in those resettlement sites. He is also answerable to the local citizens for not utilizing existing mechanisms such as the Disaster Risk

Reduction and Management Council and the Local Development Council in the formulation of the Rehabilitation and Recovery Plan.

The Sangguniang Bayan barely exercised its obligation to scrutinize the action of the executive in its activities related to housing provision. It did not ask the local chief executive to explain and rectify past actions and mistakes such as the purchase of lots which were unsuitable for resettlement. The barangay officials should have been enabled to carry out discussions in order to garner community interest.

The end users of the shelter provision of the NHA-LGU permanent shelter lack the capacity to directly influence the mayor and the Sangguniang Bayan or participate in the formulation of the GRRP. Had they known that the resettlement sites would be unsafe, they would not have desired to or agreed to live there. Due to their socioeconomic condition and the particularistic culture in the vicinity, the survivors could not articulate their needs nor were they able to negotiate. Hence, they cannot compel, let alone demonstrate, approval (or disapproval) of unresponsive actions from their local officials. An adequate understanding of disaster risk reduction would have provided useful input in establishing how services could be delivered with the resources available and within the existing political mandates.

The inadequate capacities of the local government unit/bodies to meet the challenges of climate change and disaster risk reduction is manifest. A few people are assigned to deliver multiple responsibilities. This arrangement confuses the public regarding the specific roles and responsibilities local government workers are expected to deliver.

Post-disaster accountability can be facilitated with the church, the academic community, and other relevant stakeholders. They can ably educate public institutions and local citizens on accountability. The people of Guiuan need to increase their participation and representation through governance systems to hold their elected officials responsible and accountable for their decisions and performance.

NOTE

1. For example, the NHA-LGU contract should be accessible and made available to the public.

REFERENCES

Archer, D., Almansi, F., DiGregorio, M., Roberts, D., Sharma, D., & Syam, D. (2014). Moving towards inclusive urban adaptation: approaches to integrating community-based adaptation to climate change at city and national scale. *Climate and Development*, 6, 345–356. https://doi.org/10.1080/17565529.2014.918868.

Arugay, A. A. (2005). The Accountability Deficit in the Philippines: Implications and Prospects for Democratic Consolidation. *Philippine Political Science Journal*, 26, 63–88. https://doi.org/10.1080/01154451.2005.9723491.

Bawagan, Aleli. (2015). *Shifting Paradigms: Strengthening Institutions for Community-based Disaster Risk Reduction and Management.* Quezon City: UP CSWD.

Brillantes, Alex B. Jr. (2002). Decentralized Democratic Governance Under the Local Government Code: a Governmental Perspective. In Proserpina D. Tales et al. (eds.), *Local Government in the Philippines: A Book of Readings* (Vol.3), UP.

Chalmers, A. (1997). *Strategic Management: A Research Report.* Wellington: National Library of New Zealand.

Co, Edna et al. (2007). *Phil Democracy Assessment.* Philippines: Anvil Publishing.

Creswell, J. W. (2009). *Research Design: Qualitative, Quantitative and Mixed Methods Approaches.* Thousand Oaks, CA: Sage.

Easthope, Lucy. (2014). Technologies of Recovery. *The Sociological Review* 62 (S1): 135–158.

Evans, A. (2014). *Annual Tropical Cyclone Report 2013.* Joint Typhoon Warning Center: Pearl Harbor, Hawaii.

Gotham, K. F., and Campanella, R. (2011)."Coupled Vulnerability and Resilience: The Dynamics of Cross- Scale Interactions in Post-Katrina New Orleans. *Ecology and Society* 16 (3). doi: 10.5751/es-04292-160312.

Guha-Sapir, D., Below, R., and Hoyois, P. (2016). *EM-DAT: The CRED/OFDA International Disaster Database.* Brussels, Belgium: Université Catholique de Louvain.

Haque, S.M. (1994). The Emerging Challenges to Bureaucratic Accountability: A Critical Perspective. In A. Farazmand (ed.), *Handbook of Bureaucracy.* New York: Marcel Dekker.

Hilhorst, Dorothea. (2003). Responding to Disasters: Diversity of Bureaucrats, Technocrats and Local People. *International Journal of Mass Emergencies and Disasters* 21 (1): 37–55.

Joyce. Paul. (2010). *Strategic Management for Public Services.* Great Britain: Open University Press.

Kapucu, N., Arslan, T., and Collins, M. L. (2010). Examining Intergovernmental and Interorganizational Response to Catastrophic Disasters: Toward a Network-Centered Approach. *Administration & Society* 42 (2): 222–247. doi: 10.1177/0095399710362517.

Keister, Jennifer. (2013). Political Dysfunction in the Philippines is Hurting Haiyan's Victims. *Washington Post.* http:wwww.washingtonpost.com/political-dysfunction-in-the-philippines-is-hurting-haiyan's-victims

Mangada, Ladylyn L. (2015). Grooming the Wards in Leyte-Samar Islands: What's New. In Amaryllis Tiglao Torres, Laura L. Samson, Manuel Pascual Diaz (eds.), *Filipino Generations in a Changing Landscape. Philippine Social Science Council.* Quezon City. Philippines.

National Disaster Risk Reduction and Management Council. (2014). *Final Report Re Effects of Typhoon "Yolanda" (Haiyan).* National Disaster Risk Reduction and Management Council, Quezon City, Philippines.

Pelling, M. (2011). Urban Governance and Disaster Risk Reduction in the Caribbean: The Experiences of Oxfam GB. *Environment and Urbanization* 23 (2): 383–400. doi: 10.1177/0956247811410012.

Salleh, S., and Iqbal, A. (eds.). (1995). *Accountability: The Endless Prophecy.* Kuala Lumpur: Asia and Pacific Development Center.

Shadrina, Elena. (2012). "Fukushima Fallout: Gauging the Change in Japanese Nuclear Energy Policy." *International Journal of Disaster Risk Science* 3 (2): 69–83. doi: 10.1007/s13753-012-0008-0.

Sidel, John. (1999). *Bossism in the Philippines.* Stanford University Press.

Thomas, G. (2011). A Typology for the Case Study in Social Science Following a Review of Definition, Discourse and Structure". *Qualitative Inquiry* 17 (6): 511–521. doi:10.1177/1077800411409884.

Chapter 5

Sanay Kami sa Bagyo
(We are Used to Storms)

*Unpacking "irrational" Evacuation
Decision making within the Sentient
Ecology during Typhoon Haiyan (Yolanda)*

Pamela Gloria Cajilig, Diego S. Maranan,
Kathryn B. Francis, and Gintare Zaksaite

INTRODUCTION

The dark gray afternoon clouds and soft rumble of thunder suggested rain within minutes as I (Cajilig) walked into Elvie's neighborhood along the National Highway to conduct an interview[1]. It had been one month since this Visayan town and hundreds of others were devastated by Typhoon Yolanda. The storm was one of the strongest typhoons ever recorded and officially claimed over 6,000 lives, but some believe that the true number of deaths remains a state secret (Avila, 2014 August 13). The surroundings were filled with signs of a community struggling to rise above unfathomable loss: the stench of death mixed with the earthy smell of wood shavings and fresh concrete; women and young girls hawking scant piles of limp vegetables from makeshift stalls fronting their houses; the din of hammers, drills, and welding equipment that accompanied the feverish efforts of husbands, fathers, and sons to piece back together as much of their homes as they could before the next downpour.

I was visiting Elvie to inquire about the concrete slab she and her husband Max had started to build as their new roof, when a blue plastic basin resting on top of a wooden cabinet caught Elvie's eye. "That basin . . . that's how I saved my daughter," she said. Elvie and Max had been labeled by emergency

89

managers and the public as *matigas as ulo* (hardheaded), because they refused to evacuate pre-impact despite urgent calls by the local government to leave their homes (Muna, 2013 November 7). When the storm surge engulfed the town, Elvie found herself in chest-deep water inside their bedroom while holding up their two-month-old daughter. With no second floor to escape to, she placed her daughter on top of the cabinet. As the water continued to rise, the plastic basin floated past her. Elvie decided to place their daughter in the basin and make their way out of the house in the hopes of finding higher ground.

I was about to ask Elvie how she brought herself and her daughter to safety, when we both realized that there was a drizzle outside. Elvie started to tear up and shake visibly. *"Gusto ko nang tumakbo paakyat doon"* (I want to run up over there now), she said in quavering voice, nodding her head toward a cluster of hills in the distance where many neighbors sought refuge during the flood. *"Tuwing ganyang umuulan, kahit patak-patak lang, takot akong mangyari ulit ang Yolanda* (Every time it rains, even if it's just a few drops, I'm afraid that Yolanda will happen all over again)." I asked if she wanted to talk further, but she only nodded weakly. I took that as a sign for me to wrap up the interview. I gave her my NGO's business card for any help we could provide, and thanked her. Then I hastily took a pedicab back to our staff quarters before the drizzle turned into a thunderstorm.[2]

Elvie was just one of several Typhoon Yolanda survivors with whom Cajilig engaged as part of a rapid humanitarian shelter needs assessment for a women's NGO that was funded by an international donor. That assessment was comprised of quantitative profiling of damaged houses, ten loosely structured and focus group discussions, and sixteen semi-structured and unstructured interviews, which were often accompanied by direct observation via home visits[3]. Narratives of how inhabitants experienced the storm surge began to surface as an unintended consequence of trying to understand the reconstruction priorities of homeowners within Palo, in the Leyte province.[4] Many discussions originated from the decision to refrain from evacuating prior to the typhoon, and people's subsequent experiences of the surge. These accounts were accompanied by stories of how they lost their loved ones in a moment[5]. Notably, the focus of this chapter on non-evacuees was more of a function of the unpredictable conditions of ethnographic field work, than of design. Furthermore, engagement with first responders, government officials, and other community gatekeepers as part of Cajilig's role as a humanitarian also yielded information about the larger cultural and sociohistorical contexts of these harrowing experiences that unfolded through a series of agonizing choices. These discussions also represent the creatural aspects of the human experience that are often ignored by social and cultural anthropology: our ecological positionalities, our vulnerability to the environment, and our capacity to make meaning from perceiving our surroundings through our senses.

DRAWING FROM THE ANTHROPOLOGY OF DISASTER, THE ANTHROPOLOGY OF DECISION MAKING, AND COGNITIVE SCIENCE

This chapter will examine the considerations of non-evacuees in deciding to stay home during Typhoon Yolanda. In applying the formulations based on the phenomenology of Edmund Husserl (Genuisas, 2012; Koestenbaum, 1998), we hope to diverge from formative and unicentral notions of choice in favor of an actor-centered understanding that highlights the sociocultural dimensions of decision making (Geertz, 1973), some of which have so far been underexplored by existing literature. In examining the trajectory of choices made by Elvie and her fellow inhabitants, we extensively borrow from the "substantive, developmental, and comparative platform of anthropology" in consideration of disasters as totalizing phenomena that encompass cultural, societal, and environmental concerns (Hoffman & Oliver-Smith, 2002:6,13). We view this chapter as a contribution to ethnographic expertise, "the ability to obtain contextual understanding and to act on the basis of such experience," and which has yet to be considered as essential criteria for successful disaster management (Rajan, 2002:247). An ethnographic approach is likewise suited to the study of decision making. Aʼsa Boholm and others underscore how ethnography reveals the "everyday-ness of decision making" by illuminating how decisions are socioculturally informed and imbued with meaning (Boholm et al. 2013:107). This chapter was developed with the intention of contributing to the anthropology of disaster through a foray into the anthropology of decision making, and vice-versa. In addition, we fold into our discussion consonant views from cognitive psychology (Anderson, 1995), not only in order to illustrate how ethnographic analysis can be enriched by other epistemologies, but also to signpost how decision making during disaster could be studied by other fields located within the "network of disciplines, fields, and other knowledge formations" (Maranan, 2017) in cognitive science. We recognize that cultural anthropology and cognitive science have hardly been bedfellows. However, we argue that the challenge of responding effectively to the intensifying effects of climate change is a wicked problem that cannot simply be addressed by a single discipline. It is "complex, involving multiple possible causes and internal dynamics that could not be assumed to be linear, and [it could] have very negative consequences for society if not addressed properly" (Peters 2017; Ritter & Weber, 1973).

RELATED LITERATURE AND
THEORETICAL ANCHORS

The following review of related literature is divided into three parts. The first part draws heavily from Dash and Gladwin (2007) and is an overview of literature about hurricane decision making processes. We then move on to the second part, the anthropology of decision making. In a discussion of this emerging field, we explore "horizons of choice" and the gaps in research that this term addresses. In doing so, we expound on the formulations of Boholm et al. (2013), which, in turn, are inspired by the phenomenology of Edmund Husserl. We complement the emphasis the first two sections place on decision making as socially constructed and culture-specific with an exploration of Tim Ingold's (2002; 2010) "dwelling perspective" and related concepts. These draw upon psychological theory in perceiving people as human organisms that are shaped by mutually constitutive sociocultural and environmental processes. It is by using the lens of this third section that we primarily aim to innovate upon the anthropology of decision making.

Hurricane Evacuation Decision Making

Disaster risk reduction and management (DRRM) practitioners view evacuation procedures as integral to disaster preparedness. Developing an evacuation plan is especially critical for coastal communities that are rapidly urbanizing and, at the same time, are vulnerable to climate change. The importance of evacuation is further highlighted by spectacles of destruction and death caused by the flooding that have characterized natural disasters which have gained global attention. This includes the Indian Ocean Tsunami in 2004 and Hurricane Katrina in 2006 (Esteban et al., 2015), and more recently Typhoon Yolanda in 2013. According to Dash and Gladwin's (2007) review of literature on hurricane evacuation decision making, the voluminous studies on the subject can so far be classified into three categories: warning, risk perception, and evacuation compliance. On the point of warning, there are three main strands of studies in this area: the quality of the warning messages themselves; characteristics which account for differences in the interpretation of warning messages, including characteristics which account for these (e.g., demographics and level of knowledge); and who ultimately ends up evacuating and who does not based on the interpretation of these warnings (Dash & Gladwin, 2007:69–70; Mileti et al., 1975). Furthermore, risk perception is a key factor in understanding evacuation decision-making processes, as information about hazards needs to be translated into a concrete conception of pending danger for action to take place (Dash & Gladwin, 2007:71–72; Esteban et al., 2015). Studies of risk perception explore the range of variables that influence how people determine risk, including but not limited to social characteristics (White, 1994) and the ability to personalize risk (Dash 2002). Finally, research in evacuation compliance endeavors to identify differences in the characteristics of evacuees versus non-evacuees; variables such as age, disability, presence of vulnerable family members, gender, and race may all determine the motivation to evacuate (Dash & Gladwin, 2007:72; Mileti et al., 1975; Gladwin & Peacock, 1997; Fothergill, 1996).

Typical research objectives in this area involve developing comprehensive predictive models for evacuation compliance. However, Dash and Gladwin (2007:70) point out that complexity in decision making and difficulties in categorizing decisions, especially within hurricane evacuation decision making, could frustrate the attempts to build comprehensive and accurate models. They maintain that succeeding studies must move beyond parsing out the characteristics of evacuees and non-evacuees, and toward an understanding of the factors that people consider as important to their processes of decision making.

Understanding who evacuates and who does not has been one of the preoccupations of researchers focusing on the pre-impact stages of natural and technological hazards (Dash & Gladwin, 2007:69). Non-evacuation has gained special attention as it contradicts assumptions by emergency managers that people will act "rationally" upon hearing a warning, and upon perceiving that the costs of staying clearly exceed its benefits (Dash & Gladwin, 2007:69) Meanwhile, Esteban et al. (2015) observed that while people's reasons for evacuating were fairly straightforward, examining why affected people refused to evacuate was more complex. Consequently, this chapter responds to the challenge of understanding the so-called "irrationality" of non-evacuation by adopting an actor-centered approach in examining the cultural logic that underpins non-evacuation (Langley et al., 1995; Boholm et al., 2013).

Horizons of Choice

Boholm et al. (2013) define the experiential frames with which we make decisions as *horizons of choice*, a key concept from phenomenology used by Edmund Husserl (Horizont) to address "the constitution of experience from expectations" (Boholm et al., 2013 drawing from Kuhn 1940; also see Genuisas, 2012). "Horizon" is derived from a Greek word, a verb which roughly translates to "to limit," "to divide," or "mark off by boundaries" (Genuisas, 2012:2). The term is now commonly used to refer to the line where the earth or the sea meet the sky. This line can be conceived as the limit of one's visual perception, but it is not an actual physical line; the horizon is relative to the position of the actor perceiving it, and it often appears to recede as one moves forward (Genuisas, 2012:1). Therefore, the horizon is limiting, but it is also insurmountable (Genuisas, 2012:1–2), and the same can be used to characterize Husserl's metaphorical use of "Horizont." Notably, "horizon" also refers to meanings beyond the visual in everyday speech: for good reason, we also tend to speak of horizons of knowledge, experience, and interests (Genuisas, 2012:1). This usage provides a good indication of what constitutes "horizon" in the sense of Husserl.

Consequently, horizons of choice in part refer to the realms of (intersubjectively accessible) experiences that ground our intentions (Koestenbaum, 1998; Genuisas, 2012); it is the solution space of all possible decisions that a person can take. The objects of our perception (cogitatum) are indexed against past events, our "mnemonic mass" in the sense of Blanshard (Koestenbaum, 1998:34). In psychology these have been referred to as "schemata," which can be described as cognitive frameworks of some part of the world, based on experience. These are continuously updated with every encounter with a related event (Bartlett, 1932; Piaget, 1985). At the same time, Husserl's position is that "potentiality is an aspect of the experience of any object" (Koestenbaum, 1998:33). For example, the "potential" of plastic to float in water and the potential of a basin to contain small objects forms part of the total "experience" of a "plastic basin," an everyday tool in the Philippine households which is used in both washing dishes and doing laundry, and which was instrumental to Elvie's fulfillment of the intention to save her daughter's life.

Horizons of choice are not limited to past experiences; they are concurrently about the future. Returning to Elvie's narrative, experiencing the life-saving potential of a plastic basin now forms her "mnemonic mass" of memories associated with this household item, and recollections of this specific utility of plastic basins might be reawakened in other contexts. Furthermore, horizons of choice are imbued with sociality (Boholm et al., 2013). For example, the bonds of kinship and friendship that were threatened, saved, nurtured, and lost during this relatively short time frame is a common thread within the narratives collected about physically surviving the typhoon.

Meanwhile, Boholm et al. (2013), citing Langley et al. (1995), identified three concerns regarding major theories on decision making outside the field of anthropology. The first, reification, refers to the tendency to treat a decision as a discrete object rather than a social construct (Boholm et al., 2013:100). Decisions are elusive; they have a "dubious ontology" (Boholm et al., 2013:100). Whether a decision exists is not always self-evident from the facts at hand. What exactly is a decision? And if it can be ascertained that a decision does exist, at what moment did it come into being? Is its constitution in its deliberation, verbalization, or enactment? (Boholm et al., 2013:100; also see Gladwin & Murtaugh, 2016).

The second concern is dehumanization: assuming decision making is "deprived of the emotions, imaginations, and 'irrationality' that emanate from experience and memory" (Boholm et al., 2013:100). This then leads to an assumption that people who are provided with the same information and share similar preferences will arrive at the same decision (also refer to Langley et al., 1995). However, this view neglects the role of individual differences. The perception of a particular situation will be dependent on a person's previous experience, which in most cases will be different than their peers'. This will affect the person's perception of a particular situation, judgment of risk, and costs and benefits of particular decisions (e.g., Neisser, 1967). This view also ignores the significance of social factors in decision making. Different societies (and individuals) will create their own sets of criteria against which to assess and measure risk; these social and individual schemata suggest that risk perception, and subsequent behavior, are subjective (Toft & Reynolds, 2016). Moreover, processes of decision making are enmeshed in a web of both human and non-human constituents of the larger environment, the forces of which are not within the control of the actors involved (Ingold, 2010).

Boholm also stated a third concern: isolation. It is closely related to the first concern of reification. Isolation refers to the idea that "decision making can be understood as separated from other activities of an organization or decision maker (Boholm et al., 2013:100)." Since decisions are interconnected and thus shape each other, it is seldom viable to bracket one of these decisions as a basic, discrete unit of analysis (Boholm et al., 2013:100). The processual complexity of decision making thus poses challenges in defining the precise moment when a decision is actually made, as well as difficulties in separating preparations for making choices (such as surveying available information) from the actual decision (Boholm et al., 2013:100).

A strand of studies of decision making addresses these concerns by turning to social life and naturalistic settings (Boholm et al., 2013: 101; Krzyworzeka, 2013; Sjölander-Lindqvist & Cinque, 2013). These studies embrace the reality that decision making tends to be messy: it is less structured than previously thought; it entails the negotiation of diverse, contradictory, and dynamic goals; and it is enacted through interrelated yet differently positioned actors (Boholm et al., 2013:101–102; also see Henning, 2009).

Decision Making by Sentient Beings

In *Perceptions of the Environment: Essays on Dwelling, Livelihood and Skill* (2002), Tim Ingold pushes for an anthropology that strives to overcome a false dichotomy that, on the one hand, either only recognizes human beings as biological organisms, or, on the other hand, only attends to human embeddedness in sociocultural life. Ingold realizes that analysis integrating psychology, a field he admits to having overlooked in previous work, could bridge these two halves of anthropology (Ingold, 2002:2). Ingold's ecological approach to perception is consequently drawn from the following ideas: 1) the mind is not limited by the skin (Bateson, 1973) and, 2) it is not the mind that is trapped in a body that perceives the environment, but the organism as a whole in its "exploratory movement through the world" (Ingold, 2002:5; Gibson, 1979).

Humans operate in the environment with a "sentient ecology" (Ingold, 2002:40; Anderson, 2000). This is knowledge based on feeling and comprised of the "skills, sensitivities, and orientation" through lived experience in a particular environment, which is obtained through processes of discovery, rather than through formal, authorized means (Ingold, 2002:37, 40; Boholm et al., 2013). This "sentient ecology" can also be called "intuition," which is not inferior knowledge, as Western thought and science have long assumed. Intuition is basic knowledge we all have and it is deployed as we go about our daily lives (Ingold 2002:37; also see Dreyfus & Dreyfus, 1986). To regard humans as sentient beings is to recognize that humans are "organisms-persons" that inhabit the world along with beings of manifold kinds, both human and non-human (the "dwelling perspective"; Ingold, 2002:5; Ingold, 2010; also see the discussion of our "creatural" subjectivities by Ortner, 2006). In this view, our sociality is merely a subset of our ecological relations, and these relationships, together with the sensibilities and meanings gathered as they unfold, underwrite our capacities of judgment and skills to discriminate (Ingold, 2002:40).

FIELD RELATIONS AND THE COMPLEXITIES OF DATA GATHERING IN A POST-DISASTER SETTING

Certain conditions within the field constrained the extent of interactions between Cajilig and the local community. Cajilig endeavored to be as sensitive as possible in probing experiences of the storm surge; however, the timing of her engagement with humanitarian shelter meant that the recollection of the loss and devastation of Typhoon Yolanda was still an open wound for interlocutors. Cajilig therefore needed to be attuned to non-verbal signs of distress, as her interlocutors could have agreed to continue with the interviews out of politeness. Secondly, Cajilig's positionality as a representative of an NGO distributing multiple forms of humanitarian aid to several communities provided access to a wide network of interlocutors. However, this same stance often gave the impression that she was there to provide shelter support specifically to those who responded to interview requests, an expectation that needed to be managed constantly. Understandably, much of this expectation was constituted by the extent of loss and desperation experienced by those affected, as well as by the hope of regaining some form of material comfort for themselves and their families. While the NGO planned to eventually provide shelter support, the exact form of shelter had yet to be decided. Cajilig documented the humanitarian shelter needs assessment and outcome in a separate article (see Cajilig et al., 2014). These concerns necessitated the use of handwritten notes for recording and reserving the use of audio and video equipment only for interlocutors who were comfortable with being recorded and who clearly understood the NGO's mandates and limitations.

Furthermore, in the subsequent discussions and when applicable, the narratives examined were supplemented with secondary data. In addition, they were complemented by Cajilig's own experiences and knowledge of local practices in disaster risk reduction and management, acquired through past and current participation in other projects that were not directly relevant to Typhoon Yolanda, and in which she has not been officially involved as a researcher. As opposed to participant observation, in which the extent to which the researcher intervenes is limited, these discussions rely on the entanglements of observant participation. In observant participation, fieldworkers find opportunities to understand phenomenon even as they fulfill non-research roles, such as those related to conference organizing, volunteer work, etc.; neither are they "eternal cultural apprentices" whose contributions are limited to critical questioning, nor are they "managers of development projects in an all-too-familiar top-down regime" (Gatt & Ingold, 2013:154; Also see Agar, 1996; Croll & Parkin, 1992; Hobart, 1993). This chapter, therefore, also aims to contribute to the anthropologies of disaster and decision making by illustrating how critical reflection regarding one's nonacademic practice as productive of social relations in the field can lend itself to theoretical analysis.

DECISION MAKING BEFORE AND DURING IMPACT

The following discussion is divided into two parts. The first part lays down the socio-temporal and culturally constituted (and some historically situated) beliefs that reportedly underpinned household deliberations once news of the typhoon spread. As Cajilig's interlocutors did not evacuate, they were in their homes with their families when the five-meter storm surge overwhelmed the town. Consequently, the second part of the discussion focuses on the intuitive enactment of survival strategies that are grounded in perceptions of the immediate environment and its human and non-human constituents. The discussion ends with a postscript on how individuals and institutions chose to carry on given the shared experience of Typhoon Yolanda. We conclude by suggesting ways through which this strand of exploration can continue.

"We Are Used to Typhoons"

"*Sanay kami sa bagyo*"[6] (We are used to typhoons) was a phrase Cajilig often heard in the field, and which many of her interlocutors used to partly explain their decision to stay in their homes. As such, when the Manila-based national government activated disaster preparedness measures, there were residents, veterans of decades of typhoons, who regarded these activities as excessive. (Similar findings were discussed by Dalisay & De Guzman, 2016.) Relatedly, Greg Bankoff (2002:3) maintains that a decolonized understanding of disaster acknowledges that certain populations do not necessarily view disasters as aberrant phenomena. Furthermore, "for the greater part of humanity, hazard and disaster are simply just accepted aspects of daily life. So normal, in fact, that their cultures are partly the product of adaptation to those phenomena" (Bankoff, 2002:3). The regularity with which inhabitants of the Municipality of Palo experience typhoons is explained by Leyte island's location along the Typhoon Belt of the Philippines. The country experiences an average of twenty typhoons each year, five of which are destructive (Asian Disaster Reduction Center, n.d.). Many residents, who live in areas where weather threats are frequent, will ignore disaster warnings because they develop a sense of invulnerability. This sense allows residents to lead normal lives and complete daily tasks without constantly worrying about the potential dangers that threaten them (Janoff-Bulman, 1992).

Typhoon Yolanda made its mark as one of the strongest storms in history (Santos, 2013 November 10). However, historian and newspaper columnist Ambeth Ocampo (2013 November 19) quickly reminded the public about historical records showing that more than a century ago, Leyte experienced at least two super typhoons of the same intensity. According to Ocampo, Jesuit Father Jose Algue, the second director of Manila's first weather bureau, published a 136-page monograph titled "El Baguio de Samar y Leyte 12–13 de Octubre de 1897" (The Typhoon of Samar and Leyte 12–13 October 1897). Algue and his team visited many affected municipalities, including Palo and Tacloban. Ocampo further notes that the black and white photographs contained in the monograph are not different from the images of Yolanda's aftermath that were disseminated through the media: ruins of houses and churches, and uprooted trees. On the other hand, the U.S. Library of Congress online archive shows a brief report from the Washington Herald in 1912 (November 30) mentioning the loss of about 15,000 lives in the nearly obliterated capital cities of Tacloban and Capiz.

The meaning of "disaster," therefore, is constituted by what accumulates over time as part of the givens of everyday life[7] and consequently, common sense. As such, the horizons of choice through which inhabitants responded to environmental forces of the typhoon (such as the decision of Elvie and Max to refrain from evacuation) are shaped by inflections in meaning that are, in this case, grounded in geography and history. Inhabitants of Palo did not necessarily equate "storm" with "disaster" nor increased risk, and therefore held off on evacuation. From a psychological perspective, we might explain such behaviors with reference to heuristics. When we are required to make judgments about risk in a situation where very little concrete information is available to us (such as during a disaster), we tend to make fast inferences based on what we have experienced (seen, heard, and felt) before. If storms are commonplace and residents have been able to wait out previous events, this history of experience creates "rules of thumb" that will shape present actions (Toft & Reynolds, 2006).

Meanwhile, grounding the significance of "disaster" in history brings forth the necessity of understanding decision making as a temporally nested process (Walker & Lovat, 2017; Store-Brinchmann, 2002; Boholm et al., 2013; Ingold, 2002). This view is also in line with assertions that an understanding of disasters ought to be historically situated (Garcia-Acosta, 2002; Rajan, 2002; Oliver-Smith & Hoffman, 2002). Specifically, Virginia Garcia-Acosta (2002:49–50; also see Palerm, 1980) emphasizes the need to historicize disaster to show that "history has not yet been surmounted and is still, in a strict sense, part of our present."

"Only God has the Right to Take our Lives"

In loosely structured group discussions with women, as well as high school students, religious beliefs emerged as a common influence of evacuation decision making. *"Diyos lang ang makakapagsabi kung kailan ang oras natin"* (only God can say when it's our time), several participants said, and it was a phrase that was often uttered when residents were deliberating on whether to leave. Jonas, a first-year high school student, stated that while his mother, his brother, and he wanted to evacuate before the typhoon, his father was very much against the idea. During the storm surge, the family found themselves clinging to a beam on the second floor of their house, with the water up to their necks. At that point, the rest of the family begged the father to lead them out of the house. *"Pero sabi ni Tatay hindi raw dapat kami mag-evacuate dahil Diyos lang daw ang may karapatan na kumuha ng buhay namin"* (But Father said we shouldn't evacuate because only God has the right to take our lives), said Jonas. The belief that God is more powerful than any storm may thus constitute a specific horizon of choice that excludes choosing to evacuate during a disaster.

The nesting of these beliefs within a lifeworld that considers typhoons as an everyday occurrence can thus generate powerful arguments against leaving one's home in the event of a looming catastrophe. This analysis, however, does not imply that those subscribing to the same religion will necessarily hold the same beliefs[8]. As Sherry Ortner (2006:59) notes, "Subjectivities are complex because they are culturally and emotionally complex, but also because of the ongoing work of reflexivity, monitoring the relationship of the self to the world."

People are constantly observing the world, assessing what is at stake for them, and what is at stake for others, and make decisions accordingly based on unique, but culturally constituted, structures of feeling and thought. Jude, one of our community guides, mentioned that many people were disappointed with a local seminary that closed its gates to evacuees; they were told that the place was "sanctum sanctorum" (a very holy place), and therefore not just anyone could be allowed to enter. Meanwhile, in preparation for Typhoon Ruby in the same area of the following year, around 10,000 evacuees were housed in churches across parishes in Leyte (Tupaz, 2014 December 6). Fr. Alcris Bada, who coordinated disaster efforts for the Archdiocese of Palo encouraged the faithful to not only pray, but also to "prepare and participate": *"An Dios nabulig han tawo nga nabulig han iya kalugaringon"* (God helps those who help themselves) (Tupaz, 2014 December 6.)

Local definitions of "disaster" may, therefore, also intersect with certain deep-seated beliefs within the community in relation to other aspects of cultural life, such as religion, which remain to be explored in detail by future research. The Archdiocese of Palo "has grown to be one of the largest administrative diocese of the Roman Catholic Church (Archdiocese of Palo n.d.)." Southern Leyte is also imagined as having a special place in the history of the Catholic Church in the country, as the first Holy Mass in the archipelago that would later become the Philippines was believed to be held on its island Limasawa on Easter Sunday of 1521[9]. Pope Francis visited Tacloban, the adjacent capital city of Leyte, in January 2015 to provide spiritual guidance and encouragement to those affected by Typhoon Yolanda. Catholic religion is an axis of everyday life for many families in the area; Cajilig's interlocutors who managed to recover religious items from the rubble of their homes, such as the Crucifix and statues of the Santo Niño, regarded these as the ultimate sign from heaven that God had safely guided them through the deluge.

"We Didn't Understand the Meaning of 'Storm Surge'"

Much of the loss and destruction in Typhoon Yolanda was directly caused by the same storm surge that nearly drowned Elvie and her daughter. Palo was particularly vulnerable as it is bordered by the sea and the Palo River runs through the municipality. Prior to Typhoon Haiyan's devastation, the Philippine Atmospheric, Geophysical and Astronomical Services Administration (PAGASA), the country's current weather bureau, reported the risk to local agencies and communities. However, research by Lejano, Tan, and Wilson (2015) revealed that the impending storm surge was "simply a line at the end of a routine weather bulletin." At the cost of the decision to follow routine and pro forma communication, the bureau failed to emphasize the urgency of the storm surge to key agencies and the public (Lejano et al., 2015 February 05). Several of Cajilig's interlocutors noted that they vaguely recalled hearing about the storm surge from the media, but did not understand its significance. "*Parang narinig namin sa TV [ang 'storm surge'], pero hindi namin alam kung ano yun*" (We somewhat heard [about the storm surge] from TV, but we didn't know what it was). As such, while there was information available, the technical language in which the bureau communicated the risk failed to register the need for urgent action. This failure to understand weather statements has been found in previous research examining the effectiveness of weather warnings; arguably the combined effect of regular exposure to weather warnings and lack of understanding of these warnings, generates a neutral attitude toward the threat (Drost, Casteel, Libarkin, Thomas, & Meister, 2016). Ensuring that messages are "personalized" for local residents can help to overcome these problems in communicating the severity of storms (Jibiki, Kure, Kuri, & Ono, 2016).

Dash and Gladwin (2007:70) point out that warning "is a social process and people interpret and react to warning differently based on who they are, whom they are with, who and what they see or do not see, and what they hear." Cajilig's interlocutors also said they gauged their response to typhoon warnings through observing how their neighbors responded to this information. Seeing their neighbors remain also reinforced their own sentiments that it was best to stay home. This is also consistent with the evidence from psychology: participants under stress have been found to rely more strongly on judgments of others (Driskell & Salas, 1991).

"Only the Rich can Prepare for Disaster"

During one of the group discussions, Cajilig asked about preparations made upon hearing the news about the typhoon. Luz, a barangay health worker, stated, "*Madaling maghanda sa baygo, kung may pera ka. Eh wala kaming pera*" (It is easy to prepare for disaster, if you have money. But we don't have money). There was therefore a sense that nothing they could have done to prepare for Typhoon Yolanda would have been enough; that is to say, they felt that the outcome of disaster was outside their "locus of control" (as developed by Rotter, 1954), given their lack of resources and marginal position in society. Certain members of the group were informal settlers, and therefore landless. They were afraid to leave their homes since landowners might prevent them from returning. They also feared that others would steal the few possessions that they did have, had they decided to evacuate. Having relatives who are equally poor, and who also have no homes built with robust material or with second floors, also discouraged evacuation. Consequently, families considered their financial, physical, and social capital in deliberations about whether to evacuate. These findings are corroborated by Walch (2017:8), who also observed that landlessness discourages evacuation as informal settlers feared that landowners would use the opportunity to not only bar them from returning, but to also impose a construction ban unless settlers provided some form of recompense (Walch, 2017:8). As a result, men typically choose to stay to protect their residence and possessions during disaster, while the rest of the family evacuates (Walch, 2017:8).

Walch's (2017:8) research also reveals that lack of land tenure discourages inhabitants from investing in more permanent structures for their homes, given the possibility of eviction. Nor do they have the means—the NGO's shelter damage assessment report showed that many houses in the town were built using substandard materials. The NGO disseminated shelter recommendations in the municipality, which included using thicker concrete hollow block walls, rebar, and galvanized iron sheets. Interlocutors understood the significance of these suggestions, since many households were supported by men working in the construction industry. However, people simply had no money, and government support was scant. Most homeowners started rebuilding by picking out scraps from the piles of rubble of the fragile materials that were once their homes. Inhabitants with no security of land tenure who are confronted with the risks of disaster are therefore facing a dilemma: They neither have the right and means to build themselves permanent and more resilient housing, nor do they have the option to leave.

Lived Experience and Decision Making on the Day of the Typhoon

We managed to piece together participants' rough flow of decision making on the day of the typhoon. Figure 5.1 shows that as the typhoon continued to intensify, families monitored their houses in relation to the wind and the rain. The presence of strong winds and rising water in the larger environment prompted them to assess whether roofs and walls were still intact. If there was little or no water inside the house, families stayed put while already starting to secure their valuables. If there was damage to the roof and walls, but still no water inside the house, they still stayed put while finding a corner or piece of furniture to shield them from the elements. At knee-level

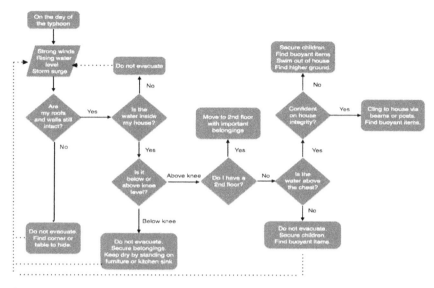

Figure 5.1   Decision-making process of non-evacuees who remained in their homes on the day of Typhoon Yolanda.

depth water, they started moving with their belongings to the second floor, if they had one. Serious contemplation of evacuation started when the water reached chest level. At this point, parents prioritized their children by ensuring they were attached to flotation devices, or to sturdy posts. Among those we conversed with, the decision to leave was ultimately left to the father. If the father was not confident about the integrity of the house, the family attempted to leave for higher ground. Families with fathers who were confident in the structure of the house opted to stay, in which case family members clung to the highest beam they could find, or to floating items like plastic jugs for distilled water and refrigerators. Notably, several male homeowners worked in construction, and were often involved in building their own houses; this was one reason as to why they had the final decision on whether to leave. One homeowner, Sally, who is married to a construction worker (Eric), said that water in their house had already reached their necks but her husband still did not want the family to evacuate. *"Sabi ng asawa ko maganda daw ang pagkakagawa niya ng bahay namin. Maganda ang materyales, malalim ang pundasyon. Buhay pa rin kami dito pagkatapos ng Yolanda."* [My husband said he made our house very well. The materials are good, the foundation is deep. We were still alive here after Yolanda]. Here, the relationship between the homeowner and the house parallels that of a craftsman and his craft. Being able to remain in the house throughout the typhoon was a testament of craftsmanship, a consideration in evacuation that has been underexplored so far in existing studies of hurricane decision making.

The flow chart above attempts to order (for the sake of discussion) processes of perception and action that were, in reality, fraught with danger, stress, and complexity. Those who opted to stay were forced to negotiate the safety of their children and belongings, and their rapidly deteriorating houses, with the brute forces of nature. This information also demonstrates that those who were affected by the forces of the typhoon were corporeal, sentient beings (Ingold, 2002:40): their experience was perceived and comprehended through embodiment, as they assessed danger and risk by interpreting the relationship of the flood level to specific parts of their bodies, such as their knees and chest.

While this example shows how humans are biological organisms that are vulnerable to natural elements, the accounts of the typhoon's impact expose the sociality of decision making. First, a flood in the house underscores how parents prioritized protecting their children from impact. Secondly, the perception of risk is gendered, as the task of judging structural integrity (and therefore the final call for evacuation) was assigned to men, given that construction in Palo is a domain of men, and given that the families we engaged with are headed by men. There is some evidence of gender differences in risk perception (e.g., Ho, Shaw, Lin & Chiu, 2008) but, unfortunately, data on how this applies to evacuation behaviors are quite scarce. Thirdly, the identification with a particular livelihood may constitute one's choices even in the stressful event of being caught in a flood, as Sally and Eric's case exhibits.

The aspects of people's decision making described above can also be seen as being geared toward the concept from psychology known as uncertainty reduction (Berger & Calabrese, 1975). When they are in situations in which aspects of the future are unknown, they will seek further information before making a choice. While a large amount of evidence for this comes from laboratory studies, some of this research has been done under (low) physical threat conditions, such as administering a shock (e.g., de Berker et al., 2016). In any case, this concept seems to suit the decision-making process detailed above: people were hesitant to make the decision to evacuate when the probability of a life-threatening level of typhoon was unknown. However, once the indications of intensity were high (i.e., water reaching chest level) and therefore uncertainty was reduced, people were more likely to evacuate.

Inhabitants realized that they were in for a different kind of typhoon when household items on the floor or ground started to float. Kris, an upper-class homeowner married to a high-ranking local government employee, started to worry when she saw their Montero, a luxury pickup vehicle, floating in their garage. The household then convened by the landing near the second floor, which would directly lead them to the third floor in case the water got any higher. Around eleven neighbors from adjacent houses (all bungalows) swam their way to Kris's house for safety. By this time, the water had nearly reached the second floor. The neighbors broke the house's glass windows from the outside so they could enter the house.

At the flood's highest level at the second floor, the group had to choose between staying put amidst the rising water, or moving up to the third floor and dealing with the 300kph gusts of wind. As the third floor was partially open, they decided to stay on the second floor as long as possible. The only safe place on the third floor was a toilet, but they wouldn't all be able to fit. They could not afford to expose themselves to the wind (which some described as sounding like a woman wailing), as it had already blown galvanized iron sheets into the floor, and there was falling debris and other potential, unidentifiable hazards. Kris recalled that water continuously rose for about four hours since the typhoon struck during early morning. This is because the storm surge flowed into the town, and then flowed back to the sea. At the end of the interview, Cajilig asked Kris: What was the most important decision you needed to make during the typhoon? *"Kung anong kortina and pwedeng maging rope"* (Which curtain to use as rope), she said, referring to the moment in which household members needed to pull in neighbors out of the flood outside and through their windows.

Kris recalled that when she and her husband moved a couple of decades ago to the government-funded housing that was a benefit accorded to her husband, the couple was very dismayed by the quality of the house. *"Kahit ang isang ten years old na may martilyo, kayang-kayang buwagin ang bahay"* (Even a ten-year-old with a hammer could tear the house down). They decided to tear down the house and build a better quality one from scratch, which is now the three-story house that was used to save their neighbors. None of the other houses in the government-funded subdivision for employees were left standing.

Other stories of survival highlighted the objects in the immediate surroundings that were essential to survival, such as the curtain for Kris and her neighbors, and the plastic basin for Elvie. Karen and Eddie, a couple who lived along the highway, realized that they needed to get themselves to higher ground when they were separated from other family members during the rush of a big wave. They knew that there was a house with three floors down the road that might take them in, but getting there was a problem as the wind and current was very strong and they could not see their way through the fog. Eddie suddenly spotted a piece of black wire from the town's electric company floating nearby and thought that this could lead them to the house:

Maputi lahat, wala kaming makita ng asawa ko, yung taong nasa harapan mo lang. Sinundan lang namin ang electric wire hanggang makarating sa bahay na mataas para hindi maanod. (It was all white, my husband and I couldn't see anything, just the person in front. We just followed the electric wire until we reached the tall house so we wouldn't float away.)

Upon reaching the building, several other neighbors who had sought refuge there pulled them out of the water.

It is interesting to note that prosocial behavior was relatively common in these cases. This draws an interesting parallel with psychological findings. Laboratory studies have found that acute stress increases prosocial behavior (e.g., Von Dawans et al., 2012), and amplifies prosocial tendencies, such that people who have higher rates of helping at baseline tend to help more under stressful conditions, while people who have lower rates of helping at baseline tend to help even less under more stressful conditions (Moussaïd & Trauernicht, 2016). There is also evidence that realistic emergency situations amplify prosocial tendencies, particularly when people share a common social identity (Alnabulsi & Drury, 2014).

Meanwhile, Joy, who co-owns a small driving school with her husband, started to worry about the weather conditions and decided to look outside. The moment she opened the door, the storm surge engulfed the house. Joy recounted the moment their family of eight managed to escape from their house:

Joy: Pag Yolanda, dito kami dumaan [pointing to broken window of jalousie]. *May TV stand dito na hagdan at doon sa roof nila* [pointing to neighbor's house outside window], *doon kami dumaan.* (During Yolanda we passed here [pointing to broken jalousie window]. There was a TV stand here (used as) a ladder and there by their roof [pointing to neighbor's house outside window], that's where we passed).
Cajilig: So 'yung tubig nasaan na? (How high was the water?)
Joy: Tindi talaga. (Very intense.) 15 feet.
Cajilig: Lumulutang na kayo sa tubig diyan? (You were floating over there?)
Joy: Opo . . . Diyan kami dumaan sa bubong . . . Yung anak ko, ginanyan ko [gesture of lifting the child up]. (Yes . . . We passed along the roof . . . I did this to my child [gesture of lifting the child up]).

Survival in this highly stressful environment was often dependent on divergent thinking and cognitive flexibility (Guilford, 1967; Ionescu, 2012) that helped individuals find alternative and life-saving uses for objects. Curtains and electric wire became rope, basins became boats, roof beams become anchors. In the case of Joy, a clerestory window became a door, the roof became a pathway, and the TV stand, a ladder. Such shifts in meaning of these objects through cross-classification of their use categories (Barsalou, 1983, 1991) are drawn not only from individual past lived experiences of these everyday objects, but also from the shared human ability to infer new functions for these objects through their tactile affordances (Hodges, Spatt, & Patterson, 1999). Meanwhile, the ability to apply this new significance requires a dynamic apprehension of these affordances—which already relationally link the object's properties to the physical abilities of the human interacting with it (Gibson, 1979)—with respect to ever-shifting and difficult environmental conditions. Drawing from Ingold, Boholm et al. (2013:106), posit that "it is this reflexivity of the human mind that enables the adaptive planning of action in the face of changing environment and life circumstances," something Tim Ingold (2002) has pertinently denoted as an "ecology of life."

It must be said that the decision to evacuate did not necessarily guarantee survival, and the same things that have the potential to facilitate resilience during disaster can also frustrate attempts to survive. During their field work for humanitarian shelter research, Father Ben, a local Catholic priest who volunteered to be a community guide, brought Cajilig and her team to two buildings in Palo that comprised an elementary school. The buildings were converted by the local government as an evacuation center for women and children. The sturdier building was reportedly better-funded with the help of an international donor, while the building of lesser quality was built with local funding. We later learned from Father Ben and local NGO staff that everyone

Figure 5.2   Life-saving household items. Many of those who experienced the storm surge improvised lifebuoys out of ordinary things, such as these plastic water jugs.

who evacuated to the well-built building had perished in the storm surge. The roofs were so well-built that the evacuees could not puncture through them when the water engulfed the building. Meanwhile, many of those who evacuated to the building of lower quality also did not make it given the enormity of the surge. However, some of them managed to survive, as punching their way through the weaker roofing material increased their chances of finding higher ground. Thus, in a calamity this extreme, one cannot easily assume that one type of building is better than another. Moreover, this account underscores the difficulty of assessing risk effectively in such a dynamic situation, as well as the necessity of analyzing how those affected improvise with their immediate environment under life-threatening circumstances.

CARRYING ON POST-DISASTER

Recognizing the temporality of horizons of choice entails not only understanding past experiences; it also involves turning attention to how individuals and institutions progress over the longer term, given the large and small interrelated decision-making processes that have transpired. Across several loci, comprehending the desolation in the wake of Typhoon Yolanda gave the overwhelming sense that things in the Philippines—humans, but also many other constituents of the environment such as mangrove forests, rice fields, fish, and buildings—are truly vulnerable to the forces of climate change. Consequently, life cannot carry on in a "business as usual" mode. As is supported by Boholm et al. (2013), the adoption of efforts that respond to the experience of Typhoon Yolanda broadens the horizons of choice of actors at the individual and collective levels, as well as incorporates a more diverse range of possibilities for future disasters. For example, middle class homeowners rebuilt their homes using materials and designs that they perceived to be more disaster-resilient than their previous choices. Some homeowners invested in concrete foundations and exterior walls, instead of using plywood. Meanwhile, others switched from gable roofs or flat galvanized iron sheet roofs to hip roofs, concrete slab roofs, and even domed roofs.

Notably, a year after Typhoon Yolanda, another storm, Typhoon Ruby, threatened to unleash a similar level of havoc on Leyte and in surrounding provinces. Having previously experienced the devastating effects of Typhoon Yolanda, many people decided to evacuate. While Typhoon Ruby fortunately veered away from the Philippine Area of Responsibility (PAR) at the last hour, one million people (1% of the Philippine population) decided to evacuate; this effort became one of the largest peacetime evacuations in the world (#RubyPH 2014 December 8). Had the typhoon continued on its original course, more people might have survived compared to Yolanda given that

Figure 5.3   Rebuilding with a new design. After the typhoon, some homeowners built a more disaster-resilient, all-concrete house with a domed roof.

this new and shared understanding of the urgency to evacuate is now part of the horizons of choice of the town's inhabitants.

At the same time, false alarms such as this one may result in people being less likely to evacuate in the future. First, individual and community actions can be predicted by the degree to which an individual *trusts* the source of a weather warning or evacuation order; "the preservation of trust is of critical importance in the context of getting people to comply with weather warnings" (LeClerc, 2014, p. 19). Importantly, psychology research suggests that trust is more easily lost than gained (e.g., Eiser, 2005) and so repeated experience to so-called *false alarms* could prove detrimental to evacuation behaviors because trust in the evacuation source erodes (e.g., Bliss & Fallon, 2006; Bostrom & Lofstedt, 2003). Secondly, action could also be affected by the effect known as the gambler's fallacy. This is the often-mistaken belief that the likelihood of a low probability event occurring again is a decreasing function of its previous occurrence, for example, the belief that after getting heads five times in a row using a coin toss, tails would be more likely to be obtained on the next toss, even though both outcomes are equally likely. Applied to evacuation behavior, the occurrence of a disaster should lead to the development of a mindset that says something like *this already happened, it's not likely to happen again* (Cohen, Etner, & Jeleva, 2008). This mindset would also result in people being less likely to evacuate in the future.[10] While these factors might reduce the likelihood of future evacuations, other factors discussed in this chapter which contributed to people not evacuating (e.g. inadequate warnings over media) could and should be improved.

Immediately after Typhoon Yolanda, the Philippine government submitted a request to The World Bank to provide support for reconstruction efforts. The World Bank sent a technical team "to help the government assess damages and needs for a long-term reconstruction plan" (The World Bank, 2013). The resulting policy note concluded that existing law is insufficient and the current structure for disaster management limits the country's capacity to deal with the impact, scale, and rapidly changing problems in disaster risk reduction and management (De Vera, 2017; The World Bank, n.d.).

Therefore, The World Bank recommended the establishment of a national disaster risk reduction agency with a "stronger mandate to coordinate, plan, finance, implement and monitor all disaster risk reduction and management (DRRM) interventions—prevention and mitigation, preparedness, response, risk reduction and resilience, and rehabilitation and recovery" (De Vera, 2017; The World Bank, n.d). Consequently, President Duterte is urging Congress to approve the creation of a Department of Disaster Resilience, an agency that would be empowered to direct subordinate agencies in endeavors related to disaster risk reduction and management (Lopez, 2018).

Currently, the challenge of reconstruction after Typhoon Yolanda remains, with only 13 percent of housing units occupied and 38 percent built (Gamil, 2017), making recovery more difficult and posing additional considerations for preparedness and response. However, with the environmental education that resulted from the experience of the typhoon, the entire sentient ecology and its horizons of choice will inevitably morph through time. There are certain signs of this transformation. After Typhoon Yolanda, information about how to prepare disaster kits for the home proliferated in Philippine social media—and continue to do so—while "storm surge" is now part of the vocabulary of ordinary citizens. Meanwhile, Metro Manila, which contributes 36 percent to the country's GDP, is particularly vulnerable to earthquakes (Masigan, 2017). Emergency managers, city officials, schools, offices, and homeowner associations across the megalopolis participate in the annual Metro Manila Shake Drill, which includes education about safe evacuation (de Vera et al., 2015). At the time of this writing, Typhoon Ompong (Mangkhut) threatens to wreak Yolanda-level destruction, possibly more, on ten million inhabitants of Philippine northern coasts within 48 hours (International Federation of Red Cross and Red Crescent Societies, 2018). In response, the government is implementing early evacuation protocols which have resulted in massive evacuation, while the Department of Public Works and Highways have started road clearing operations to give way to emergency response teams (Reyes, 2018). Meanwhile, several rice farmers have opted to harvest prematurely rather than undergo the consequences of allowing their crops to drown (UNTV News and Rescue, 2018 September 12). This education of attention (Ingold, 2002) not only transformed inhabitants of Palo, but even those who reside elsewhere in the country. Maintaining this kind of adaptive flexibility, along with state efforts to ensure that disaster recovery does not exacerbate or reproduce systems of inequality, could prevent "punctuated entropy," in which the system collapses further with each disaster, eventually rendering any kind of recovery impossible (Dyer, 2002).[11]

CONCLUSION

This chapter aimed to address the challenges of understanding the decision of non-evacuation in the face of a hurricane by adopting a multifaceted approach that enriches the anthropology of decision making with theories of cognition. In doing so, we have underscored the social, ecological, and psychological processes that constitute the limitations and possibilities of horizons of choice, through which the lived experience of disaster unfolds. Following Ingold (2002), this view perceives people as social beings who are entrenched in relationships of power, as well as sentient beings who inhabit a dynamic environment along with other humans and non-humans. Our view resonates with theories and frameworks of decision making from the field of cognitive studies that view cognition as emergent, interactive, augmentable, relational, multilevel, and temporal (Kristensen, Loesche, & Maranan, 2017). We also hope that this actor-centered lens enables an appreciation of the continually evolving cultural logics that underpin the decisions of non-evacuees, thus dispelling impulses to simply write them off as *matigas ang ulo* ("hard-headed"), or "irrational." We note that by "evolve" we refer simply to the dynamic process by which organisms adapt in response to the ever-changing sentient ecology, and not some inevitable progression toward an ideal state.

As the circumstances through which the data for this chapter were gathered were largely coincidental, we recognize that this analysis is by no means exhaustive. We suggest a more formal inquiry into the topic that would build on the multiple disciplinary collaboration that we have initiated in this discussion, while remaining sensitive to the moral turmoil experienced by those affected by disaster. We also recommend further exploration into the epistemological complexities and possibilities of gathering data on decision making within the ethical and practical challenges of doing research in the context of disaster. In the spirit of Edmund Husserl, we consider this piece as a contribution to cogitatum, in and of itself, one imbued with potentiality for new knowledge about disaster and decision making to further unfold.

NOTES

1. For confidentiality purposes, all interlocutors' names are pseudonyms.

2. Upon returning to the staff quarters, Cajilig requested that Elvie be included in the NGO's psychosocial recovery program.

3. Loosely structured group interviews are naturally occurring informal conversations that occur in a research site. This technique takes into account people's practices of *pag-uusyoso* (to find out what's going on), specifically when a crowd gathers around a researcher and research participants while research-oriented activity is taking place. Typically, members of the crowd, including the originally involved research participants, sporadically interject and step out of the interaction. Research participants may also drift in and out of the discussion to attend to household chores, childcare duties, or livelihood-related activities (Cajilig, 2013:39).

4. The dominant language in Palo is Waray-Waray, but the interviews were conducted in Filipino and Taglish. There was little time for Cajilig and the team to learn the local language given the urgency of delivering humanitarian aid. Filipino and English are the national languages in the Philippines. Filipino, which is based on Tagalog, is commonly used in mainstream media. Meanwhile, Taglish is a language that combines Tagalog and English and is also widely spoken. Interlocutors, including migrants from other provinces, were all fluent in these languages, although the use of Filipino and Taglish prevented Cajilig and her team from engaging those who only speak Waray-Waray.

5. Given their traumatic nature, our process for selecting narratives included ethical considerations. We endeavored to practice thick description (in the sense of Geertz, 1973), while being sensitive to the distress and pain our interlocutors felt in their most vulnerable moments. We thus opted to exclude the most poignant accounts, mostly those which contained very detailed experiences of loved ones perishing in the storm surge, from the objectification inherent in theoretical analysis.

6. Notably, the veracity of climate change continues to be a hotly contested topic, and world leaders such as Donald Trump continue to contest its reality (Gustin, 2018).

7. Or the lifeworld, as Husserl might hold; see Zahavi, 2003.

8. Also, not everyone in the areas affected identify as Roman Catholic.

9. It should be noted that this is contested (Serrano, 2002).

10. There might also be a conflicting interplay here between the gambler's fallacy and the availability heuristic, whereby people make judgments about the frequency of an event based on how easily an example comes to mind. As such and according to the availability heuristic, the occurrence of a disaster should lead to the development of a different mindset that says something like *this happened, this could happen again*. As such, distinct actions are predicted by the gambler's fallacy versus the availability heuristic (Cohen et al., 2008; Vasiljevic, Weick, Taylor-Gooby, Abrams, & Hopthrow, 2013).

11. Typhoon Ompong registered a casualty count of ninety-five (Rappler, 21 September 2018). There was minimal coverage about the death toll and missing persons for Ompong compared to Typhoon Yolanda, a possible indication that non-evacuation in this case was not a major concern among government authorities. Instead, news

coverage on the aftermath of Ompong focused on massive agricultural loss (ex. Dullana, 19 September 2018), with farmers likening the struggle to make optimal decisions regarding their crops to "gambling with nature" (Dullana, 18 September 2018).

REFERENCES

15,000 Die in Philippine Storm. (1912, November 30). *Washington Herald.* https://do i.org/10.1017/CBO9780511783531.

Agar, M. (1996). *The Professional Stranger.* London: Academic Press.

Alnabulsi, H., & Drury, J. (2014). Social identification moderates the effect of crowd density on safety at the Hajj. *Proceedings of the National Academy of Sciences,* 111(25), 9091–9096.

Anderson, D. (2000). *Identity and Ecology in Arctic Siberia: The Number One Reindeer Brigade.* New York: Oxford University Press.

Anderson, J. R. (1995). *Cognitive Psychology and Its Implications* (4th ed.). New York: W.H. Freeman.

Asian Disaster Reduction Center (ADRC). (n.d.). Retrieved September 1, 2018, from http://www.adrc.asia/nationinformation.php?NationCode=608.

Avila, Bobit S. (2014, August 23). How many casualties from typhoon 'Yolanda?' Retrieved September 2, 2018, from https://www.philstar.com/opinion/2014/08 /23/1360818/how-many-casualties-typhoon-yolanda.

Bankoff, G. (2003). *Cultures of Disaster: Society and Natural Hazards in the Philippines.* London; New York: Routledge Curzon.

Barsalou, L. W. (1983). Ad hoc categories. *Memory & Cognition, 11*(3), 211–227.

Barsalou, L. W. (1991). Deriving categories to achieve goals. In G. H. Bower (Ed.), *The Psychology of Learning and Motivation: Advances in Research and Theory.* New York: Academic Press, Vol. 27, 1–64.

Bartlett, F. C. (1932). *Remembering: A Study in Experimental and Social Psychology.* Cambridge University Press.

Bateson, G. (1973). *Steps to an Ecology of Mind: Collected Essays in Anthropology, Psychiatry, Evolution and Epistemology.* St. Albans: Paladin.

Berger, C. R., & Calabrese, R. J. (1974). Some explorations in initial interaction and beyond: Toward a developmental theory of interpersonal communication. *Human Communication Research,* 1(2), 99–112.

Bliss, J. P., and C. K. Fallon, 2006: Active warnings: False alarms. In M. S. Wogalter (Ed.), *Handbook of Warnings.* Lawrence Erlbaum Associates, 231–242.

Böholm, Å., Henning, A., & Krzyworzeka, A. (2013). Anthropology and decision making: An introduction. *Focaal,* 2013(65). https://doi.org/10.3167/fcl.2013.650109.

Bostrom, A., and R. E. Lofstedt, 2003: Communicating risk: Wireless and hardwired. *Risk Analysis,* 23, 241–248.

Cajilig, P. (2013). Practices of identification in the creation and consumption of novelty T-shirts (MA thesis).

Cajilig, P., Salva, O., & Maranan, P. (2015). If the house fits: The political ergonomics of design thinking for post-Yolanda shelter development. *Aghamtao: Journal of the Uganayang Pang-Aghamtao/Anthropological Association of the Philippines*, 24, 61–85.

Clifford, J. (1983). On Ethnographic Authority. *Representations* (2), 118–146. https://doi.org/10.2307/292838.

Cohen, M., Etner, J., & Jeleva, M. (2008). Dynamic decision making when risk perception depends on past experience. *Theory and Decision*, 64(2–3), 173–192.

Croll, E., & Parkin, D. (Eds.) (1992). *Bush Base: Forest Farm. Culture, Environment and Development*. London: Routledge.

Dalisay, S. N., & De Guzman, M. T. (2016). Risk and culture: The case of typhoon Haiyan in the Philippines. *Disaster Prevention and Management: An International Journal*, 25(5), 701–714. https://doi.org/10.1108/DPM-05-2016-0097.

Dash, N. (2002). Decision-making under extreme uncertainty: Rethinking hazard related perceptions and action. Ph.D. dissertation, Florida International Univ., North Miami, Fla.

Dash, N., & Gladwin, H. (2007). Evacuation decision making and behavioral responses: Individual and household. *Natural Hazards Review*, 8(3), 69–77 https://doi.org/10.1061/(ASCE)1527-6988(2007)8:3(69).

De Berker, A. O., Rutledge, R. B., Mathys, C., Marshall, L., Cross, G. F., Dolan, R. J., & Bestmann, S. (2016). Computations of uncertainty mediate acute stress responses in humans. *Nature Communications*, 7, 10996. doi: 10.1038/ncomms10996.

De Vera, B. O. (2017, October 16). World Bank cites 'Yolanda' rehab woes. Retrieved September 5, 2018, from http://newsinfo.inquirer.net/938181/world-bank-cites-yolanda-rehab-woes.

De Vera, B. O., Aurelio, J. M., & Brizuela, M. B. (2015, July 31). 1st-ever Metro shake drill 'dream fulfilled' [News site]. Retrieved September 13, 2018, from https://newsinfo.inquirer.net/709312/1st-ever-metro-shake-drill-dream-fulfilled.

Denham, S. L., & Punt, M. (2017). Abstract of 'Cognitive Innovation: A View from the Bridge.'" *Leonardo*, 50(2), 184–185. https://doi.org/10.1162/LEON_a_01386.

Dreyfus, H. L., & Dreyfus, S. E. (1986). *Mind Over Machine: The Power of Human Intuition and Expertise in the Age of the Computer*. Oxford: Basil Blackwell.

Driskell, J. E., & Salas, E. (1991). Group decision making under stress. *Journal of Applied Psychology*, 76(3), 473.

Drost, R., Casteel, M., Libarkin, J., Thomas, S., & Meister, M. (2016). Severe weather warning communication: Factors impacting audience attention and retention of information during tornado warnings. *Weather, Climate, and Society*, 8(4), 361–372.

Dullana, R. (2018, September 18). Cagayan farmers on Ompong-hit crops: 'Like losing gamble vs nature' [News and opinion]. Retrieved February 25, 2019, from http://www.rappler.com//nation/212261-cagayan-farmers-typhoon-ompong-crops-losing-gamble-vs-nature.

Dullana, R. (2018, September 19). Typhoon Ompong leaves nearly 76,000 homes damaged in Cagayan [News and opinion]. Retrieved February 25, 2019, from https://www.rappler.com/nation/212324-typhoon-ompong-damage-infrastructure-agriculture-cagayan-september-19-2018.

Eiser, J. R., & White, M. P. (2005). A psychological approach to understanding how trust is built and lost in the context of risk. Paper presented at of Social Context and Responses to Risk Conference on Trust, London School of Economics, 12th December 2005.

Esteban, Miguel, Valenzuela, V. P., Yun, N. Y., Mikami, T., Shibayama, T., Matsumaru, R. . . . Nakamura, R. (2015). Typhoon Haiyan 2013 Evacuation Preparations and Awareness. *International Journal of Sustainable Future for Human Security*, 3(1), 37–45. https://doi.org/10.24910/jsustain/3.1/3745.

Fothergill, A. (1996). "Gender, risk and disaster." *International Journal of Mass Emergencies and Disasters*, 14(1), 33–56.

Gamil, J. T. (2017, November 7). Only 13% of 'Yolanda' housing occupied, 38% built. Retrieved from https://newsinfo.inquirer.net/943740/philippine-news-updates-yolanda-yolanda-housing.

Garcia-Acosta, V. (2002). Missing expertise, historical disaster research. In A. Oliver-Smith & S. Hoffman (Eds.), *Catastrophe & Culture: The Anthropology of Disaster*. Houston: School of American Research Press. School of American Research Advanced Seminar Series, 237–260.

Gatt, C., & Ingold, T. (2013). From description to correspondence: Anthropology in real time. In W. Gunn, T. Otto., & R. C. Smith (Eds.), *Design Anthropology: Theory and Practice* (pp. 139–158). New Delhi, India: Bloomsbury Academia.

Geertz, C. (1973). *The Interpretation of Cultures: Selected Essays*. New York: Basic Books, Inc.

Geniusas, S. (2012). *The Origins of the Horizon in Husserl's Phenomenology*. Dordrecht; New York: Springer.

Gladwin, H., & Peacock, W. G. (1997). Warning and evacuation: A night for hard houses. In B. H. Morrow & H. Gladwin (Eds.), *Hurricane Andrew: Gender, Ethnicity and the Sociology of Disasters*. New York: Routledge, 52–74.

Gladwin, Hugh, and Michael Murtaugh. 1980. The attentive-preattentive distinction in agricultural decision making. In Peggy F. Barlett (Ed.), *Agricultural Decision Making: Anthropological Contribution to Rural Development*. New York: Academia Press, 115–136.

Gustin, G. (2018, February 5). Troubled by Trump's climate denial, scientists aim to set the record straight | InsideClimate News. Retrieved September 10, 2018, from https://insideclimatenews.org/news/04022018/climate-science-trump-denial-meteorological-society-expertise-ipcc-simplify-communication.

Henning, Annette. (2009). Decisions with impact on energy reduction opportunities: Swedish manufacturers and buyers of new single-family houses. Unpublished paper presented at the AAA 108th Annual Meeting, Philadelphia, USA, 2–6 December.

Ho, M. C., Shaw, D., Lin, S., & Chiu, Y. C. (2008). How do disaster characteristics influence risk perception? *Risk Analysis: An International Journal*, 28(3), 635–643.

Hobart, M. (1993). Introduction: The growth of ignorance? In M. Hobart (Ed.) *An Anthropological Critique of Development: The Growth of Ignorance*. London: Routledge, 1–32.

Hodges, J. R., Spatt, J., & Patterson, K. (1999). "What" and "how": Evidence for the dissociation of object knowledge and mechanical problem-solving skills in the human brain. *Proceedings of the National Academy of Sciences of the United States of America*, 96(16), 9444–9448.

Hoffman, Susanna M. & Oliver-Smith, A. (Eds.). (2002). *Catastrophe and Culture: The Anthropology of Disaster*. Santa Fe, NM: School of American Research Press.

Howard, A., & Ortiz, S. (1971). Decision making and the study of social process. *Acta Sociologica*, 14(4), 213–226. https://doi.org/10.1177/000169937101400401.

Ingold, T. (2002). *The Perception of the Environment: Essays on Livelihood, Dwelling and Skill* (1st ed.). USA and Canada: Routledge. https://doi.org/10.4324/9780203466025.

Ingold, T. (2010). Bringing Things to Life: Creative Entanglements in a World of Material. National Center for Research Methods Working Paper. Morgan Center, University of Manchester, Manchester, UK.

International Federation of Red Cross and Red Crescent Societies. (2018, September 12). Philippines: 10 million people lie in path of "destructive" Typhoon Mangkhut. Retrieved September 13, 2018, from https://media.ifrc.org/ifrc/press-release/phi lippines-10-million-people-lie-path-destructive-typhoon-mangkhut/.

Ionescu, T. (2012). Exploring the nature of cognitive flexibility. *New Ideas in Psychology*, 30(2), 190–200. https://doi.org/10.1016/j.newideapsych.2011.11.001.

Janoff-Bulman, R. (1992). *Shattered Assumptions: Towards a New Psychology of Trauma*. New York, NY: The Free Press.

Jibiki, Y., Kure, S., Kuri, M., & Ono, Y. (2016). Analysis of early warning systems: The case of super-typhoon Haiyan. *International Journal of Disaster Risk Reduction*, 15, 24–28.

Koestenbaum, P. (1998). Introductory essay. In Edmund Husserl (Ed.), *The Paris Lectures* (P. Koestenbaum, Trans., pp. IX–LXXVII). Dordrecht, Boston, and London: Kluwer Academic Publishers.

Kristensen, M. S., Loesche, F., & Maranan, D. S. (2017). Navigating cognitive innovation. *Avant*, 8 (Special Issue (Off the Lip: Collaborative Approaches in Cognitive Innovation)), 45–55. https://doi.org/10.26913/80s02017.0111.0005.

Krzyworzeka, A. (2013). Decision-making in farming households in eastern Poland. *Focaal*, 2013(65). https://doi.org/10.3167/fcl.2013.650111.

Kuhn, Helmut. (1940). The phenomenological concept of "horizon". In Marvin Farber (Ed.), *Philosophical Essays in Memory of Edmund Husserl* (pp. 106–123). Cambridge, MA: Harvard University Press.

Langley, Anne, Mintzberg, Harold, Pitcher, Patricia, Posada, Elizabeth, & Saint-Macary, Jan. (1995). Opening up decision making: The view from the black stool. *Organization Science* 6(3): 260–279.

LeClerc, J. (2014). Communicating weather and climate uncertainty: Exploratory research in cognitive psychology (Doctoral dissertation).

Lejano, R., Tan, J. M., & Wilson, M. (2015, February 5). Learning from Typhoon Haiyan. *Nature* [Academic Journal]. Retrieved August 30, 2018, from https://www.nature.com/articles/518035d.

Lopez, V. (2018, July 31). Palace submits admin version of bill creating Department of Disaster Resilience. Retrieved September 1, 2018, from http://www.gmanetwor k.com/news/news/nation/662453/palace-submits-admin-version-of-bill-creating -department-of-disaster-resilience/story/.

Maranan, D. S. (2017). Haplós: Towards technologies for and applications of Somaesthetics (Ph.D. Thesis). Plymouth University, UK. Retrieved from http://hdl.handle.net/10026.1/10170.

Masigan, A. J. (2017, February 12). The story behind PH's 6.8 GDP growth. Retrieved September 13, 2018, from https://business.mb.com.ph/2017/02/12/the-story-behind-phs-6-8-gdp-growth.

Mileti, D. S., and Sorensen, J. H. (1987). Hazards and precautionary behavior. In D. Weinstein (Ed.), *Taking Care: Understanding and Encouraging Self-Protective Behavior*Cambridge: Cambridge University Press, , 189–207.

Moussaïd, M., & Trauernicht, M. (2016). Patterns of cooperation during collective emergencies in the help-or-escape social dilemma. Scientific reports, 6, 33417. DOI: 10.1038/srep33417.

Muna, A. (2013, November 7). Netizens urge prayers amid Yolanda's wrath | ABS-CBN News. *ABS-CBN News*. Retrieved from https://news.abs-cbn.com/nation/metro-manila/11/07/13/netizens-urge-prayers-amid-yolandas-wrath.

Neisser, U. (1967). *Cognitive psychology*. East Norwalk, CT, US: Appleton-Century-Crofts.

Ocampo, A. R. (2013, November 19). Tacloban, not once but thrice | Inquirer Opinion [News site]. Retrieved September 1, 2018, from http://opinion.inquirer.net/65685/tacloban-not-once-but-thrice.

Ortner, S. B. (2006). Subjectivity and cultural critique. *Vibrant—Virtual Brazilian Anthropology*, *v3*(n1), 30.

Palerm, A. (1980). *Antropología y Marxismo*. Mexico, DF: Centro de Investigaciones Superiores del Instituto Nacional Antropología e Historia/Editorial Nueva Imagen.

PDRF | Philippine Disaster Resilience Foundation. (2018). Retrieved September 1, 2018, from https://www.pdrf.org/.

Peters, B. G. (2017). What is so wicked about wicked problems? A conceptual analysis and a research program. *Policy and Society*, 36(3), 385–396. https://doi.org/10.1080/14494035.2017.1361633

Piaget, J. (1936). *Origins of Intelligence in the Child*. London: Routledge & Kegan Paul.

Rajan, S. (2002). Missing expertise, categorical politics, and chronic disasters: The case of Bhopal. In A. Oliver- Smith & S. Hoffman (Eds.), *Catastrophe & Culture: The Anthropology of Disaster*. Houston: School of American Research Press. School of American Research Advanced Seminar Series, 237–260.

Ranada, P. (2017 March 01). Duterte signs Paris climate deal. *Rappler*. Retrieved on March 22, 2017.

Rappler.com. (2014, December 8). #RubyPH: One of "largest peacetime evacuations" in PH history [News site]. Retrieved September 1, 2018, from http://www.rappler.com//move-ph/issues/disasters/typhoon-ruby/77421-ruby-large-peacetime-evacuation-philippines.

Rappler.com. (2018, September 21). At least 95 dead due to Typhoon Ompong [News and opinion]. Retrieved February 25, 2019, from http://www.rappler.com//nation/212481-typhoon-ompong-death-toll-september-21-2018

Reyes, Dempsey. (2018). 'Ompong' Triggers Massive Evacuation. *The Manila Times*, September 13, 2018. https://www.manilatimes.net/ompong-triggers-massive-evacuation/440778/

Rittel, H. W. J., & Webber, M. M. (1973). Dilemmas in the general theory of planning. *Policy Sciences*, 4, 155–169.10.1007/BF01405730.

Rotter, J. B. (1954). *Social Learning and Clinical Psychology*. New York: Prentice-Hall.

Santos, R. J. (2013, November 10). Yolanda and the world's strongest storms. Retrieved September 6, 2018, from http://www.rappler.com//science-nature/4 3351-world-strongest-cyclones-history.

Serrano, Ben. (2006, April 2). Butuan to pursue claim it was site of First Mass in RP 485 years ago. Retrieved September 6, 2018, from https://www.philstar.com/headlines/ 2006/04/02/329389/butuan-pursue-claim-it-was-site-first-mass-rp-485-years-ago.

Sjölander-Lindqvist, A., & Cinque, S. (n.d.). When wolves harm private property: Focaal. *Focal Journal of Global and Historical Anthropology*, 114–128.

Støre Brinchmann, B., Førde, R., & Nortvedt, P. (2002). What matters to the parents? A qualitative study of parents' experiences with life-and-death decisions concerning their premature infants. *Nursing Ethics*, 9(4), 388–404. https://doi.org/10.1 191/0969733002ne523oa.

The World Bank. (2013, November 15). Reconstruction after Typhoon Haiyan. Retrieved September 5, 2018, from http://www.worldbank.org/en/country/phil ippines/brief/philippines_reconstruction_after_typhoon_haiyan_yolanda

Toft, B., & Reynolds, S. (2016). *Learning from Disasters*. Leicester, UK: Perpetuity Press Limited.

Tupaz, V. (2014, December 6). Ruby evacuation: Thousands flock to churches. Retrieved September 5, 2018, from http://www.rappler.com//move-ph/issues/d isasters/typhoon-ruby/77153-ruby-evacuation-churches.

Typhoon and Tidal Wave in the Philippines. (1898, January 12). *Barrier Miner*, p. 3.

UNTV News and Rescue. (2018, September 12). Rice farmers opt for early harvest ahead of "Ompong"—UNTV News. *UNTV News*. Retrieved from https://www.unt vweb.com/news/rice-farmers-opt-for-early-harvest-ahead-of-ompong/

Vasiljevic, M., Weick, M., Taylor-Gooby, P., Abrams, D., & Hopthrow, T. (2013). Reasoning about extreme events: A review of behavioural biases in relation to catastrophe risks. Other. *Lighthill Risk Network*. Retrieved from https://kar.kent. ac.uk/id/eprint/33993.

Von Dawans, B., Fischbacher, U., Kirschbaum, C., Fehr, E., & Heinrichs, M. (2012). The social dimension of stress reactivity: Acute stress increases prosocial behavior in humans. Psychological science, 23(6), 651–660. doi: 10.1177/0956797611431576.

Walch, C. (2018). Typhoon Haiyan: Pushing the limits of resilience? The effect of land inequality on resilience and disaster risk reduction policies in the Philippines. *Critical Asian Studies*, 50(1), 122–135. https://doi.org/10.1080/14672715.2017.14 01936

Walker, P., & Lovat, T. (2017). *Life and Death Decisions in the Clinical Setting*. Singapore: Springer Singapore. https://doi.org/10.1007/978-981-10-4301-7.

White, G. (1994). Paths to risk analysis. In S. Cutter (Ed.), *Environmental Risks and Hazards*. Prentice-Hall, Upper Saddle River, NJ, 69–74.

Yonge, G. D. (1966). Structure of experience and functional fixedness. *Journal of Educational Psychology*, 57(2), 115–120. https://doi.org/10.1037/h0022967.

Zahavi, D. (2003). *Husserl's Phenomenology*. Stanford, CA: Stanford University Press.

Chapter 6

Surviving the Old Tides

Disaster Resilience Among Food-Insecure Older Adults in an Urban Poor Settlement in Manila

Maria Carinnes P. Alejandria

BASECO COMPOUND AS A POCKET OF URBAN MARGINALIZATION

Traversing Roxas Boulevard near the old streets of Intramuros, one can see the infrastructure development of Manila city, from its paved roads to manicured lawns and skyscrapers. The city's development byline of "Manila always onwards, never backwards" echoes in these markers of economic progress. However, as one looks closely into the seams of the city's landscape, one is confronted with the tucked undersides of development that have become pockets of marginalization. Situated behind the golf courses of Intramuros, the BASECO Compound is a striking example of these pockets that have been painstakingly hidden from the tourist's gaze in an attempt to perpetuate an "onwards" Manila theme.

BASECO Compound, or Barangay 649, is a 52-hectare area of land with an estimated population of around 61,000[1]. Due to the compound's unique geographic position, it is often referred to as an estuarial community, being bound by two of the country's largest bodies of water: Pasig River and Manila Bay. The area is continually diminishing as the estuary claims the land that primarily consists of concrete debris, sand, broken shells, and garbage. This land composition gave the area a low load-bearing capacity that cannot support massive infrastructures (Steinberg & Lindfield, 2011). Consistent reclamation efforts have allowed for the initial 25–30 hectares of land known as the Engineer's Island to be expanded with the addition of *isla*

119

laki, isla liit (big island and small island), and the breakwaters to about 52 hectares (See figure 6.1).

Over a timespan of fifteen years, the watery area that separates the Engineer's Island, Isla Liit, and Isla Laki has been reclaimed by the settlers of BASECO by covering it with sand hauled from the shore, garbage, and other debris (see figure 6.2). Locals continue to fill the low-lying areas of

Figure 6.1   Satellite map of BASECO (2001). *Source:* Google Maps.

Figure 6.2   Satellite map of BASECO (2016). *Source:* Google Maps.

the compound with whatever debris is available. For the past four years, the depressed pathways in the inner blocks have been filled with sandbags and garlic peelings, the latter being a byproduct of what is currently the most common form of livelihood in the area. There are still parts of the inner compound that become easily submerged in floodwater and can often remain in such a state for weeks. One has to tread lightly on these watery areas as the depth of some parts could be up to an adult's waist. Locals have created makeshift pathways to minimize the exposure of the passersby to the murky and contaminated waters.

The earliest recorded settlers in the area migrated there in the early 1960s. This first wave of migrants consisted of the workers of the then National Shipyard and Steel Corporation (NASSCO), which was later renamed to Bataan Shipping and Engineering Company (BASECO) after the Romualdez's took ownership in 1964 (Murphy, 2012). These workers were later joined by their families, increasing the population in the area by over 100 percent in a period of only two years. It could be said that the BASECO Compound is a migrant barangay, as the majority of the residents moved from other parts of the country to participate in the economic development that was rapidly occurring in Metro Manila.

Although the shipyard went bankrupt in the 1990s, a constant influx of migrants to the BASECO Compound has been documented (Mercado, 2016). The compound's proximity to economic hubs such as Divisoria and Quiapo has made it a primary option for urban migrants who cannot afford the high rental cost of residences in the area. Of the thirty older adults who participated in this study, twenty-two claimed to have migrated to the area for economic reasons. Eight of them reported that they were recent migrants to the compound, having been requested by their relatives to join them in Manila to either provide childcare or be taken care of. Demographically, BASECO has a growing older adult population that is typically ascribed the primary caregiver role to their grandchildren due to a phenomenon of a missing second generation. This phenomenon, which was also observed in countries in Africa that have been heavily affected by the AIDS crisis (Guest, 2003; Kihiu, 2007; Riley & Lupafya, 2011), has created a the diminishing population of second-generation individuals who either left the compound for economic opportunities in other localities or left for social reasons which may include remarriage and threats to security due to current government policies. As a result, older adults of the BASECO Compound have been redefining the Philippine concept of an economically passive older adult, as most are still actively engaged in livelihood activities to support their households.

The concepts of resilience and vulnerability to disasters and hazards are often framed within the context of "static phenomena" that is rooted in communities with established systems of support and infrastructure. This framing poses limitations on the understanding of communities and settlements in which systems for averting risks and mitigating disasters are lacking. These populations have an informal basis of land tenure and a high vulnerability to food insecurity.

This chapter considers the experiences of disaster among older adults and their household in an urban poor settlement in Manila. More specifically, this work explores the processes that older adults take to negotiate with their community and government to secure food for their family during times of flooding. Ethnographic data indicates that reliance on the household economy and social capital were higher in 2014–2016 than the acceptance of government-based interventions (which are often locally perceived as inadequate or inefficient). Another point of note is that typical food security strategies such as food sharing and food loan were practiced less frequently during periods of flooding because these practices were replaced by the consumption of alternative foods, such as seafood washed ashore, drowned animals, and food donated by NGOs. From the narratives of selected older adults who experienced dislocation and relocation due to flooding brought by storm surges or mere tidal shifts, I argue that their vulnerability to both flooding and food insecurity are systemic forms of state violence that are predicated by urban planning based on tropes of gentrification and political patronage that disenfranchise the undocumented residents.

VULNERABILITY TO HAZARDS

Being bound by two of the country's largest bodies of water, the BASECO Compound is at high risk of being affected by natural hazards like typhoons, storm surges, and tidal shifts. Weather variabilities are always expected by residents to have an impact on their daily lives, especially the most vulnerable blocks. One key cultural indicator of the locals' acceptance of their risky environment is the prevalence of flood-related possessions such as knee-high plastic boots, clothes stored in plastic bags, and evacuation cards carefully sealed in plastic containers. The deepest flood water that I witnessed while working in the area was thigh-deep. It was troubling to walk into for two main reasons: the uncertain depth of water in some parts, and the multiple contaminants present in the water given the lack of sewage system in the area. Most of the locals affected by the floods seemed tolerant of their environment. One could even see children recreationally swimming in flood water (Ancheta & Gonzalez, 2015). Economically, flooding affects the residents' access to food sources like seafood from the estuary and the sari-sari store. It also disrupts food-sharing arrangements among extended families as food sources diminish and walkways are difficult to traverse due to murky flood water and muddy ground. Food deliveries can also be delayed due to impassable inner roads. This gap in supply increases product prices significantly. Hence, flooding is typically equated to worsening food insecurity for most households.

Despite the efforts of the barangay to implement evacuation measures, some residents refuse to evacuate during times of flooding. The narratives that Reyes (2016) collected on the perception of older adults of their vulnerability during periods of disaster in BASECO have shown that the task of ensuring the safety of the household's belongings is often relegated to the older adults. This prevents them from evacuating during such periods and consequently places them at high risk. The primary reason for selecting the older adult to perform such a role is their physical inability to proceed to the evacuation center which is about three kilometers away from their blocks. These individuals would often refuse to be evacuated by local government officials due to a perceived threat of theft of their belongings. The seemingly unperturbed response of the older adults concerning the potential environmental threats to their physical safety and health has been observed in other societies (Ban et al., 2017; Hori & Shaw, 2012; Yu, Cruz, & Hokugo, 2017). Cherniack (2008, p.1) highlighted this in his review of medical literature on the impact of natural disasters among older adults stating, "individuals may be more resilient to some of the psychological manifestations of disasters with more frequent exposure, often including the elderly." The normalization of flooding in the BASECO Compound led to a lack of concern among most of its residents. They appear to be desensitized to the posed risks. I observed how locals have been living a seemingly double life: one life during dry periods and a different life during flooding periods. From the clothing they keep, to the food that they eat, to the means by which they gather their food; the residents' lived experiences shift with the tides of the estuary.

Despite the associated risks of living in the compound, the population in the area continues to increase. From the unpublished estimates recorded by the barangay, the population of the BASECO Compound has ballooned from 45,017 residents in 2001 to 50,918 in 2010. With an annual growth rate computed at 10.77 percent, the population is expected to rise to about 70,000 by 2018. One of the key drivers of the population increase in the BASECO Compound is internal migration for economic reasons. Mercado (2016) argues in his work in the area that the locals have a high perception of risk and vulnerability to natural hazards, but they remain living in this high-hazard zone due to socioeconomic constraints that prohibit them from relocating to a safer environment. However, he adds that BASECO residents' concerns were confined to just themselves, their family, and their community, and the past disasters that they have experienced. They do not have particular concerns regarding hazards that have not yet transpired, such as earthquake, liquefaction, or tsunami (Mercado, 2016, p. 500).

Although literatures have correlated economic status with resiliency during disasters (Drabek, 2007; Frialde, 2014; Prashar & Shaw, 2012), the resiliency exhibited by the residents of the compound during the aftermath of disasters goes beyond their socioeconomic stability. In previous research I conducted in the area (Ancheta et al., 2015; Alejandria-Gonzalez, 2018), the resiliency of the locals is determined by the sociocultural capital that they have. This includes a strongly exhibited subscription to local concepts of *pakikisama* (friendly interpersonal relationship; Saito, 2010, p.1) and *pagdamay* (share the fate; Agpalo, 1999, p.51), such that a household's survival during difficult periods is determined by the extent of its connection with other households or social organizations. The narratives collected by Diamante (2015) and Reyes (2016) highlighted that sharing resources during periods of flooding is a common community-based response among the locals as much as default dependence on social organizations for relief packages. The most vulnerable households in this case are those who have fewer relatives and those who are not affiliated to any organization, be it religious or social. Older adults who live independently and have no membership to any organization are at higher risk of food insecurity and displacement during periods of flooding. They also possess the lowest capacity to recover after such events due to their lack of support system.

KALAM AND *DISKARTE* DURING FLOODING

In earlier work, I explored experiences of food insecurity among selected older adults in the compound. These studies have yielded multilayered contexts around experiences of food insecurity, locally referred to as *kalam*[2]. The means by which an individual addresses *kalam* is usually referred to as *diskarte*. Locals believe that as long as a person has a form of diskarte, such as scavenging or taking a loan, the extent of his/her experience of *kalam* will be significantly lowered. In this work, diskarte is also viewed as a form of resilience. These three concepts (*kalam, diskarte,* and resilience) are interrelated, as the extent to which one is experienced by an older adult is dependent on the diminished value of the other. More specifically, a finding of this research project was that the greater a person's capacity to apply or access a *diskarte*, the lesser his/her experience of *kalam* is. This also implies that a person who has much more access to *diskarte* is more resilient during periods of resource scarcity like in times of flooding. The concept of *diskarte* as a form of resilience has also been noted by other scholars who have explored the intersection of a resource-limited environment and localized coping strategies (Paz, 2008); (Ushijima & Zayas, 1994); (Paguntalan, 2002).

Resilience is a vital aspect of the lived experiences of food insecurity for the older adults in the BASECO Compound. Coates, Swindale, and Bilinsky

(2007, p.7) identified this variable as a key element in understanding the extent of food insecurity of a particular group: "Resource augmentation coping strategies are important to consider, however, in gaining a more detailed picture of the experience of food insecurity (access) in any particular context." Its value in this work is equal to undertaking the extent of their vulnerability to food insecurity given their local contexts and geography. To venture into the discussion of my informants' practices of resilience is to reframe their position as active agents in their social field (Bourdieu, 1984). Resilience can be multifaceted: from psychological to ecological. In their study of posttraumatic stress, Ozbay et al. (2007) defined psychological resilience as "a process of adapting well in the face of adversity." Foxen (2010), citing Harvey's ecological theory of resilience, discusses the importance of examining the specific communities from which individuals draw their identity and feelings of belonging, and argues that reactions to different forms of stressors"are best understood in light of the values, behaviors, skills and understandings that human communities cultivate in their members"(Harvey, 1996, p.4).

In an earlier work (Alejandria-Gonzalez, 2018), informants identified seven key food-coping strategies as their constant forms of *diskarte* during periods of food insecurity. These include food loan, alternative work, food sharing, consumption of socially stigmatized food, acceptance of dole out, missed and reduced food intake, and silence. However, access to or application of these *diskarte* is affected by various conditions.

This chapter discusses the impact of flooding as a form of disaster on the degree of food insecurity experienced by the older adults with specific regard to their access to the available *diskarte* within their community. The differentiation of access to food security strategies during dry and flooding periods contributes to discourses related to 1) aging and perception of risks during disasters, and 2) aging and agency. In the first discourse, this work argues that older adults have high awareness of the risks associated with flooding and the necessary actions that must be taken to avoid these risks, such as evacuation of the entire household to safer areas. However, due to their prescribed and perceived roles as caregivers and, at times, head of the household, they are required to cope with the threat of flooding using different strategies. This is where this work provides its contribution to the discourse of aging and agency.

The following section demonstrates how food-coping strategies that are common during dry periods change during periods of flooding, and the associated contexts for these shifts.

Food loan

During "dry" periods, the most commonly practiced form of coping strategy among the informants is taking food loans from sari-sari stores. All of the thirty older adults interviewed reported that they have practiced taking food loans from sari-sari stores and karinderia (small eateries). The food item that is commonly loaned is rice. Sari-sari stores and karinderia would allow loans for patrons of their businesses. A person who is unknown to the owner of the store would not have the option of taking a loan as these forms of transactions are informal with loans being listed down on a piece of paper that is kept by the owner; proof of any kind is not necessary to take out a food loan. This procedure has been adopted from a predominant community-based market process in the country called the *suki* system (Caliguing & Sa-Ao, 2008). In this process, store owners provide preferential treatment to selected customers who are exclusively purchasing merchandise from them. This process creates a form of socioeconomic bond between the retailer and the buyer that allows for a margin of trust and accountability. This resounds the Carrier's (2018) definition of moral economy as "[activities] in the mutual obligations that arise when people transact with each other over the course of time" such that the retailer is expected to provide the *suki* customer with cheaper-priced quality items, while the customer is expected to exclusively purchase from the retailer. In cases when a *suki* customer is unable to pay for the merchandise that he/she was buying, the retailer could be expected to provide the customer with payment options such as protracted payment.

In the BASECO Compound, sari-sari stores have a maximum credit line that they implement on their transactions with their *suki*. An *utang* (loan) is expected to be paid as soon as the *suki* gets *delhensya* (money acquired through available strategies). In cases when the *suki* was known to have acquired *delhensya* and yet failed to pay her/his *utang*, this *suki* loses the trust of the retailer which may lead to the future inaccessibility of this mechanism. For most of the stores that were interviewed in the inner blocks, the allowable *utang* of their *suki* ranges from 100 to 300 pesos. Exceptions are given to *suki* who are known for having a stable source of income. This is similar to the observations of Malapit (2012, p.1) on the informal loan system in two of Manila's urban poor communities where she argued that "informal lenders seem to rely more on reputation and credit history to screen prospective borrowers." The highest credit line given to one of the informants is 3,000 pesos due to the employed status of the informant's daughter who pays the store every two weeks. Such practices are also common among most of the karinderia that were interviewed. When asked if they extended credit lines for older adults in the community, the response was usually negative. This is due to the financial instability of the older adults who are not sure when a *delhensya* would be available for them.

Brisson (2012) has identified the value of informal loans taken from community members in addressing food insecurity among low-income mothers in the cities of Boston, Chicago, and San Antonio in the United States. This is supported by the claim of Fitzpatrick & Coleman-Jensen (2014, p.1) that "improved credit access could reduce food insecurity and improve well-being" among food-insecure households. In the BASECO Compound, informal loans such as food loans taken from sari-sari stores or karinderia have served as a lifeline for older adults and their households. As one of the informants narrated on their access to valuable foods, *"bihira lang talaga kami makakain ng baboy o manok, pagmay magpautang dun palang"* (We rarely eat pork or chicken. We only get to eat these when someone gives us a loan). However, this strategy becomes elusive as the household's credit history fails due to an inability to secure a stable source of income.

During periods of flooding, this vital source of food security becomes inaccessible as sari-sari stores and karinderia close due to evacuation of the residents and the relocation of food merchandise to higher grounds in an attempt to save them from floodwater. The few stores that remain open implement a strict no-loan policy especially for affected older adults who have no known financial supporter. As Lita, a store owner, reasoned:

mahirap magpautang sa kanila pagganyang may baha na kasi syempre unahin ko muna yung siguradong kita. Kailangan ko din kasi ng pera pagganyang baha na para may siguradong paghuhugutan.

(It is quite difficult to give them food loan during flooding because I will need to prioritize those who can pay. During flooding, I also need to earn cash so that I have a sure source of money).

Alternative Work

As the main cause of *kalam* among the informants is their low, if not lack, of income, some have addressed their household's food insecurity by participating in available alternative work. Some of the prevailing forms of livelihood in the area that are accessible for older adults are garlic peeling, scavenging, baggage carrying, selling miscellaneous items, and performing personal services like grooming, laundry, and ironing of clothes. At the age of seventy-five, Aling Nona does the laundry of six households in the compound. She earns 250–300 pesos per day. She says that due to this income, she is reliably able to feed her three dependent grandchildren. She asserted that she does not see herself as food-insecure because her family eats well. However, based on international standards of food security, Aling Nona could be considered food-insecure, especially because the food that the family typically consumes is micro-nutrient deficient such as instant noodles, flour-based cracklings, and at times diluted coffee.

The most visible and common form of economic activity participated in by older adults in the area is that of *pagbabawang* (peeling of garlic husks). An older adult can earn up to 70 pesos per sack of garlic which he/she will peel in less than 24 hours. In some households, almost every member of the family participates in the activity, including children as young as five years old. Nanay Gloria has been involved in *pagbabawang* for three years already. She claimed that "*kung wala kami, makakuha kami ng dalawang sako bawang. [Yung kita] Ilang araw na rin namin yan makakain*" (When we have no money for food, we would get two sacks of garlic for peeling. Our income from that can help us buy food for several days). Nanay Nenita is actively involved in two informal occupations, *pagbabawang* and home service nail grooming. She said that she prefers the latter over the former as *pagbabawang* is time-consuming and yields low income compared to performing grooming services which earn her almost the same amount for less time. She would at times exchange her services for food: "*nangutang ako sa mga kakilala ko dyan sa labas, sa mga customer nangutang ako nun ng saging na saba yung banana cue yun na lang ang pinakain ko sa kanila. Tapos nagpa manicure ako*" (I give manicure services to my customers and take a food loan like banana cue which I give to my grandchildren). Another popular livelihood activity is scavenging for *kalakal* (recyclable materials) that are sold to junk shops. An older adult can collect *kalakal* from the dumpsites and earn 40–70 pesos per day.

Alternative work could be viewed as *delhensya* such that it is an informal livelihood occupation which allows the worker to access financial rewards that could be used to augment their household needs. Participation in the informal economy in an urban setting remains a key driver in the employment-related internal migration of rural dwellers. This has also been observed among urban poor settlers in Guatemala who migrated from the rural areas: "Because of the centralization of the economic and political system, Guatemala City still attracts the rural poor, who can find a livelihood in informal economic activities there" (Rosenbaum & Eggleston 2006, p.264). This is a parallel experience cited by some of the older adults interviewed for this work. Tatay Norberto ended up in factory work after migrating from Surigao to Manila. He narrated of his migration, "*Dahil mahirap ang buhay namin sa probinsya nung araw, kaya nakapagbalak ako mag Maynila*" (Life in the province was hard. It was why I thought of moving to Manila). Some of the informants have had work in their provinces prior to moving to Manila. However, due to several factors like climate change, economic shift, and rural development policies, their livelihood sources related to retail, agriculture, and fishing became less sustainable. This is a common narrative among migrants where the loss of the stable sources of income they had in the province has catapulted them to migrate to the city.

During periods of flooding, all of the forms of alternative work enumerated earlier become inaccessible, except for scavenging. It is at this time that scavenging for *kalakal* is at its height and one can see locals who depart the evacuation area a day or two before clearance in order to collect *kalakal* that have washed ashore. Tatay Lino, 72, related how he has consistently defied evacuation rules by leaving the evacuation center earlier to get ahead of other scavengers in collecting *kalakal: "umaalis talaga ako ng mas maaga kesa sa kanila kasi mas marami akong napagpipilian pag nauna ako"* (I really do leave the center earlier than others because I get to have more choices from the washed up debris). Older adults would always be in competition with child scavengers on a regular day. It is only during periods of flooding that older adults experience reduced competition from their much younger counterparts as barangay officials are stricter in allowing children to return to their homes prior to the release of the official clearance from the local disaster mitigation unit. Lola Priscilla, 58 and a *kalakal* scavenger, said that she is happy whenever the estuary overflows and floods the compound because it makes her work easier when debris from the Pasig River and other tributaries wash up along the *Aplaya* shoreline.

Food Sharing

In the compound, the practice of food sharing is based on the notion of *paki-kisama* (the act of empathizing) among households that are part of a social network. These networks could be as small as two households and may be as big as six households joined together either by kinship or shared history. For the household of Nanay Rosie, food sharing is a constant strategy that is practiced with other households inhabited by cousins and a long-time neighbor. Being the eldest female in her household, the role of producing food for Nanay Rosie's household consumption has been assigned to her, while her spouse who works as a company driver inconsistently provides financial support. In this context, Nanay Rosie is tasked not just with food preparation but also with food acquisition for the entire household of thirteen members. Since she contracted tuberculosis two years before the interview, she had not been able to access alternative forms of work due to the general disinclination of employers to hire her out of a fear of contagion. With a low and unstable income, Nanay Rosie has been dependent on sharing food with her network. In one of our conversations, she narrated that, when her two sons are lucky in catching fish from the estuary or the bay, she shares the catch with her network. She estimates that this happens twice per week. On other days, they depend on the food that their network gives them. I asked her if she has ever withheld food from her network. To this she replied that even when the catch that her sons bring home is only sufficient for their consumption, she still takes a portion to give to her network. She fears that if she withholds food from her network, they may do the same during her time of need.

The concept and practice of resource sharing in urban poor communities has been observed to be an exclusive domain of selected members that is amplified by their proximity to one another (Parham, 2012). This creates exclusive sections of food-sharing households that collectively combat food insecurity. The concept of *pakikisama* is stronger among *kapitbahay* (neighbors), especially considering that their houses are overlapping as space is limited. Such spatial arrangement also limits the extent of privacy enjoyed by each home. This is the reason why Nanay Rosie opts to share her limited resources. Her neighbors would without doubt be aware when she got food for her family.

Food sharing is locally referred to as *hingi* (to ask for). When one household does not have food, a member will go to the *kapitbahay*, neighbors, to ask for extra food that they may have. Usually this role is performed by children, women, and the older adults. A food that is commonly given as part of this support mechanism is rice in the form of *bahaw* (left over rice) or *tutong* (burnt rice that is stuck on the pan). It is rare that newly cooked rice is given to *kapitbahay* who are asking for food. This is typically reserved for the immediate household members. Asking for *ulam* (viand) was observed among kin-based support groups. A non-related *kapitbahay* would often access food sharing for basic needs like rice and water. Asking for *ulam* in this context is often deemed abusive or opportunistic by the gifting household.

The concept of sharing and preparation of food has been identified as a key coping strategy among food-insecure households and is chiefly determined by the extent of a household's social network (Cohen & Garrett, 2010). It is the norms of sharing present in the community that can determine the resiliency of food-insecure individuals. Hadley, Belachew, Lindstrom, and Tessema (2009, p.89) argue for this stating that "spaces of vulnerability are patterned by local level gender norms, [and] norms of sharing and reciprocity." However, other studies have shown that this particular strategy loses its practicability among severely food-insecure households as "[they] withdraw from food-sharing obligations when resources become too scarce to support dependents beyond the household" (Wutich & Brewis, 2014). An obligation to prioritize the needs of household members takes precedence over a desire or obligation to be a supportive member of the community. Hence, a lack of food sharing among households of the older adults during periods of disaster is common. With reduced food supplies available and common sources of food inaccessible, households concentrate on the distribution of their food supply to its immediate members. *Pakikisama* is also less invoked during such periods as a means of accessing food sharing networks. I asked Nanay Rosie if her neighbors harbor negative feelings when she rejects sharing with them during flooding. Her reply was, *"ano naman ibibigay ko sa kanila, e wala rin kami. Pasensyahan muna kami"* (What am I supposed to give them when we also have nothing? We will just have to bear with each other).

Consumption of Socially Stigmatized Food

One of the key aspects in gauging the food security of an individual is their "access to culturally acceptable food" (Ramsey, Giskes, Turrell, & Gallegos, 2011). This definition considers the variation in cultural taboos related to food. For example, some societies may consider an individual food-insecure if s/he eats beef while such practice is well tolerated in another society. The underlying principle in this definition is that an individual will not consume socially proscribed food unless s/he is experiencing food insecurity. The concept of acceptability also extends to the process by which foods are gathered such that a food-secure person has "an assured ability to acquire acceptable foods in socially acceptable ways (e.g., without resorting to emergency food supplies, scavenging, stealing)" (Bombay Urban Industrial League for Development, 2010). Food security literature considers this act as a signifier of food insecurity. However, this work presents it as a local marker of food security as food is still considered available and accessible. This addresses the experience of *gutom*. This aspect of the disaster literature is underexplored; most have focused on the general lack of typically acceptable food items (Geier, 2014; Bhopal et al., 2018; Greenough et al., 2002).

This premise sheds a critical light on the prevalent coping strategy in the compound: the collection of socially stigmatized food like *tirtir, retaso, and tahong* (mussels). *Tirtir* or *pagpag* is the most socially stigmatized food in the compound due to the process by which it is collected by the sellers. *Tirtir* is typically consisted of leftover fried chicken of food establishments that are collected by scavengers from the garbage bags lined up for collection along the street. Papay, 60 and a *tirtir* collector, uses this *diskarte* as his primary means of providing for his four grandchildren. He feeds *tirtir* to them and resells it to patrons in the compound. Compared with fresh chicken, *tirtir* is cheap, so it is in demand by income-insecure households who use it as a way to cope with the food demands of its members. The cheapest package, which costs 10 pesos per half-kilo bag, is often added as a *sahog* (ingredient) to a dish of sautéed vegetables. These *retaso* (scavenged vegetables) are purchased for approximately 10 pesos per bag. This nutrient-enriched dish is worth 20 pesos and will provide a family of six to ten people with sizeable portions.

Just like the *tirtir* collectors, *retaso* collectors are highly dependent on the quality and volume of the rejected vegetables that they scavenge in Divisoria. Discarded fruit and vegetables are available for scavenging from the streets as early as four o'clock, the morning preparation time of fruit and vegetable stall holders. Older adults like Aling Mary, 65, would prepare their sacks and shared *kariton* (wooden pushcart) as early as two in the morning to walk the 3.5 kilometer distance from the BASECO Compound to Divisoria to search for food. Aling Mary used to complain about fainting spells and breathing problems that she associated with being an elderly person who was constantly hungry and vulnerable to weather variability. She died on March 2016 of heat stroke. Her neighbors reported seeing her that day, pacing the Aplaya area with her empty sack. I was told that she had not eaten that day and was attempting to collect *tahong* for her and her disabled son.[3]

Papay shared a similar outcome, in that he died of health issues that had been exacerbated by a prolonged period of food insecurity. When he was still alive, Papay would often joke to me about being a "rockstar" in Block 6 because everybody knew him and he had a lot of "fans." He was referring to being the sole retailer of *tirtir* in the block and how people patronized his tirtir packages which usually sold out within an hour of being on sale. He quit scavenging for *tirtir* during the last quarter of 2015 as he had decided to return home to Masbate after having received financial support from his sister who had migrated to Australia through marriage. Papay stayed at home until his daughter died on March 2016. Her passing prompted his return to BASECO. He stayed in the area until October 2016, when he died from an untreated infection to which he was susceptible given his working environment, not to mention his floodwater-soaked house.

Both Aling Mary and Papay utilized scavenging as a coping strategy to combat their households' food insecurity. For Aling Mary, the need to collect food, even from a dumpster, is fueled by the need to support her son. For Papay, it was for the sake of his four grandchildren. Whenever confronted about the potential negative effects of eating *tirtir* on one's health, Papay would always assert, *"hindi ito madumi. Niluluto naman yan uli"* (This is not filthy. We cook it again anyway). In another conversation, he proudly argued that I should not classify him or his household as food-insecure (*nangan-gamba sa pagkain at nagugutuman*) because they ate expensive food every day. He said this while taking a bite of a leftover pizza that he was able to salvage from the trash bags of Shakey's restaurant.

Other residents do not engage in the highly stigmatized work of scavenging. However, the free food offered by the estuary is of keen interest to households that are experiencing food insecurity. Upon visiting BASECO, one of the first things that would be noticeable is the divers who either catch fish or collect mussels. This activity is performed by individuals of all ages. However, health and physical limitations of old age prevent older adults from participating in diving for food. Most of older adults who collect *tahong* go to the breakwater and collect whatever they can in the area. In a discussion with Tatay Alfredo, he contended that exercising diligence and optimism is likely to result in sourcing seafood.

Alfredo: Pagka wala nga silang pambili ng bigas papapak na lang sila ng tahong eh.madali namang kumuha ng tahong sa dagat eh. Kapag masipag ka lang dito na manguha ng tahong makakakain ka.

(When we have no money to buy rice, we only eat mussels since it is easy to collect them from the sea. As long as you are industrious enough to collect mussels, you will surely have something to eat)

Researcher: Bale 'Tay nasubukan niyo na po kayo po mismo yung kumuha ng tahong sa dagat?

(Have you ever tried collecting mussels from the sea yourself?)

Alfredo: Oo diyan ay kinakapa lang minsan sa putik yung malalaking ano kakapa-in mong ganyan. Iluluto mo. Yun na lang po ang pang-ulam tahong.

(Yes. Sometimes you just have to feel it from the mud. You can feel the big ones. Those are the ones that you cook and pair with rice.)

Researcher: Tapos po 'Tay yung kinakapa niyo po na tahong kinakain niyo na po 'yon kaagad o binebenta niyo muna 'yon?

(Do you eat the mussels you collect or do you sell those?)

Alfredo: Syempre pagka sapat-sapat lang talagang pangkain lang talaga. Pagka medyo marami binibigay sa kapitbahay ganun. Hindi naman po maramihan para ibenta eh, pangkain lang po sa pamilya.

(What we get are just about enough to feed our family. When there's an excess, we share those with our neighbors. We don't get to collect that much for us to be able to sell some. What we are able to get is just enough for our family's consumption)

I consider the collection of *tahong* as an activity related to scavenging, given the condition of the estuary as a dumping ground for both sewage and residents' garbage. The toxicity of the water due to pollution makes the consumption of seafood harvested from it health threatening. Despite this, residents continue to exercise this food-gathering strategy. Eighner (2013) defines scavenging as "a modern form of self-reliance," such that a marginalized individual is able to assert his/her own agency in addressing the food insecurity that s/he is experiencing. The acceptability of places and acts associated with scavenging derives from the scavenger's achievement of "a moral 'sense of one's place' through a habitus that leverages the material dimensions of place itself" (Barnard, 2016). There were numerous instances when I witnessed both Papay and Aling Mary conduct their activities as though they were part of what society considers acceptable behavior. On many occasions, I saw both navigating their "territories" with the ease and comfort that one may imagine experiencing while shopping for groceries in air-conditioned stores. The act of scavenging as a coping strategy for food-insecure homes has been documented in food-insecure areas in Kenya (Kimani-Murage et al., 2014; Mudege & Ezeh, 2009), the United States (Woltil, 2012), and India (Snell-Rood, 2013). Although food scavenging is generally practiced in the Global South, the rise of dumpster divers in the region can be viewed as an indicator of increasing food security in that region (Eighner, 2013).

Unlike food sharing and food loans, the consumption of socially stigmatized food was seen as a common practice of older adults during periods of flooding. During the aftermath of weather disturbances, the prices of fish reduce in BASECO, as fish from fish pens in Rizal and Laguna overflow, releasing species like bangus and tilapia. The fish eventually reach the Pasig River. As Nanay Nenita said, "*nakakabili ako dito ng bangus pag-umuulan kasi ang mura*" (I get to buy milkfish here in the compound during rainy seasons because they're cheap). Some of the fisherfolk in the area catch tilapia in the estuary. Locals say that these are the *takas* (escapees) of fish pens in Rizal and Laguna that made their way to the Pasig River. In July 2014, the Makati city government warned its residents about eating tilapia and bangus that were caught in the Pasig River. The concern was around the toxic environment that these fish have lived in because it may result in health issues for humans when consumed. For example, the high levels of methylmercury in the river when ingested through consumption of fish caught in it can have adverse effects on the nervous system of children and may even promote cancer among adults (Frialde, 2014). Nevertheless, locals would purchase the fish caught by their neighbors from the estuary due to the significantly lower prices of these compared to the fish on sale at the market. For example, a tilapia caught in the estuary would be sold for 40 pesos per kilo. This is 43 percent cheaper than its retail value in the market.

The supply of *tirtir* and *retaso* remain unaffected by flooding in the area as they are usually sourced from fast food chains outside the compound and as far away as Divisoria. Bringing in the collected *tirtir* and *retaso* is a challenge as roads and alleys in the compound can remain submerged under floodwater for a minimum of a week. In this situation, older adults often choose to sell their collected food to resellers, keeping a small portion aside for their own household's consumption.

Acceptance of Dole Out

In the report of HUDCC (2014), one of the key issues that the organization identified in dealing with informal settlers is the latter's dependency on assistance from supporting organizations such as NGOs and other members of the private sector. The portrayal of informal settlers as highly dependent on structures and government agencies is consistently the subject of various literatures. From their dependence on policy-makers (Lombard, 2014) to food relief and similar aids from NGOs (Venkatesh, 1994), informal settlers have been depicted as disempowered individuals who have become reliant on welfare systems. A growing literature has been challenging this assertion, arguing that the basis of the issue is the paradigm in which donor organizations have been operating. Hilhorst (2001, p.9) argues that the reduced participant approach to humanitarian aid has created a disengaged recipient community that created a system with an individual-based approach to relief: "people were not encouraged to act like citizens with entitlements as well as moral obligations to play a role in the protection of more vulnerable people and the reconstruction of the community." This results in patronage systems within the community as individuals access aid through personal ties forged with donors and their representatives. In India, Mosse (2005) documented how aid was being reconfigured in a recipient village using a patronage system. Such a patronage system runs in direct contrast to collective action, which is a more progressive approach to development. In the Philippines, the issue on dependency has been well debated as early as 1978 in the work of Lim who looked into the creation of the immutable central power in Manila during Marcos's New Society "at the expense of the poor." Current literature on the Philippines' urban poor and their exercise of agency have highlighted their contribution to tourism (Yotsumo, 2013), their agency amidst the drug war (Yusay & Canoy, 2018), and their collaboration with global networks to secure their housing needs (Herrle & Ley 2016).

In the BASECO Compound, several nongovernmental organizations and private donors are operating on poverty alleviation-related projects that target specific sectors of the community, especially during periods of disaster, whether human-made (fire) or natural (flooding and water spout). Some of these are Korean Christian missionary groups, the HOPE Foundation, World Vision, Gawad Kalinga, Habitat for Humanity, and university-based community development offices. The research center in which I work has been involved in community development projects in the area through my leadership. In the projects that my center has implemented in the area, a key guideline we have followed is the engagement of community members in the planning and implementation stages. For example, the two wells that were constructed in Aplaya and Gasangan arose from the identified issue of water security in the area. Both wells were constructed using materials paid for by the center while the labor cost was shouldered by the community members. This paradigm simultaneously empowers and assigns responsibility to community members. However, this paradigm is not followed by other partner agencies operating in BASECO. From uncoordinated medical missions to food packages that contain food items that do not address the food insecurity of the locals, multiple donor groups have been undertaking non-collaborative development work in the compound. This creates a strong patronage system in the area such that those who have social ties with the compound's leaders are given information ahead of the others on the details of aid distribution or special events. Violent encounters during uncoordinated distribution of food packages usually erupt as individuals attempt to procure the limited supply provided by donor organizations.

Occurrences of flooding caused by typhoons generate the holding of multiple charity events where food packages and hygiene products are distributed to locals. Individuals who have wider social connections are more likely to access several events and consequently acquire relief packages distributed there. When the contents of a package are deemed non-essential, these are then sold at a discounted price to neighbors who did not access the event. In some cases, these items are exchanged for essential items from sari-sari stores. While doing fieldwork in December 2015, a local offered me a package containing ingredients for spaghetti. She told me that she would exchange it for 100 pesos even though the package was worth almost 200 pesos. She later informed me that she has no means of cooking spaghetti as she does not even have wood for fire. This is a clear case of poor planning for community collaboration in the intervention planning stages.

For other locals, the portrayal of them being reliant on dole outs is absurd. Nanay Inday argued that it is not efficient to depend on dole outs: "*hindi ka naman pwede mag-antay lang sa biyaya ng iba. Minsan di naman sila dumadating*" (You cannot just rely on dole outs from others. Sometimes they don't show up). My observation corroborates this argument. NGOs and even government representatives have no sustainable project which delivers food to vulnerable households. At most, there were feeding programs that targeted school children for several months. This selective and non-sustainable approach leaves other members of the family food-insecure. There are other private organizations that distribute food packages to the compound's residents on a weekly to monthly basis. These packages do not alleviate the food insecurity within those households but allow the family to have sufficient time to gather their resources in order to acquire food resources.

Another interesting view on dole outs that I have observed among some of my informants is the negotiation of their identity in order to extend their social influence. One example is attending church services to get the coveted four kilos of rice that is given to all attendees after the event. Here, locals can be seen as negotiating their identity to access the limited resources offered by an institution. Older adults, due to their senior citizen status, can access dole outs easier than their younger counterparts. The policy of prioritizing the elderly in lines and sequences has allowed them to attend more aid distribution events than their younger counterparts.

Missed and Lessened Food Intake

One of the most immediate and common responses to food insecurity in the household is the prioritization of food distribution. In situations when food supply is limited, individuals who control a household's food distribution may impose prioritization in the distribution of food to family members. Those family members who are deemed less productive or with less potential to contribute to family resources are given lesser portions of food and the contributing members are given a greater share. Older adults are typically slotted in the less functional member category as they are not capable of contributing to the financial stability of the household due to the physical limits associated with aging. Non-working women are also placed in this category. Working members, most often men, schoolchildren, and pregnant women are given priority in food allocation due to their health condition or their need for energy to perform their roles.

Food distribution is a concept that has been explored as a manner of coping strategy in food-insecure homes by a number of authors (Chen, Huq, & D'Souza, 1981; Messer, 2009; Rivera, Aliping, Sentral, & Pilipinas, 2013). Food distribution is also used to measure the extent of an individual's food insecurity as triggered by household interactions (Burchi, Fanzo, & Frison, 2011). Following this approach, the households included in this study have been implementing unequal food distribution measures that are usually based on the perceived contribution of the member to the financial stability of the group. In this study, the impact of unequal food distribution within the household was examined as the experience of not being able to eat certain meals of the day (breakfast, lunch, dinner), or being able to eat smaller portions of food or a substitute during the said meals. These processes were labeled as *missed meals* and *lessened food intake*. Both are nearly equal in practice as narrated by the older adults, such that missing breakfast is common and eating smaller portions of food is almost a norm.

During interviews, narratives around reduced food intake included highlighting the substitution of food with liquid, such as hot water, soup, or coffee. Prioritization of food allocation for children and working family members was also a common theme. As a (grandmother) *lola* mentioned, *"magutom na ako wag lang sila, minsan sabaw sabaw lang ako, kape-kape, pero sila pinapakain ko talaga"* (I would rather be hungry instead of them. Sometimes I just take soup or coffee but I make sure that they eat). For others who are highly dependent on their working family members, missing food becomes an all too common scenario when the provider fails to give their support. As one participant stated, *"pagdi ako binigyan ng mga anak ko sa tanghalian, magpapass muna ako"* (If my children do not give me food during lunch, then I'll skip it). In some earlier work, I collected data on the food calendar for twenty elderly people who are also part of this current study. In that work, I learned that there were meals participants missed due to the unavailability of food, while there were other "meals" which consisted of nothing more than hot water.

Another type of meal substitute commonly practiced by food-insecure households is the sharing of one packet of instant noodle soup diluted in triple the recommended amount of water. Children and working members are given portions containing more noodles than those perceived as contributing less to the household. Coffee is another food substitute that is often diluted in over-portioned water.

Older adults reported that during flooding events, they remained behind to secure the household possessions while the remainder of the household left for an evacuation center. The elderly people claimed that during that period, they would eat a small portion of the food, once per day, that their family members had left with them. As stated earlier, older adults are often given the task of securing the household's movable properties from looting during flooding. These older adults are subjected to intense experiences of *kalam* as they are usually left with a packet of biscuits or some old bread. Since neither cooking food nor boiling water is possible due to wet firewood, these older adults are deprived of hot meals and clean drinking water.

Silence as a Practice of *Pagtitiis*

Pagtitiis is a Filipino value that is equated to the practice of enduring. It has been documented as a response of individuals who are under distress and are expected to continue their performance of their prescribed roles. In the work of Taqueban (2012), *pagtitiis* has been identified by Filipina domestic workers as a key practice in surviving the difficulties associated with serving households in the Middle East who have different cultures and beliefs. Among the disaster survivors of Ateneoville following the onslaught of Typhoon Ondoy, one of the traits that was identified as having helped survivors to cope was *pagtitiis* (Adviento & Guzman, 2010). This trait is believed to be taught to children, especially to females who are expected to practice *pagtitiis* in their marriages despite any difficulty or even threat to their security (Estrellado & Loh, 2016). In most contexts, *pagtitiis* is practiced in a way similar to those of familial obligations.

In the BASECO Compound, the practice of *pagtitiis* is done in consonance with specific habits such as being silent, sitting to the side, or any act that may be considered as a form of submission to one's circumstances. During interviews, informants have often equated the term *pagtitiis* and *pagtahimik* as responses to a lack of food in their households. Statements like "*pagwala tiis-tiis lang*" (when we have nothing we just have to endure) and "*pagkulang kelangan magtiis*" (when food is insufficient, we need to endure) provide insight on the transitory nature of the practice of *pagtitiis*, in other words, it is expected that the event will pass. Silence has become a common response to the lack of food sources inside the home. It can be seen as a form of *pagtitiis* and as a form of keeping face with one's neighbors. For some informants, their status as food-insecure is a source of shame. Nanay Flora commented that she would keep quiet whenever she had no food: "*Di na ko kumikibo, natutulog na lang ako. Nakakahiya naman manghingi*" (I just keep silent. I just sleep it off. It's embarrassing to ask for food).

Resignation to lack of economic opportunities that could address food insecurity has been characterized as "starving in silence" in other societies as a byproduct of the state's marginalizing policies (Vernon, 2007). For the vulnerable, silence in the midst of hunger and poverty is debilitating. The practice of silence when confronted with hunger has been equated with voicelessness and powerlessness:

> Poor people's lives are characterized by powerlessness and voicelessness, which limit their choices and define the quality of their interactions with employers, markets, the state, and even Nongovernmental Organizations (NGOs). Powerlessness results from multiple, interlocking disadvantages, which, in combination, make it extremely difficult for poor people to escape poverty.

> (Sophie & Acharya, 2014, p.116)

Pagtitiis in form of silence is an experience of voicelessness within the household and the greater community in which the older adults of BASECO negotiate their daily struggles with food insecurity. This coping strategy is probably the most marginalizing of all seven strategies identified in this work, in the sense that it directly results in dissociation from an individual's community which is expected to be the frontline support system of vulnerable households. Observably, this is also the last resort that most of the informants have taken to address their hunger. It is at this stage that they have resigned to their state of constant powerlessness to improve their circumstances. This same behavior has been documented among some urban poor residents in Payatas (Su & Sia Su, 2008) who have accepted scavenging as a norm of economic survival.

CONSTRUCTING DISASTER
VULNERABILITY AND RISK

Only about 15 percent of the residents in the BASECO Compound have legal documents that provide them the status of a formal settler. These households have security of tenure, which allows them to easily access government-sponsored aid during periods of flooding. They are also prioritized during evacuation. The undocumented majority of BASECO's population receives an application number provided by the barangay that is used to prove that they have been residents of the compound for a minimum of ten years. With this number, they are given color-coded cards that they are expected to use during evacuation in times of flooding. An older adult who has a barangay-tagged home is given a priority card that allows them to have first access to the evacuation center and the relief supply. Children are also given this same card, followed by pregnant women. However, due to the prescribed roles for older adults, most of them do not use their card for evacuation.

The BASECO Compound primarily comprises informal settlers and its population keeps on increasing, yet government-sponsored infrastructure developments continue to be completed. From a four-story evacuation center that could accommodate 3,000 individuals to inner roads being sealed, the area presents itself as an urban poor community which consists of documented settlers. Unlike other informal settlements, BASECO residents seem unperturbed by the supposed threat of eviction by the government, and they especially appear unconcerned that the area is highly prone to natural disasters. Socrates (2016, p.31) discusses the general perception of the residents toward eviction stating:

> [The] [m]ajority of the respondents admit that they *do not feel threatened* of the possibility of eviction, due to these reasons (1) *part of the census tagging in 2001,* (2) there were news about eviction but *no official report,* (3) *Willing to leave,* and lastly *(4) BASECO is being developed.*

The houses closest to the shore[4] were tagged by the barangay in 2001, giving them partial tenure security despite the constant threat of flooding by any form of weather variability or tidal shifts. As the estuary reclaims the land, these houses become closer to the shore and, consequentially, closer to the threat brought about by flooding. All of the households along Aplaya have at least one elderly person who is often left behind to secure the family's belongings during flooding. Nonetheless, not a single household that was interviewed had plans of relocating due to the threat of flooding. Nanay Rosie said, "*sanayan lang naman yan. Pagtalagang mataas ang baha, yun medyo nakakatakot pero hindi ibig sabihin nun ay aalis na kami*" (it is just a matter of getting used to it. When the floodwaters are really deep, we do get scared. But it does not mean that we will relocate). When I asked Nanay Inday, a former barangay local representative, why the government had not produced a demolition or relocation project, she told me, "*e di nawalan sila ng botante*" (because they would lose voters). The BASECO Compound has been a political battleground for aspiring local officials of the city of Manila, due to its voting population numbering approximately 60,000 people. Locals have often cited that the reason for their non-eviction is their political power especially during local elections.

Relocation has often failed here due to the economic viability of the relocation sites. In the case of the BASECO Compound, residents remain in the area despite the constant threat of flooding because of its strategic location that puts it in proximity to the major economic centers of Manila. With a less inclusive form of economic development in a country that creates exclusive centers, residents of economically marginalized regions moved to urban areas, a phenomenon that creates rippling issues ranging from overpopulation, to informal labor abuses, to informal settlements. Since urban planning policies prohibit the occupation of locations identified as danger zones, these spaces become the prime choice for individuals who cannot afford the cost of living spaces in the city. It is against this backdrop that the older adults of the BASECO Compound have been negotiating their identity to survive the *kalam* that they experience daily.

CONCLUSION

The intersection between disaster risk and vulnerability to the experiences of food security has been at the core of this chapter. I argue that the daily lives of this study's participants have been defined both by their environment and by the policies that have confined them within the periphery of state support. The shift in their environmental conditions that is predicated by multilayered contexts that include climate change and more often exclusive development policies have widened the gap in their perceived state of food security and their actual experiences. A similar frame has been observed in the experiences of urban households in South Africa as they respond to a constant state of food insecurity which is often exacerbated by disasters resulting from climate change (De Lange, 2015). Similarly, I argue in this study that localized forms of resiliency have allowed for the community and its members to cope with the threats of food insecurity. These localized strategies which extend from the consumption of socially stigmatized food items to a renegotiation of food-sharing networks have posed questions on the generalizing definition of food security that is employed in the food security literature. The question of who has the power to define when a person is food-insecure is brought to the fore as locals differentiate between the experiences of *gutom* and *kalam*, stating that the former is a constant state which is a byproduct of their socioeconomic condition of being urban informal settlers, while *kalam* is what could be considered a state of being food-insecure because it is an intensified experience of *gutom* that results from non-access to even the most socially stigmatized food items which may include *tirtir* and *retaso*. It is also in this period of *kalam* that the majority of the usual food-coping strategies are inaccessible. The findings of this study provide an alternate definition of food security and require an interrogation of current disaster risk reduction and sustainable development policies. The cases presented in this chapter illustrate the intensity of the shocks that avoidable events like flooding can inflict on vulnerable households.

NOTES

1. Based on November 2016 barangay record.

2. Older adults preferred to use the term *kalam* over *gutom*, because a translation of "food insecurity" for the latter implies a constant state for most, while *kalam* is an extreme form of *gutom*. *Kalam* typically means having nothing to eat at all.

3. Aling Mary was buried in an unmarked grave in the city cemetery while her son was taken by the representatives of the Department of Social Welfare and Development. Her house was demolished by the neighbors who proceeded in claiming the land as an extension of their undocumented property.

4. (Aplaya; approximately 40 feet).

REFERENCES

Adviento, M. L., & Guzman, J. de. (2010). Community Resilience During Typhoon Ondoy the Case of Ateneoville. *Philippine Journal of Psychology, 43*(1).

Agpalo, R. E. (1999). The Philippine Pangulo Regime. *Philippine Political Science Journal, 20*(43).

Alejandria-Gonzalez, M. C. (2018). Food Insecurity and Resilience: Experiences of Hunger and Poverty among Elders in a Manila Slum. In Alejandria-Gonzalez, Maria Carinnes; Ghosh, Subharati; Sacco, Nicolas (Eds.), Aging in the Global South: Challenges and Opportunities. Washington DC: Rowman and Littlefield

Ancheta, A., Batan, C., Balita, D. A., & Gonzalez, M. C. (2015). *"Baha at Mga Bata": Exploring the Filipino Children's Perceptions and Experiences of "Flood" as Stories of Vulnerabilities.* University of Santo Tomas, Manila City.

Ban, J., Lan, L., Yang, C., Wang, J., Chen, C., Huang, G., & Li, T. (2017). Public Perception of Extreme Cold Weather-Related Health Risk in a Cold Area of Northeast China. *Disaster Medicine and Public Health Preparedness, 11*(4), 417–421.

Barnard, A. V. (2016). Making the City "Second Nature": Freegan "Dumpster Divers" and the Materiality of Morality. *American Journal of Sociology, 121*(4), 1017–1050. http://doi.org/10.1086/683819.

Bombay Urban Industrial League for Development. (2010). *Eat Less Sleep Less, and Work More: Situational Analysis of Food Insecurity in Urban Slums of Mumbai.* Mumbai.

Bourdieu, P. (1984). *Distinction: A Social Critique of the Judgment of Taste.* Routledge. http://doi.org/10.1007/s13398-014-0173-7.2.

Brisson, D. (2012). Neighborhood Social Cohesion and Food Insecurity: A Longitudinal Study. *Journal of the Society for Social Work and Research*, *3*(4), 268–279. http://doi.org/10.5243/jsswr.2012.16.

Burchi, F., Fanzo, J., & Frison, E. (2011). The role of food and nutrition system approaches in tackling hidden hunger. *International Journal of Environmental Research and Public Health*, *8*(2), 358–373. https://doi.org/10.3390/ijerph8020358.

Caliguing, E. M., & Sa-Ao, B. C. (2008). Suki System as a Marketing Strategy at the Baguio City Public Market. *Research Journal*, *XVI*, 137–141. Retrieved from http://www.eisrjc.com/documents/Suki_System_As_A_Marketing_Strategy_1325748887.pdf.

Carrier, James G. (2018). Moral Economy: What's in a Name. *Anthropological Theory*. https://doi.org/10.1177/1463499617735259.

Chen, L. C., Huq, E., & D'Souza, S. (1981). Sex Bias in the Family Allocation of Food and Health Care in Rural Bangladesh. *Population and Development Review*, *7*(1), 55. http://doi.org/10.2307/1972764.

Cherniack, E. P. (2008). The impact of natural disasters on the elderly. *American Journal of Disaster Medicine*, *3*(3), 133–9. Retrieved from http://www.ncbi.nlm.nih.gov/pubmed/18666509.

Coates, J., Swindale, A., & Bilinsky, P. (2007). *Household Food Insecurity Access Scale (HFIAS) for Measurement of Food Access: Indicator Guide*. Washington. Retrieved from www.fantaproject.org.

Cohen, M. J., & Garrett, J. L. (2010). The food price crisis and urban food (in)security. *Environment and Urbanization*, *22*(2), 467–482. http://doi.org/10.1177/0956247810380375.

De Lange, D. (2015). *The Relationship Between Food Security and Disaster Risk Reduction at the Urban Household Level in the South African Context.*

Diamante, C. J. (2015). *Food Insecurity: The Experiences of Hunger Among the Households Living In A Manila Slums.* University of Santo Tomas.

Drabek, T. E. (2007). *Sociology, Disasters and Emergency Management: History, Contributions, and Future Agenda. Disciplines, Disasters and Emergency Management: The Convergence and Divergence of Concepts, Issues and Trends in the Research Literature.* Retrieved from http://books.google.co.za/books?id=3XyTLUgXmBIC&pg=PA335&lpg=PA335&dq=Drabek+Sociology,+Disasters+and+Emergency+Management:+History,+Contributions,+and+Future+Agenda&source=bl&ots=DRIrgNR2dE&sig=HflRKQsSti58FdoolaIBEzX1nTs&hl=en&sa=X&ei=Vhl_U937E4uO7QbpnY.

Eighner, L. (2013). On Dumpster Diving. *New England Journal of Public Policy Lars New England Journal of Public Policy*, *24*(1). Retrieved from http://scholarworks.umb.edu/nejpp.

Estrellado, A. F., & Loh, J. (MI). (2016). To Stay in or Leave an Abusive Relationship. *Journal of Interpersonal Violence*, 88626051665791. http://doi.org/10.1177/0886260516657912.

Fitzpatrick, K., & Coleman-Jensen, A. (2014). Food on the Fringe: Food Insecurity and the Use of Payday Loans. *Social Service Review*, *88*(4), 553–593. http://doi.org/10.1086/679388.

Foxen, P. (2010). Local Narratives of Distress and Resilience: Lessons in Psychosocial Well-Being among the K'iche' Maya in Postwar Guatemala. *The Journal of Latin American and Caribbean Anthropology, 15*(1), 66–89. http://doi.org/10.11 11/j.1935-4940.2010.01063.x.

Frialde, M. (2014, July 18). Makati Warns: Don't Eat "toxic" Pasig River Fish. *Philippine Star*, p. 3. Manila. Retrieved from http://www.philstar.com:8080/metro/2014/07/18/1347486/makati-warns-dont-eat-toxic-pasig-river-fish.

Guest, E. (2003). *Children of AIDS: Africa's Orphan Crisis*. Pluto Press.

Hadley, C., Belachew, T., Lindstrom, D., & Tessema, F. (2009). The Forgotten Population? Youth, Food Insecurity, and Rising Prices: Implications for the Global Food Crisis. *NAPA Bulletin, 32*, 77–91.

Harvey, M. R. (1996). An Ecological View of Psychological Trauma and Trauma Recovery. *Journal of Traumatic Stress, 9*(1), 3–23. http://doi.org/10.1002/jts.2490090103.

Hilhorst, D. (2001). *Saving Lives or Saving Societies? Realities of Relief and Reconstruction*. Wageningen: Wageningen University.

Hori, T., & Shaw, R. (2012). Global Climate Change Perception, Local Risk Awareness, and Community Disaster Risk Reduction: A Case Study of Cartago City, Costa Rica. *Risk, Hazards & Crisis in Public Policy, 3*(4), 77–104.

HUDCC. (2014). *Developing a National Informal Settlements Upgrading Strategy for the Philippines*. Quezon City. Retrieved from http://www.hudcc.net/sites/default/files/styles/large/public/document/NISUS Final Report_July2014.pdf.

Kihiu, P. G. (2007). *The AIDS Orphan Crisis in Kenya: Caring for Kikuyu Children in Escarpment* (Doctoral dissertation, Asbury Theological Seminary, Wilmore, KY). Retrieved from https://place.asburyseminary.edu/cgi/viewcontent.cgi?article=1008&context=ecommonsatsdissertations.

Kimani-Murage, E. W., Schofield, L., Wekesah, F., Mohamed, S., Mberu, B., Ettarh, R., … Ezeh, A. (2014). Vulnerability to Food Insecurity in Urban Slums: Experiences from Nairobi, Kenya. *Journal of Urban Health : Bulletin of the New York Academy of Medicine*, 1–16. http://doi.org/10.1007/s11524-014-9894-3.

Lim, R. (1978). The Philippines and the "dependency debate": A Preliminary Case Study. *Journal of Contemporary Asia.* https://doi.org/10.1080/0047233788539 0101

Lombard, M. (2014). Constructing Ordinary Places: Place-Making in Urban Informal Settlements in Mexico. *Progress in Planning, 94*, 1–53. http://doi.org/10.1016/j.progress.2013.05.003

Malapit, H. J. L. (2012). Are Women More Likely to be Credit Constrained? Evidence from Low-Income Urban Households in the Philippines. *Feminist Economics, 18*(July), 81–108.

Mercado, R. M. (2016). People's Risk Perceptions and Responses to Climate Change and Natural Disasters in BASECO Compound, Manila, Philippines. *Procedia Environmental Sciences, 34*, 490–505.

Mercado, R. M. (2016). People's Risk Perceptions and Responses to Climate Change and Natural Disasters in BASECO Compound, Manila, Philippines. *Procedia Environmental Sciences, 34*, 490–505. http://doi.org/10.1016/j.proenv.2016.04.043.

Messer, E. (2009). Rising Food Prices, Social Mobilizations, and Violence: Conceptual Issues in Understanding and Responding to the Connections Linking Hunger and Conflict. *NAPA Bulletin, 32,* 12–22.

Mosse, D. (2005). *Cultivating Development an Ethnography of Aid Policy and Practice.* London: Pluto Press.

Mudege, N. N., & Ezeh, A. C. (2009). Gender, Aging, Poverty and Health: Survival Strategies of Older Men and Women in Nairobi Slums. *Journal of Aging Studies, 23*(4), 245–257. http://doi.org/10.1016/j.jaging.2007.12.021.

Murphy, D. (2012). *BASECO and Its Proclamation.* Quezon City. Retrieved from http://www.ombudsman.gov.ph/UNDP4/wp-content/uploads/2012/12/BASECO_PROC1_HTML.pdf.

Ozbay, F., Johnson, D. C., Dimoulas, E., Morgan, C. A., Charney, D., & Southwick, S. (2007). Social Support and Resilience to Stress: From Neurobiology to Clinical Practice. *Psychiatry (Edgmont (Pa. : Township)), 4*(5), 35–40. Retrieved from http://www.ncbi.nlm.nih.gov/pubmed/20806028.

Paguntalan, A. M. C. (2002). *Nimble Fingers, Clenched Fists: Dynamics of Structure, Agency, and Women's Spaces in a Manufacturing Company.* Quezon City, Philippines: University of the Philippines Center for Women's Studies.

Parham, E. (2012). The Segregated Classes: Spatial and Social Relationships in Slums. In M. Greene, J. Reyes, & A. Castro (Eds.), *Proceedings of the Eighth International Space Syntax Symposium* (pp. 1–19). Santiago: PUC.

Paz, C. J. (2008). *Essays on Well-Being, Opportunity/Destiny, and Anguish.* UP Press.

Prashar, S. K., & Shaw, R. (2012). Disaster Resilience of Slums in Delhi through Appropriate Risk Communication. *Asian Journal of Environment and Disaster Management (AJEDM)—Focusing on Pro-Active Risk Reduction in Asia, 4*(1), 99. http://doi.org/10.3850/S179392402012001093.

Ramsey, R., Giskes, K., Turrell, G., & Gallegos, D. (2011). Food Insecurity Among Australian Children: Potential Determinants, Health and Developmental Consequences. *Journal of Child Health Care : For Professionals Working with Children in the Hospital and Community, 15*(4), 401–16. http://doi.org/10.1177/1367493511423854.

Reyes, H. (2016). *Experiences of Vulnerability During Flooding: Narratives Of Selected Elderly In Port Area, Manila.* University of Santo Tomas.

Riley, L., & Lupafya, E. (2011). Rethinking the Orphan Crisis: Community-Based Responses to Orphan Care in Malawi. In M. Denov, R. Maclure, & K. Campbell (Eds.), *Children's Rights and International Development* (pp. 221–239). New York, NY: Palgrave MacMillan.

Rivera, J. P. R., Aliping, N. B., Sentral, B., & Pilipinas, N. (2013).The Implications of Government's Poverty Reduction Programs on the States of Poverty and Hunger in the Philippines. *Journal of International Business Research, 12*(2), 73–97.

Rosenbaum, B., & Eggleston, S. (2006). Women's Participation in Non-Government Organizations: Implications for Poverty Reduction in Precarious Settlements of Guatemala City. *City and Society, 18*(2), 260–287. http://doi.org/10.1525/city.2006.18.2.260.Women.

Saito, I. (2010). Pakikasama: A Filipino Cultural Trait. *Rissho University Psychology Institute, 8*, 43–53. Retrieved from http://commons.lib.jmu.edu/cgi/viewcontent.cg i?article=1041&context=master201019.

Snell-Rood, C. (2013). To Know the Field: Shaping the Slum Environment and Cultivating the Self. *Ethos, 41*(3), 271–291. http://doi.org/10.1111/etho.12022.

Socrates, F. A. (2016). *The Contexts of Construction of BASECO Compound as an Informal Settlement.* University of Santo Tomas.

Sophie, L., & Acharya, S. K. (2014). The Hunger, Poverty and Silence: The Synergy of Threats to Development and Progress. *International Journal of Development Research, 4*(1), 115–117. Retrieved from http://www.journalijdr.com/sites/default /files/Download 1299.pdf.

Steinberg, F., & Lindfield, M. (2011). *Inclusive Cities.* Mandaluyong. Retrieved from https://www.adb.org/sites/default/files/publication/29053/inclusive-cities.pdf.

Su, G. L. S., & Sia Su, G. L. (2008). Determinants of Economic Dependency on Garbage: The Case of Payatas, Philippines. *Asia-Pacific Social Science Review.* https://doi.org/10.3860/apssr.v7i2.500

Taqueban, E. M. (2012). Salam: Of Dislocation, Marginality and Flexibility. *Social Science Diliman, 8* (December), 1–28.

Ushijima, I., & Zayas, C. N. (1994). *Fishers of the Visayas.* Quezon City, Philippines: University of the Philippines Press.

Venkatesh, S. A. (1994). Getting Ahead: Social Mobility Among the Urban Poor. *Sociological Perspectives, 37*(2), 157–182. http://doi.org/10.2307/1389318.

Vernon, J. (2007). *Hunger A Modern History.* Cambridge: The Belknap Press of Harvard University Press.

Woltil, J. (2012). The Impact of Emotional Social Support on Elders' Food Security. *Sociation Today, 10*(2), 1–24.

Wutich, A., & Brewis, A. (2014). Food, Water, and Scarcity. *Current Anthropology, 55*(4), 444–468. http://doi.org/10.1086/677311

Yotsumoto, Y. (2013). Formalization of Urban Poor Vendors and their Contribution to Tourism Development in Manila, Philippines. *International Journal of Japanese Sociology.* https://doi.org/10.1111/ijjs.12000

Yu, J., Cruz, A. M., & Hokugo, A. (2017). Households' Risk Perception and Behavioral Responses to Natech Accidents. *International Journal of Disaster Risk Science, 8*(1), 1–15.

Yusay, C. T. C., & Canoy, N. A. (2018). Healing the Hurt Amid the Drug War: Narratives of Young Urban Poor Filipinos in Recovering Families with Parental Drug Use. *The International Journal on Drug Policy.* https://doi.org/10.1016/j.drug po.2018.10.009.

Chapter 7

"Baha at mga bata" (flood and children)

Exploring Selected Filipino Children's flood Experiences, Vulnerable contexts, and Resilience

Arlen A. Ancheta, Clarence M. Batan, Dan Angelo B. Balita, and Maria Carinnes P. Alejandria

INTRODUCTION

In recent years, the ecological landscape of urban Manila has been marred by both natural and human-made disasters, which have caused damage not only to properties but have also claimed human lives (Gaillard, 2011). Among these calamities is the phenomenon of flooding (Zoleta-Nantes, 2000, 2002), locally known in the country as "pagbaha" or simply, flood, or "baha." As an archipelago located in the Northwestern Pacific, the Philippines is geographically prone to weather disturbances at varying intensities, making coastal areas the most vulnerable. A case in point is Manila Bay, famous for its sunset, natural harbors and ports (Alejandro, Santos, & Yuson, 2006; Project Management Office of Manila Bay Environmental Management Project [MBEMP], 2001). It is the prime maritime center supporting trade and commerce on the island of Luzon. However, it is exposed to natural calamities as it is located along the typhoon path, prompting unstable levels of vulnerabilities among various sectors of its coastal communities.

One of these vulnerable sectors is the children, or in local Filipino language, "mga bata." As some Western-based studies attest, children are more susceptible to hazards, needing protection especially during disaster events (Seballos, Tanner, Tarazona, & Gallegos, 2011; Tanner & Seballos, 2012). However, even during times of disasters such as floods, children, too, carry a sense of agency (Walker et al., 2012) that may be important to explore in order to understand how their voices are configured into the complex lives of these vulnerable communities.

This study attempts to make sense of the relation between the two salient dimensions of disaster discourse in urban Manila: (a) "baha" (flood), and (b) "mga bata" (the Filipino children). Similar to the British study on children's flood stories (Walker et al., 2012), this chapter describes "baha at mga bata"—the Filipino children's perceptions and experiences of flooding. Stories have been collected from the voices of selected children in the BASECO compound located in the port area, Manila. The children belong to an urban estuarial community where flooding has become a natural fabric of social life.

In the context of the current debate on climate change and disaster management, this study argues that BASECO children's conceptions of "baha" and their relative flood experiences unravel stories of vulnerabilities and the way children's negotiations signal their sense of agency, highlighting both the benefits and consequences of living in flooded areas. In so doing, the study provides insights about how children as agents may possibly enhance the preparation and implementation of Community Based Disaster Risk Reduction (CBDRR) programs in some communities experiencing similar flooding events.

BASECO, Flooding Landscape as Urban Coastal Community

BASECO, politically under the authority of Barangay 649, Zone 68, is located at the south harbor of Manila's port area, a reclaimed section along Manila Bay's shorefront at the mouth of the Pasig River. As an estuarial community, it is bounded in the North by the Pasig River, in the West by Manila Bay, and in the South by the South Harbor (Guevara, Mayor, & Racelis, 2009). BASECO, as a former shipping dock and a 52-hectare square kilometer area, is home to about 60,000 persons based on 2015 census where riverside and shorefront areas are occupied by informal settlement families.

Located downstream of Manila, BASECO is highly vulnerable from flooding as graphically depicted in figure 7.1. Unfortunately, this same area receives all the floating garbage from the Pasig River to Manila Bay. Garbage from the Pasig River can be traced to Laguna Lake, passing through several cities in Metro Manila. People in BASECO fear that when a high tide coincides with a strong typhoon, unpredictable flooding can occur, increasing community vulnerability. As an estuarial barangay, BASECO experiences tidal changes. During a high tide riverside and shorefront areas expect flooding, though it recedes during low tide. Though "baha" (flooding) may be regarded as a natural element of the urban slum due to its frequent occurrence, people are alarmed during periods when the high tide and heavy rains converge. At these times, water currents are strong, and safety is uncertain.

Figure 7.1 Kevin's visual depiction of flood in BASECO. *Source*: Primary Data from Fieldwork.

The case of the BASECO compound is parallel to worldwide trends of slumification which involves a process of encroachment of informal settlement within a private or public land area. As a reclaimed area initially intended for shipping activities, gradually it was occupied to create a community of migrants, who came from various provinces in search of job opportunities in the National Capital Region.

Vulnerability of Urban Coastal Community

Vulnerability can be defined in many ways across many issues such as food insecurity, climate change, and natural and coastal hazards (Zou & Thomalla, 2008). It entails varying degrees of exposure, sensitivity, and capacity or resistance (Donner & Rodriguez, 2013; Huang, Li, Bai, & Cui, 2012; United Nations University, 2013) from several structural factors. But for this study, we refer to the working definition of Klein and Nicholls (2005) in the context of coastal hazards where they define *vulnerability* as the "degree of capability to cope with the consequences of climate change and sea-level rise" (cited in Zou & Thomalla, 2008:21). Hence, vulnerability as used in this study, refers to the capability of the urban coastal community to cope with the consequences of climatic change events, like violent typhoons causing coastal flooding. Children together with women and the elderly are considered socially vulnerable (Tapsell, 2010) as they are dependent on able-bodied men during flooding events. Arguably, they lack political access (Woodrow, 1989) to initiate evacuation and must simply wait for the men to transfer them to an evacuation center.

Such is the case of urban coastal community that has been undergoing development, resulting in increasing population and the depletion of "buffer zones" (e.g., mangroves, trees, sand dunes) (Donner & Rodriguez, 2008). In effect, the urban coastal community became open to various environmental and social problems, such as: (a) land subsidence due to excessive extraction of ground water depleting soil composition (Marfai & Hizbaron, 2011); (b) rapid urbanization, due to increased numbers of informal settlement families looking for cheap rentals and job opportunities.; (c) greater flood risk aggravated by overflowing of river channels due to erosion, siltation, and clogging of solid waste (Donner & Rodriguez, 2008; Djihad, 1990, cited in Nantes, 2000); (d) exposure to natural hazards like storm surges and sea-level rise (Lane, Wheeler, & Graber, 2013; Kaplan, 2009); and (e) diseases or illnesses (Kazmierczak & Cavan, 2011) due to exposure to pollutants and contaminants.

As in the case of the emergence of informal settlements in BASECO, the area has thus been exposed to many vulnerable conditions. For instance, while the barangay community naturally experiences tidal flooding, it is also simultaneously vulnerable to overflow of rivers surrounding the area (See figure 1). The mobility of community members, including children, is thus severely affected as the phenomenon interweaves in their day-to-day lives in recent years. Worst, BASECO has no natural barrier as the shoreline communities are exposed to strong waves and garbage surging from Manila Bay. This makes a double-edged vulnerability scenario for the BASECO community. On the one end, this community suffers from a long spell of coastal flooding, and on the other, from the foul unhealthy smell and various forms of illnesses brought about by the unsurmountable amount of garbage dumped in their midst.

"Ang Mga Bata": Children and Vulnerability

As of 2010, half of the world's urban population is in Asia; whereas almost half of the world's children live in urban areas. "Ang mga bata," or the children, are considered among the most vulnerable sectors in times of any disaster. Recognized as a helpless sector, the role of adults and authorities to take care of children dominates the consciousness in the landscape of disaster phenomenon (Dabrowska & Wismer, 2010; International Save the Children Alliance, 2008; Lane et al., 2013; Morrow, 1999; New York University Child Study Center, 2006).

A study conducted by Tanner and Seballos (2012) identified two main concepts in research about children and disasters: (1) vulnerability and (2) protection. In a literature review, they found an emphasis on children's susceptibility in various hazards and consequently identified a requirement for the provision of protection. Experts categorize the vulnerability and protection of children in various contexts as "coercion, violence and or physical harm, mental illness, human trafficking, family separation, and quality education" (Javaid, Arshad, & Khalid, 2011). The concepts of psychological, physical, and educational vulnerability (Peek, 2008) also arise. However, Walker et al. (2012) were disturbed by these premises sweeping the helplessness of children's agency.

In recent years, interest in understanding children's experience in disasters emerged (Peek & Stough, 2010) to provide a better grasp of children's vulnerability and capacity (Peek, 2008). As observed, most studies in disasters deal with macro-level analyses where less focus is given to children. Although attempts have been documented to grasp the subjective realm of flood risks, (Burningham, Fielding, & Thrush, 2008; Fatti & Patel, 2013; Linnekamp, Koedam, & Baud, 2011; Walker et al., 2012) there are limited studies that regard children as agents of change (Lawler & Patel, 2012; Martin, 2010) and consider the voices of children's in disaster situations. A prime study example is Walker et al. (2012) who argue about the salience of children's agencies relative to community development since the 1990s. Similarly, in the Philippines, Zoleta-Nantes's (2002) study on the differential impact of flooding recognizes the voices of street children respondents in disaster discourse. It argues that various vulnerabilities, capacities, experiences, or exposure of different sectors such as children influence perceptions of flooding. In a sense, the present study intends at providing a contextualized understanding of flood or "baha" narratives of selected children (mga bata) respondents at BASECO. The aim is to further contribute to the disaster discourse, particularly on better understanding the phenomenon of flooding seen from the perspective of children.

METHODS

This case study (Creswell, 2009) explores children's voices in the context of BASECO. The research underwent three phases of data gathering. The first phase involved a focus group discussion (FGD) of ten randomly selected children aged seven to eleven years old. In the presence of the community social workers, they were instructed to draw their experiences with flooding and the effects on their health conditions.

Phase 1. Kevin, one of the informants, narrated that he was warned by his parents to avoid any flooding, for two reasons: "tibo" (punctured skin due to stepping on sharp shards of glass, wood or metal) and "lunod" (drowning). Thus, as can be seen from figure 7.2, they either wear protective plastic knee-length boots or stay in the elevated parts of their house. Interestingly, Kevin drew a fish in the water. The fish was also observed in the drawings of four other children, all claiming that fish, together with plastic materials and wood debris, are washed ashore by coastal flooding. The picture is also a reflection that children observe the movement of "baha" in the overflowing of the Pasig River and rising of the sea level from Manila Bay due to high tide. The children called Manila Bay *dagat* (the sea).

Apart from the debris, the children relayed that insects and other vermin would surface during floods. Jema's drawing shows cockroaches on the windows and a tree floating on brackish floodwater. All the children viewed floodwater as dirty and containing "germs," as warned by their parents. According to the children, they are not allowed to wade in or play with floodwater: "*baka daw po magkasakit kami kasi may germs* (they say we might get sick because of germs)."

Figure 7.2 Jema's visual depiction of flood in BASECO. *Source*: Primary Data from Fieldwork (Ancheta, et al., 2019).

Figure 7.3   Jema's visual depiction of flood in BASECO. *Source*: Primary Data from Fieldwork (Ancheta, et al., 2019).

Phase 2. The second phase of data gathering consisted of a series of interviews with local officials and NGOs working in the area. It provided an overview of the social, political, health, and environmental conditions of the locale.

Phase 3. Respondents of the study were children around ten years old, more than half of whom were female. Almost all children were in latter primary education typical of their age. Almost all their parents were employed as contractual workers with no security of tenure. They did not have benefits like regular employees; and their level of education was insufficient to hold a good paying salary. In this phase of the fieldwork, an intensive interview with the children about their experiences in flooding was conducted. The study gathered the children's views about the nature and extent of their experiences with their fears, happy moments, and direct contact with floodwaters, as well as activities in the evacuation centers. Twenty-five children connected to *World Vision* and *Kabalikat sa Pag-unlad ng BASECO* were the respondents of the in-depth interview. Socio-demographic data on gender, age, educational attainment, and parental education and occupation were collected. Ethical standards in interacting with children were observed and consent forms from the parents of these children respondents were secured. Using visual method (Tanner & Seballos, 2012), the children were asked to recall their experiences with floods. The children highlighted the activities they experienced during community social events, where they used stickers to identify the pictures depicting their encounters.

Oral history methods were also employed to collect some accounts of the residents during each phase. They were viewed as an important part of the study as they illustrate the culture of flooding in BASECO.

RESEARCH RESULTS

Children Respondents' Sense of Space and Vulnerable Contexts

This section reports our findings about children respondents' understanding of BASECO as their "community" and their notions of "baha" (flood) in relations to two analytical dimensions: (a) childhood processes, which in Filipino refers to as "pagkabata," and (b) vulnerability contexts. Our intent here is to provide contexts of BASECO children's social space and their notions of flood to demonstrate how these notions shape their childhood experiences, which seems to impact these children's relative vulnerable conditions.

The data matrix below in table 7.1 summarizes BASECO children's concepts of community and "baha" (flood) that were axially compared with two

Table 7.1 Data Matrix of Selected BASECO Children Respondents.' Concepts of Community and Flood ("Baha") By Childhood Processes ("Pagkabata") and Vulnerability Contexts

Concept	Notions	Childhood Processes "Pagkabata"	Vulnerability Contexts
BASECO as community	*full of garbage ("maraming basura") *being flooded ("bumabaha") *disorderly ("magulo")	*place of our house ("lugar ng aming bahay") *place of our family (lugar ng aming pamilya")	*sense of safety ("ligtas na lugar") *prayer ("magdasal") *evacuation ("paglikas") *disaster ("sakuna") *house destroyed ("nasisira ang bahay") *death ("pagkamatay")
flood ("baha")	*due to typhoon and heavy rains ("dahil sa bagyo at malakas na ulan") *due to garbage ("dahil sa basura")	*place of play (lugar ng laruan") *growing-up with garbage ("paglaki kasama ang basura") *difficulty walking due to floods ("nahihirapan maglakad dahil sa bata") *drowning ("nalulunod')	*unsafe playing grounds *delay schooling/forced out of school ("natitigil sa pag-aaral/ di na nakakapag-aral") *sickness ("nagkakasakit") *death ("pagkamatay")

salient focuses of this chapter, (a) childhood processes ("pagkabata") and, (b) vulnerability contexts. Some interesting insights from this data matrix direct attention to four research insights. First, selected children respondent's notion of BASECO as their "community" suggests a relatively high level of environmental awareness. These children know and report about living amidst a community full of "basura" (garbage) that is being flooded, seemingly shaping their everyday lives. They were also aware of the level of "disorder" in BASECO community. Second, selected children respondents appear to understand "baha" (flood) as brought about by natural causes such as typhoons and heavy rains but also reported that flood was "due to garbage." This accounts for the informed level of ecological understanding of these selected BASECO children who appear to know how the phenomenon of flood in their community is a disaster that is both natural and man-made.

The third finding relates how our respondents' "pagkabata" (childhood experiences) are shaped and negotiated along marginalized contexts of slumification and the phenomenon of flood. This brings attention to how these selected BASECO children construct their notions of social space where on the one hand, they see BASECO as providing a place for their house and family, and a place where they play. Yet on the other hand, from the perspectives of these selected BASECO children, this same space directs attention to the marginality of their "growing-up" processes in conditions where they spend their childhood in the midst of garbage, flood, and reported incidences of "drowning." Fourth, the knowledge of selected BASECO children of their "vulnerability" appear to strongly litter their narratives. In articulations of BASECO as a flooded area, selected children respondents report vulnerable conditions such as a sense of safety ("ligtas na lugar"), the need for prayer ("magdasal"), and preparedness for evacuation ("paglikas"). These same children were also well-aware of the disastrous impact of flood such as their house being destroyed ("nasisira ang bahay"); the community as unsafe playing grounds; being delayed or being forced-out of school ("natitigil sa pag-aaral/ di na nakakapag-aral"); sickness ("nagkakasakit"); and worst, death ("pagkamatay"). These vulnerable situations entrench the experience of marginalization of these selected BASECO children whose childhood experiences are shaped by the disastrous flood experiences.

Selected Vignettes of "Baha" (Flood) and "Mga Bata" (Children)

This section relates selected vignettes of selected BASECO children respondents' negotiations with "baha" (flood) further narrating their vulnerable contexts. Our aim here is to demonstrate how the phenomenon of flood shapes childhood experiences and how these growing-up processes appear to impact their health, schooling, struggle for livelihood (even as children), and how the same processes offer an opportunity to *feel* and *build* a sense of family and community amidst marginality.

"Baha" (Flood) on Playing, Earning and Learning

If there is one place where coastal flooding is most vividly experienced by selected children respondents it would be at Block 1, popularly known as *Aplaya*, located along the shorefront of BASECO, fronting the Manila Bay. *Aplaya*, is the first line of defense against weather disturbances from the bay area, and geographically vulnerable to coastal flooding and tidal changes. Without exaggeration, to the bare eyes, *Aplaya* is dangerously murky due to rotting water hyacinth, all types of garbage including human and animal wastes.

Despite this danger, BASECO children (including those we interviewed) are often seen playing along *Aplaya's* beach, which over the years was tagged by residents as "tae" (feces) indicative of human and animal wastes dumped along this shore. As observed, some children play along the shore and with flood waters but are fully aware of its consequences. As articulated by Long, one of the children respondents who seemed to know its dangers narrate about fellow children's experiences saying, "Masaya sila na naliligo sa baha, pero malungkot na sila 'pag nagkasakit na" (They surely enjoy playing with flood waters, but they become sad when they get sick).

But playing was not the only reason why children linger around *Aplaya*. As reported by children respondents, some of them also collect "kalakal" (recyclable materials) like plastic cups and bottles to earn some money. These materials are sold to junk shops where a day's worth of collection could generate up to Php 43.00 equivalent to less than one dollar. Interestingly, our respondents also saw opportunities during high tides. While high tides worsen flood conditions in BASECO, this same natural occurrence brings more trash into the shore, providing more opportunities for increased collection of recyclable waste. As observed, when there is more trash, some BASECO children would often absent themselves from school to collect recyclable materials. And when asked why these children respondents choose to gather recyclables instead of attending classes, they admirably explained that their meager earnings were intended to financially help their respective families.

When it comes to BASECO children's health and welfare, "baha" (flood) poses another degree of vulnerability to them. As reported by children respondents, they are all aware of the possible health consequences of flooding. Hence, these children were observed to have learned avoiding these floodwaters as much as they could such as wearing made-up protective gears. However, even when these children are with their parents or warned by their parents to stay away from flood waters, there were occasions where some areas of BASECO, especially those near the shoreline, were severely flooded, threatening the health conditions not only of the children but the entire community. For those who were most affected, they chose to evacuate in a nearby evacuation center provided by the local government.

For our children respondents, "baha" (flood) appears to highlight these children's negotiations with acquiring basic education. School classes are usually suspended whenever severe flooding occurs, but our respondents demonstrate the relative high value they give to the schooling process and the challenges they endure during flood events. For instance, Pipay, one of our children respondents, reported taking good care of her school supplies and her pair of shoes. She recounted the many occasions where her shoes were all soaked up due to walking through flood waters, but these incidences appear to have not disheartened her from going to school. She wittingly narrated that whenever her pair of shoes got wet, she will just wash them and hang them dry ("Ipapatuyo lang po.)"

As observed in BASECO, whenever some areas are flooded, schooling children would just have to be more careful by raising their bags of school supplies, and some by taking off their pair of socks and shoes while walking through the murky flood waters. Parents, especially mothers, are usually seen helping these children but there were instances as narrated by Princess, where some younger children were offered piggy back ride by older children while others with extra money pay for a tricycle ride (a three-wheeled local transport) just to reach their schools to attend classes. Unfortunately, when rains and floods persist for days, this means an extended suspension of classes where BASECO children stay at evacuation centers or at their flooded home particularly for those who opt not to leave their houses.

"Baha" (Flood) from the Perspectives of Children Respondents

So how do BASECO children respondents make sense of "baha" (flood)? From our interviews, we observed two emerging themes. First is the "sense of danger and urgency" where children respondents reflect their high level of environmental consciousness about the phenomenon of flooding. Second is the "sense of community and solutions" where children respondents articulate how they see the value of their families and neighbors and their perceived solutions relative to their flood experiences.

The apparent "sense of danger and urgency" of children respondents is informed and shaped by their actual experiences of typhoons and heavy rains which consequently led to severe flooding complicated by uncollected garbage problem. As discussed above, these children are aware of the consequences of this disastrous situation to their community and to their lives.

For instance, our children respondents growing up in severely flooded area of BASECO, had frightening disaster memories of Typhoon Ondoy (Ketsana) in 2009, which they experienced firsthand. But these children also reported knowing about the Japan tsunami in 2011 and Typhoon Yolanda (Haiyan) in 2013. They were fully aware of the dangers of living along the coastline; they certainly knew their houses and communities were vulnerable from the disastrous occurrence of any typhoons and earthquakes in the futures. At an early age, these children knew about the urgency of action during times of dangers such as flooding, and the concept of "evacuation" which meant for this children, temporary relocation, a space for safety and security.

Interestingly, the similar experience of flooding as expressed by children respondents brings forth their witnessing of community participation as a disaster response. This "sense of participation and solutions" point seems to direct attention to the local concept of "bayanihan," which means a spirit of communal unity. In BASECO, this is prominently expressed in forms of assistance for security and safety during flood events as witnessed by children respondents. Children respondents also reported being aware of the assistance offered by government agencies, nongovernmental organizations (NGOs), people's organizations (POs), and "barangay" local officials during the times of rescue and evacuation.

As children may be seen vulnerable during the times of disaster, our children respondents nonetheless demonstrated how they, too, offered some form of assistance during these trying times. These solutions reflect their relative sense of agency despite their age and how in their perspectives, they could help mitigate the flood problem at BASECO. Children respondents first reported about "praying" to reduce the pouring of heavy rains, which meant lower probability of severe flooding. They also reported praying for the safety of their families and neighbors. But more concretely, children respondents narrated that during flood events, they also found ways to help neighbors such as building improvised bridges made of wood and stones; piggybacked fellow children attending schools; assisted elders by building makeshift walls to protect their houses from flooding; and when flood recedes, gathered recyclables not only to earn from these scraps but according to some children respondents, to help reduce uncollected garbage in their community.

DISCUSSION

Growing up in BASECO, as viewed from our selected children respondents, demonstrates on the one hand, how everyday life may be shaped amidst naturally and humanly induced disaster such as "baha" (flood) unraveling the dimensions of their vulnerable contexts. On the other, this research exercise also offered another way of listening to children's voices directing attention to their sense of awareness and their sense of agency observed during flood events.

By problematizing the concepts of "baha" (flood) in relation to "mga bata" (children), we observed how vulnerability argument in sectors such as children, may be enhanced by giving equal attention to the notion of "resilience," which underscored the narratives and voices of our children respondents. Thus, this section discusses how both literatures and findings tend to point out the interspersing discourse about children's vulnerability and resilience found in BASECO's flooded areas. In doing so, building up from previous studies on children and flood (Walker et al., 2012; Tanner and Seballos, 2012; and Muto et al., 2011) our hope is to contribute furthering the discourse of childhood and children relative to the larger issues of disaster responses, experiences, and risk management.

The first contextual feature of children's vulnerability in this BASECO case study directs attention to the issue of space, that is, children (and their families) living in areas that are dangerously susceptible to natural calamities such as typhoons and heavy rains that bring about flooding. Such spatial vulnerability is due to hazardous events complicated by another contextual feature of improper garbage disposal system where areas like BASECO are thus further entrenched to experiencing more and extended flooding exposures. The third vulnerability feature overflows to these children's spaces of "play" and "schooling." Here, as if with no choice, BASECO children live with flood waters and have found ways to transform this space into playgrounds. Aware of the dangers of flood, the same phenomenon impinges on children's schooling, which may have surely impacted their quality of learning and education.

In understanding children's vulnerability, it is interesting to note the expected sense of powerlessness these children experience during disasters and the expected sense of protection that should be given to them. As pointed out by Tanner and Seballos (2012), the more susceptible children are to hazards, the more they need protection from coercion, violence and/or physical harm, mental illness, human trafficking, and family separation, and even in acquiring quality education (Javaid, Arshad, & Khalid, 2011). However, as aptly discussed by Walker et al. (2012), upon reviewing the vast number of literatures emphasizing the vulnerability of children's agency, their findings suggest that only few studies on the voices of children about disaster show them as agents of change and that although children are perceived as important in community development these children remain voiceless.

Our intentional approach to listen to the "voices" to our BASECO children respondents, following Walker et al.'s (2012) critique, allow us to observe and witness how such vulnerability features are negotiated and mitigated by these children's sense of awareness and sense of agency relative to their flood narratives.

As articulated earlier in our research findings, it is fascinating to note how our children respondents' environmental awareness of the problems and consequences of flood at BASECO. This awareness on the "dangers" of flood, as reported, did not deter these children to transform their vulnerable area into a playground. A finding that according to Muto et al. (2011), may be alluded to the fact that these children have adjusted to a "water-based lifestyle." This means that playing in the water becomes a norm, especially for children residing near the easements and shoreline.

But while "playing" in flood water seems to reflect dispositions of childhood, our findings discovered how playing can be a means of collecting recyclables that in turn becomes a source of earnings not primarily for themselves but to assist their respective families. We see this gesture of transforming vulnerable situations of flood events into opportunities of livelihood, which in the most ideal situation would be perceived as a violation of their basic human rights to survive. Rather, in this context, we see this negotiation as a dimension of resilience shaped by the disastrous condition of flooding practicing their agency to help ease the marginality of their respective families.

Another dimension of resilience we observed in our data, is the ability of our children respondents to express their capabilities contrary to how they are labeled as "as weak, inability to form their lives, passive and pathetic" (Lein, 2009, p. 2). As reported by our respondents, during flooding season, they too, aid their fellow children, parents and elders. Their "water-based" life must have shaped their adaptation strategies.

The optimism of these children in overcoming flood is also indicative of their spirit of resilience. This sense of hopefulness is enhanced by the presence of nongovernmental organizations (NGOs) and people's organizations (POs) with local officials whom these children witness working at BASECO. These efforts are experienced by children during evacuation, and other community projects such as relief operations and medical missions.

In this context, we continue to desire learning the extent to which these community agencies empower children to take actively take part, say as volunteers, in these intervention programs? As clearly manifested in this research, selected BASECO children respondents were all so well aware of their vulnerable contexts that they creatively negotiate through their sense of agency and resilience.

CONCLUDING INSIGHT

This chapter hopefully demonstrates how the children's experiences of "baha" (flood) led to further understanding the varying vulnerable structures and conditions that shaped-up their growing-up process. It highlights these children respondents' sense of environmental awareness as well as their sense of agency in negotiating their lives as children in flooded areas like BASECO.

The chapter also describes the salience and potential of listening to children's voices as active agents in responding to the larger issues of disaster responses, experiences, and risk management. Specifically, as in the case of BASECO, our findings suggest that children have the potential to make valuable contributions to the local-based CBDRR program in terms of recognizing children as active part of building community resilience and giving these children active roles during disasters.

By rethinking children beyond their perceived vulnerability, weakness, and incapacities, a child-friendly, rights-based, empowering CBDRR program in BASECO and in other disaster-prone areas may result in healthier, meaningful, safe, and protected childhood experiences even in places where elements of marginality abound.

REFERENCES

Alejandro, R. G., Santos, V. R. S., & Yuson, A. A. (2006). *Manila Bay: The Cross-roads of Asia*. Philippines: Reynaldo G. Alejandro & Unilever Philippines, Inc.

Burningham, K., Fielding, J., & Thrush, D. (2008). It'll never happen to me': understanding public awareness of local flood risk. *Disasters, 32*(2), 216–238. doi: 10.1111/j.1467-7717.2007.01036.x

Coastal Land use in the Manila Bay—Types and classification of coastal land use in the centre and outer sphere of influence of a metropolis, 48 Cong. Rec. 76+ § 76 (1998).

Creswell, J. (2009). *Research Design: Qualitative, Quantitative, and Mixed Methods Approaches* (3rd ed.). United States of America: SAGE Publications.

Dabrowska, E., & Wismer, S. K. (2010). Inclusivity matters: Perceptions of children's health and environmental risk including Old Order Mennonites from Ontario, Canada. *Health, Risk & Society, 12*(2), 169–188. doi: 10.1080/13698571003632445.

Donner, W., & Rodriguez, H. (2008). Population composition, migration and inequality: The influence of demographic changes on disaster risk and vulnerability. *Social Forces*, *87*(2), 1089–1114.

Fatti, C. E., & Patel, Z. (2013). Perceptions and responses to urban flood risk: Implications for climate governance in the South. *Applied Geography, 36*(0), 13–22. doi: http://dx.doi.org/10.1016/j. apgeog. 2012.0 6.011.

Gaillard, JC. (2011). *People's Response to Disasters: Vulnerability, Capacities, and Resilience in the Philippine Context*. Angeles City, Pampanga: Center for Kapampangan Studies, Holy Angel University.

Guevara, Marita Concepcion Castro, Mayor, Ana Mariia Felliisa Gallang, & Racelis, Mary. (2009). *The Philippine Pilot Study of the Child Friendly Community Participatory Assessment Tools*. Quezon City, Philippines: Childwatch International

Research Network, United Nations Children's Fund—Innocenti Research Centre, Children's Environments Research Group, Bernard van Leer Foundation.

Huang, Y., Li, F., Bai, X., & Cui, S. (2012). Comparing vulnerability of coastal communities to land use change: Analytical framework and a case study in China. *Environmental Science & Policy*, 23, 133–143. doi:10.1016/j.envsci.2012.06.017.

International Save the Children Alliance. (2008). *In the Face of Disaster: Children and Climate Change*. London, UK: International Save the Children Alliance.

Javaid, Z., A., M., & Khalid, A. (2011). Child protection in disaster management in South Asia: A case study of Pakistan. *South Asian Studies (1026–678X), 26*(1), 191–202.

Kazmierczak, A., & Cavan, G. (2011). Surface water flooding risk to urban communities: Analysis of vulnerability, hazard and exposure. *Landscape and Urban Planning, 103*(2), 185–197.

Klein, R. J., & Nicholls, R. (2005). Climate change and coastal management on Europe's coast. In J. Vermaat, L. Bouwer, K. Turner, & W. Salomons (Eds.), *Managing European Coasts: Past, present and future* (pp. 199–226). Berlin, Germany: Springer, Berlin, Heidelberg. https://doi.org/10.1007/3-540-27150-3_11.

Lane, Kathryn, Charles-Guzman, Kizzy, Wheeler, Katherine, Abid, Zaynah, Graber, Nathan, & Matte, Thomas. (2013). Health effects of coastal storms and flooding in urban areas: A review and vulnerability assessment. *Journal of Environmental and Public Health, 2013*.

Lawler, Jill, & Patel, Mahesh. (2012). Exploring children's vulnerability to climate change and their role in advancing climate change adaptation in East Asia and the Pacific. *Environmental Development, 3*(0), 123–136. doi: http://dx.doi.org/10.1016/j.envdev.2012.04.001.

Lein, H. (2009). The poorest and most vulnerable? On hazards, livelihoods and labelling of riverine communities in Bangladesh. *Singapore Journal of Tropical Geography*, 30(1), 98-113. https://doi.org/10.1111/j.1467-9493.2008.00357.x.

Linnekamp, F., Koedam, A., & Baud, I. S. A. (2011). Household vulnerability to climate change: Examining perceptions of households of flood risks in Georgetown and Paramaribo. *Habitat International, 35*(3), 447–456. doi: http://dx.doi.org/10.1016/j.habitatint.2010.12.003.

Project Management Office, Manila Bay Environmental Management Project (MBEMP). (2001). *Manila Bay coastal strategy*. Manila, Philippines: Author.

Marfai, M., & Hizbaron, D. R. (2011). Community's adaptive capacity due to coastal flooding in Semarang coastal city. Annals of the University of Oradea – Geography Series, 21, 209–221.

Martin, M. (2010). Child participation in disaster risk reduction: The case of flood-affected children in Bangladesh. *Third World Quarterly, 31*(8), 1357–1375. doi: 10.1080/01436597.2010.541086.

Morrow, B. H. (1999). Identifying and mapping community vulnerability. *Disasters, 23*(1), 1.

Muto, M., Moroshita, K., & Syson, L. (2011). Impacts of climate change upon Asian coastal areas: The case of Metro Manila. Retrieved from https://www.jica.go.jp/jica-ri/publication/other/jrft3q0000002aif-att/Impacts_of_Climate_Change_to_Asian_Coastal_Areas_The_Case_of_Metro_Manila.pdf.

New York University Child Study Center. (2006). *Caring for Kids After Trauma, Disaster and Death: A Guide for Parents and Professionals* (2nd ed.). United States of America: New York University.

Peek, L. (2008). Children and disasters: Understanding vulnerability, developing capacities, and promoting resilience—An introduction. *Children, Youth and Environment, 18*(1), 1–29.

Peek, L., & Stough, L. M. (2010). Children With Disabilities in the Context of Disaster: A Social Vulnerability Perspective. *Child Development, 81*(4), 1260–1270. doi: 10.1111/j.1467-8624.2010.01466.x

Racelis, Mary, & Aguirre, Angela Desiree M. (2005). *Making Philippine Cities Child Friendly: Voices of Children in Poor Communities.* Quezon City, Philippines: Institute of Philippine Culture, Ateneo de Manila University.

Seballos, F., Tanner, T., Tarazona, M., & Gallegos, J. (2011). *Children and disasters: Understanding impact and enabling agency.* Retrieved from http://www.childreninachangingclimate.org/uploads/6/3/1/1/63116409/impacts_and_agency_final.pdf.

Tanner, Thomas, & Seballos, Frances. (2012). Action Research with Children: Lessons from Tackling Disasters and Climate Change*. *IDS Bulletin, 43*(3), 59–70. doi: 10.1111/j.1759-5436.2012.00323.x.

Tapsell, S., McCarthy, S., Faulkner, H., & Alexander, M. (2010). *Social Vulnerability to Natural Hazards.* London: CapHAz-Net WP4 Report, Flood Hazards Research Center-FHRC.

United Nations Children's Fund (UNICEF). (2012). The State of the World's Children 2012: Children in an Urban World. www.unicef.org/sowc2012: United Nations Children's Fund (UNICEF).

United Nations University. (2013). *From Social Vulnerability to Resilience: Measuring Progress Towards Disaster Risk Reduction.* Retrieved from United Nations University Institute for Environment and Human Security: SOURCE.

Walker, Marion, Whittle, Rebecca, Medd, Will, Burningham, Kate, Moran-Ellis, Jo, & Tapsell, Sue. (2012). 'It came up to here': Learning from children's flood narratives. *Children's Geographies, 10*(2), 135–150. doi: 10.1080/14733285.2012.667916.

Wee, B. S., & Anthamatten, P. (2014). Using photography to visualize children's culture of play: A socio-spatial perspective. *Geographical Review, 104*(1), 87–100. doi:10.1111/j.1931-0846.2014.12006.x.

Wisner, B., Gaillard, J.C., & Kelman, I. (2012). Framing disaster: Theories and stories seeking to understand hazards, vulnerability and risk. In B. Wisner, J. C. Gaillard, & I. Kelman (Eds.), *The Routledge Handbook of Hazards and Disaster Risk Reduction* (pp. 18–34). London: Routledge.

Zoleta-Nantes, Doracie B. (2000). Flood hazards in Metro Manila: Recognizing commonalities, differences, and courses of action. *Social Science Diliman, 1*(1), 60–105.

Zoleta-Nantes, Doracie B. (2002). Differential impacts of flood hazards among the street children, the urban poor and residents of wealthy neighborhoods in Metro Manila, Philippines. *Mitigation & Adaptation Strategies for Global Change, 7*(3), 239.

Zou, Lele & Thomalla, Frank (2008). *The Causes of Social Vulnerability to Coastal Hazards in Southeast Asia.* Stockholm Environmental Institute.

Chapter 8

Drought, Food Insecurity, and Cultures of Hunger in the Philippines

Will Smith

INTRODUCTION

Famine, as with other forms of disaster, has been well-examined as the prod-uct of social, rather than simply environmental, forces. However, despite a long-standing emphasis by critical scholars on the socially produced nature of food insecurity resulting from either historical-structural issues of colo-nialism and development (e.g., Watts 1983; Davis 2002) or the household politics of food access (e.g., Dettwelyer 1993), issues of malnutrition remain defined and understood in primarily biological terms by national governments and international development and aid organizations. Conceptual models of hunger deployed by international developmental agencies, such as the United Nation's Food and Agriculture Organization, remain dominated by nationally focused arithmetic. These methodologies subtract the total number of calories required by a population from the net food production in that country (Ilcan and Phillips 2006). As Edkins (2000, 22) notes, "modern approaches regard famine as a question of food and generally assume an unproblematic and uncomplicated notion of food. Food is 'fuel for the human machine': what is important is its caloric and nutritional value. Questions of nutritional status and minimum needs are addressed and malnutrition is identified." The result is a regime of caloric-fungibility in which all foods are broken down into equally exchangeable units of potential food energy. While this focus is a justifiably pragmatic response aimed at optimizing human survival in the face of extreme circumstances and limited economic resources, it does occlude the ways in which malnutrition and food shortage are always more than biomedi-cal in nature. Though often construed as a basic human universal, "hunger" and the need for food are social phenomena shaped not only by metabolic processes but culturally specific understandings of well-being, the body, and nutrition (Young 1986; De Boeck 1994). Despite a widespread recognition of cross-cultural "food preferences" in the food security literature (Pinstrup-Andersen 2009), the cultural construction of hunger and its connection to human health rarely meaningfully features in the study of food shortage as a social phenomenon (Pottier 1999, 14). While there is also an emerging literature that considers what an indigenous food sovereignty might look like, emphasizing the de-colonizing potential of indigenous agroecological food systems in formulating alternatives to industrial neoliberal food production (Grey and Patel 2015), this critique is rarely deployed to critically reevaluate what is actually *meant* by hunger, shortage, or famine or how these dominant formulations shape governmental interventions (cf. Scheper-Hughes 1988). In this chapter, I point to some of the limitations of biomedical perspectives of nutrition and the possibilities of a more culturally informed approach to food security policies by focusing on the relationship between hunger and rice in the Philippines.

Drawing on ethnographic fieldwork and oral histories generated with Pala'wan people on the Philippine island of Palawan, I consider the sometimes ambiguous boundaries between famine, understood in the biological sciences in terms of deficiencies in specific nutrients and overall caloric intake, and what might be considered a social famine; the absence of food or foods necessary for maintaining a much wider culturally defined sense of well-being. This encompasses ways in which particular kinds of food are viewed as essential to maintain particular social relations, forms of internal or cosmological balance, among other imperatives poorly captured by global development policies. In particular, and less well considered even within the anthropological literature in terms of food security, is how the varied meanings of food also connect—often implicitly—to culturally specific understandings of famine and food shortage (de Boeck 1994, 258). The case study material for this chapter focuses on the production and value of rice in an indigenous Pala'wan community in the south of Palawan Island. For many indigenous people, the social and cultural values of rice mean that it is a vital, though often unobtainable, element of daily diets in ways that are not captured by biomedical perspectives on nutrition. While rice is often uncritically assumed to be a naturalized part of local diets and farming landscapes, the agricultural history of the archipelago suggests that the prevalence of rice is a recent phenomenon informed by political imperatives and social values rather than an adaptive inevitability. I argue that the intangible values surrounding rice remain a powerful mediating force in experiences and responses of food shortage. In making this argument, I explore indigenous values of rice, and the significance of these values for both everyday livelihood decision making and responses to disaster events, such as the impact of the 1997/8 El Niño drought on Palawan Island.

RICE HISTORIES IN SOUTHEAST ASIA

Food scarcity and insecurity, often seen as a symptom of poverty, are a recurring feature of life for many households in the Philippines (e.g., Kerkvliet 1990, 67–68; Alejandria, this volume). While reasons for food insecurity are often complex and locally specific, systematic crop failure in local agricultural systems has historically been a source of chronic food shortages in urban and rural areas for much of the archipelago's history, frequently resulting in widespread morbidity and mortality. The relative variability and intensity of climatic conditions, in combination with other pressures on agricultural production, are often identified as a key driver of crop failure and food insecurity (Lansigan 2000). Cyclonic activity, for example, often diminishes agricultural production. Landslides and strong winds that arise from cyclonic activity directly damage crops, in addition to disrupting food distribution infrastructure. The impacts of these events, while intense, are often relatively localized to areas facing the typhoon's path. In contrast, most instances of food insecurity are associated with cyclical El Niño droughts which tend to impact large portions of Southeast Asia and much of the Philippine archipelago (Bankoff 2003; Warren 2018). The extended dry seasons associated with El Niño events have a dramatic impact on rice yields throughout the nation, especially in areas where irrigation infrastructure remains limited (Dawe et al. 2009). Like all disasters, these experiences of food insecurity are of both natural and social origin. For example, culpability for nineteenth-century famines in the Philippines could equally be located in colonial policies that encouraged commodity cropping at the expense of subsistence crops as in El Niño dynamics (see McLennan 1982; Doeppers 2016). Contemporary experiences of food insecurity and hunger are similarly rooted in the highly uneven ownership of land and neoliberal agricultural policies that leaves tenant farmers vulnerable to environmental change (McAfee 1985; Borras Jr 2007).

However, while the political origins of food crises are the subject of sustained investigation, there has been little examination of the ways in which local understandings of nutrition and hunger shapes perceptions and experiences of famine, national policies of food security, and local agricultural decision making. The agricultural choices of rural producers are frequently viewed as driven by the desire to maximize yield, a strategic response to conditions of oppression or marginalization or the unmoving demands of tradition. However, as Virginia Nazarea (1995) has pointed out in her detailed examination of rice farmers in Laguna, small-holder agricultural decision making is not just made on the basis of either cold agronomic efficiency or in response to political conditions of marginality, but also the lively desire for taste and flavor. As such, there is "need to reorient our perspective on farmers to admit a view of them as consumers rather than just as producers and to take the gastronomic preferences into account" (Nazarea 1995, 185). In recognizing the ways in which flavor is a powerful motivator for rural households, I suggest that the desire for rice in the Philippines is largely naturalized in both national media and international aid and development policy, meaning that the political origins and cultural significance of rice preferences remains under-interrogated in the analysis of food shortages. As such, perennial national concerns surrounding food security policies in the Philippines focus almost exclusively on the production of rice; the question of achieving food security, posed frequently by media commentators and government officials as "why does the Philippines import rice?" (Davidson 2016), is answered by gesturing to contemporary technical and political failures and dysfunction rather than a reexamination of the nation's overwhelming preferences for rice.

Rice, one of the world's most popular foods, is a crop that readily embodies tensions between adaptive biological utility, national symbolism, political-economic strategy and cultural meanings of nutrition (e.g., Ohnuki-Tierney 1994). The prevalence of rice in global diets is often explained in utilitarian terms. Under ideal climatic conditions and with intensive capital and labor inputs, irrigated rice provides a high yield per land unit in river deltas and areas of Southeast Asia with high annual rainfall (Hutterer 1983, 175). However, despite its many advantages, rice production in both irrigated and rain-fed forms is relatively labor and capital intensive when contrasted to the production of alternative crops (Boomgaard 2003, 58), requiring laborious field maintenance, terracing, and systems of transplanting. Compared to the cultivation of tubers, corn, or even other starchy grains, rice farming systems are highly sensitive to variations in rainfall, changing light conditions and are vulnerable to a broader range of pests. In many areas of Southeast Asia, the spread and popularity of rice is therefore poorly accounted for by arguments for ecological adaptiveness (Barton 2012). Tellingly, Michael Dove has noted that his swiddening Kantu' interlocutors on Borneo "also portray rice as greedy" suggesting that "such groups also possess some critical awareness of the downsides of grain cultivation" (Dove 1999).

In terms of biomedical calculations of nutrition, rice is less than an optimal choice even when compared to similar cereal options such maize. Diets high in processed rice have long been a point of public health concern (Juliano 1983). The infamous prevalence of thiamine deficiency, or beri-beri, in Southeast Asia during the nineteenth century is attributed to the rise of mechanized rice milling and conjoined dominance of rice as a staple food crop for urban dwellers. Rice-dominated diets in the region remain nutrient deficient, and this ongoing concern has sparked intense interest in the genetic fortification of rice to counter widespread vitamin deficiencies that arise from dependency on processed white rice. For consumers and farmers throughout Southeast Asia, the centrality of rice in everyday diets (both idealized and achieved) is instead frequently explained in reference to its superior taste, cosmological significance and as a formative component human personhood (e.g., Dove 1999; Carsten 1995, Boomgaard 2003; Volkman 1985; Janowski and Kerlogue 2007). In surveying the spread of rice throughout the region, Richard O'Connor (1995, 186) notes that "rice advances across Southeast Asia as if it were addictive. Farmers slight root and tree crop staples to grow this better liked and more prestigious crop . . . all of this argues for treating wet rice as a complex that has a life of its own, not just a crop that spreads by rational calculation."

However, this "agency" of rice in agricultural histories should also be tempered by the archaeological and ethno-historical evidence that points to a relatively recent and political origin of rice monoculture in Southeast Asian agriculture to the exclusion of root crops only within the last few hundred years. This shift toward a diet made up largely of rice is often bound up with histories in which colonial governments encouraged rice production as a taxable good cultivated by fixed, and therefore governable, subjects (Scott 2009). In colonial Malaysia, for example, Ronald Hill (2012, 56) has characterized the growing dominance of rice cultivation and trade as the "child of imperial interests" where growing populations in British Southeast Asian possessions created enormous demand for food imports and stimulated a market for easily transportable rice crops. Similarly, in the Philippines, early colonial accounts make nlimited reference to wet-rice cultivation that can be, instead, viewed as a response to colonial economic policy (Newson 2009, 184)[1]. The Spanish encomienda system, which granted land and bonded native labor to loyal Spanish subjects, stimulated the production of wet-rice agriculture alongside other commodity crops as an easily extractable form of tribute (Anderson 1976; Constantino and Constantino 1975, 124). The current dominance of rice, especially in insular Southeast Asia, is therefore held in tension between the biophysical difficulties of its cultivation, its intrinsic properties that define its desirability and colonial histories which have propelled the crop to near universal dominance.

RICE AND THE SOCIAL CONSTRUCTION OF MALNUTRITION IN THE PHILIPPINES

Given the widespread, though recent, importance placed on rice consumption within diverse cultural worlds, it is unsurprising that it is a food closely connected to localized notions of health, the body and nutrition. In the Philippines, the relative difficulty and intensity of irrigated rice production has meant that the transformation of rice from occasional luxury to an everyday necessity has been relatively recent, even among local elites. Until the nineteenth and twentieth centuries the majority of rice was produced through swidden agriculture and was only a relatively minor, though highly valued, component of diets rich in tubers and other non-rice cereals (Junker 1999, 234). In contemporary Philippine society, there remains a rigid hierarchy of carbohydrate preference with rice at the apex (with few regional exceptions). In poorer households, where rice cannot be parboiled and served as a discrete element of a meal along with a flavor-rich viand or *ulam*, it is often boiled into a rice porridge or mixed with other grains, such as corn. Despite a recent re-broadening of urban Filipino diets, the inability to procure rice for household consumption is widely seen as a marker of extreme poverty and deprivation or associated with media reports of famine. In addition to the weighty economic symbolism of rice, the cereal is an essential component of everyday folk-nutrition that cuts across class distinctions (e.g., Law 2001, 275). Not only are meals frequently seen as incomplete without rice, but human beings are seen to require rice for optimal bodily functioning. For example, only rice can provide the adequate sustenance for extensive periods of labor, and other foods are not seen to be able to satiate appetite to the same degree[2] (Aguilar 2005).

Outside of the urban core in rural and indigenous communities, rice often assumes an even larger role, not only in diets, but in agricultural practices mediating in social relations and spirituality. For example, Brosius (1988, 98) suggests that for the Ifugao rice is a "central cultural idiom" around which social differentiation, kinship and ritual practice are organized. Correspondingly, rice occupies a central role in locally specific understandings of diet and well-being. Kwiatkowsk (1998) also describes that rice is key substance in the regulation of emic notions of health. The Ifugao term *feter*, often glossed as famine, may refer to both time of "absolutely no food" and the diminishment of rice stocks by supernatural forces (Kwiatkowski 1998, 157). This significance of rice in ritual, social relations and understandings of well-being is found throughout the archipelago in ethnographic accounts (Jocano 1968; Rosaldo 1981; Gibson 1986; Minter 2010), and is a prominent feature of many indigenous communities on Palawan Island (Fox 1954).

RICE IN PALA'WAN LIVES AND LIVELIHOODS

The Pala'wan are an ethno-linguistic group who reside primarily on state-owned forestlands in the river valleys of southern Palawan Island. Though there is ongoing debate over the scope and putative linear nature agrarian changes in rural Southeast Asia (Dressler and Pulhin 2010), Pala'wan people are often identified as experiencing a "transition" from swidden agriculture, a rotational form of agricultural production in which sections of forest are annually felled and burned, toward more sedentary and intensive forms of agricultural production such as irrigated paddy rice. In barangay Inogbong, located in the municipality of Bataraza, the lives of approximately 500 Pala'wan who reside in the state-owned uplands and their livelihood histories have been shaped by experiences of exchange, cooperation, and conflict with colonial settler authorities and migrant lowlanders. Early written accounts from explorers and colonial officials, alongside indigenous oral histories, emphasize dominion of Tausug datus from the Sulu Sultanate over the coastal regions of southern Palawan for much of the nineteenth and early twentieth centuries (Macdonald 2007, 12–15). This exclusion of indigenous Pala'wan people from coastal regions positioned the Tausug as intermediaries in the forest product trade with China who could extract trade goods and swidden rice from upland households. Following World War II and the establishment of postcolonial national government, Christian settlers from the elsewhere in the Philippines began to formally acquire land titles and legally dispossess Pala'wan households from much of the coastal plain. As indigenous households were relegated to the state-owned uplands, they were increasingly targeted by forest policy which viewed swidden agriculture, or *kaingin*, as a destructive waste of state resources. As discussed elsewhere (Smith and Dressler 2017), swidden agriculture has indeed been constrained in Inobong through a range of punitive measures and a reframing of environmental subjectivities over the course of decades.

However, in addition to these structural constraints on production, I also suggest that the desire for rice is another important yet under-considered aspect in explaining agricultural decision making. Across indigenous communities on the island, rice is considered a divine food originating in human sacrifice, which grants it a spiritual potency unmatched by other substances (with the partial exception of honey) (e.g., Novellino 2011). As such, rice is a prominent part of Pala'wan spirituality, and regularly features in mythology and ritual practice in Inogbong. Similarly, the fulfillment of many mundane and extraordinary obligations is dependent on the exchange or production of rice. Shortages of rice, therefore, have profound cosmological implications. While I elsewhere also argue that the meanings attached to rice and the sociality of swidden agriculture may help explain ongoing vitality of "customary" agricultural practices (Dressler et al 2018), rice is also an important feature of Pala'wan notions of hunger and nutrition that warrants closer investigation as a motivator of "economic" behavior.

Macdonald (2007, 45) suggests that Pala'wan conceptions of hunger are driven by an idealized triadic relationship between hunger (*urap*), appetite (*sublek*), and taste (*rasa*). The flavorful components of meals which can satisfy appetite and taste are diverse and may come in the form of simply prepared vegetables (aubergines, edible greens, onion, among others), small amounts of fish bartered from seaside communities or the rare consumption of hunted meats. In contrast, hunger can only truly be satiated through the consumption of rice and is an ideal feature of each meal. While Pala'wan swiddens are intercropped with a range of crops such as cassava, sweet potato, taro, millet and sorghum (in addition to a range of vegetables), these staples are considered vastly inferior in terms of their flavor and ability to sustain optimal human well-being. During fieldwork, my personal prefer-ence for common starchy substitutes such as boiled plantains or grated and baked cassava in place of rice was treated with a combination of dismay and mirth.

For most indigenous households, intercropped swidden fields can provide adequate caloric intake and a wide diversity of fruits, vegetables, and starches. Hunger, in the biomedical sense of caloric deficiency, is rare—though protein is clearly a rarity and diets are becoming increasingly less diverse as a result of transitions away from swidden. Rice is central feature of all swidden fields, and most households will plant between three and ten varieties of upland rice. This diversity is sometimes explained as a risk mitigation strategy, though just as often Pala'wan will emphasize the desire for a range of flavors and textures specific to certain varieties. The texture and color of glutinous rice varieties also have specialized ritual application. However, contemporary Pala'wan swidden fields are not productive enough to fulfill aspirations of consuming rice at each meal. As elsewhere in the Philippines, despite the value of rice it is unlikely that the cereal has ever constituted the primary base of subsistence in indigenous swidden systems, a position supported by com-parative ethnographic work with indigenous Pala'wan and Tagbanua peoples. Macdonald (2007, 36) has noted that "although highlanders grow upland dry rice and emphatically claim to be rice agriculturists, in fact they are dependent on tubers and root crops, particularly cassava." Neither is this necessarily a recent state of affairs. As late as the early 1900s, Manuel Hugo Venturello, a prominent Spanish-Filipino politician on Palawan Island, (1907, 514) noted that rice was largely a luxury for both Filipino settlers and indigenous peoples on Palawan Island: "The harvests of rice, though of a most excellent quality, are scarcely sufficient to satisfy the most urgent necessities of the poor and miserable inhabitants, who in the majority of cases nourish themselves with various tubers found in the woods, or planted by the natives." Like other indigenous groups on the island, swiddens in Inogbong may only provide for one or two months of regular rice consumption each year and Pala'wan diets are heavily supplemented by cassava, plantains, corn, and other more pro-ductive crops (Warner 1979, 73). As a result, while hunger—also rendered in conversation with non-Pala'wan in Tagalog as *gutom*—can refer to the chronic lack of food in general it more frequently refers the absence of rice from one's diet (see also Revel 1990, 66).

Avoiding this culturally framed definition of hunger is an important component of livelihood decision making. For example, in household surveys conducted over 2011–2012, respondents routinely identified that the primary reasons for engaging in waged labor in lowland migrant rice fields, an increasingly central component of indigenous livelihood strategies, was to purchase rice for household consumption, followed by school fees and clothing. Histories of indigenous peoples on Palawan also repeatedly point to the desire and willingness to go into large amounts of debt for rice as a key reason for the entry of indigenous peoples into commodity chains on extremely unfavorable terms—often in ways that defy explanations grounded purely in terms of caloric returns. For example, James Eder (1978) has suggested that during the 1970s indigenous Batak people on Palawan Island often forwent collecting and processing wild tubers for "arduous" participation in collecting almaciga (manila copal) for sale, despite lower caloric returns for effort expended. Similarly, in Inogbong, shifts away from swidden agriculture to alternative livelihoods, such as irrigated paddy rice production or commercial agroforestry, are framed in terms of granting a greater supply of rice for household consumption. While I do not suggest that this is the sole motivating factor in shaping agrarian trajectories, there is clearly more scope in the analysis of livelihood decision making for the role of food preferences, particularly in seeking to understanding extraordinary situations of food insecurity.

FOOD PROVISIONING, HUNGER, AND THE EL NIÑO DROUGHT EVENTS

I want to here briefly turn to Pala'wan people's experiences of drought during the 1997/8 El Niño event and the ways in which indigenous understandings of rice can complicate how hunger is understood in development practice. The El Niño-Southern Oscillation (ENSO) phenomenon refers to the intra-decadal shifting of Pacific sea-surface temperatures and related atmospheric disturbances. In Southeast Asia, the El Niño phase of ENSO dynamics, in which warm water off the coast of South America produces an anomalous pressure differential across the Pacific Ocean, has long been associated with diminished monsoonal rainfall activity and sustained drought events. While the El Niño phase occurs cyclically, appearing at irregular intervals each decade, the drivers of the relative intensity of each El Niño event is poorly understood, meaning that there is a high degree of uncertainty surrounding the impact of El Niño events on farming landscapes. Compounded by highly uneven agrarian political-economies, unpredictably intense El Niño events have historically been a key driver of food insecurity and famine events in the Philippines from the colonial period to the present (McLennan 1982). Though each warming event brings a measure of hardship for farming households, the most severe drought in the region was the 1997/8 El Niño event. The sustained lack of rain during 1997, lasting into the subsequent monsoonal period, resultantly produced a marked decline in Philippine rice production—exacerbating existing dependency on imported rice from elsewhere in the region to provide for domestic consumption. Though urban centers were largely shielded from both food and water insecurity through preferential important and domestic allocation policies (Dawe et al 2009, 294, 301), communities in the rural peripheries of the archipelago suffered from sustained food insecurity and economic distress as the result of widespread crop failures (Bankoff 2003).

In Inogbong, the 1997/8 El Niño was often explained, like contemporary climatic variation, as the product of incestuous relationships in the community (Smith 2018). While drought is understood as a recurring feature of upland life, the 1997/8 event is recalled as a unique and devastating experience within oral histories generated in Inogbong with Pala'wan people. As elsewhere in the archipelago, the failure of the 1997 monsoonal rains to arrive had a dramatic impact on agricultural production among Pala'wan households in the upland of the barangay. According to oral histories, swidden plots— the primary source of subsistence for most indigenous households—experienced an almost complete crop failure. Usually hardy tubers, such as cassava, withered alongside more sensitive rice and corn seedlings. In addition to the impact on household agricultural production, the severe length of the drought impacted income-generating activities that could have been used to purchase food such as cash-cropping and waged labor in migrant fields. How, then, did households secure food? In some cases, Pala'wan households reported leveraging a moral economy of food exchange with their relatives in the deep forest interior where the impact of the drought was less acute. However, the most commonly described subsistence strategy was foraging or hunting for forest foods. These foods included wild tubers, fruit crops, varied sources of sago and to a lesser extent wild grains, vegetables and otherwise unpalatable foods such as banana heart or bat. One key tuber was *Dioscorea hispida* (*kedut*), which requires extensive processing in order to remove excessive and poisonous alkaloids. Elsewhere in the Philippines, the improper preparation of such wild tubers was associated with widely reported poisonings (Bankoff 2003, 104). In recalling the hardships experienced during the period, one indigenous leader recalled the significant risk and effort involved in collecting enough kedut;

> by the grace of God we survived that hardship. We just had to be patient and resourceful. Just like what I've told my nephew Jeeboy; just have patience. And

even when the rains come [again], he still went to the mountain to get something to eat . . . He's getting the kedut, I will just tell you his experience. It was raining one day when he decide to collect kedut in the mountain and when they crossed the river, the water's current is strong and in both his hands he is holding the sack with kedut and the other is holding an ipil tree [*Intsia bijuga*]. I told him you are risking your life if you do that, but lucky for him he is still alive.

Descriptions of hunger during this period do not necessarily mean a complete absence of food but point to a reconfigured economy of risk and unpleasantness that surround securing and eating undesirable foods. For example, in reflecting on her own experiences with the drought, a Pala'wan women described hunger (gutom) and difficulty (hirap) not in terms of the complete absence of food but the reliance unpleasant or undesirable combinations, as well as the laborious processing involved in making kedut edible:

In my own experience I really had a hard time because I just gave birth to my son and what I ate was banana hearts (ubod ng saging), and then the unripe mango (mampalang) with fish . . . there is fish in the pond and then we also sometimes catch bats and then fish. . . . We can also get the sarawak [a root crop] but not good quality because it is hard, and also the poisonous kedut. We also get it, provided that you know how to prepare it because if you don't know it might kill you . . . You must remove the skin and then it must be sliced very thinly and then soak it in water for two nights. Two nights in the stagnant water and then two nights in flowing water, so four nights before you can cook it.

In a Pala'wan man's account, he similarly lingers on the unpalatable foods that were consumed during this period. Common to many explanations of hunger during this time, being "hungry" and "having no food" is equated with subsisting on unpleasant foods:

I don't know why it happened, but all I can remember is that all the people were hungry because no food was available. Even the banana and coconut did not bear fruit. And my children only ate mango for breakfast, lunch and dinner. . . . No other food was available, sometimes the heart of the banana tree.

At the same time, the desire for rice was a key motivator for seeking out cash income. What little income could be gleaned from the diminished amount of labor involved in paddy rice production and participating in illegal logging activities was used to purchase "smelly" National Food Authority relief rice in the lowlands. The perceived poor quality and malodorous smell of relief rice, distributed by the National Food Authority, is a widespread feature of oral histories from this period in Inogbong. The distress experienced from consuming less than ideal rice was experienced throughout the Philippines in both urban and rural communities during 1997/8 (Aguilar 2005).

DISCUSSION AND CONCLUSION

Despite the widespread recognition that famine and food insecurity are the product of social rather than simply natural forces, the role of "culture" in shaping local and international perspectives on seemingly fundamental concepts in the food security literature ("basic needs") remains under examined. Though in broad terms national and international relief efforts take into account varying geographic food preferences, "sensitivity to cultural perspectives on food requires more than the simplistic 'people x enjoy food y'" (Pottier 1999, 16). Rather than a powerful explanatory tool that could guide disaster relief and help reevaluate developmental livelihood interventions, the expansion of food security definitions during the 1990s to include the cultural preferences for food has often been treated as needlessly obfuscating to the "real business" of preventing hunger (e.g., Pinstrup-Andersen 2009, 6). In contrast, ethnographic research has suggested that questioning the social construction of taste, hunger, and nutrition—for agricultural communities, relief organizations and states that plan food security policies—can be central to explaining and preventing famine as a more broadly understood phenomenon (Romanoff and Lynam 1991, 39; Shipton 1990, 369–370)

In advocating for a more nuanced exploration of hunger in understanding food insecurity, this chapter has focused on the social and cultural values of rice in the Philippines. Rice is closely linked in the Western imagination to the diets of diverse Asian communities, and is deemed a naturalized part of household livelihoods and agricultural landscapes. As I have described on Palawan Island, questioning this naturalization in any particular place can unearth contingent social and political histories of food and health that defy simplistic people-place connections regarding agricultural production and consumption. To explore these complexities, I have examined the ways in which rice forms part of idealized diets among indigenous Pala'wan households in the barangay of Inogbong on Palawan Island.

In reflecting on Pala'wan experiences with diverse forms of hunger, I make two points; first, notions of food security, and related concepts rooted primarily in Western biomedical perspectives with highly reductive understandings of food preferences, often map poorly on local realities. Pala'wan experiences in 1997/8, in addition to the annual or daily periods in which rice is absent from household diets, demonstrate some of the complexities in deploying the notion of food security as a policy tool. Whatever value the rhetoric of food security might have in guiding policy is therefore dependent on first translating complex local notions of food and health. Secondly, descriptions of livelihood change and coping strategies deployed in times of crisis in Inogbong suggest that local perceptions of food are important in understanding agrarian histories and long-term strategic responses to drought. In studies of peasant societies, food preferences are often assumed to be immutable, yet as discussed here the recent orientation of Southeast Asian agriculture toward rice production and daily rice consumption can be viewed as an example of the power of flavor on a sustained and grand scale—albeit infused by histories of colonial extraction and commodification. For Pala'wan people, I suggest that the ideal of consuming rice with each meal is an important part of household decision making, both during disasters and in everyday livelihood planning.

NOTES

1. Indeed, the antiquity of the famed Ifugao rice terraces has recently come under debate, further highlighting the recentness of what are now deemed a fundamental feature of rural Philippine landscapes (Acabado 2009).

2. In contrast, American colonial officials saw rice as a deficient foodstuff unfit for human consumption. As a result, public health campaigns during the early twentieth century worked to replace rice in Filipino diets with corn and other American imports (Ventura 2015).

REFERENCES

Acabado, S. (2009). A Bayesian approach to dating agricultural terraces: a case from the Philippines. *Antiquity*, 83(321), 801–814.

Aguilar Jr, F. V. (2005). *Rice in the Filipino diet and culture*. Discussion Paper Series No. 2005–15. Philippine Institute of Development Studies, Makati.

Anderson, E. (1976). The encomienda in early Philippine colonial history. *Asian Stud*, *14*(1), 25–36.

Bankoff, G. (2003). *Cultures of Disaster; Society and Natural Hazard in the Philippines*. Routledge Curzon, London

Barton, H. (2012). The reversed fortunes of sago and rice, Oryza sativa, in the rainforests of Sarawak, Borneo. *Quaternary International*, 249, 96–104.

Boomgaard, P. (2003). In the shadow of rice: Roots and tubers in Indonesian history, 1500–1950. *Agricultural history*, 582–610.

Borras, S. (2007). 'Free market', export-led development strategy and its impact on rural livelihoods, poverty and inequality: The Philippine experience seen from a Southeast Asian perspective. *Review of International Political Economy*, 14(1), 143.

Brosius, J. P. (1988). Significance and social being in Ifugao agricultural production. *Ethnology*, 27(1), 97–110.

Carsten, J. (1995). The substance of kinship and the heat of the hearth: feeding, personhood, and relatedness among Malays in Pulau Langkawi. *American ethnologist*, 22(2), 223–241.

Constantino, R., & Constantino, L. R. (1975). *A History of the Philippines*. NYU Press, New York.

Davidson, J. S. (2016). Why the Philippines chooses to import rice. *Critical Asian Studies*, 48(1), 100–122.

Davis, M. (2002). *Late Victorian holocausts: El Niño famines and the making of the third world*. Verso, London.

Dawe, D., Moya, P., & Valencia, S. (2009). Institutional, policy and farmer responses to drought: El Niño events and rice in the Philippines. *Disasters*, 33(2), 291–307.

De Boeck, F. (1994). 'When Hunger Goes Around the Land': Hunger and Food Among the Aluund of Zaire. *Man*, 29(2), 257–282.

Dettwyler, K. A. (1993). The biocultural approach in nutritional anthropology: case studies of malnutrition in Mali. *Medical anthropology*, 15(1), 17–39.

Doeppers, D. F. (2016). *Feeding Manila in peace and war, 1850–1945*. University of Wisconsin Press, Madison.

Dove, M. R. (1999). The agronomy of memory and the memory of agronomy: ritual conservation of archaic cultigens in contemporary farming systems. In V. Nazarea (ed.) *Ethnoecology: Situated knowledge/located lives*. University of Arizona Press, Tucson, pp. 45–70.

Dressler, W. H., Smith, W., & Montefrio, M. J. (2018). Ungovernable? The vital natures of swidden assemblages in an upland frontier. *Journal of Rural Studies*, 61, 343–354.

Dressler, W., & Pulhin, J. (2010). The shifting ground of swidden agriculture on Palawan Island, the Philippines. *Agriculture and Human Values*, 27(4), 445–459.

Eder, J. F. (1978). The caloric returns to food collecting: Disruption and change among the Batak of the Philippine tropical forest. *Human Ecology*, 6(1), 55–69.

Fox, R 1954, *Tagbanua religion and society*, PhD. Thesis, University of Chicago.

Gibson, T. (1986). *Sacrifice and sharing in the Philippine highlands: Religion and society among the Buid of Mindoro*. Athlone, London.

Grey, S., & Patel, R. (2015). Food sovereignty as decolonization: Some contributions from Indigenous movements to food system and development politics. *Agriculture and Human Values*, 32(3), 431–444.

Hill, R. D. (2012). *Rice in Malaya: a study in historical geography*. NUS Press, Singapore.

Hutterer, K. L. (1983). The natural and cultural history of Southeast Asian agriculture: Ecological and evolutionary considerations. *Anthropos*. 78, 169–212.

Ilcan, S., & Phillips, L. (2006). Circulations of insecurity: Globalizing food standards in historical perspective. In *Agricultural Standards* (pp. 51–72). Springer, Dordrecht

Janowski, M., and Kerlogue, F. (eds.). (2007). *Kinship and Food in South East Asia*. Nias Press, Cophenhagen.

Jocano, F. L. (1968). *Sulod society*. University of the Philippines Press, Manila.

Juliano, B.O. (1993). Rice in Human Nutrition. Food and Agriculture Organization of the United Nations: Rome.

Junker, L. L. (1999). *Raiding, trading, and feasting: The political economy of Philippine chiefdoms.* University of Hawaii Press, Honolulu.

Kerkvliet, B. J. (1990). *Everyday politics in the Philippines: Class and status relations in a Central Luzon village.* University of California Press, Berkeley.

Kwiatkowski, L. M. (1998). *Struggling with development: the politics of hunger and gender in the Philippines.* Westview Press, Boulder.

Lansigan, F. P., De los Santos, W. L., & Coladilla, J. O. (2000). Agronomic impacts of climate variability on rice production in the Philippines. *Agriculture, ecosystems & environment, 82*(1), 129–137.

Law, L. (2001). Home cooking: Filipino women and geographies of the senses in Hong Kong. *Ecumene, 8*(3), 264–283.

Macdonald, C. J. (2007). *Uncultural behavior: An anthropological investigation of suicide in the southern Philippines.* University of Hawaii Press, Honolulu.

McAfee, K (1985), The Philippines: A Harvest of Anger, in D.B. Schirmer and S.R Shalom (eds.) *The Philippines Reader.* South End Press, Boston, pp 292–301.

McLennan, M. (1982), 'Changing human ecology on the central Luzon plain: Nueva Ecija, 1705- 1939', in McCoy A & de Jesus (eds.), *Philippine social history: global trade and local transformations.* Ateneo de Manila University Press, Quezon City, pp. 57–90.

Minter, T. (2010). *The Agta of the Northern Sierra Madre. Livelihood strategies and resilience among Philippine hunter-gatherers.* Leiden University, Leiden.

Nazarea, V. D. (1995). *Local knowledge and agricultural decision making in the Philippines: Class, gender, and resistance.* Cornell University Press, Ithaca.

Newson, L. A. (2009). *Conquest and pestilence in the early Spanish Philippines.* University of Hawaii Press.

Novellino, D (2011), 'Toward a "common logic of procurement": unravelling the foraging-farming interface on Palawan Island (the Philippines)', in Barker G & Janowsky (eds.), *Why cultivate? anthropological and archaeological approaches to foraging-farming transitions in southeast Asia*, McDonald Institute for Archaeological Research, Cambridge, pp. 105–119.

O'Connor, R. A. (1995). Agricultural change and ethnic succession in Southeast Asian states: a case for regional anthropology. *The Journal of Asian Studies, 54*(4), 968–996.

Ohnuki-Tierney, E. (1994). *Rice as self: Japanese identities through time.* Princeton University Press.

Pinstrup-Andersen, P. (2009). Food security: definition and measurement. *Food security, 1*(1), 5–7.

Pottier, J. (1999). *Anthropology of food: the social dynamics of food security.* Polity Press, Cambridge.

Revel, N (1990), *Fleurs de paroles:histoire naturelle Palawan.: La maitrised'un savoir et l'art d'une relation.* Peeters, Paris.

Romanoff, S., & Lynam, J. (1992). Commentary: cassava and African food security: some ethnographic examples. *Ecology, Food and Nutrition, 27*, 29–41.

Rosaldo, R. 1981. The Social Relations of Ilongot Subsistence. In Olofson, H. (ed). Adaptative Strategies and Change in Philippine Swidden-Based Societies. Forest Research Institute: Laguna.

Scheper-Hughes, N. (1988). The madness of hunger: sickness, delirium, and human needs. *Culture, Medicine and Psychiatry, 12*(4), 429–458.

Scott, J. C. (2009). *The art of not being governed: An anarchist history of upland Southeast Asia.* Yale University Press, New Haven.

Shipton, P. (1990). African famines and food security: anthropological perspectives. *Annual Review of anthropology, 19*(1), 353–394.

Smith, W. (2018). Weather from incest: The politics of indigenous climate change knowledge on Palawan Island, the Philippines. *The Australian Journal of Anthropology, 29*(3), 265–281.

Smith, W., & Dressler, W. H. (2017). Rooted in place? The coproduction of knowledge and space in agroforestry assemblages. *Annals of the American Association of Geographers, 107*(4), 897–914.

Ventura, T. (2015). Medicalizing Gutom: Hunger, Diet, and Beriberi during the American Period. *Philippine Studies: Historical and Ethnographic Viewpoints, 63*(1), 39–69.

Venturello, M. H. 1907. *Manners and customs of the Tagbanuas and other tribes of the Island of Palawan.* The Philippines. Smithsonian Misc. Collect. 48, 514–558.

Volkman, T.A. (1985). *Feasts of Honor: Ritual and Change in the Toraja Highlands.* University of Illinois Press, Chicago.

Warner, K. (1979). Walking on two feet; Tagbanwa adaptation to Philippine society. Ann Arbor, University of Michigan. PhD Thesis.

Warren, J. F. (2018). Typhoons and droughts: food shortages and famine in the Philippines since the seventeenth century. *International Review of Environmental History, 4*(2), 27–44.

Watts, M. (1983). *Silent violence.* University of California Press, Berkeley.

Young, M. W. (1986). "The worst disease": The cultural definition of hunger in Kalauna. In L. Manderson (ed.) *Shared wealth and symbol: Food, culture and society in Oceania and Southeast Asia.* Cambridge University Press, Cambridge, pp. 111–126.

Chapter 9

Ethnographic Approaches to Locating Disaster

Honey Harvesting, Livelihoods, and Everyday Uncertainty on Palawan Island

Sarah Webb

INTRODUCTION

In my ethnographic research I have not explicitly sought to focus on disasters. And yet in my research activities I constantly encountered the kind of everyday mentions of disasters which could be considered an ordinary part of daily life in the Philippines. These included both events regular and expected—like the consistent discussion of typhoons, where they were in the Philippines, and what their local impacts might be—as well as those which were perhaps less expected, such as the circulation of hoax text messages that acid rain was falling locally, prompted by an actual crisis concerning nuclear reactors in Japan. In this chapter I seek to focus on some conceptual and methodological aspects of these dynamics which I hope will be useful to those conducting research on disasters in the Philippines. Here I offer the perspective of someone who has encountered disasters empirically, but not intentionally, in the Philippines because I suggest this might provide a different view to studies which consider the Philippines primarily in terms of a place where disasters can be found. Predominantly, I discuss the relevance of ethnographic approaches to disasters, particularly in terms of questioning where disasters might be located in research. In questioning the "where" of locating disasters within research projects, what I am really discussing is the ontology and epistemology of how we as researchers position disasters within our research projects—what we consider to be disasters, and how we consider it possible to investigate disasters within the lives of those they impact. In doing so, the chapter aims to contribute to an emerging body of work from anthropologists, sociologists, historians, Philippine studies scholars, and others who are establishing the importance of ethnographic and everyday approaches to understanding disasters in the Philippines. Such work has done much to influence the formulation of my central position—that questioning where disasters might be located requires acknowledging how disasters are embedded within the broader uncertainties of everyday life in the Philippines. In discussing this point I argue that ongoing concerns about livelihoods are of paramount importance for understanding how diverse Filipinos live with disasters.

What then are the potential conceptual and methodological contributions of ethnographic approaches to disasters in the Philippines? The focus on depth and specificity valued in ethnographic approaches provides researchers with the possibility to explore how disasters are not only experienced, but also articulated in the daily lives of particular people. This means an opportunity to critically investigate what can be considered to be a disaster, and examine the politics of how disasters are defined, by whom, and question who benefits from such definitions. Furthermore, such approaches can assist scholars to reconceptualize the relationship between what is ordinary and extraordinary—an issue especially relevant in the context of the Philippines, where disasters have long been discussed as normal and expected even as they have always been felt unevenly. The kind of biographical focus that becomes possible with ethnographic approaches allows researchers to acknowledge the heterogeneous nature of how disasters are experienced and articulated by diverse Filipinos. This is a crucial dimension of understanding disasters in the Philippines, given that the politics of how disasters are defined and managed has proven to have long term and dramatic impacts on peoples' lives. As the editors of this volume suggest, experiences of disasters extend beyond popular narratives, into areas less broadly visible and less easily recognizable. Ethnographic approaches therefore offer one avenue for investigating not only how the extraordinary is apparent in the everyday, but also the politics of such distinctions. This has become of increasing relevance to the study of disasters following a shift toward acknowledging that the disruption of disasters is not limited to sudden, contained events but must also extend to what has been termed "slow disasters" which are of significant impact but are often less visible because they are gradual and incremental.

In the chapter which follows I provide one example of such an ethnographic approach by discussing a series of moments from fieldwork focused on livelihoods on central Palawan Island. What I seek to emphasize is how "extraordinary" events that are easily recognizable as disasters, such as world wars and volcanic eruptions, are not necessarily found within neat explanations of how disasters are conceptualized, experienced, and anticipated. I show how such events might feature as elusive mentions bound up within what might at first appear to be tangential livelihood pursuits such as the seasonal harvesting of honey, but which ethnographic research demonstrates are actually crucial to understanding how disasters are located within everyday life. But more than this, I demonstrate how events which could be more easily recognized as a disaster (like a volcanic eruption) might be used by people not to discuss the impacts of that disaster per se but to explain other, more locally salient "slower disasters" such as long term, multidimensional livelihood uncertainty and precarity. In this example I suggest that making sense of such accounts in the work of attempting to locate disasters requires not necessarily looking for further examples of volcanic eruptions. Rather, what is required is an attempt to understand those complex contexts of everyday uncertainty and risk in which Tagabanua families on central Palawan Island attempt to make a living.

ETHNOGRAPHIC APPROACHES AND
EVERYDAY UNCERTAINTY

There is nothing radical about suggesting that ethnographic attention to the everyday is an important approach to considering disasters in the Philippines, or indeed elsewhere. It has long been acknowledged that disasters cannot be considered independently from daily life (Wisner, 1993). Key works have demonstrated how disasters are socially constructed and concern questions of everyday politics (Hilhorst et al., 2013; Bankoff, 2004). Even as mass communications increasingly render particular events recognizable and accessible as disasters, simultaneously many other disruptions to daily life are not subject to such attention. This tension suggests that questions of how, and by whom, something might be considered a disaster matter. Dorothea Hilhorst identifies two dimensions of such politics which are of particular relevance to this discussion. First, that the politics of defining disaster often involve questions of scale—that is, disasters are assumed to be something beyond the capacity, and often consequently even ownership, of those directly impacted (Hilhorst, 2013, pp. 5–6). Secondly, that disasters are embedded within broader social fields of uncertainty and risk which shape not only the experiences and perspectives of those involved but also broader distinctions between what is ordinary or extraordinary (*ibid*, pp. 2–3; see also van Voorst, Wisner, Hellman, & Nooteboom, 2015). It is by drawing ethnographic attention to the everyday that such researchers have attempted to investigate how such distinctions emerge (Hilhorst, 2013, 7). How might the everyday, then, be a place where preparations for disaster might be located as conspicuously non-visible, for example, as survival kits stored in closets or the slippage of high-calorie compact food products into the everyday as they become a staple for busy workers in Japan (Sayre, 2011).

How different people within and across locales make distinctions about uncertainty and risk in everyday life therefore becomes important for considering the politics of disasters in the Philippines. Key works have proposed that certain kinds of disasters have long been part of everyday life in the archipelago (Bankoff, 2003; Warren, 2016). Studies suggest that as a result, understanding disasters requires considering the kinds of existential questions through which people make sense of their lives. Across the significant ethnic and religious diversity of the Philippines, questions such as *"why do storms come?"* are formulated and considered within multiple understandings of human culpability and more-than-human worlds (Bobis, 2017). In considering the Philippines broadly, anthropologist Raul Pertierra proposes that many Filipinos have important and pervasive hesitations toward considering the governance of the world completely knowable, predictable and closed (2003, pp. 5–6). Rather, Pertierra argues, there exist key cultural attitudes supporting an openness to possibility, including the "ordinary acceptance" of "miraculous events" (*ibid*, p. 12). One key insight from ethnographic approaches can be considering how such epistemological issues and their associated ontological assumptions can potentially shape the way that researchers attempt to understand and locate disasters. Recent work on disasters in the Philippines has, for example, questioned how nature has been conceptualized as an historical actor (Aguilar et al., 2016, p. 647). Ethnographic studies of Philippine societies have shown how events such as volcanic eruptions which are often assumed to be exclusively natural and unambiguously predictable are produced as complex cultural phenomena (Dumont, 1992, esp. pp. 121–122). Such approaches offer researchers much to assist in questioning our expectations about finding neat or complete explanations of how disasters are experienced and understood.

In terms of understanding how disasters might be embedded within everyday life in the Philippines, broad perspectives are certainly worth considering. However, doing so should not occur at the expense of recognizing that understandings of uncertainty are heterogeneous, and that many distinctions regarding risk have a basis in social differentiations. In a recent special issue problematizing the focus on disasters as spectacle, Nicole Curato and others have argued for attention to slow-moving disasters in the Philippines. In citing examples of such research, Curato explains the significance of everyday approaches which are too often dismissed as trivial despite their important insights: "their seemingly banal character often demotes these issues as nothing more than the micro-politics of everyday life, even though it is these life experiences that immediately shape the uneven character of communities' collective memory" (2018, p. 60). This recent work discusses the importance of everyday approaches to understanding not only the political economy of disasters, but also how political economy can be exacerbated by disasters. In studies which have examined reconstruction and retail as locally salient markers of recovery from typhoons and earthquakes, researchers have noted such recovery initiatives often involve the removal of those deemed to no longer belong in such spaces—for example, poorer residents or vendors (Curato, 2018, pp. 61–62; Matejowsky, 2002). These are, of course, exclusions which have significant impacts on these peoples' livelihoods (*ibid*). In examining intersecting forms of inequality in post-Haiyan recovery, Mirca Madianou has argued that in some instances recovery processes can have a greater impact than the event of the disaster (2015, p. 2). Such examples demonstrate how the "everyday-ness" of disasters in the Philippines is situated within the cultural dimensions of class across the nation. Based on ethnographic research into news media consumption and suffering, Jonathan Ong argues that the notion that disaster is something everyday and normal is one which "pertains only to the experience of the Filipino poor" for whom "the news functions in their lives as a continuing documentation of the everyday struggles of the Filipino poor, rather than individual clips of exceptional tragedy" (Ong, 2015, p. 131).

What this literature on the everyday politics of disasters shows is that specific groups and individuals often have quite different evaluations of uncertainty based on their lived experiences and understandings of what is ordinary. Although there has been widespread interest in "rediscovering" indigenous worldviews as part of a broader Filipino heritage, particularly within discourses on living sustainably, specific aspects of these perspectives are often largely acknowledged only when they accord with mainstream views (Bankoff, 2004, pp. 93–94). For many indigenous peoples and so-called cultural minorities in the Philippines, marginalization in terms of broader conceptualizations of disasters takes two key forms: first, exclusion from broader conversations about what might constitute disasters and forms of everyday uncertainty in the Philippines. Second, members of such groups often experience key disruptions to everyday life which are largely unseen and unacknowledged in comparison to certain events rendered visible and accessible to Filipinos across the nation and abroad through mass communications.

What then does it mean to navigate specific forms of everyday uncertainty for some indigenous peoples in the Philippines? How does this relate to local forms of everyday politics, particularly those concerning livelihoods? And how might considering pursuits which involve everyday uncertainty provide insights into how ethnographic approaches to the everyday can assist researchers in understanding disasters? In the following sections I address these questions by focusing on accounts of Tagbanua searches for honey hives. Although a highly valued and desirable product, harvesting honey is a seasonal activity which involves navigating risk and uncertainty at multiple levels. While at first these accounts might appear to concern pursuits tangential to the kinds of events commonly recognized as disasters, together they provide an example of how researchers ethnographically investigating everyday uncertainty might encounter elusive mentions of world wars or volcanic eruptions within other discussions. The following section aims to focus on the opportunities that such elusive mentions might offer to researchers. In addition to demonstrating how mentions of disasters might emerge as part of everyday conversations unprompted by explicit questions about disasters from researchers, such accounts can provide important insight into how disasters might be connected to what is locally salient within everyday life. In the case discussed here this means the ongoing livelihood precarity experienced by marginalized indigenous families which is exasperated by a local political economy shaped through environmental governance, tourism, and a history of land grabs. The biographical focus of these accounts demonstrates how shared meanings and experiences are heterogeneously experienced in the lives of diverse Filipinos.

ETHNOGRAPHICALLY LOCATING DISASTERS

Artemio

Artemio is a Tagbanua man in his late sixties. I lived with Artemio and his wife Cecilia in a household that often included some of their children and grandchildren for several periods during this research. The following excerpt comes from a multi-hour conversation, several years after we first met. Like other accounts which follow, Artemio briefly mentions a significant disruptive event as part of a broader narrative on honey harvesting and livelihoods. Here he is describing his first recollection of his father harvesting a *pukyutan* (honeybee) hive during Artemio's childhood.

> So when my father get the *anira* [part of beehive] and *lanao* [honey] in the *biaw* [container] they put it in the pan and then they squeeze the *lanao* and I ask my father, "Father, what is this?" and then he said "this is a *pukyutan*." According to my father's grandfather this is the *pukyutan* that most of the Tagbanua people is eating that is why most of the Tagbanua people do not need to buy more medicine because at that time there are no medicine in Puerto after the World War Two. That is why he said to me this will serve as our medicine. That is the first time that I observed my father to eat it."

I use this account to introduce my presentation and discussion of ethnographic data because it demonstrates the way that, for many Tagbanua elders, World

War II continues to serve as an important marker of social memory. Many Tagbanua elders refer to the past in terms of before, during, and after World War II. Following the war was a time of significant social, economic, and environmental change locally, particularly when the region became regarded as a Philippine land frontier in the 1950s. This was also a key period of exacerbation for many of the issues of political economy such as uneven access to formal land ownership which have come to shape contemporary Tagbanua experiences of marginalization and livelihood precarity (Dressler, 2009). The war itself was a particularly disruptive event locally, and elders still discuss this as a time when Tagbanua families would have fled into the forested uplands to avoid Japanese soldiers along the coast. In 2011, some months prior to the previously mentioned conversation, Artemio and I had been drawing a local map of key *sitios*, and discussing how they were connected through forest trails as part of my ethnographic investigation into where honey might be found. The bottom of the map was annotated with field notes pertaining to our discussion while making the map which referenced where Tagbanua living in different areas identified on the map would have hidden during World War II. The map notes that a trail between two areas was "new" in the sense that it was only made after World War II. An inscription states that "the ppl [people] are avoiding the seashore." This example serves as an introductory illustration of how such disruptive events might briefly flow into the course of discussions about the everyday uncertainties of finding honey during ethnographic fieldwork, and how these moments can challenge dichotomous distinctions between what is ordinary and extraordinary in terms of how they are articulated in the everyday lives of certain Filipinos. It also provides some background to the subsequent accounts by showing how honey harvesting specifically, and livelihoods more generally, have been embedded for a significant amount of time within contexts of uncertainty and risk for those generation of Tagbanua who are now elders. This context is important for considering the significance of how more contemporary discussions of livelihoods are shaped through both social memory and imagining the future, as per Alberto's following account.

Alberto

Alberto is a Tagbanua man in his fifties, who resides with his wife Ruth and often some of their young grandchildren in a *sitio* which is mainly accessible only by boat. I lived in their household several times during this research. Like many Tagbanua men of his age, Alberto engages in numerous livelihood activities at different times, including harvesting forest products, planting rice, fishing, and wage labor. He and his wife have also held local positions in municipal government and the tribal council. One day in 2011 Alberto and I were speaking about a common topic of everyday conversations about livelihoods, forest products, and (what as an anthropologist I would describe as) the political economy of their local governance. On this occasion Alberto took up a lengthy and uninterrupted discussion of the difficulties of transporting and selling *bagtik* (almaciga resin, Manila copal), which included an overview of the subversive strategies required to navigate state-imposed regulations, and an explanation of why certain circumventions were necessary. The quote following is one part of this broader conversation.

> *kasi yan ang pangunahing hanapbuhay ng mga tao dito, kasi ang sabi ni Captain extra hanapbuhay lang daw yun, pero hindi mula't sapul yan ang hanapbuhay ng tao dito, amakan at honey, pero ang honey weder weder lang, pag m[a]y bulaklak ang kahoy may honey pag may taon na walang bulaklak ang kahoy halimbawa 2012 hindi mamulaklak ang kahoy walang honey. 2003–2004 walang honey, lalo na yong pumutok yong bulkang Pinatubo last 5 years kasi natuyo ang bulaklak ng kahoy walang madapuan ang honeybee.*

Because that [*bagtik*] is the main livelihood of the people here, the [Barangay] Captain says it is only an extra livelihood, but no, from the beginning that has been an essential livelihood of the people here, honey is also [a kind of long-standing livelihood] but honey is only seasonal, when the trees have flowers there will be honey but there are years when the trees have no flowers, for example, [if in] 2012 the trees do not flower there will be no honey. [In] 2003–2004 there was no honey, and especially the blast from the [Mount] Pinatubo eruption last five years, because the tree's flowers were dried the honeybees could not land [on them].

Alberto's account provides a strong example of how mentions of disasters and the associated ongoing impacts might empirically emerge in conversations about what could at first appear to be unrelated topics. In suggesting that in the coming year there might be no honey, Alberto references periods in the past when this was the case, including following the eruption of Mount Pinatubo—presumably referring to the early 1990s. After this brief mention of the volcano, Alberto's narrative immediately returns to the necessity of finding ways and means to transport and sell *bagtik*, given that local residents have such limited livelihood opportunities. I was surprised, as others might be, at the mention of Pinatubo during this conversation and the suggested geographic and temporal impact of that event on Palawan. However, as an ethnographer attempting to make sense of this reference, I take my cues from Alberto's narrative itself (what does he go on to discuss at length following this part of his narrative, what might this suggest about what he deems relevant and important about the discussion?) as well as my broader experience talking to Tagbanua families (where Pinatubo is not a common topic of conversation but discussion of livelihood precarity is ubiquitous). Given this, there is also another key way to consider this reference—that the eruption of Pinatubo might be an event embedded within broader, ongoing livelihood uncertainties for indigenous peoples on central Palawan Island.

How then, can this ethnographic example be used to consider the everyday dimensions of risk and uncertainty that disasters are situated within in the Philippines? Specifically, how can we locate disasters as part of wider concerns about livelihoods across the archipelago? To continue thinking with the example of Pinatubo, the importance of doing so has been illustrated in research focused on the eruption and subsequent threats of lahars which has argued that perceptions of risk need be placed within a daily context where other hazards include poverty and livelihood constraints. For many in the vicinity of Pinatubo, decisions regarding the risk of remaining in the area or relocating were weighed against the risk of livelihood insecurities or access to capital such as land (Gaillard, 2008). In discussing responses to warnings about the eruption, Filomeno Aguilar mentions that a key concern for some Aeta residents reluctant to leave was that lowland Filipinos might destroy their houses and crops (2016, p. 613).

What then are the connections and differences in terms of disaster, risk, uncertainty, and livelihoods across these examples? First, Alberto's account and Gaillard and Aguilar's discussions all speak to the centrality of livelihoods. At the time of his account, Alberto too resided in an area where indigenous peoples were living with the fear that their forest products or other property might be deliberately stolen or destroyed. And while Alberto's account does not describe the same weighing of risks as Aguilar and Gaillard's examples in terms of relocation, all three allow researchers to consider the question of *what is recognizable as a disaster*? Because a volcanic event is hardly the only disaster described in any of these stories. Rather than understand each of these as a story about a volcanic eruption and its impacts as one form of disaster, I want to now shift the discussion to thinking about the context such events are embedded within—ongoing concern and uncertainty regarding livelihoods—and how these can be ethnographically considered.

This shift refers to methodological implications at two levels. First, we saw that Alberto's account could demonstrate the value of how an ethnographic approach could *generate* important empirical data that might not emerge through other kinds of methods. As a researcher, it did not occur to me to ask Alberto about the impact of Mount Pinatubo's eruption in the 1990s on subsequent honey production over time or how this came to shape his everyday experiences of uncertainty. Furthermore, the way that the reference to Pinatubo appeared as part of Alberto's narrative provides a different account than might have been given even if I were to have asked direct questions on these topics. This is an important methodological consideration, but in suggesting a shift in focus I am talking about going beyond the generation of data to discuss methodology at a second level, in terms of the *treatment and interpretation* of data and how this can be used to shape subsequent investigation and analysis. Here, what I am suggesting is that ethnographic approaches can assist in beginning to unpack what it is that Alberto is discussing in his account. Rather than looking from his reference toward the event of Pinatubo, I suggest what is important is to explore what it was that Alberto was using this reference to Pinatubo to explain. In an attempt to do so, I now turn this discussion to focus on the uncertainty regarding livelihoods that is a key feature of daily life for the Tagbanua families I worked with. At this point we move from more recognizable forms of disaster such as events like world wars and volcanic eruptions to those dynamics supporting precarity which are in many ways less visible and recognizable, but which the above ethnographic material demonstrates are locally relevant forms of unpredictability, uncertainty, and risk.

SEARCHING FOR FOREST HONEY AND THE DYNAMICS OF EVERYDAY UNCERTAINTY

As Alberto's account suggests, Tagbanua livelihoods are enmeshed within complex dynamics of uncertainty in terms of the associated difficulties of specific activities, their potential contribution, and availability over time. Different livelihood activities are valued in different ways according to these dynamics, and as Alberto's account also shows, these evaluations can differ for different individuals or change over time in response to particular circumstances. What perhaps endures for most Tagbanua families is that livelihoods broadly and specific livelihood activities both refer to ongoing pursuits to provide and survive under conditions of resource scarcity and marginalization, rather than offering a comfortable means of provision. More broadly, the question of achieving sustainable livelihoods in the region has been conceptualized as an issue of poverty and conservation which has preoccupied government agencies, civil society, researchers, and the public at numerous scales but has unfortunately largely been focused on apolitical, technical solutions (Ferguson, 1994). The key issue with this is that such approaches have systematically failed to acknowledge the broader political economy which has produced the marginalization of Tagbanua and other indigenous or poor families through large scale resource extraction, poor market relations, land grabs, state governance of the forest trade, and recently tourism (Dove, 1983; Eder, 1990; Dressler, 2009). Livelihood uncertainty, then, is an ordinary part of everyday life in this context. However, there are significant local social differentiations in terms of how specific livelihood activities and everyday uncertainties are imagined and managed.

As Alberto describes, harvesting honey from dipterocarp forests is a livelihood activity that is highly seasonal—it is available only during part of the year, and the production of honey ebbs and wanes over multiyear cycles. Many of the Tagbanua families with whom I work discuss honey in ways which give it a kind of regular presence, even though it is more often materially absent from the home. This discursive presence of honey educes the normalcy of honey's potential to flow into the forest, and from there into the homes of Tagbanua people. The possibility for honey to have this kind of presence is intimately related to honey's origins as a form of Tagbanua inheritance, and its ability to support Tagbanua people as a source of food, sweetness, nutrition, medicine, and cash income. The value of honey also contributes to the dynamics of its absence, as it is often consumed or sold quickly. Tagbanua parents would laughingly tell me that they do not stock honey because their children love it so (meaning, that once it has entered the household, it is quickly eaten by children). Honey is therefore a substance which has a kind of everyday and enduring presence, even though it is regularly unavailable.

In writing ethnographically about these dynamics, and attempting to use this ethnographic material to consider the politics of distinction between what is ordinary and extraordinary, I draw on work from material culture studies and the anthropology of absence and presence. A key theme in this work suggests that absence and presence are interrelated to the point of being mutually constitutive in the construction and experience of social life and social memory. Just as the absent event of World War II has a presence in shaping Artemio's account of honey harvesting or Pinatubo's eruption has in shaping Alberto's discussion of the past, present and future,

> what may be materially absent still influences people's experience of the material world. We argue for a need to see the relationship between the present and the absent as more complex than simply consisting of two antonymic categories. Rather, as an ambiguous interrelation between what is there and what is not, absences are cultural, physical and social phenomena that powerfully influence people's conceptualizations of themselves and the world they engage with. (Bille, Hastrup, & Flohr Sørensen, 2010, p. 4)

These insights are particularly useful in considering how finding honey is a pursuit which fundamentally involves navigating uncertainty. One of the initial reasons honey is so often absent is because it is seasonal, and the volumes of honey produced vary significantly across multiyear cycles. For many Tagbanua, the production of honey is multifaceted, with factors such as climate and the movement of bees shaped by a complex hierarchy of more-than-human social relations. Searching for hives requires experience to mitigate a range of extensive risks, a willingness to spend time looking for hives (which might not be found), and the endurance to wait for located hives to be ready for harvest (which could in the meantime be harvested by someone else or destroyed by frequent storms). Once found, actually harvesting a hive means scaling high trees, successfully smoking bees from the hive, cutting part of the hive, and lowering it down without spilling honey or allowing the wax to touch the ground. It is for these reasons that searching for hives is considered by some to be an unappealing quest. What I will now use the example of honey harvesting to convey is a key point discussed throughout this chapter—that ethnographic research on disasters and the everyday can provide important insight into how uncertainty and risk are not considered in the same ways by all, even within local areas. What is deemed undesirable by some is valued highly by others for entirely different reasons. These diverse conceptualizations of uncertainty are connected by different social actors to a range of larger issues and events which ultimately relate to a common concern—imagining the provisioning of daily life in the past, present, and future. This concern is central to understanding how different Filipinos distinguish between what is ordinary and extraordinary, and how, given this, they navigate uncertainty and risk in their everyday lives.

TALKING ABOUT FINDING HONEY

Diego

Diego is in his thirties, and living with his wife and children in a *sitio* where many Tagbanua families live. We conducted our interview in the workshop next to his house where he constructs furniture from local forest products such as rattan. He quickly dismisses honey as a livelihood, telling me that it was not his job, and explaining that he is not Tagbanua. Like many who have more recently made their homes in the area, he regards looking for hives as an undesirable and unprofitable livelihood activity (even though he describes having honey as being desirable, particularly owing to his experience in giving it to his sick children as medicine—a practice recommended to him by his own parents). The following statements are his responses to my questions about why he does not harvest honey, whether he had ever harvested a hive, and why he did not regularly look for hives even though he had described an interest in having honey:

> "*kasi may tao rin talaga na mahilig halos mag hapon ubusin na nya, araw-araw din yan naghahanap kung*" (some people like collecting honey, they would look the entire day, everyday); "*sa trabaho ba, baka ubusin yun isang araw tapos wala kang makita yan, kasi may trabaho din dito sa baba e, kasi may*

pinagkakakitaan din" (in terms of work, collecting honey often takes a day and you sometimes end up without anything, here in the lowlands there is work and income); *"sayang yung isang araw tapos wala ka pang matagpuan"* (the whole day will be wasted if we can't find [any honey]); *"kung wala kang kasanayan yan hindi ka makakita"* (if you are not skilled in that work, it will be hard for you to find some).

Similar statements were made to me by other neighbors of Tagbanua families. Such people might buy honey for consumption within their household or resell it for a profit. However, they would regard the notion of spending extensive time searching for hives, potentially without result, as largely unprofitable and compared to other, more certain livelihood activities, "a waste of time" (see also Eder, 1987). Some individuals commented that they felt a great pity for Tagbanua families, given that this was their livelihood. The way that this is often articulated is to say that "they" ("the *katutubo*," indigenous or innate) have no other livelihood. What is particularly important to note here is that, as Alberto's account indicates, Tagbanua families actually do not exclusively harvest honey as their only livelihood activity or source of income. And yet harvesting honey has such a high social value among so many Tagbanua households that, in contrast to the descriptions of their neighbors, it is common to hear people proudly describe honey in terms of contribution to their livelihood. For these Tagbanua, particularly older women and men, the uncertainties and difficulties of searching for hives is discussed in ways markedly differently to the descriptions of neighbors like Diego. The following accounts demonstrate how there are aspects of the uncertainty and risk associated with specific livelihood activities which are not necessarily evaluated in negative terms (even though significant livelihood precarity is a ubiquitous, ongoing concern for Tagbanua families). This ethnographic revelation adds a further level of complexity to considering the everyday ways in which different Filipinos navigate uncertainty and risk.

Manong Enrico and Manang Gloria

Manang Gloria and Manong Enrico are an elderly Tagbanua couple in their eighties. We conducted our interview inside their home, and begun by discussing a story about the origin of bees. Manang Gloria qualifies this story as being only partial by explaining that the complete story was known by the old people (meaning their ancestors). In talking about honey hunting, Manong Enrico says that an essential part of becoming *manlalbet* (an expert honey harvester) is learning to look for hives. In explaining this, he suggests that not only is honey (as a substance or a livelihood) a form of inheritance, but that becoming *manlalbet* is itself a form of inheritance. He describes the latter through an example of working the whole day in the forest and always looking up to the branches of the tree as a way of learning to become *manlalbet*. Tagbanua women generally do not harvest high hives, and I ask whether women also learn to find hives. Manong Enrico replies, "of course!," "they are taught by their parents how to find hives"—"they must know how to find hives," he says. I ask him whether he deliberately looks for hives or just comes across them when he is in the forest, and Manong Enrico replies: *"mayrong sadya merong hindi rin, kasi pag naglalakad ka gubat kahit hindi ka naghahanap minsan makakita ka"* (sometimes [one might] really look for it but sometimes not, because when you go walking in the forest sometimes you are not looking [for hives] you just see it along the way).

Manong Pablo

Manong Pablo is a Tagbanua man in his sixties. I interviewed him, his wife Manang Oblivia (an authority on many matters concerning bees), and several of their adult children many times during the course of this research. On this day we were talking at his house and Manong Pablo also described becoming *manlalbet* as a form of inheritance, and similarly linked this becoming to extensive experience searching for hives. He explained that one becomes *manlalbet* by looking for hives, and that if someone is called *manlalbet* this indicates an expertise in looking for hives. After an extensive discussion of the seasonal dynamics and annual fluctuations of honey, I asked Manong Pablo, *"Ilang beses na kayo nag hahanap ng lanao ngayong taon?"* (how many times have you tried looking for honey this year?) to which he replied, *"Maraming beses din. Kahit anong oras yan basta alam namin na merun pa yan nag hahanap kami"* (Several times. It doesn't matter what time it is. As long as we know that there is still honey, we still search for it).

Manong Pablo is widely regarded as a very industrious man. As he and other Tagbanua elders indicate, to search for honey without result is hardly considered as a "waste of time." That is, the uncertainty of searching for hives is not necessarily a deterrent to this pursuit (as it was for Diego). Rather, for these Tagbanua, searching can be productive beyond harvesting specific hives. As one younger Tagbanua man explained, the dynamics of searching could itself even be a source of amusement. He told me that it could be very fun to go searching for hives in a group, giving an example of the excitement felt when one called out to others that they had found a hive.

HONEY, LIVELIHOODS, AND UNCERTAINTY

In this chapter I have argued that ethnographic approaches can assist researchers to understand why livelihoods might be of central relevance to considering disasters in the Philippines. Throughout the discussion I have referred to some significant concerns regarding the precarity of Tagbanua livelihoods. In drawing these ethnographic accounts to a close, it must be mentioned that although there might be forms of everyday uncertainty and risk associated with finding hives that are viewed positively by some Tagbanua, many of these same people also express concern about other seriously worrisome forms of uncertainty. One of these is, as introduced by Alberto, is the potential for honey to become less available in the future. A particular worry for many Tagbanua elders is a commonly held perception that there are fewer bees and less honey now than there was in the past. In informal conversations, Tagbanua variously attribute this to multiple, and not necessarily mutually exclusive, potential reasons. These include notions that fluctuations are a normal and expected part of honey production cycles, and that variations both reflect and must be addressed through relations with a complex hierarchy of spirits. These relations are themselves embedded within the present dynamics of local everyday life, with specific reasons for low production referenced to increasing numbers of tourists (especially because spirits are known to dislike the smell of petrol from the pumpboats going inside the popular local tourism site of the Underground River); pesticides from rice paddy fields (given that spirits, and bees, do not like the chemicals); and, people using incorrect honey harvesting techniques (particularly not smoking hives in the proper manner). Furthermore, even though forest honey has become a valuable Palawan product in lifestyle and tourism markets, Tagbanua have disproportionally suffered blame over anxieties of broader fake honey markets and have borne the subsequent brunt of lower sales and decreased pricing (Webb, 2018). In such ways, even though honey harvesting is highly socially valued by many Tagbanua, its sale remains embedded within the uneven local political economy which has produced the ongoing livelihood precarity which is a predominant feature of everyday life for Tagbanua families.

CONCLUSION

Acknowledgment of the broader context of everyday uncertainties is essential to any consideration of disasters in the Philippines. Emerging work is demonstrating the importance of everyday approaches, given that the politics of defining and managing disasters has significant, long-term impacts on peoples' lives. In this chapter I have argued that ongoing concerns about livelihoods are of paramount importance for understanding how diverse Filipinos live with disasters. Here I have discussed accounts of Tagbanua searches for honey hives—a livelihood activity embedded in multiple forms of uncertainty—to outline some of the potential conceptual and methodological contributions which ethnographic approaches can offer researchers interested in disasters in the Philippines. I have suggested that methodologically, ethnographic approaches can provide researchers not only opportunities to generate important empirical data, but also that such empirical material can play a central role in subsequent investigation and analysis of data. For example, the ways in which specific people experience and articulate events in their daily lives can assist researchers in reconceptualizing distinctions between what is ordinary and extraordinary. This reconceptualization is central to the work of what I have referred to in this chapter as the questioning of where disasters might be located within research projects.

What this discussion of ethnographic material demonstrates is that there are complex relationships between uncertainty and risk, the ordinary and the extraordinary, and the study of disasters. It is through outlining some of this complexity that I have sought to illustrate a key point from the literature raised earlier in this chapter: that disasters are embedded within broader social fields of uncertainty and risk which shape broader distinctions between what is ordinary or extraordinary (Hilhorst, 2013, pp. 2–3). This ethnographic discussion began with an account which introduced how the extraordinary event of World War II continues to serve as a powerful marker within social memory for a generation of Tagbanua elders, to the point that it enters into the discussion of more ordinary types of uncertainty, such as searching for honey hives—an activity embedded within a context of livelihood precarity exacerbated in the period following this event. It was in seeking to explain contemporary livelihood precarity that Alberto came to mention the local impact of Pinatubo's eruption. In making sense of the everyday perceptions of uncertainty and risk that Alberto's account raises, I offer a summary background into the broader context of how honey harvesting is socially valued as well as providing the reader with a series of accounts which illustrate the heterogeneous attitudes toward the uncertainty and risks of honey harvesting as a livelihood activity held by a range of local residents. These diverse perceptions show how some everyday forms of risk and uncertainty might not necessarily be understood only in negative terms by certain residents, but also how valuing honey harvesting as a livelihood activity does not mean that there are not concerns about how honey harvesting is embedded within long-term livelihood precarity.

The point I wish to raise for future studies of disasters in the Philippines is how ambiguous and ephemeral mentions of disaster might be in the flows of ethnographic research activities such as interviews, informal conversations, and making maps. These mentions ultimately frustrate any desires for full explanations of events, their range of effects, or their absolute causes. Yet depending on the ontological and epistemological underpinnings of research projects, such frustrations can offer researchers an opportunity rather than a limitation, because they allow the chance to critically question our assumptions about what disasters are, and how we might expect to locate them as part of peoples' lives within our research projects.

REFERENCES

Aguilar, F.V. (2016). Disasters as contingent events: Volcanic eruptions, state advisories, and public participation in the twentieth-century Philippines. *Philippine Studies*, 64(3–4), 593–624.

Aguilar, F.V., Pante, M.D. & Tugado, A.F. (2016). Disasters in history and the history of disasters: Some key issues. *Philippine Studies*, 64(3–4), 641–656.

Bankoff, G. (2003). *Cultures of Disaster: Society and Natural Hazard in the Philippines*. London, Routledge Curzon.

Bankoff, G. (2004). In the eye of the storm: The social construction of the forces of nature and the climatic and seismic construction of God in the Philippines. *Journal of Southeast Asian Studies*, 35(1), 91–111.

Bille, M., Hastrup, F. & Flohr Sørensen, T. (2010). Introduction: An anthropology of absence. In M. Bille, F. Hastrup, & T. Flohr Sørensen (Eds.), *An Anthropology of Absence: Materializations of Transcendence and Loss* (pp. 3–22). New York, Springer.

Bobis, M. (2017). Salba istorya/salba buhay: Save story/save life: Collaborative storying in the wake of typhoons. In A. Collett, R. McDougall, & S. Thomas (Eds.), *Tracking the Literature of Tropical Weather: Typhoons, Hurricanes, and Cyclones* (pp. 151–176). Springer International Publishing.

Curato, N. (2018). Beyond the spectacle: Slow-moving disasters in post-Haiyan Philippines. *Critical Asian Studies*, 50(1), 58–66.

Dove, M. R. (1983). Theories of swidden agriculture, and the political economy of ignorance. *Agroforestry Systems*, 1(2), 85–99.

Dressler, W. H. (2009). *Old Thoughts in New Ideas: State Conservation Measures, Development and Livelihood on Palawan Island*. Manila, Ateneo de Manila University Press.

Dumont, J. P. (1992). *Visayan Vignettes: Ethnographic Traces of a Philippine Island*. United States of America, University of Chicago Press.

Eder, J. F. (1990). Deforestation and detribalization in the Philippines: The Palawan case. *Population and Environment*, 12(2), 99–115.

Eder, J.F. (1987). *On the Road to Tribal Extinction: Depopulation, Deculturation, and Adaptive Well-Being Among the Batak of the Philippines*. Berkeley, University of California Press.

Fox, R.B. (1954). *Religion and Society Among the Tagbanuwa of Palawan Island, Philippines* (Doctoral dissertation, Department of Anthropology, University of Chicago).

Fox, R.B. (n.d.). Tagbanuwa fieldnotes 1947 to 1953. In the *Fred Eggan Papers 1870–1991*, Special Collections Research Center at the University of Chicago Library, box 143, folder 4.

Gaillard, J. (2008). Alternative paradigms of volcanic risk perception: The case of Mt. Pinatubo in the Philippines. *Journal of Volcanology and Geothermal Research*, 172, 315–328.

Madianou, M. (2015). Digital inequality and second-order disasters: Social media in the typhoon Haiyan recovery. *Social Media + Society*, 1(2), 1–11.

Matejowsky, T. S. (2002). Globalization and retail development in the post-disaster context: A comparison of two Philippine communities. *Research in Economic Anthropology*, 21, 311–341.

Ong, J. C. (2015). *The Poverty of Television: The Mediation of Suffering in Class-Divided Philippines*. Anthem Press.

Pertierra, R. (2003). Science, technology and everyday culture in the Philippines. *Pilipinas*, 40, 3–14.

Sayre, R. (2011). The un-thought of preparedness: Concealments of disaster preparedness in Tokyo's everyday. *Anthropology and Humanism*, *36*(2), 215–224.

van Voorst, R., Wisner, B., Hellman, J., & Nooteboom, G. (2015). Introduction to the "risky everyday". *Disaster Prevention and Management*, 24(4).

Warren, C.P. (n.d.). Field notes—Warren—Batak of Palawan, undated. In the *Charles Warren Papers, 1950–1989*, the Special Collections and University Archives Collection at the University Library, University of Illinois at Chicago, box 8, folder 106.

Warren, J.F. (2016). Philippine typhoons since the seventeenth century. In G. Bankoff & J. Christensen (Eds.), *Natural Hazards and Peoples in the Indian Ocean World* (pp. 105–141). New York, Palgrave Macmillan.

Webb, S. (2018). Greening honey: Producing the underground origins of a forest wonder. *Journal of Material Culture*, doi: 1359183518782717.

Chapter 10

Community-Engaged Resilience in an Island Community

Case of Fisherfolks in Pamarawan Island, Malolos, Bulacan, Philippines

Alain Jomarie G. Santos, Zosimo O. Membrebe Jr, John Christian C. Valeroso, and Arlen A. Ancheta

INTRODUCTION

In the 2018 World Risk Index, the Philippine archipelago was ranked third among countries most vulnerable to disasters. A significant number of the country's small island and coastal communities are greatly vulnerable to impacts of climate change and hydro-meteorological hazards (Hiwasaki et al., 2014). Due to the island communities' geographical, hydrological, and demographical features, they are rendered perennially at-risk to natural disasters, such as effects of storm surges, floods, landslides, tsunamis, drought, and famine. The resulting catastrophic economic and physical damage, as well as loss of lives emphasizes the importance of resiliency and economic security in an island ecosystem.

Among residents of island communities, an obvious economic impact of this vulnerability is livelihood insecurity. Because locals cannot address the declining aquatic resources due to unpredictable change in weather patterns and garbage pollution caused by anthropogenic sources, island development is slow (Berse, 2016). Exposure to natural hazards also aggravates adverse impact on human lives and productivity.

One of the most vulnerable island communities is Pamarawan, an island barangay located off the coast of Malolos, a coastal town in Bulacan Province in Central Luzon. The island is a prolific producer of shrimps and crabs.

Aside from open sea fishing, the island has fish ponds for freshwater fish. However, the island is prone to sea level rise due to tidal changes, and low-lying areas of the island are frequently submerged. The geographical isolation of Pamarawan contributes to the low economic returns of fishing activities. Moreover, the locals are economically restricted due to natural upheavals of the rising sea water and flooding; hence, their catches are declining.

SMALL ISLAND ECOSYSTEMS

An island as a piece of land surrounded by water is a tempting object of any study due to the apparent clarity of boundaries and insularity (Kerr, 2005). An island may be an area with a clear jurisdiction but is also defined by spatial limitations, thus inhabitants struggle and contend for food, water, and shelter.

Small islands and coastal zones have highly diverse ecosystems, which serve not only as a food source for the community, but also as a habitat for many species. This diversity also suggests the possibility of overexploitation and contamination of the resources in the area as a result of coastal populations, infrastructure, and investment (Bijlsma et al., 1995). Due to the growth of economic activity, the coastal systems' ability to adapt to the changes in the environment (e.g., climate, human activities, sea levels, etc.) is compromised, thus resulting in the degradation of natural amenities. Size, isolation, and resource limitations are just among the challenges and pressures these coastal systems frequently face if they are to aim for sustainability (Kelman, 2007).

Island ecosystems therefore require social, economic, and political parameters to sustain them. Having limited resources within their reach, island communities could benefit from effective and sustainable island management and inclusive development.

RESILIENCY

The island ecosystem of Pamarawan, as a vulnerable community, must embed resiliency so as not to disrupt their economic activities. Externalities such as weather disturbances, garbage surges, tidal changes, chemical spillage, and other hazards threaten the community specifically in the sustainability of their economic security.

The International Labor Organization (ILO) defines "Economic Security" as a principle that constitutes basic social security, defined by access to fundamental needs of infrastructure relating to wellness, education, housing, information, and social protection, as well as employment or work security. Economic Security in a vulnerable island community is buoyed in a strong resilient community and environment. Resiliency is the ability to recover from shocks and situation pressures in a timely and effective way (Unger, 2011). Consequently, a resilient community would enhance economic security brought about by economic resiliency. Economic resiliency is the ability of a community to perform its function despite any shock (Rose, 2007).

Several authors suggest that community resiliency incorporates components from both physical and social realms, whereby most individuals are as successful as their communities as a whole (Cohen et al., 2013; Unger, 2011). Resilient communities undergo four phases in disaster which are: mitigation, disaster preparedness, response, and recovery (Maguire and Hagan, 2007). Each phase is critical in enhancing the resiliency abilities of every individual in the community.

The Theory of Complex Adaptive Systems pertains to disaster resilience in its surfacing phase. This theory elucidates inherent closeness between the theory of complex adaptive systems and the concept of resilience, which strengthens the importance and information in the study of disaster risk management that would sustain resilience. Zhou et al. (2010) state that "dynamic resilience can be enhanced by adjusting, adapting to hazards, and learning from the disasters according to the theory of the adaptive cycle," while Manyena et al. (2006) state that disaster resilience can be seen as the innate system capacity of a community, or populace susceptible to shock or stress, to rebound and adapt in order to keep going. The theory of Complex Adaptive Systems suggests that risk management would fortify resilience; hence the role of the decision-makers in disaster mitigation during the emergence stage is critical in preparation and mitigation of risk.

Membrebe and Briones (2016) suggest that for Filipinos to address disaster risks and problems, it is essential that educating an individual on disaster preparedness and risk reduction will create more responsible individuals and inhabitants in a disaster-prone area like the Philippines. On the other hand, Chandra et al. (2017) also suggest that education is important but argue that it must be incorporated by exchange of information to develop more systematic planning in disaster-prone communities.

A useful mechanism which has been identified in lessening the damage to coastal systems because of human activities is integrated coastal zone management, normally initiated by a local government unit. This system will entail a continuous and developmental process that identifies and implements mitigating actions to attain sustainability and adapt to climate change, particularly in coastal zones and small island community such as Pamarawan. It will not only help in preserving and safeguarding the natural resources of the coastal system, but it will also benefit the coastal population regarding food source and livelihood. However, no matter how promising this project is, constraints such as community participation and economic disruptions are inevitable.

In the study of Briguglio (1995), factors were identified that contribute to the threat of small island developing states, namely: limited size, insularity and remoteness, susceptibility to natural disasters, and environmental factors. Inhabitants are challenged by a sense of insecurity, insufficient food, and loss of livelihood. *Sense of security* means restricting the impact of uncertainties and risks which affect the people's daily lives while providing a social environment where people's sense of belonging to a range of communities is defined, and where they benefit from fair treatment and opportunities in the workplace while developing their capacities in what the International Labor Organization refers to as decent work. Decent work is important as it would help people alleviate their current standard of living. As author Barbara Ehrenreich said as she experienced underemployment, "No one ever said that you could work hard—harder even than you ever thought possible—and still find yourself sinking ever deeper into poverty and debt" (2001).

Socioeconomic effects are likely to decrease household income and lead to greater poverty (Israel & Briones, 2014). A correlation has been established between natural disasters and poverty based on the 2011 Community-Based Monitoring System data set for 70,326 households from Pasay City, Metro Manila (*ibid*). The research discovered that 7 percent of the per capita household income was lost because of disasters like floods and typhoons. In contrast, wealthier households are more likely to take the initiative in undertaking proactive adaptation measures (*ibid*).

RESEARCH METHODOLOGY

This research study used mixed methods to determine community resilience, as well as fishermen's economic security. Creswell (2015) describes the method as a way in which both quantitative and qualitative data were gathered by the investigators, combining the two and drawing interpretations based on the combined strengths of both sets of data to address the research problems. A combination of quantitative and qualitative data was necessary as the research aimed to provide a balance in community resiliency and economic security of the chosen island community (*ibid*).

Qualitatively, the researchers conducted a focused group discussion and several field observations with the leaders of the fisherfolk during their immersion in the Pamarawan community from October 2016 to January 2017. The series of questions posed to the fisherfolk were based on fishing skills and categorized as: *namamanti* (uses fishnet fishing); *namamaklad* (fish pen workers); *manunudsod* (prawn fishing using fishnet); and *namamangka* (boatman). The four types of fisherfolk were all interviewed to understand the community's fishing system, their struggles with natural disasters and responses to them, as well as understanding their concept of resiliency. The researchers also asked the same questions of the thirty-three heads of household included in the structured survey.

Quantitatively, this research determines the factors that likely support economic resiliency in the identified island community of Pamarawan. Factors affecting economic resiliency were measured using logistic regression, which is a special form of regression used in determining the impact of independent variables with dependent variables that have binary responses.

The logistic regression model of this research is illustrated in equation below:

$$Res = ln\frac{P_i}{1-P_i} = Z_i = \beta_0 + SEC_1X_1 + Info_2X_2 + Edu_3X_3 + Tools_4X_4 + Risk_5X_5$$

$$+ Age_6X_6 + u$$

Where:

Res = Respondent's answer if they were able to recover from the disaster they have encountered (Binary dependent variable which is answerable by "Yes" or "No")

SEC = Respondent's measured socioeconomic class based on Socioeconomic Classification Marketing Opinion Research Society of the Philippines (MORES)

Info = Respondent's answer about the information they get in times of disaster (This will be on a scale of 1–10, 10 having the most information)

Edu = Respondent's educational attainment

Tools = Number of tools (emergency materials) that a household possesses in times of disaster

Risk = Respondent's answer about their perceived risk in times of disaster (This will be in a scale of 1–10, with 10 being the most vulnerable)

Age = Respondent's age

The study used clustered random sampling (Calmorin et al., 2007) where the population is grouped into clusters or small units. The basis of the values in the clustered random sampling is the number of households listed in the January 2015 barangay profile. Qualifying questions allow the researchers to remove from the list respondents who are ineligible, based on the predetermined criteria of the research (Siniscalco & Auriat, 2005). Therefore, all respondents in this research have the following characteristics: (1) Head of the household (2) Resident of the island for at least ten years (3) Identifies fishing as their livelihood for more than ten years (4) Has experienced disaster more than ten times and (5) Not included in the initial interview during the field observation and focused group discussion. Out of forty-two potential respondents, only thirty-three were considered, as they are the household heads who were able to meet the identified qualifiers.

The Island of Pamarawan

Pamarawan is one of the islands situated between the river delta of Malolos and Manila Bay; its distance from the capital city of Manila is 25 kilometers. Like the rest of the island communities scattered along the Philippine archipelago, Pamarawan is exposed to natural disasters. According to the 2016 Barangay Profile, the island has a lot area of 264 hectares, including fishponds (see figure 1). It has a population of 4,003, consisting of 804 households. The main sources of livelihood are fishing and salt-making. Pamarawan is considered one of the poorest barangays in the province of Malolos (Malolos City Government, 2011).

The barangay captain is the singular chief authority, and the island lacks the major human resources and major facilities required to make the place a livable environment. It offers just one public elementary school, one public

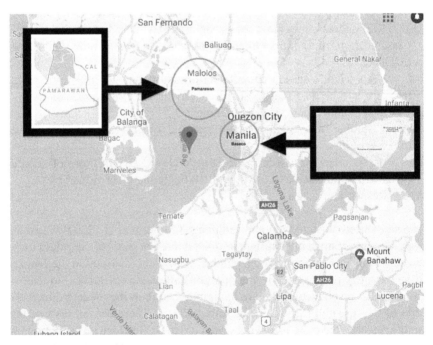

Figure 10.1 Map of Pamarawan. *Source*: City Planning and Development Office of Malolos (n.d.), Bulacan.

high school, a single floor health center, a two-kilometer cemented road, two churches, and one small fish landing port. The only access to mainland Malolos is via a 45-minute banca ride from the Pamarawan fish landing to Panasahan, another fish landing in Malolos.

Fishing Skills

The locals in Pamarawan are skilled fisherfolk; the male members of the community dominate the fishing activity while women are in charge of the shrimp and fish marketing. Fishing activities are undertaken between midnight and early morning. Shrimp and fish catches are brought to the Pamarawan fish landing where the "baculero" (capitalists) are waiting to buy the catch at a wholesale price. Price negotiation at the Pamarawan fish landing is through bidding by *bulungan* (whispering), a traditional way of negotiating fish prices.

The fisherfolk have their own motorized banca and an assortment of tools for catching shrimps of different sizes. Their fishing tools include *panti* (gill-nets), *sudsud* (dredging tool), and *baklad* (fish corral). Gillnets are used in catching fish; dredging tools are used in catching alamang (small shrimp), kapac, and crabs; and shrimps and crabs are trapped in the fish corrals. Fishing is undertaken both inland and at sea.

Shrimp fishing is dictated by weather conditions. Fisherfolk do not travel in the open sea during heavy rains, strong winds, and heavy waves, but Pamarawan is fortunate to have inland fishponds that sustain the communities during the wet season and salt beds during the dry season. Those who cannot go out to the open sea are hired to monitor the fish ponds.

Living Side by Side with Water and Disaster in Pamarawan

Access to basic services is difficult in Pamarawan; medical facilities are inadequate, and the community is dependent on artesian wells for their water supply. The island community is submerged in water during high tide. The streets are narrow and some houses are made of lightweight materials, such as wood and galvanized iron. Houses are small, hence children play their empty shell games in the street.

Unemployment and unstable income are the major sentiments of the locals, who lack financial resources and support from various local government units. These units are not proactive enough in implementing new programs to support residents of the island communities, other than supporting fishing employment. The lack of access to financial institutions results in demanding economic situations for people wishing to augment their daily subsistence requirements, as they tend to borrow from moneylenders who charge exorbitant interest rates.

While unpredictable weather conditions are a limiting factor on fishing activities, man-made disturbances such as floating garbage and *pulang tubig* (red tide) also affect community residents, as well as the main livelihood activity. Floating garbage blocks the gill nets and destroys the bancas' motors. Garbage is a major problem: the island community has no disposal facility, and refuse is transported by a garbage boat to mainland Malolos.

A survey was conducted to present a holistic picture of Pamarawan in living with natural disaster. Out of thirty-three respondents, twenty-six household heads or 79 percent were male, twenty-one of whom were employed and five were unemployed. Among the seven female respondents, three were employed and four were unemployed. Thirteen out of the thirty-three respondents belonged to Class D income bracket, which comprised the majority of the respondents, followed by ten respondents in Class C2 and nine from Class E. Only one respondent could be considered in Class C1, which shows that majority of the people from the community lack most of the basic necessity and income for their daily needs. The majority of the respondents also lacked college education: only one respondent graduated from college and thirteen out of the thirty-three respondents only finished sixth grade.

Table 10.1 below shows the cross tabulation of respondents' ages and their responses to questions about recovery from the most recent disaster they had experienced. The table provides two important findings: first, the majority of the people in the community were relatively old. The respondents' comments show that most of the individuals who completed their college degree on the island then leave the community in search of better economic opportunities and eventually they settle outside of the island. The second observation was that the majority of the respondents could be categorized as "resilient" after a disaster; however, there were still individuals who experienced difficulties in coping with disasters, regardless of their age. Furthermore, the majority of the respondents who were aged fifty and above were found to be the most resilient.

Table 10.1 Logistic Regression Results

Variable	Coefficient	Odds Ratio	z value
Constant (Resiliency)	−15.01	0.00	−2.54**
SEC	1.63	4.35	1.93*
Information	0.45	1.57	1.75*
Educational Attainment	0.96	2.61	1.65*
Preparation Tools	0.13	1.14	0.81
Perceived Risk	0.09	1.10	0.62
Age	−0.29	0.75	−0.78

**Significant with 95% confidence level.
*Significant with 90% confidence level.
LR statistic = 17.78; Prob Chi^2 = 0.0068; Pseudo R^2 = 0.3911.

Respondents were asked to rate the level of disaster risk reduction information they received from government agencies during disasters. On a scale of 1–10, the mean response is 6.82, which means that they received a moderate level of information. The respondents often mentioned that their most common source of information about natural disasters was television news. Consequently, island residents have to look for other means by which to get full information in times of disaster.

The researchers noted twenty-seven elements that a community must possess, to be resilient and disaster ready, and found that the subject-community was 65 percent prepared for a natural disaster. Items noted to be lacking in most of the households were a first aid kit, cooking supplies, and compilation of pertinent documents such as government-issued certificates (birth, marriage) and IDs, property titles, bank documents among others. The mean answer of the respondents to perceive risk or their general perception of community's vulnerability in times of disaster was 7.24. The mean may still be considered as moderate due to the diverse perceptions of some respondents (Standard Deviation = 3.2). However, it is worth noting that 40 percent of the respondents (fourteen out of thirty-three) gave a rating of 10, which may imply that people find their current condition very risky in times of disaster. The respondents were also asked to rate the level of disaster risk reduction information they received from government agencies during a disaster. Participants were found to possess a moderate level of information.

The researchers used logistic regression in determining if socioeconomic class, level of information, education of household head, preparation tools, perceived risk and age, would increase the likelihood of being resilient in the island community. As shown in table 1 above, researchers inferred that socioeconomic class, level of information about disaster risk reduction, and educational attainment would significantly increase the likelihood of community resilience. In terms of resiliency during a disaster, a community's low socioeconomic status can be mitigated by increased access to information and the presence of residents with a higher level of education. This validates the application of the Theory of the Complex Adaptive Systems, which precursors the need for readiness at the early stage of the disaster to establish resiliency regardless of the socioeconomic class. The study shows that respondents who have a lower socioeconomic classification (SEC) are more resilient than those who have a higher SEC. This result is inconsistent with the regression analysis of Israel and Briones (2014) in the households in Metro Manila. This result is different in an island community because people with a lower SEC have fewer household possessions and they are more accustomed to disaster-related catastrophes such as flooding. Disaster risk reduction tools and risk perception would increase the likelihood of being resilient, although they are statistically insignificant. Age does not have a significant impact on a community's resilience.

Health is also a major concern since a majority of the older population suffers from cardiovascular conditions, including hypertension. These health concerns could be attributed to the staple food consumed, as their diet is high in seafood such as shrimps and crabs, but low in fruit and vegetables, which they cannot afford to buy, especially during lean fishing months.

Despite a meager daily income and a high unemployment rate (63%), it was observed that the majority of the locals engaged in gambling and drinking. At present, Pamarawan is challenged by poor road conditions, difficulties in commuting during the wet season, tidal flooding, poverty, lack of stable income during the off-fishing season, and lack of facilities to support the island fishing industry.

In addition, the barangay has not been implementing proper waste management. Refuse may be seen everywhere, including floating on the high tide and lying along the sidewalks during low tide. Solid waste management is one of the major environmental concerns currently confronting the island's inhabitants. This is due to the absence of a waste disposal facility, a lack in the residents' initiatives to conduct proper waste disposal, and non-segregated waste practices. Plastic is everywhere and piles of garbage either rip or destroy gill nets and block shrimps and crabs from entering the fish corrals. Floating garbage coming from various sources reduces the shrimp catch of the fishermen.

Fisherfolk in Pamarawan consider flooding a disastrous and hazardous event on the island. They cannot sell and negotiate prices in the market as they have no fish and shrimp catch. Most of the fisherfolk do not earn an income sufficient to meet their daily needs; thus, they would venture into the open sea even in harsh conditions. When strapped for cash, many of them approach informal lenders, commonly known in the Philippines as *five-six (5–6)*, a local slang for a fly-by-night financing scheme, which lends money at a 20 percent interest rate. The *5–6 lending* serves as an emergency source of finances to the fisherfolk, as the majority of them are not qualified to acquire a bank loan due to their limited earning capacity and lack of property to offer as collateral. Another lending option for residents is a credit cooperative which charges minimum interest. It is popularly known as CARD, the Center for Agriculture and Rural Development (CARD, Inc.). Founded in December 1986, it is a social development organization that provides a range of community development services to landless women in poverty. Most of the fisherfolk availed of loans from this organization for various reasons; however, the loan facility is considered a short-term solution to be accessed in times of financial stress.

COMMUNITY-ENGAGED RESILIENCE

People in an island community, because of the geographic isolation, usually rely on each other with regards to various needs, whether its food, physical help or emergency assistance. Good relationship with the people in the community would foster community-engaged resilience. The locals in Pamarawan have a strong community support system. *Pakikisama* or camaraderie as a basic gesture in helping those who are in need is a common practice. This social support system is a vital economic coping mechanism in the community. In Pamarawan island where everybody knows everybody, the community members in general help each other when neighbors lack basic needs. An example of this social support is evident in the way food is shared among fisherfolk. If the catch of one household is not enough to be sold in the market, at least they have food to consume for the day and can ask their neighbors for some rice. The main problem during a disaster period, however, is the availability of rice, a staple food in the Philippines, as well as the gasoline needed for their motor boats to operate.

The conversion of fishponds to salt beds is an alternative source of economic security during the summer months. This activity provides a bridging source of income for those who are unable to go out fishing on the open sea. If weather conditions for fishing are unfavorable, the children, women, and fisherfolk can gather crabs or shrimps along the shores to augment family income.

The diverse fishing skills of the locals such as *pamamanti* (the use of gill nets), *panunudsud* (the use of dredging tool), and *pamamaklad* (the use of fish corral) are devices for economic resilience. There are many tools that they can use in harvesting the shrimps and crabs from the sea. If a fish corral is destroyed by strong waves, then the fisherfolk can use gill nets or dredging tools as alternatives. Aside from fishing, some fisherfolk are engaged in transportation work. Others drive an electric tricycle around the island or their motorized banca to transport the locals to mainland Malolos. During the fishing off-season, fisherfolk repair their nets, fish corrals, and motorized banca. These practices by the locals promulgate community-engaged resilience as far as food security is concerned.

CONCLUSION

Island ecosystems are vulnerable to natural disasters. The study reveals that the locals lack information and education on disaster risk management. The people tend to be complacent and fatalistic. The people in Pamarawan would benefit from increased information and knowledge about disaster risk strategies to manage the threats of natural disasters. The community leaders must be involved in building a culture of information and preparedness. Regular and sustained information workshops regarding resilience and disaster preparedness must be offered to the locals. This finding is consistent with the findings of research conducted in Visayas and in Mindanao, which suggested the importance of education and information exchange to develop systematic planning in disaster-prone communities (Chandra et al., 2017; Membrebe & Briones, 2016). Education, coupled with adequate information, provides the locals with improved understanding and disaster risk mitigation options. Locals have traditionally adopted a complacent attitude, saying *"sanay na kami sa bagyo at baha"* [We are used to typhoons and floods]. However, the impacts of climate change-induced disasters are severed and unpredictable.[1] With climate change, every disaster is different in terms of intensity and frequency.

It was also observed that the island has limited open and coastal spaces necessary to build environmental resilience and infrastructure growth. Sustainability of space is important in an island ecosystem because it serves as a buffer between the sea and limited land use. The locals therefore should be guided on the importance of space. As Ancheta et al. (2016) mention, "sustainability would create a livable city that would have the elements of green space and open access for public use." Mangroves are decreasing around Pamarawan and due to the increasing population, and space is a scarce resource. The mangroves that used to protect the island have been replaced by housing and inadequate protections against erosion.

The fisherfolks' occupation makes them vulnerable. The study revealed that most of the fisherfolk are vulnerable to several diseases such as respiratory illnesses and skin infection. They are likewise vulnerable to economic instability due to their insecure income and possible dangers they encounter at work on the sea, aside from the fact that they don't have any other skills apart from fishing which has been a traditional livelihood source. Most dream of their families living off the island and enjoying a better standard of living. Low income from fishing as a nature-dependent livelihood is a factor that made the locals pay less attention on the community's natural environment, as evidenced by massive floating garbage polluting the shoreline of the barangay which are not cleaned up for proper waste disposal. They are also strongly vulnerable to becoming victims of natural disasters physically, emotionally, and financially.

Financial access and capital formation are factors that also uphold resiliency. Because of the fishing disruption brought about by natural and manmade disasters, locals tend to have instability in economic income. This income insufficiency drives them to source funds from informal lenders which is just a stop gap solution. The exorbitant interest from the loans makes it more difficult for them to achieve financial stability. Microfinance can help rural households in upgrading their livelihood (Manta, 2016) and is recommended in addressing the needs of the family. Higher education increases the income of microfinance institution clients (Ikpefan, Taiwo & Areghan, 2016). As such, microfinance is not the only way to alleviate poverty; however, it may be a good starting point for small island communities. Microfinance will not only provide financial assistance for capital, but will also provide health, education, and housing assistance. Since small islands are usually remote areas, with fewer resources compared to others, microfinance can help people in these communities learn how to efficiently manage their resources.

The Local Government Unit in the island barangay wants the community to have options and alternative opportunities to reduce the risks fisherfolk often experience. Resilience should be strengthened among the locals, who believe that opportunities (especially for women) enhance resiliency in the community. Women in the island can promote financial resilience through livelihood support programs, disaster resilience through proper emergency response trainings, and environmental resilience through women-initiated mangrove planting and coastal clean-up. It was that women are not harnessed or engaged as valuable players in building the resiliency of coastal communities because of the patriarchal orientation in every household. They have been practicing community-engaged resilience but are not aware of it and its proper process. This is reflected in how the community designates flood lines as risk warning; alternative livelihoods from inland fishponds to salt-making following the change of season. However, these are not enough as the locals need capacity building in disaster risk reduction. The locals are sensitive to the needs of the island and the sea in general, but they lack the capacity to articulate these needs as many are not well-informed. They are contented to be *manganganti (*fishermen using gill nets*), manunudsud (*small shrimp and crustacean catchers*),* and *mamamaklad (*fishpen workers*),* thus their hope lies with the youth, who they hope will study and leave the island for opportunities elsewhere.

Locals are now complaining that garbage interferes with fishing activities, threatening the economic, health, and social well-being of the Pamarawan, as well as nearby communities. The island's poor waste management system pose as a deterrent to healthy environment and water system that would promote good health and clean habitat for the aquatic resources such as fish and crustaceans. A waste management system needs to be supported by the local government and a functioning material recovery facility to manage the waste disposal in the island.

Pamarawan is just one of the thousands of small islands in the Philippines and community-engaged resilience needs to be embedded among the locals as they know what resources they have, what potential they have, and what resources to protect in the community. Institutional support is required to empower the community to survive unpredictable natural disasters. The usefulness of the Theory of Complex Adaptive Systems in understanding the required adaptability and ability to be flexible when facing emerging disasters is important in becoming a resilient community. It emphasizes that disaster resilience varies in approach as it is based on various sociocultural, economic, and governance reasons due to the differences among communities in the hazards they are facing. However, regardless of the differences, it is critical that the decision-makers and the community are well-informed and properly engaged in order to strengthen resilience.

NOTE

1. Typhoon Haiyan that devastated Tacloban City in 2013 was an example of this catastrophe that caused massive loss of lives, properties, and environmental destruction.

REFERENCES

Ancheta, A.A., Membrebe, Z.O., Santos, A.G., Valeroso, J.B., & Vizmanos, C.B. (2016). Sustainability of forest park as space break: A case study of Arroceros forest park in congested city of Manila. *International Journal of Sustainable Development, 9 (5),* 63–81.

Berse, K.B. (2016). In between the everyday and the invisible: Climate change perception and adaptation among Filipino Children. *Journal of Politics and Governance, 6,* 58–82.

Bijlsma, L., et al. (1995). Coastal zones and small islands. *Cambridge University Press, 9* 289–224.

Briguglio, L. (1995). Small Island States and their Economic Vulnerabilities. *World Development, 23 (9),* 1615–1632.

Calmorin, L & Calmorin, M. (2007). *Research Methods and Thesis Writing.* Manila: Rex Book Store.

Center for Agriculture and Rural Development. (2014). *Who We Are? CARD INC.* Retrieved October 21, 2016 from: https://www.cardmri.com/cardinc/.

Chandra, A. et al. (2017). A study of climate-smart farming practices and climate-resiliency field schools in Mindanao, the Philippines. *World Development, 2017,* 1–17.

Cohen, O. et al. (2013). The conjoint community resiliency assessment measure as a baseline for profiling and predicting community resilience for emergencies. *Technological Forecasting and Social Change,* 1–10.

Creswell, J.W. (2015). *A Concise Introduction to Mixed Methods Research.* California: SAGE Publications Inc.

Ehrenreich, B. (2001). *Nickel and Dimed: On (Not) Getting By in America*. New York: Metropolitan Books.

Gujarati, D.N., & Porter, D.C. (2010). *Essentials of econometrics*. (Fourth ed). New York: McGraw Hill.

Gujarati, D.N. (2004). *Basic Econometrics* (Fourth ed.). New York: McGraw Hill.

Hiwasaki, L., Luna, E., Syamisidik, & Shaw, R. (2014). Local and indigenous knowledge for community resilience: Hydro-meteorological disaster risk reduction and climate change adaptation in coastal and small island communities, *UNESCO*, 60.

Ikpefan, O., Taiwo, J.N., & Areghan, I. (2016). Microfinance and poverty alleviation in Southwest Nigeria: Empirical evidence. *Journal of South African Business Research, 2016,* 1–19.

Israel, D.C., & Briones, R.M. (2013). *The Impact of Natural Disasters on Income and Poverty: Framework and Some Evidence from Philippine Household*. Makati: Philippine Institute for Development Studies.

Israel, D.C., & Briones, R.M. (2014). *Disasters, Poverty and Coping Strategies: The Framework and Empirical Evidence from Micro/Household Data—Philippine Case*. Makati: Philippine Institute for Development Studies.

Israel, D., & Bunao, D. (2016). *Research on Urban Resilience to Natural Disasters of Households, Firms and Communities in the Philippines*. Makati: Philippine Institute for Development Studies.

Kelman, I. (2007). Sustainable livelihoods from natural heritage on islands. *Island Studies Journal, 2 (1)*, 101–114.

Kerr, S.A. (2005). What is small island sustainable development about? *Ocean & Coastal Management*, 48, 503–524.

Maguire B., & Hagan P. (2007). Disasters and communities: Understanding social resilience. *The Australian Journal of Emergency Management, 22*, 16–20.

Membrebe, B.Q., & Briones, C.F. (2016). Disaster relief foods and food consumption practices of low–income inhabitants in Eastern Visayas, Philippines. *International Journal of Academic Research in Environment and Geography, 3 (1)*, 29–37.

Rose, A. (2007). Economic resilience to natural and man-made disasters: Multidisciplinary origins and contextual dimensions. *Environmental Hazards, 7,* 383–398.

Siniscalco, M.T., Auriat, N., & Ross, K. (2005). *Quantitative research methods in educational planning: Questionnaire Design [module]*. Paris: UNESCO International Institute for Educational Planning.

Ungar, M. (2011). Community resilience for youth and families: Facilitative physical and social capital in contexts of adversity. *Children and Youth Services Review, 33* 1742–1748.

Ungar, M. (2011). The social ecology of resilience. Addressing contextual and cultural ambiguity of a nascent construct. *The American Journal of Orthopsychiatry, 81*, 1–17.

Chapter 11

Harnessing Participatory and Community-Based Approach in Disaster Recovery Planning in Areas Affected by the Earthquake in Bohol

Emmanuel M. Luna, Rosalie Quilicol,
and Victor G. Obedicen

BACKGROUND

In October 15, 2013, a 7.2 magnitude earthquake hit the province of Bohol and affected thirty municipalities and the City of Tagbilaran. The earthquake resulted in surface rupture, ground shaking, liquefaction, landslides, and sink-holes. A coastal uplift was observed in some communities where the ocean shore retreated about 50 meters back. The earthquake caused widespread damage to buildings and infrastructure, notably roads, bridges, houses and even icons of Bohol culture and heritage. The earthquake claimed 211 lives and injured 877 while eight people were reported missing. It also displaced 73,721 families or 373,325 persons and destroyed more than 66,000 houses. (Province of Bohol 2014; NDRRMC 2013).

Emergency responses were undertaken by government agencies and humanitarian organizations. However, three weeks later, super-typhoon Haiyan hit Leyte and other provinces in the Visayan region on November 8, 2013. The storm surge devastated the city of Tacloban and adjacent munici-palities. The new disaster drew greater public attention and diverted much humanitarian assistance from Bohol to Leyte.

In response to these disaster situations, the University of the Philippines (UP) launched funding support program for projects to help the communities affected by the two disasters. Supported by the University fund, the College of Social Work and Community Development (CSWCD) implemented a six-month action research from January–June, 2010 to help the poor communities affected by the earthquake. The action research dealt with the problem: How can participatory and community-based approaches be adopted in undertaking disaster recovery and in rebuilding communities affected by the earthquake in Bohol?

The short-term participatory action research (PAR) experience in this project shows how theoretical formulations can be operationalized in a disaster situation. Considering the urgency of the situation and the fact that the communities were devastated by the earthquake, it is imperative to see how local participation can be enhanced. As shown in the succeeding narrative of the process and outcomes of the PAR, the earthquake resulted in the physical devastation of the communities, but it brought out inherent resources that helped them in their recovery.

THE NEED TO ENGAGE THE POOR
IN DISASTER RECOVERY

The CSWCD believes in participatory development and it was deemed important to apply this in disaster recovery context. The PAR initiative was anchored on theoretical and empirical observation about how disaster impact the poor and how they respond to disaster events. Disaster impacts are multidimensional and affect people from various socioeconomic groups. For disasters of huge magnitude, the poor have the greatest difficulty in recovering because of the lack of resources or access to resources that would enable them to move on. For example, when typhoon Ketsana flooded Metro-Manila in September 2009, poor communities in low lying areas and along the lake remained in evacuation centers until January of 2010. On the other hand, rich families affected by the flood and lack of electric power supply simply moved to other homes, or stayed in hotels during the emergency While the local people are often the first to be impacted by disaster, they are also the first responders at the familial and community level (Luna 2009 and 2011; Delica-Wellison and Gaillard 2012).

In a developing country such as the Philippines, inequality is very prevalent and disaster impact is also unequally experienced. Thus, disasters are viewed, not as natural but "more as a matter of power and social justice" (Mascarenhas and Wisner 2012, citing Wisner, et al. 2004). The powerlessness of the poor is manifested in their material well-being, as well as in their lack of access in decisions and policy-making processes affecting their lives. They have forfeited their right to intervene and participate (David 1984). At the macro level, the country's growth could be dragged down by calamities and can push the households into "transient poverty" (Remo 2013). The poor become poorer as disasters destroy their livelihood and access to basic services.

Immediately after the outset of disaster, there is usually a massive influx of emergency assistance in the forms of money, people and volunteers, relief goods, technical assistance for rescue operations, evacuation and provision of life support systems (Luna 2001). However, as time passes, the volume of aid is reduced despite the ongoing needs of the impacted community. This can be explained by various sociocultural factors such as shift in media coverage, decreasing interest, perceived return to normalcy, political conflicts and humanitarian concerns including the occurrence of new disasters and aid fatigue. Significantly, there is a tendency to forget the disaster event when it is no longer covered in the media which, in turn, shapes disaster-related international finance (Dean 2017).

Given the needs that have to be addressed, the management of an emergency situation is considered poor when the agencies and organizations that are supposed to respond are uncoordinated and there is no control over the situation (Lopez-Carresi 2012). Greater losses take place and this affects the phase of recovery which has to follow immediately after emergency response. However, critical conditions take place when disasters happen one after the other, forcing the humanitarian workers to focus always on meeting the emergency needs.

PAR have been undertaken since the 1970s when participatory development became the alternative to economic growth and the modernization model of development. It was applied in several programs for health, irrigation, agriculture, urban poor, workers, and most programs for marginalized sectors. By the 1980s, participatory and community-based approaches to disaster management became popular in the Philippines. The role local communities could play in reducing vulnerabilities was recognized in responding to emergency disaster response and later, in disaster risk reduction (Heijmans and Victoria 2001; Delica 2003; Luna 2004; Delica-Willison and Gaillard 2012; Luna 2014; Delica-Willison, de la Cruz and Molina 2017). Participation was also adopted in disaster studies through what has become known as "action research." In PAR, the "A" is action intended to reduce disaster risk through the participation of both the researcher and the local people (McCall and Peters-Guarin 2012).

Community participation has become embedded in disaster risk reduction measures meant to address conditions and vulnerabilities faced by communities. Community participation is imperative in managing resources for risk reduction to ensure that programs and projects are based on the actual needs of the community. It is a way to incorporate the people's local and indigenous knowledge and practices in mitigating disaster risks. Community participation empowers vulnerable communities to plan and implement initiatives to lessen their vulnerabilities and strengthen their capacities (UNISDR 2007).

Community participation can be concretized in community-based disaster risk reduction management (CBDRRM) processes meant to transform passivity and powerlessness into action and resilience. It is an alternative to the reactive and "dole out" approach that often remains pervasive following emergencies in the Philippines. Rather than following on managing the impacts of disasters, CBDRRM encompasses risk reduction before, during, and after disaster events. CBDRRM is a strategy to reduce people's vulnerabilities, ensure public safety, and reduce the impacts on lives, property, resources, and environment due to hazards, empowers individuals and community institutions, and transform structures and relationships that generate inequity (Heijmans and Victoria 2001; Delica 2003; Luna 2004 and 2014; Delica-Willison and Gaillard 2012; Luna 2004 and 2014; Shaw 2016; Delica-Willison, de la Cruz and Molina 2017). The Asian Disaster Preparedness Center defines CBDRRM as:

> A process of disaster risk management in which at risk communities are actively engaged in the identification, analysis, treatment, monitoring and evaluation of disaster risks in order to reduce their vulnerabilities and enhance their capacities. This means that the people are at the heart of decision making and implementation of disaster risk management activities. The involvement of the most vulnerable is paramount and the support of the least vulnerable is necessary. (ADPC 2003 cited in Abarquez and Murshed 2004)

After the disaster emergency response, the next stage in CBDRRM is the recovery. Disaster recovery are decisions and actions taken after a disaster with a view to restoring or improving the pre-disaster living conditions of the stricken community, while encouraging and facilitating necessary adjustments to reduce disaster risk. It adopts the principle of "build back better." The recovery task of rehabilitation and reconstruction begins soon after the emergency phase has ended, and should be based on preexisting strategies and policies that facilitate clear institutional responsibilities for recovery action and enable public participation. Recovery programs, coupled with the heightened public awareness and engagement after a disaster, afford a valuable opportunity to develop and implement disaster risk reduction measures and to apply the "build back better" principle (UNISDR 2007; UNISDR 2015).

The International Recovery Platform based in Kobe, Japan developed guidelines for recovery planning in nine areas: shelter, health, infrastructures, livelihoods, psycho-social issues, gender, climate change, environment, and governance. There is also an innovative approach, the Pre-Disaster Recovery Planning (PDRP) that prepares communities for recovery, even prior to the disaster event. The PDRP reduces disaster impact and facilitate the recovery process, and may be considered as any planned attempt to strengthen disaster recovery plans, initiatives, and outcomes before a disaster occurs (UNISDR 2005). However, lack of awareness and understanding of PDRP concepts and the processes remains high in disaster management in the Philippines. Instead, when disaster strikes, there is a proliferation of reactive responses (Luna 2014). The process of recovery becomes more challenging due to the absence of preconceived plans on how to deal with the losses and conditions arising from disaster impact.

THE PARTICIPATORY DISASTER RECOVERY PROCESS

Two months after the earthquake and after the emergency state, the PAR team of the college started preparing for the action research toward recovery by reviewing reports on the earthquake data and impact. The municipality of Loon was chosen as the site of the PAR upon the recommendation of the provincial officials who recognized that it was one of the more severely impacted municipalities in the province.

The municipality of Loon, composed of sixty-seven barangays, was the hardest hit by the earthquake. The earthquake resulted in landslides, tension cracks, sinkholes, ground rupture, liquefaction, and tidal flat uplift. These impacts destroyed basic and strategic public and private infrastructure; rendered thousands of households homeless; and drastically halted and later slowed down government operations and delivery of public services like water and power supply, healthcare and education, among others, as well as goods and services that are essential to daily survival. There were 1,820 totally damaged houses and 6,370 partially damaged houses. The casualty in Loon was seventy-two, or 32.28 percent of the total casualties in the province, relatively high compared with other municipalities (Loon Municipal Rehabilitation Plan 2013).

The community residents were grateful that the earthquake happened early in the morning on a day that was declared as a holiday. They said that there would have been more casualties if it happened on a regular working and school day.

After meeting and project orientation at the provincial level, the PAR team met with the municipal mayor of Loon. The mayor agreed to participate in the project and designated personnel who could assist the researchers. With the assistance of the municipal staff, the three most affected communities in the municipality were chosen as the research sites, subject to the confirmation by the community leaders. The communities represented different resource zones, namely urban, coastal, hilly and upland areas.

The researchers visited the communities, met the local leaders and conducted ocular surveys. The community leaders agreed to participate in the project and took care of the preparation for a one-day initial meeting for assessment of the situation and damages of the earthquake. The participants in the FGDs were the community leaders representing different groups such as men, women, youth, private sector, religious groups, persons with disability, and senior citizens. The participants were oriented about the project and the roles that they would be playing in the process. They agreed to participate and shared their experiences, the challenges they met, and their suggestions to improve the conditions.

As the community assessments progressed, the local leaders became increasingly engaged in the conduct of a disaster recovery planning workshop. They identified the participants from each community. The participants included local government (LGU) officials involved in planning for disaster recovery. The outcome of the initial assessment of the damages, responses, needs, as well as the outputs of the disaster recovery workshop were documented and presented to the community leaders and LGU officials. The final activity in each community was the conduct of a seminar on DRR, Community-Based Disaster Risk Reduction and Management, and on the DRRM Law in the Philippines. A workshop held in each of the three communities identified the community's participation in recovery efforts, lessons learned, barriers to recovery, and their recommendations.

CASES OF COMMUNITY RECOVERY

Case 1: Barangay Napo

Barangay Napo is a coastal community that is adjacent to the central district of the municipality called *poblacion*. It is located at the back of the church that totally collapsed during the earthquake. Although the community is part of the *poblacion* that is already urbanized, the people rely mostly on fishing and farming. The barangay has a land area of 474,890 hectares. The 2011 population was 1,480, with 722 male and 758 female. There are 271 households and 345 families. This means that there are many households which are composed of multiple families (Brgy. Napo File. n.d.).

Only one resident died at the church that collapsed in the *poblacion*. All the houses were affected by the earthquake; 50 percent of them collapsed while the others had partial damages. The barangay hall had several cracks and the community stage was damaged. Other facilities that were destroyed were the classrooms, street lights, chapel and the barangay road. Two classrooms were impacted by large sinkholes which emerged inside the buildings. The community was thankful that there was no class at the time of the earthquake, or there would be more injuries and casualties among the children.

In terms of livelihood, the fisherfolks were afraid to go on fishing because it was reported that there were cracks at the bottom of the sea. They no longer know the terrain under the water. Initially, the water became blurred and the fish caught diminished, resulting in the increase of the price of the fish. The locals said that the sea receded. The earthquake caused the coral reef to rise up above the sea level, thus expanding the sea coast by about 300 meters into the sea. This was problematic to the fisher folks because they had to carry their boat for a long distance. The exposure of the reef and the sudden deepening of the sea beyond the shore affected the sea shell gatherers, especially the women and children. They could no longer gather sea shells.

The community received assistance from various government agencies like the Department of Social Welfare and Development, National Food Authority and Department of Health. The local government units (LGU) and local and international humanitarian organizations provided relief goods, tents, temporary school rooms, materials for shelter and medical services. They also provided stress debriefing services. During the FGD and planning workshop with the residents from Brgy. Loon, they identified and prioritized damage that required attention and assessed the status of the recovery. The needs prioritized were housing, facilities, school, environment, livelihood, prices of goods, and the barangay roads. The rehabilitation of the community infrastructures such as the barangay roads, community hall, health center, school classrooms, and the stage at the community square were beyond the community's financial capacity. Although the barangay had a budget called the Internal Revenue Allocation (IRA) from the national government, the amount was not enough to enable the barangay to reconstruct the facilities. The community leaders sought all possible linkages that could assist them. They considered applying for a loan which could be paid through the IRA. However, they recognized that securing a loan has long-term implications such as paying high interest and inadequate funds for basic services.

The temporary classrooms were made of tents and were not conducive to learning due to high temperatures. Seven classrooms and a faculty room were needed. The Mines and Geoscience Bureau (MGB) instructed the community leaders to put on hold any construction of the school building, pending structural analysis of the soil. They were encouraged instead to construct structures made of light local materials from bamboo and coconut trees called *pawid* and *sawali*.

Since most of the residents depend on fishing and sea shell gathering for their income, the expansion of the shoreline was a significant problem. They thought of digging a canal that will enable them to transport their boats in going out to the sea. However, the fishery experts from the government advised them that this proposal has to be studied first. The fisherfolk were also not organized. A fisherfolk with a banca can earn P 250.00 per day.

But with the decreasing catch, they were not able to earn this amount. They needed fishing materials such as nets. They suggested other alternative livelihood pursuits such as swine raising, carpentry and doing catering services.

Case 2: Barangay Lintuan

Brgy. Lintuan has a land area of 820,438 hectares. The community has coastal flat land and rolling terrain toward the hillside. Being along the shoreline, the common occupation of its constituents is fishing. The community has 1,076 population, 220 households, and 229 families (Brgy. Lintuan, n.d.) There is a day-care center and an elementary school in the community. The basketball court, the day-care center, the school and the stage are all located at the side of multipurpose open pavement. Important occasions such as graduations, foundation day and fiesta are all celebrated here. The barangay hall is beside the compound where the basketball court and schools are situated. The Catholic chapel is located just across the street. This community square is patterned in the traditional arrangement where all the important political and social structures are clustered together for easy coordination and conduct of important barangay activities.

No person died during the earthquake. However, a woman's arm was severed because she was hit by a beam of her house that collapsed. Some male residents of the barangay rescued her, despite the risk that they might also get trapped inside should there be an aftershocks. The people lamented that after the rescue, it was the local police who were recognized for the rescue operation instead of the men of the community. The family of the female survivor, however, rewarded the man who was able to rescue their daughter by providing a scholarship to one of his children.

Due to the destruction of major roads and bridges, the access to the municipality became difficult. There was a delay in the provision of assistance such as food and temporary shelters in Brgy. Lintuan immediately after the earthquake. The neighbors helped each other through the *bayanihan* labor-sharing system, the Filipino practice of helping each other through volunteerism and collective action. A resident and a community health worker shared that on the day the earthquake happened, all the residents no longer wanted to stay inside their houses because of the fear of frequent and strong aftershocks. They identified an open space deemed safe and stayed there together with some other families. Since their food was good only for a few days, a neighbor whose husband was working abroad adopted them and provided their daily sustenance for almost two weeks, until relief goods from the barangay were distributed.

During the FGD, the community participants prioritized their livelihood. With the sea receding, fisherfolks had difficulty and the catch had also lessened. The second priority is the community facilities, which unfortunately could not be reconstructed and thus required new facilities to be constructed. The walls and ceiling of the barangay hall were partially damaged. The stage at the community square was severely damaged. To construct temporary shelters, some of the residents put up small houses made of light materials while waiting for resources to rebuild their houses. Three school buildings were declared to be off limits or restricted for use.

The participants were keenly aware of what needs should be addressed. While they recognized that assistance should be sought from external sources such as government organizations (GOs), nongovernmental organizations (NGOs) and the private sector to hasten the recovery process, they believed that it is necessary for them to engage in *bayanihan* in the community efforts to recover by reconstructing the roads, rebuilding their homes or putting up makeshift schools. During the participatory disaster recovery planning workshop held in March 2014, participated in by community leaders, LGU officials and NGOs engaged in recovery efforts, each barangay presented their recovery plans. Contrary to the initial observation in the January 2014 FGD where the Brgy. Council and the constituents of the barangay in general were seemingly still affected or traumatized from their experience, hence were incapacitated to even call for a general assembly and engage in recovery planning, the leaders who attended the planning workshop were able to articulate the immediate challenges faced by the community. During the workshop, they identified the barriers toward their recovery such as the lack of funds and equipment, and the lack of monitoring from agencies providing assistance. They learned the value of readiness and preparedness in times of disaster, and less obvious lessons such as the value of personal appearance in following up request for assistance from government offices.

Case 3: Barangay Bahi

Brgy. Bahi is one of the upland barangays of Loon, Bohol. It has a land area of 157.5 hectares, with much of its topography being rolling hills. It has a population of 451 individuals (Brgy. Bahi 2013) Brgy. Bahi is an agricultural community with many of the residents dependent on planting palay and copra for their livelihood. The impact of the earthquake in the community was beyond the physical damages. While the damaged infrastructures were the primary concern, the disaster affected the people's welfare, the delivery of social services, and the local economy. Many community members also experienced physical and psychological distress. They had health problems such as measles, diarrhea, coughs, and cold. Students were also not able to go to school because the day-care center and road bridge were destroyed. Some children experienced trauma as manifested by crying whenever there were aftershocks. Some elders panicked, shouted, or ran whenever there were aftershocks.

The houses and the barangay facilities such as the community chapel, the Barangay Council Hall, the day-care center, the agricultural trading center, the covered court, and the power lines were destroyed. There was no electricity for two weeks. The day-care center temporarily stopped holding classes until a makeshift center was put up. The community leaders were not able to hold office immediately. Some of their office files were also destroyed. Agriculture was affected because the earthquake caused some rice fields to misalign. Coconut trees were uprooted or disturbed causing lesser yield for farmers.

The barangay LGU was over-burdened and overworked due to the additional work of following up on relief assistance and operations, maintaining administrative functions like council meetings and general assemblies in difficult situations, and making reports despite damaged office facilities. School class sessions were shortened but additional class days were added. Despite these difficulties, one glaring capacity exhibited by the community immediately after the disaster and on its way to recovery was its barangay governance spearheaded by the Barangay Council. Initially, to counter the threat of food insecurity, it was the Barangay Council that provided rice for the families. They later on advised the people to consume other fruits like banana even if those were sourced from farm lands other than their own.

The barangay had already initiated activities to recover from the earthquake. The Barangay Council spearheaded in the clean-up operations of the debris and repairs of damaged infrastructures. The barangay hall area was back hoed and debris cleared. The people cleared the stage area through the cash for work program. They were able to construct the roof and posts of the community chapel and placed temporary walls using resources that came from donations. The road concreting was done to repair the damaged sections through the cash for work program. They repaired the damaged streetlights and the water supply system. They have put up temporary walls using marine plywood for the day-care center. The kitchen and stockroom have been cleared of debris.

The Barangay Council has provided food assistance to the constituents accessed through the calamity funds. The Barangay Council facilitated the distribution of vitamins, and the administration of vaccinations to prevent measles and mumps for children 1–15 years old and pregnant mothers. The Barangay Council also distributed piglets for hog raising to some members of the barangay for livelihood. Another capacity is the inherent resourcefulness of the people from the community. They accessed and managed limited resources to address hunger and diseases, in rebuilding their homes, clearing out debris, and resuming economic activities. Because of the limited assistance from outside, the people resorted to borrowing money from relatives and friends, rather than wait for assistance from the government that was very slow in responding to their needs.

The residents immediately repaired their houses and sought financial resources to buy materials, although their funds were not enough to cover all their needs. Some residents salvaged the materials from the houses and built temporary shelters. The social relationships in the barangay helped in surviving the aftermath of the earthquake. Some couples suggested that as a result of communal recovery efforts they had grown closer and had fewer fights. Parents became more protective of their children, for example, parents bringing and fetching their children to and from school because of their fear of aftershocks. The disaster event strengthened cooperation and sharing of resources among neighbors.

Community members were able to access and utilize a variety of human, social, financial, material, and natural resources. The human resources included the resourcefulness of the people of the community during and after the emergency situation. After the earthquake the people from Bahi relied on each other for support to get through the initial shock of the earthquake by sharing resources such as food, fuel, and even shelter. The Barangay Council was also able to use its connection and familiarity with the Municipal LGU to secure relief for their constituents. The people said that their belief in god was also a source of strength. They believed that it was god's will that they were not injured. The experience also served as an awakening for the community to attend to their spiritual life.

The Internal Revenue Allotment of the Barangay Council provided immediate relief as this was used to purchase food and other necessary expenses for repairs of barangay facilities. However, the financial resources were not enough and they required external assistance. Being in an agricultural community, the people were able to thwart hunger because they had stored rice and other agricultural products for food. There were also local materials such as wood, bamboo, and coconut lumber which they used to set up temporary shelters.

Integrated Analysis and Conclusions

The major activities conducted during the PAR enabled the project team and the community leaders to produce information on the effects and impacts of the earthquake, formulate a simple recovery plan for the community, and get an update on the current recovery status and initiatives of the community. The conduct of the municipal participatory planning workshop contributed in enhancing awareness among the local staff on the recovery needs of the communities. There was minimal written information available about the communities and the absence of written documents was aggravated by the collapse of the community barangays where the documents were kept. The PAR was able to document the disaster events through storytelling by community members. The sharing of experiences by the community members on the earthquake provided local accounts of what transpired during the earthquake, how the community responded, and the challenges and needs they faced, their initial responses, and the plans for their recovery.

The people at the interior and less accessible upland community did not receive relief goods and had to content themselves with the community leader's initiative to meet their needs. Those who were visible at the evacuation centers or were staying in the fronts of their houses at the *poblacion* or the highway were the ones who received more relief goods. The damage and impact of the earthquake that were highlighted by the mass media and the public were the road infrastructure, heritage churches, and beautiful houses. Little media exposure was given to the livelihood and housing conditions of the ordinary residents.

In the communities, the damages that affected the people most are the destruction of their houses, school classrooms, barangay halls, day-care centers, lighting facilities, community stage, and the displacement of their livelihood. Those who manifested shocks and trauma received inadequate support. Some debriefing was done by some agencies at the start but these were not sustained. During the FGS, the children participants still cried while narrating their experiences. The people in the communities were poor but the disaster impact caused them to become poorer. The municipality has vast open land where the families staying in vulnerable places can be relocated. However, due to land ownership, it was difficult to find suitable places for resettlement. The principle of "building back better" was far from the reality.

Community Capacities and Resources

Bayanihan, the Filipino collective and voluntary action by the people aimed at helping each other spontaneously manifested in the three barangays immediately after the earthquake and during the rebuilding phase. The people built temporary shelters right after the earthquake using improvised materials such as nipa, mats, tarpaulin, and tents. They made an inventory of food available and these were shared with families without food. The men were involved in rescue operations. The community residents mobilized internal resources beyond what the local government can provide. They held a program to celebrate the founding of the community and to raise funds, collected offerings during mass and accepted donations for the renovation of their chapel. The reconstruction and fixing of some of the facilities such as roads and street-lights were done by the people themselves.

The local governance through the Barangay Council leaders was very effective in responding to the needs immediately after the earthquake. They used the calamity fund of the barangay to purchase rice and other food. They coordinated the preparation and distribution of cooked food. They came out with resolutions seeking for assistance from the LGU and attended the LGU meetings and planning activities toward recovery. The effectiveness of local governance can be attributed to the manageable size of the community, the residents being relatives and part of the extended families, and the dynamic relationship among the barangay leaders and the barangay constituents. They supported each other.

Sustaining community tradition is a way to recover from a collective trauma experienced due to a disaster. The holding of traditional festivities such as the annual foundation or barangay day was a way of recovering from emotional losses. The musical number, colorful banners to identify groups of people, community dancing and festive eating reflects the cultural aspect of the community of not losing hope and looking forward with a new start. The decision to hold the festive tradition helped them to be more proactive and forward looking. It also showed that the community had the means to make the necessary preparations for the event.

An attitude of sharing among the community existed in helping those who were affected. When the housing materials such as galvanized iron sheets and plywood came for the families whose houses were assessed as totally damaged, those who were not included in the list were also given assistance by each family by sharing one or two iron sheets and plywood for those not in the list. In the process, all the families in the community received housing materials. Relief goods are not just material assistance but are also interventions that can help in the psycho-social recovery. A relief good symbolizes a helping hand and care that can help people feel that there are others from the outside who remember and share in times of disaster (Luna 2006, 2000).

There was also a natural mechanism for recovery. Before, the people were very worried that the mangrove along the shore would die because the sea water receded. However, by June 2014, sea water had expanded and reached the mangrove area. The trees started to recover.

The responses and actions of the people show that they have local and indigenous knowledge that they can utilize for disaster risk reduction, specifically for response and recovery. There have been several researches conducted on local knowledge and practices since the 1970s that show that local knowledge can address risks and increase the resilience of the communities (Hiwasaki, et al. 2014). Both the Hyogo Framework for Action (2005–2015) and the Sendai Framework for Disaster Risk Reduction 2015–2030 acknowledge the significant role of local, indigenous, and traditional knowledge in disaster risk reduction. Thus, in doing disaster recovery planning, it is important to consider the local and indigenous knowledge in drawing out measures for recovery.

Formulation of a Disaster Recovery Action Plan

Pre-disaster recovery planning was not a practice at the provincial, municipal, and community levels. The recovery activities were conceived only after the disaster event. Hence, most of the efforts were geared toward response, and the recovery planning followed. The Barangay Disaster Risk Reduction and Management Committees were not functional at the time of the earthquake. What prevailed was the "natural" or instinctive role of the leaders to act and lead the community facing danger and devastation based on preexisting social norms and forms of collective cooperation. With the inputs provided during the Municipal Participatory Planning Workshop, the participants were able to map out a recovery plan that served as basis for their recovery and moving forward. The workshop gave the municipal government officials more opportunities to better understand what was happening at the community level. Through the PAR, the LGU and the community had more exchanges and dialogues, instead of just planning at the municipal level by using data from forms distributed to the communities. With the PAR, the community leaders learned the value and appreciated the importance of putting their experiences and plans into writing. Before, they relied more on oral tradition in setting their plans. The recovery plan drafted during the workshop served as a guide for the community to monitor the process and status of their recovery.

The recovery efforts of the government were focused more on the distribution of materials for housing and funds for the rehabilitation of infrastructure facilities. The provision of livelihood was crucial for individual recovery but the people did not receive it, or only little assistance was provided. Apart from the inadequate resources, livelihood strategies operate at the micro or community level and within complex social relationship, thus it is difficult for the government agencies to intervene without coordinating with the local communities or nongovernmental organizations working in the area (Jigyasu 2012). Participatory approaches in local assessment and recovery planning are therefore inevitable to institutionalize a system that will work for both the community and government agencies.

Without appropriate voices from below, there could be recovery projects that are conceived to be beneficial to the poor but are impractical and not feasible. A humanitarian organization providing housing assistance in one of the communities required a cash counterpart amounting to P 14,000. Many beneficiaries decided to forego the housing assistance because of their inability to provide the required counterparts. Without livelihood and other sources of income, it would be impossible for the people affected by disaster to come up with cash counterparts. The provision of cash rather than material assistance can be more effective because this provides greater flexibility in asset rebuilding.

A seemingly unimportant project that was prioritized was the reconstruction of the community stage in the multipurpose square. However, for the community, this was an important project because the stage is used for activities such as graduation, foundation day, and other community festivities. This simply reflects the cultural importance of a simple kind of infrastructure in the lives of the people. Filipinos generally find meaning and significance in rituals, ceremonies, celebrations, festivities, and other community gatherings that contribute to the identity and wholeness of the person. Reconstructing facilities that contribute to cultural development is a key to rebuilding the inner self of a person. There is very little awareness and even high resistance to the idea about the social and cultural aspects of risks and disasters (Hewitt 2012), despite earlier assertion that "natural" disasters are social rather than natural phenomenon. Viewing disaster as a social phenomenon allows proactive strategies and stipulates that "the recovery process is a process in which the population improves its level of adaptation to its environment and also lowers its future vulnerabilities" (Dynes 1992:15).

Support and Commitment in Pursuing Participatory Community Disaster Recovery Planning

The experience in the PAR project showed that the Barangay Local Government Unit (BLGU) played the primary role in distributing relief, identifying needs of the barangay constituents, and seeking assistance from various resource agencies. The barangay officials were able to use the annual income given by the national government known as the Internal Revenue Allocation (IRA) to communities for recovery purposes. While residents are confined as beneficiaries of whatever assistance the BLGU can provide, there were residents who moved to recovery by reconstructing their houses using their own resources and with minimal assistance from external organizations. It was understood that the local and national government had the intention to help as shown in the recovery plan. However, the process was very slow. The rehabilitation of community infrastructures depended on the national budget. However, due to bureaucratic procedures, the disbursement took too long. The funds for the recovery came only in June 2014, eight months after the earthquake.

The recovery process must be viewed holistically and should not be limited to infrastructure only. Other aspects such as psycho-social and environment should be considered and sustained. There is a need to equip and develop the capacity of the LGU in planning and monitoring recovery efforts.

Participatory monitoring is needed because communities tend to be passive and complacent in terms of accountability and in engaging themselves in the monitoring of the recovery and rehabilitation activities.

For several decades already, community participation in DRR has been given immense attention in academic discourse and literature, conferences, and international mandates. The Hyogo Framework for Action (HFA) 2005–2015 had made community and volunteer participation as a crosscutting issue to be taken into account in pursuing DRR.

However, despite the mandate to incorporate community participation in DRR, it was observed in the process of tracking the progress of HFA that "community participation in DRR policies and plans is not mandated in any of the (countries) reviewed" (Wilkinson, Twigg, Weingartner and Peters 2017:18). Thus, the Sendai Framework for Disaster Risk Reduction 2015–2030 stipulated in its guiding principles that DRR "requires an all-of-society engagement and partnership. It also requires empowerment and inclusive, accessible and non-discriminatory participation" (UNISDR 2015). In the Philippines, the Republic Act 10121 known as the "Philippine Disaster Risk Reduction and Management Act of 2010," declared that it is a policy of the State to "engage the participation of the civil societies, the private sector and volunteers in the government's disaster risk reduction programs" (RA 10121, Sec.2m). However, as shown in the PAR outcome, the local community had indigenous practices and were actively engaged in addressing their needs, but had very limited participation in decision making in the government's recovery planning process. Therefore, it is necessary for practice beyond theoretical formulation and that the mandates be translated into local actions. Engaging the community in DRR-related projects provides opportunities for enhancing their capacities. Documenting and sharing their practical experiences promotes greater awareness that theories should be applied and redefined by learning and listening to their voices.

Local communities devastated by disaster need external support from the outside. However, this requires developing their capacities and institutionalizing systems for local recovery. This is imperative to avoid falling into the risk of depending on external aid (Jigyasu 2012). Thus, humanitarian organizations, government agencies, the academe, and all other entities wanting to mobilize material and financial resources to meet the basic needs of disaster victims must have

an empowering perspective in the process of giving. Receiving aid like dole outs helps alleviate emergency needs, but can create more devastating effects such as dependency and powerlessness. Producing services with the direct inputs of the disaster-affected families is both physically and inwardly rewarding. It symbolizes the rebuilding of their lives with their own will. (Luna 2009:24)

This statement made almost a decade ago still holds true today, indicating that there has been slow progress in enhancing community participation, and there is still much to do today.

REFERENCES

Abarquez, Imelda and Murshed, Zubair (2004). *Community-Based Disaster Risk Management*, Bangkok: Asian Disaster Preparedness Center.

Asian Disaster Preparedness Center (ADPC) (2003). *Course Reference Manual of the Eleventh Community-Based Disaster Risk Management Course (CBDRM-11)*, Bangkok. ADPC.

Barangay Lintuan. (n.d.). [Community File]. Lintuan, Bohol, Philippines: Author.

Barangay Napo. (n.d.) [Community File]. Alicia, Bohol, Philippines: Author.

Barangay Bahi. (2013). [Community Fie]. Bahi, Bohol, Philippines: Author.

David, Karina C. (1984). Community organization and people's participation. *Lambatlaya*, Third and Fourth Quarters.

Dean, Annika (2017). "Funding and Financing for Disaster Risk Reduction Including Climate Change Adaptation" in Kelman, Ilan, Mercer, Jessica and Gaillard, JC (eds). *The Routledge Handbook of Disaster Risk Reduction Including Climate Change Adaptation*, London and New York: Routledge.

Delica-Wellison, Zenaida, de la Cruz, Loreine B., and Molina, Fatima Gay (2017). "Communities Doing Disaster Risk Reduction Including Climate Change Adaptation" in Kelman, Ilan, Mercer, Jessica and Gaillard, JC (eds). *The Routledge Handbook of Disaster Risk Reduction Including Climate Change Adaptation*, London and New York: Routledge.

Delica, Zenaida (2003). "Community-Based Disaster Risk Management: Gaining Ground in Hazard-Prone Communities in Asia." *Philippine Sociological Review*, 51:41–64.

Delica, Zenaida and Gaillard, J (2012). "Community Action and Disaster" in Ben Wisner, JC Gaillard, and Ilan Kelman (eds). *The Routledge Handbook of Hazards and Disaster Risk Reduction*, London and New York: Routledge.

Dynes, Russell (1992). "Disaster Reduction: The Importance of Adequate Assumptions About Social Organization" in Idema, Marlies and de Bell, Harold (eds). *Proceedings of the Seminar Training for Disaster Reduction II. Cairo, 2–5 September 1991*. The Netherlands: Disaster and Emergency Reference Center.

Earthquake and Megacities Initiatives (2014). "The 15 October 2013, Bohol, Philippine Earthquake". Technical Report Initial Release.

Heijmans, Annelis and Victoria, Lorna (2001). *Citizenry-Based and Development-Oriented Disaster Response: Experiences and Practices in Disaster Management of the Citizens' Disaster Response Network in the Philippines*. Quezon City: Center for Disaster Preparedness.

Hewitt, Kenneth (2012). "Culture, Hazard and Disaster" in Wisner, Ben, Gaillard, JC and Kelman, Ilan (eds). *The Routledge Handbook of Hazards and Disaster Risk Reduction*, London and New York: Routledge.

Hiwasaki, L., Luna, E., Syamsidik, Shaw, R. (2014). *Local and Indigenous Knowledge for Community Resilience: Hydro-Meteorological Disaster Risk Reduction and Climate Change Adaptation in Coastal and Small Island Communities*, Jakarta: UNESCO.

International Recovery Platform (IRP), United Nations Development Programme (UNDP) and International Strategy for Disaster Reduction. (n.d.). *Guidance Note on Recovery*, Kobe, Japan: IRP, UNDP, ISDR.

Jigyasu, Rahit (2012). "Socio-Economic Recovery" in Wisner, Ben, Gaillard, JC and Kelman, Ilan (eds). *The Routledge Handbook of Hazards and Disaster Risk Reduction*, London and New York: Routledge.

Khan, Amir Ali (2008). "Earthquake Safe Traditional House Construction Practices in Kashmir" in Shaw, R., Uy, N. and Baumwoll, J. (eds). *Indigenous Knowledge for Disaster Risk Reduction: Good Practices and Lessons Learned from Experiences in the Asia-Pacific Region*, Bangkok: UNISDR.

Lopez-Carrezi, Alejandro (2012). "Emergency Management Principles" in Wisner, Ben, Gaillard, JC and Kelman, Ilan (eds). *The Routledge Handbook of Hazards and Disaster Risk Reduction*, London and New York: Routledge.

Luna, E. M. (2014). Community-based disaster risk reduction and disaster management. In A. Lopez-Carresi, M. Fordham, B. Wisner, I. Kelman, & J. C. Gaillard (Eds.), Disaster management: International lessons in risk reduction, response and recovery (ch. 4). Milton, UK: Routledge.

———— (2011). "Community Education for Building Communities: Framework and Cases from the Philippines" in *Social Work Research Institute. Social Work in Disaster Risk Management 2010*. Tokyo, Japan: Social Work Research Institute, Japan College of Social Work.

———— (2009). Community development as an approach to reducing risks among flashflood-affected families in Albay, Philippines. Disaster Studies Working Paper 24, London: Aon Benfield UCL Hazard Research Centre. Available in https://www.researchgate.net/publication/238657781_COMMUNITY_DEVELOPMENT_AS_AN_APPROACH_ TO_REDUCING_RISKS_AMONG_FLASHFLOODAF-FECTED_FAMILIES_IN_ ALBAYPHILIPPINES/download

———— (2006). Power from within to overcome vulnerabilities; A Philippine case on the endogenous system of response to river flooding. *Science and Culture*, 72(1&2), 45–51.

———— (2004). Rising from the field: The concept and practice of community–based disaster risk management in the Philippines. *Proceedings of the Third Disaster Management Practitioners' Workshop for Southeast Asia* (pp.56–64). Bangkok: Asian Disaster Preparedness Center (ADPC).

———— (2001). Disaster mitigation and preparedness: The case of ngos in the Philippines. *Disasters*, 25(3), 216–226. https://doi.org/10.1111/1467-7717.00173.

———— (2000). A case study on the endogenous system of response to river flooding in Bula, Camarines Sur: Towards an appropriate and integrated development (Doctoral dissertation, University of the Philippines-Diliman, Quezon City, Philippines). Retrieved from http://lynchlibrary.pssc.org.ph:8081/bitstream/handle/0/4185/12_Endogenous%20System%20of%20Response%20to%20River%20

Flooding%20as%20a%20Disaster%20Subculture_%20A%20Case%20Study%20 of%20Bula.pdf?sequence=1&isAllowed=y.

Mascarenhas, A and Wisner, B (2012). "Politics: Power and disaster" in Wisner, Ben, Gaillard, JC and Kelman, Ilan (eds). *The Routledge Handbook of Hazards and Disaster Risk Reduction*, London and New York: Routledge.

McCall, Michael K and Peters-Guarin, Graciela (2012). "Participatory Action Research and Disaster Risk" in Wisner, Ben, Gaillard, JC and Kelman, Ilan (eds) *The Routledge Handbook of Hazards and Disaster Risk Reduction*, London and New York: Routledge.

Municipality of Loon. (2013). *Municipal Recovery Planning Workshop Documentation [Government Report]*. Loon, Bohol, Philippines: Author.

Municipality of Loon. (2013). *Municipal Rehabilitation Plan [Government Report]*. Loon, Bohol, Philippines: Author.

National Disaster Risk Reduction and Management Council (NDRRMC) (2013). SitRep no. 33 re Effects of Magnitude 7.2 Sagbayan, Bohol Earthquake (On-line) Retrieved from http://www.ndrrmc.gov.ph/attachments/article/1108/updsitrep33.pdf

Province of Bohol. (2014). *Post-Great Bohol Earthquake Rehabilitation Plan [Government Report]*. Bohol, Philippines: Author.

Remo, Michelle (2013). "Calamities May Push More Pinoys Into Poverty-NEDA." *Philippine Daily Inquirer*. November 10, 2013, p. A6.

Philippines. (2010). Republic Act no. 10121.

Shaw, Rajib (2016). "Community-Based Disaster Risk Reduction" in *Oxford Research Encyclopaedia, Natural Hazard Science*, Oxford: Oxford University Press USA.

Twigg, John (2004). *Disaster Risk Reduction: Mitigation and Preparedness in Development and Emergency Planning. Good Practice No. 9*, London: Humanitarian Network Practice

United Nations International Strategy for Disaster Reduction (UNISDR). (2015). *Sendai Framework for Disaster Risk Reduction 2015–2030*, Geneva: UNISDR.

——— (2007). *Word Into Action: A Guide for Implementing the Hyogo Framework.* Geneva: UNISDR

——— (2005). Guidance Note on Recovery: Pre-Disaster Recovery Planning. Retrieved from www.unisdr.org/we/inform/publications/31963

Uy, Sam Ath (2004). "Nature and Practice of Community-Based Disaster Risk Management in Southeast Asia: Cambodia" Pp.55–60 in *Proceedings Third Disaster Management Practitioners' Workshop for Southeast Asia*, Asian Disaster Preparedness Center, Bangkok: ADPC.

Wilkenson, E., Twigg, J., Weingartner, L. and Peters, K (2017). *Delivering Disaster Risk Reduction by 2030 Pathways to Progress*, London: Overseas Development Institute.

Wisner, B., Blaike, P., Cannon, T. and Davis, I. (2004). *At Risk: Natural Hazards, People's Vulnerability and Disasters*, London: Routledge.

Chapter 12

Climate Hazard Effects on Socio-Environmental Health and Adaptation Strategies in Two Coastal Communities in Palawan Island, Philippines

Patrick A. Regoniel, Frederick G. Precillas, Melissa Theodora U. Macasaet, and Nelly Mendoza

INTRODUCTION

The Philippines has an undesirable merit of being a country which is prone to disaster. The magnitude of extreme climatic events has increasingly been felt over the last years. Most of these events are life-threatening and impact the economy, cultural heritage, and ecosystems. Some notable events are fires (Piñol et al. 1998, 345–357), physical damage to crops (Rosenzweig et al. 2002, 197–202), wind damage to trees (Quine 1995, 379–403), and landslides among others (Atienza et al. 2010, 85–91; Smith 2013). These climatic events also affect human health (Kunkel et al. 1999, 1077–1098; McMichael 2003; Patz 2005, 310–317; Luber and McGeehin 2008, 429–435) and, in extreme situations, result in the loss of human lives (Kalkstein 1991, 96, 145; Jonkman 2005, 151–175; Jonkman and Kelman 2005, 75–97).

Situated within the typhoon belt, the Philippines is an archipelagic country comprising many small islands. It is highly susceptible to climatic events such as typhoons, storm surges, and floods (Adrianto 2002, 393–413; Mercer et al. 2007, 245–256; Turvey 2007, 243–264). An average of twenty tropical cyclones form and cross the Philippine Area of Responsibility (PAR) annually (de Guzman et. al 2014, 111–119). Around 89 percent of the Filipino people live within 100 km of its coastal areas (ADB 2009). The islands of the country are characterized by steep slopes which are prone to landslides when heavy rains pour into logged or unstable lands. An illustrative example is the Ormoc landslide tragedy that killed thousands of people (Atienza and Hipolito 2010, 85–91). Severe lashes of typhoons and increasing levels of sea water result in the limited habitable coastal plains becoming narrower and more prone to disasters. Sea level rise (SLR) caused by the expansion of the oceans as a result of global warming (Church et al. 1991, 438–456; Meehl et al. 2005, 1769–1772; Solomon et al. 2009) gradually take its toll on the livelihood of communities (Wu et al. 2002, 255–270). Small islands, deltaic settings, and coastal ecosystems in Southeast Asia are particularly vulnerable to SLR (Nicholls and Mimura 1998, 5–18). The advancing waters can have a significant impact on the tourism industry (Titus et al. 1991; Agnew and Viner 2001, 37–60; Bigano et al. 2008, 765–791) as it causes damage to and destruction of tourist destinations. Sources of fresh groundwater become less available as saltwater intrudes into shallow coastal aquifers (Sorensen et al. 1984, 179, 214; Pezeshki et al. 1990, 33, 287–301; Chang 2011, 1283–1291). Some of the most serious and pervasive threats that humanity faces today are brought about by climate change.

The climate change vulnerability of the Philippines is an element of its development patterns and geographic location (Fisher 2013). The Philippines, as a developing country with limited resources to be adaptive either socially, technologically, or financially, is more likely to suffer as the impacts of climate change increase and intensify, accelerating toward becoming catastrophic. As noted by Birkmann and Wisner (2006), vulnerability is an important element in effective disaster risk reduction strategies. For the last ten years, the Philippines has suffered from a number of deadly typhoons, earthquakes, volcanic eruptions, and other natural disasters. Typhoon Haiyan, locally known as Yolanda, and the earthquake that hit Central Visayas are documented evidence of the inexhaustible disasters faced by the Filipino people. Accordingly, this research investigates the vulnerability of coastal communities to disaster, particularly barangays Binduyan and Babuyan of Puerto Princesa. Primarily, the exposure to and ability to cope with the impacts of climate change are ascertained to help address the need for better resilience against climate change and to assess the socio-environmental health effects of climate hazards experienced by the residents of the two communities. Resilience does not mean that people do not endure any climatic stress, rather, that a resilient and adaptive community functions quicker after an adverse event and the accompanying stress is a transitory case (Norris et al. 2007). The promotion of resilient and adaptive communities demands a change of focus from natural hazards and extreme events to the identification, assessment, and ranking of vulnerability (Lavell et al. 2003; Birkmann 2006a; Birkmann 2006b; IPCC 2012).

The effects of the climate hazards that Binduyan and Babuyan recently experienced are identified in this research. The vulnerabilities of the two coastal communities are used to generate options for adaptation to address the threats of climate change. Adaptation measures have to be accompanied by disaster risk reduction and management interventions to enable vulnerable communities to survive with both climate change and natural disaster risks, such as typhoons, floods, rain-induced landslides, and sea level rise, among others.

The research team utilized data gathering methods such as participant observation, key informant interviews, focus group discussions, and community mapping. The study's informants include long-term residents, community leaders including the barangay chairperson, barangay council officials, leaders of people's organizations, and government employees and officials. Encounters consisted mostly of informal interviews. The team interviewed twelve key informants. The focus group discussion (FGD) involved multiple sectors, including local government officials, a barangay nutrition scholar, barangay security personnel, farmers, fisherfolk, representatives from the business sector, health workers, women, and youth. A total of thirty stakeholders (fifteen in Babuyan and fifteen in Binduyan) participated in the focus group discussions. They were asked to list important climate-related events in their community, and the sector's perceived level of vulnerability to flooding as a major climate hazard affecting their community. After they had done so, the whole group was asked to prioritize the different sectors from most vulnerable to least vulnerable. The list of events was validated with information from the City Social Welfare and Development Office.

The aim of including local people in this research was to understand their local knowledge and experience of the climatic events over time. Participatory approaches to disaster management and preparedness often necessitate a basis in local knowledge and practices because communities in disaster-prone areas have accumulated experiences over time (Battista and Baas 2004, p 10), and, as such, their knowledge is necessary in creating policies and adaptive measures. According to participatory discourse, incorporating local knowledge when formulating policy around disaster risk management has the potential to make a significant contribution to the success of the planning and its implementation. It is also an opportunity to promote locals' participation with higher-level institutions in disaster management (Battista and Baas 2004, p 8) with a view to improving aspects of the project such as performance, acceptance, and sustainability. Community is always the key actor but also the primary beneficiary in the disaster risk reduction process (Yodmani 2001; Osti and Miyake 2011).

Participants were also asked to pinpoint on their community maps the relative location of areas affected by climate hazards. Babuyan barangay officials generated a sketch of the affected areas, while in Binduyan, the locations were labeled with Post-it Notes on their existing community map, and then photographed. The same number of participants in the FGDs joined the community mapping.

The data collected during the first meeting were processed, and cost and benefits assumptions were generated, based on key informant interviews and secondary literature. Cost-effectiveness has been used for many research projects. It is understood as an effective way to limit damage and losses when equated to response and recovery (Shyam 2013). The cost effectiveness ratios (CER) for the different climate hazard adaptation options in the two communities were estimated. Cost estimates, particularly on the hard adaptation options, were made on a per unit basis. The most efficient adaptation option has the least CER value. The formula used in computing the cost effectiveness ratio was:

$CER = C_x/C_n$ where C_x is cost of option x and E_n = number of households or area of property spared from climatic hazards.

The team also explored both short and long-term strategies and their cost-effectiveness. The intention in using this approach was to reduce the negative impacts of disaster hazards, such as flooding, landslides, extreme temperature, droughts, and typhoons. Benefits can be calculated not only in money saved, but also in more secure livelihoods and lives. After processing the data and performing an analysis, the team returned to the study site and validated the results of the study, as well as facilitated the stakeholders' preferred climate hazard adaptation option.

THE BINDUYAN AND BABUYAN COMMUNITIES

The households of Barangay Binduyan are predominately situated alongside the national highway and are clustered in the wider coastal portions at the northeastern part of its boundary. The sources of income and livelihood of this barangay are agriculture, aquaculture, and the tourism industry, which offers a number of resorts and beach-front property developments. As we stroll through the community, it is noticeable that the roots of coconut trees are already exposed. This is visible, physical evidence of SLR. Also, over the past two years, the rising sea has reached the community basketball court that were several meters away from the coast. There are discarded plastic wares, and floating and submerged garbage is common. Some of these are entangled in the coral reefs, which are exposed during low tide.

Barangay Babuyan, on the other hand, is composed of two clusters of households: one is a densely populated coastal area on the northeastern

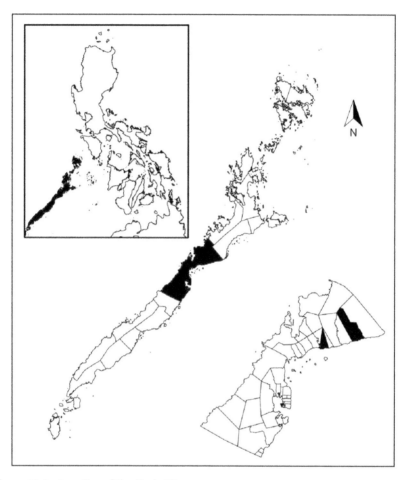

Figure 12.1   Location of the Study Sites.

boundary, and the other is widely dispersed along the sides of the national highway which is on the southern boundary. The community has ponds for fish culture. They farm tilapia and bangus. The ponds comprise approximately 80 hectares and are owned by those who have capital or "big-time" as some informants relayed. In recent years, there has been a decline in the production of these ponds. The coastline of Babuyan has sparse *bakawan* or mangroves. Community raised that for the past years, some members cut mangroves for home use while some use it to produce charcoal. Aside from these geographical characteristics, Babuyan has a 20.68 km river which drains toward Honda Bay. The Babuyan River passes through several barangays in Puerto Princesa City, including Lucbuan, Maoyon, Marufinas, San Rafael, Tagabinit, and Tanabag. There is a total of 161, 912 persons residing within the immediate vicinity of the river, with Babuyan being the most-populated barangay in the river basin area, according to a survey conducted by the National Statistics Office (NSO) in 2010.

These two communities are situated near Honda Bay at the middle-eastern (9°44'N, 118°44'E) side of mainland Palawan, which is one of the most significant sources of reef fisheries in the country. The nearshore region, bounded by the 15 km municipal waters, is a major fishing ground for 1,968 small-scale fisherfolk coming from the eighteen coastal barangays of the City of Puerto Princesa, as well as those from adjoining barangays and commercial fisherfolk outside of this zone. During the 1970s the abundant coastal and marine resources of Honda Bay attracted migrants. Over the past four decades, several settlements have emerged along the coastline. As the population has increased in the settlements the land has become less available, resulting in the poor and marginalized people occupying disaster-prone areas such as steep slopes and exposed sections of the coast. In recent years, the central portion of the island appeared to have suffered more severe storms and surges. Much of the original upland and coastal forests that afford protection against the elements have also been cut down for housing and other economic uses. Thus, typhoons, flooding, and other climate hazards that appear to have intensified over time have left coastal barangays vulnerable to disasters such as flooding in low-lying and nearshore areas, and prone to waterborne diseases, which appear to have increased in frequency.

CLIMATIC EVENTS THROUGH THE YEARS: BABUYAN AND BINDUYAN'S HISTORICAL EVENT MARKERS

Babuyan community members identified the aggressive and life-threatening phenomenon that struck their barangay, affecting their socio-environmental sectors and people's well-being. Some of the FGD participants remembered the 1998 flooding associated with Typhoon Norming. The floods destroyed agricultural areas of the barangay and left about P5.6 million worth of overall damages to Palawan's agricultural products (Vanzi 1998). The typhoon washed out roads and destroyed households, leaving Puerto Princesa in a state of calamity.

Participants also recalled the effects of Typhoon Feriang, which struck in 2001. At that time, 439 community members suffered injury and loss as when wind gusts of 120kph struck the area. Drought was experienced in the following year and nine farmers were given calamity seed assistance. Typhoon Ineng paralyzed the livelihoods of around 433 fisherfolk and farmers when it hit the community in 2003. It occurred during the same year when grassfire razed agricultural land and products, affecting 111 farmers. Most of the grassfires that people experienced were caused by irresponsible community members or some passersby who threw their cigarette filters into dried *cogon* grass.

In 2007, Typhoon Lando with its strong wind gusts destroyed fishing boats, affecting 260 families. 1,325 community members evacuated and were given rice assistance. An increase in malaria cases in the area was observed between 2002 and 2007. Typhoon Tonyo in 2008 destroyed the guardhouse of the Puntod Ilis Marine Sanctuary and affected seventy-eight community members. Farms of 1,085 farmers and fishponds and bancas of forty-three fisherfolk were destroyed by the strong winds, heavy rain, and flooding. Participants recalled that in 2009, there was an increase in reported medical cases and illnesses such as typhoid fever, flu, dengue, diarrhea, colds, and coughs. Participants identified that the reason for some medical cases was because of the condensed household that spreads illnesses easily from one household to another. Crops were destroyed by pests and affected farmers in 2010.

Binduyan community members vividly recalled Typhoon Pepang, which lashed the area in 1995. Three years later, another remarkable typhoon named Welfring destroyed the roofs of houses. Community members also recalled the rise of sea temperatures in 1998 that led to siltation, killing fish and shellfish along the shore. Typhoon Norming in 1998 left the barangay with its roads and houses devastated. The community mourned as they lost one family when this typhoon struck their area. One decade later, a major landslide occurred near the national highway. About 100 hectares of land was razed by grassfire in 2009. In the year 2010, the number of harvested squid and octopus declined.

An historical timeline reveals climatic events which influenced the lives of the fisherfolk and farmers. Notable events include evidence of high sea surface temperature in 1998, strong typhoons in 1995 and 1999, erosion in 2008, and grass fires in 2009. Typhoons appear to have been much more frequent and intense during the last ten years. These events placed community members at risk and socio-environmental sectors vulnerable to hazards.

VULNERABILITY OF SOCIO-ENVIRONMENTAL SECTORS OF BABUYAN AND BINDUYAN

Before the start of the nineteenth century, community members accepted that natural disasters were accepted as God-given events. This belief has slowly altered and science has identified nature as the source of many disasters (Quarantelli 2000). This change in view triggered an emergence of adaptive measures to disasters to limit the damage and loss. Societies began to understand the risks to human beings and socio-environmental sectors wrought by extreme climatic events. As society experiences harm as a result of some drastic changes in the climate around the world, it becomes vulnerable to hazardous climatic events. Generally, socio-environmental sectors of the rural

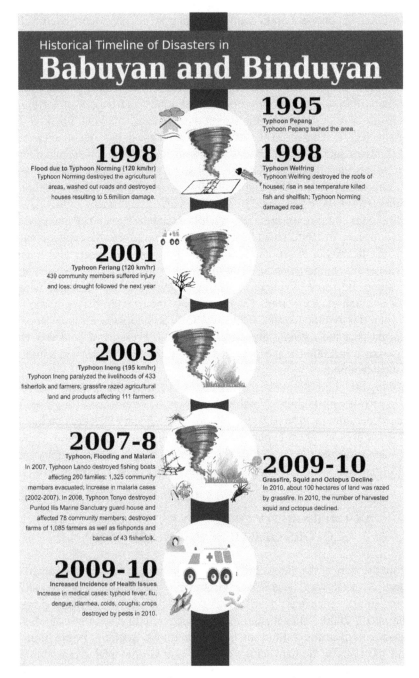

Figure 12.2 Historical Timeline of Disasters in Babuyan and Binduyan.

areas have high vulnerability to climate hazards because they are dependent directly on the resources that they have in their society.

As defined by UNFCCC (2007), vulnerability refers to the exposure of a community or a region to the hazards of and an inability to cope with the impacts of climate change. Barangay Babuyan and Binduyan, for instance, are exposed to environmental contingencies and stress which community members find difficult to manage. The notable events over the last decades that have been identified by the participants of the research were validated through the information that were recorded and documented by City Social Welfare and Development Office.

Typhoons, flooding, and droughts were among the major climate hazards experienced by the two communities. Participants agreed that the most vulnerable sector to extreme climatic events is agriculture. Residents from both barangays recognized the direct and negative impacts of climate change on their yield. In Binduyan, for instance, typhoons affect the production of cashews and bananas. Rice fields and production in the lowland areas are not spared from this hazard. With the temperature increase, the same sector is highly vulnerable to drought, disturbing the crop production of the two communities. Drought may cause grassfires as some careless people may accidentally throw away cigarette filters, which can start a fire. When drought is experienced, both humans and non-humans suffer. Sources of food are affected and may cause the start of health or medical problems in the community. Moreover, fisherfolk are also affected because they cannot go out to fish. Boats and fishing gear are damaged and some are lost in tidal waves.

In Babuyan, the second most vulnerable sector identified by participants was health. Informants associated illnesses with changes in weather. Residents experienced recurring illnesses such as flu, cough, colds, dengue, and muscle pains after each climatic event that they were exposed to. Due to the high temperature, community members suffer from hypertension and sore eyes. Health was also identified as an area of concern by Binduyan participants, who reported similar illnesses, however they ranked it as third most important.

Infrastructure ranked second in Binduyan because the main lines of the water supply system get destroyed during typhoons or heavy rains. On the other hand, Babuyan ranked this sector sixth on their list. Generally, the water supply systems of the communities are affected since during a climatic event, water systems overflow and sometimes fill with gravel and leaves. Barangay roads and bridges (footbridges) often become damaged and inaccessible, causing the supply to be blocked and water difficult to transport after calamities strike the area. This accords with the services that ranked fourth in Babuyan and fifth in Binduyan respectively. Transportation, somewhat connected to the services and infrastructure sector, ranked seventh in the list of Babuyan for accessibility reasons. Common means of transportation are unavailable during severe storms and floods. However, in Binduyan, this sector was not identified to be vulnerable.

Communication interruptions occur during typhoons. Trading, in the form of "buy and sell," is likewise affected due to the lack of farm and fisheries products to sell. This may result in loss of income. The community members of Binduyan, however, take advantage of the typhoons. According to them, the number of pebbles increases after climatic events. This aftermath pebble or stone-gathering supplements the residents' income. They sell them to generate profit in lieu of their main source of income.

Fishpond operators estimate the sea level rise in Barangay Babuyan to be about a meter during the last ten years. As a response, they have increased the height of their dikes to enclose their fishponds and prevent incoming water during high tides and storm surges. Stakeholders in Barangay Babuyan ranked the vulnerability of aquaculture at third place. Around 70 hectares of fishponds become inundated during typhoons. Fisherfolk in Barangay Binduyan are not bothered by this issue as the barangay does not have suitable areas for fishpond construction.

Most houses built in the communities are constructed of light materials and are easily destroyed by typhoons and floods. This sector is considered as vulnerable by stakeholders and ranked fourth and fifth in Binduyan and Babuyan respectively. The manufacturing sector ranked eighth in Babuyan, while in Binduyan, it ranked sixth. Both communities identified similar impacts such as the inability to produce sufficient roofing materials made of coconut leaves and some other products produced in the area.

By identifying climatic events, Binduyan and Babuyan participants were also able to determine the vulnerability of the sectors affected and map out which areas are susceptible or prone to climactic disaster. The participants from Binduyan prepared a spot map of their barangay, and they used this to superimpose the different hazards the community was exposed to, specifically in those areas that were affected by grassfires, flooding, erosion, landslides, and droughts. They also noted the areas where incidents of sickness like malaria, flu, high blood pressure, fever, and malnourished children could be found.

The rainy season in Babuyan signals the onset of health problems for some. Climate hazards pose a risk for the occurrence of infectious diseases. Illnesses such as typhoid fever, diarrhea, flu, cough and colds, sore eyes, dengue, pruritus or itching, and malaria are experienced by some. Malaria is transmitted by water-related vectors such as the Anopheles mosquito which carries two species of sporozoans (*Plasmodium falciparum* and *P. vivax*). The increased cases of malaria in 2002 to 2007 suggest an increased distribution range of malaria-carrying mosquitoes due to increasing temperature (Haines et al. 2006, 585–596).

The lack of sanitary comfort rooms and inappropriate waste disposal practices also threaten community members' health. High coliform has been recorded and is due to pigpens constructed near the sea compound. Pathogenic microorganisms in contaminated fresh water bring waterborne diseases in these two communities. Bathing, washing, drinking, or ingesting contaminated food may result in infection (Louis et al. 1990, 719–728). The saltwater intrusion also affects shallow coastal wells, causing saltiness in drinking water. Flooding and storm surges cause saltwater intrusion in open and ground level wells. This source of water is subjected to many waterborne diseases, especially when natural disasters happen. There are reported and documented waterborne diseases due to climate hazards such as flooding and storm surges in Binduyan, including typhoid fever and diarrhea.

Just like in Babuyan, mosquitoes transmitted malaria to some residents in Binduyan. Residents also noted that hypertension cases increased in the area and, apparently, higher than usual temperature levels caused this health issue. Grassfires and droughts during hot months periodically raze agricultural lands. In 2008, a major landslide blocked road access to the barangay. This event prevented the residents from quick access to medical services in times of emergency.

COST-EFFECTIVENESS OF ADAPTATION STRATEGIES TO CLIMATE HAZARDS IN BABUYAN AND BINDUYAN

Adaptation strategies to climate hazards should be practiced to help society manage the accompanying uncertainties. This is through good planning and appropriate response to the climatic events that produce hazard to humans. As discussed earlier, the history of the events in Binduyan and Babuyan shows gradual climactic changes which became more aggressive and extreme over time. The communities are adjusting accordingly and gradually adapting. Community members raised several options, consisting of new and previously undertaken resource management activities which had the support of the national government, nongovernment organizations, and the local government of Puerto Princesa. Stakeholders in Barangay Babuyan identified their objectives with adaptation strategies and plan to implement any or all of them to mitigate the effects of climate hazards.

To protect the households from storm surges and loss of property, and to minimize soil erosion, it was mentioned that there is a necessity to construct a concrete breakwater. This structure will be placed in the mouth of the Babuyan River as an option to reduce incoming wave intensity, which contributes to erosion and flooding in the area. The community plans to source external funding for this project. The cost per household of the breakwater is

Table 12.1 Cost Effectiveness Analysis of Identified Climate Hazard Adaptation Options

Size	Objective	Adaptation Options	CER (US$)*
Babuyan	1. To protect households (HH) from storm surges, loss of property, and minimize sand erosion	Construct breakwater	276,552.95/HH
		Build dike/levee	32,278.39/HH
		Reforest coast with mangrove propagules	19,457.83/HH
	2. To prevent river overflow and minimize siltation	Rehabilitate riverbank with vetiver grass and supplementary materials	34,020.93/ha
		Construct dikes	32,232.28/ha
		Rehabilitate riverbank with vetiver grass	4,310.47/ha
	3. To protect households from inland flooding	Relocate affected households to a safer place	2,234.11/HH
		Reforest the uplands	925.77/HH
		IEC/Establish early warning system and provide temporary evacuation center	119.52/HH
Binduyan	1. To protect households from strong waves and storm surges	Breakwater construction	11,634,582.61
		Reforest coast with mangrove propagules	9,323.30/HH
		Relocate vulnerable households	1,249.69/HH
		Construct a seawall	885.66/HH

*per unit of benefit.

$276,552.95. The construction of a dike was also suggested. This structure needs to be a length of approximately 500 meters. It is expected to prevent coastal erosion, overflow of fishponds, and soil erosion in coconut plantations. The cost of the structure will be $32,278.39 per household.

Community planting was also suggested. There is a need to reforest the coast with mangrove propagules. This mitigation strategy seeks to address coastal erosion and protect the coastline. The community believes that reforestation can shelter them from strong winds and waves brought about by typhoons. Previously, they had identified five hectares of the coast, covering 6.3 kilometers of the shoreline, as an area to be planted with mangrove propagules. The projected cost was approximately USD 19,457.83 per household. Also, five hectares of land was identified by community members for a reforestation program. Planting trees in the watershed will accord protection from flooding during heavy rains. The cost has been calculated at around USD 925.77 per household.

The cost of hard adaptation options, such as breakwater and dike construction, to protect households from storm surges, strong waves, and loss of property are less cost-effective in Barangay Babuyan than seawall construction in Binduyan. In Babuyan, mangrove reforestation was identified as the most cost-effective strategy for protecting homes and properties, and in minimizing sand erosion in the barangay where mangroves appear to have flourished. Mangroves can serve as a buffer against storms. However, the protective function of mangrove reforestation will take a longer period to be beneficial to the community. On the other hand, in Binduyan, seawall construction had the lowest cost-effectiveness ratio among the identified options.

To prevent the river from overflowing and to minimize siltation, participants focused on rehabilitating riverbanks with vetiver grass and supplementary materials, costing approximately $ 34,020.93 per household. The use of bioengineering technology in riverbank rehabilitation entails planting deeply rooting vetiver grass to hold the soil in riverbanks together. The whole system is strengthened if supplemented with other plants such as bamboo, or mechanical structures such as PVC pipes, wire nets, coconets, and similar materials. Dredging or clearing the riverbed of accumulated sand and gravel deposits, which blocks the water from flowing downstream, addresses overflows in farm areas as well as riverbank erosion. River dredging has the least CER. This strategy is the most cost-effective among the options presented by the stakeholders. On the other hand, riverbank rehabilitation using vetiver grass, combined with mechanical methods, has the highest CER, due to the high cost of materials required to complete such project.

There was also a suggestion that there is a need to implement an information, education, and communications (IEC) campaign and establish a temporary evacuation center to protect households from inland flooding. The estimated cost is $119.52 per household. An IEC campaign, as part of an early warning system, could reduce the negative impacts of extreme weather events. This initiative complements an existing early warning system that warns every member of the community of impending disasters. This early warning as an adaptation method has been effective and has already been implemented in some coastal communities in the Philippines, such as in the Province of Albay in the Bicol Region. A temporary evacuation center should also be constructed to accommodate households affected by typhoons or flooding. Some areas were discovered to be highly prone to landslides. These vulnerable households, especially those on mountain slopes, should be relocated. The cost of this adaptation strategy totals $2,234.11 per household. External funds for the acquisition of the property for the relocation site should be sourced out. Financial assistance should also be considered for the affected households, amounting to PHP 50,000.00 ($1,188.78).

Barangay Binduyan stakeholders identified disaster mitigation strategies similar to those of Babuyan. They include breakwater construction, mangrove reforestation, seawall construction, and relocation. Among the different adaptation options, mangrove reforestation is considered the most cost-effective strategy for protecting homes and properties as well as in minimizing sand erosion in areas where mangroves are known to grow well. Two officials of the two barangays supported hard adaptation options like breakwater and dike construction, provided that adequate funds are available.

The results of our analysis provided leaders and decision-makers with a concrete basis for project implementation toward mitigating the effects of climate change. Barangay officials tend to favor options with lower CERs since their barangay funds can cover the cost, while those with high CER were reserved for future implementation, especially those without firm-funding commitments. Resource availability is one of the major considerations in identifying the adaptation options for the community to improve their resilience to the impact of climate change, particularly to sea level rise.

At the barangay level, the planned adaptation strategy with the lowest CER will have the highest chance of implementation, assuming that the cost can be covered by the available funds of the barangay and at the same time the strategy is prioritized by the barangay officials. The budget for the implementation of the chosen planned adaptation option comes from the Barangay Infrastructure Funds (BIF) and Internal Revenue Allotment (IRA). The Barangay Disaster Risk Reduction Management Plan (BDRRMP) should also include the planned adaptation options since 30 percent of the calamity fund can be used for a Quick Response Fund while the remaining 70 percent can be used for preparedness, mitigation, and recovery under RA 10121.

At the city level, projects that address preparedness, mitigation, and recovery from disasters and climate change impacts are funded from the 70 percent of the Calamity Fund for the year, as long as it is an identified disaster risk reduction or climate change adaptation measure in the Disaster Risk Reduction and Management (DRRM) Plan. Both at the City and barangay level, the presentation of cost-effectiveness ratio for planned adaptation options will assist the barangay and city government leaders in deciding which option to implement.

The costs of adaptation heavily depend on the level of the climatic events, but some estimates are feasible. Recent studies estimated the global costs for adaptation in several forms (World Bank 2009) and they identified the three most expensive areas: coastal areas, infrastructure, and water supply and flood fortification. These three have been discussed in this chapter. As mentioned, we recommend that the government provide assistance to the three most expensive sectors in these communities, to implement or employ the aforementioned adaptation strategies. This approach will further protect community members' lives and build resilience capabilities.

CONCLUSION

The residents of Babuyan and Binduyan felt the negative effects of climate hazards in recent years. The most vulnerable sector is agricultural production, the failure of which will undermine the meeting of the nutritional needs of the communities, especially children. Coastal residents sustained property damage brought about by storm surges. Households lying close to rivers or nearshore areas and low-lying areas are prone to hazards brought by flooding and erosion. Several areas in the barangays indicated the outbreak of waterborne diseases. The community identified adaptation strategies to address these hazards. The stakeholders prefer mitigation measures that are cost-effective, achievable, and within their financial capabilities.

Barangay Binduyan community members should be encouraged to engage in a mangrove reforestation project to protect households from storm surges, loss of property, and sand erosion over the long term. Whenever possible and if funds allow, they may pursue hard adaptation options as a quick fix to the threat of sea level rise, with added benefits such as fish landing facilities. Despite the low cost-effectiveness ratio of river dredging, it is recommended that the community should opt for strategies with a lesser environmental impact, such as the planting of vetiver grass along the riverbank to prevent frequent river overflow. Whenever necessary, river dredging would complement this option. Early warning systems and provision for temporary evacuation centers appeared to be the most practical adaptation strategy. This is to protect households from inland flooding. However, uncertainty in weather forecasting makes this difficult. Thus, the community should further explore alternative options to ensure residents' safety.

In Barangay Binduyan, seawall construction appeared to be the most cost-effective adaptation option in protecting households from strong waves and storm surges. This option would be most effective if combined with mangrove reforestation. The planting of mangroves in suitable areas along the shoreline will be highly beneficial to coastal residents. In general, it is recommended that the community should base their decision primarily on the affordability of the adaptation strategies without sacrificing the environmental sustainability of the preferred option.

Adaptation is highly site-specific. Adaptation options in Binduyan are not necessarily the same in Babuyan. Choices made to reduce a community's vulnerability to the impacts of climatic events may be imperfect and temporary.

However, these strategies will prolong the existence of distinctive cultural heritage sites for the enjoyment of the present and future generations. The quality of life and place contribute to community resilience (Horowitz 2016). Decisions about adaptation strategies and actions can be made at a range of levels, from the national government down to the community members (Carter and Raps 2008). In terms of policy and implementation, the support of the local government can contribute to expeditious adaptation action.

REFERENCES

Adrianto, L., & Matsuda, Y. (2002). Developing economic vulnerability indices of environmental disasters in small island regions. *Environmental Impact Assessment Review*, 22(4), 393–414.

Agnew, M. D., & Viner, D. (2001). Potential impacts of climate change on international tourism. *Tourism and Hospitality Research*, 3(1), 37–60.

Asian Development Bank (ADB). (2009). *The Economics of Climate Change in Southeast Asia: A Regional Review*. Mandaluyong, Philippines: Asian Development Bank. Retrieved from http://www.adb.org/Documents/Books/Economics-Climate-Change- SEA/PDF/Economics-Climate-Change.pdf

Atienza, E. F., & Hipolito, D. M. (2010). Challenges on risk management of sediment-related disasters in the Philippines. *International Journal of Erosion Control Engineering*, 3(1), 85–91.

Bigano, A., Bosello, F., Roson, R., & Tol, R. S. (2008). Economy-wide impacts of climate change: a joint analysis for sea level rise and tourism. *Mitigation and Adaptation Strategies for Global Change*, 13(8), 765–791.

Birkmann, J. (ed.) (2006a). *Measuring Vulnerability to Natural Hazards—Towards Disaster Resilient Societies*, United Nations University.

Birkmann, J. (2006b). Measuring vulnerability to promote disaster-resilient societies conceptual frameworks and definition. Institute for Environment and Human Security Journal, 5, 7–54.

Birkmann, J., & Wisner, B. (2006). Measuring the un-measurable. UNU-EHS SOURCE, 5. Retrieved from http://www.ihdp.unu.edu/file/get/3962.pdf.

Carter, L., & Raps, B. (2008). Adapting to climate change: It is just better planning. *Basins and Coasts*, 2(1). 29–23.

Chang, S. W., Clement, T. P., Simpson, M. J., & Lee, K. K. (2011). Does sea-level rise have an impact on saltwater intrusion? *Advances in Water Resources*, 34(10), 1283–1291.

Church, J. A., Godfrey, J. S., Jackett, D. R., & McDougall, T. J. (1991). A model of sea level rise caused by ocean thermal expansion. *Journal of Climate*, 4(4), 438–456.

de Guzman, L. E. P., Zamora, O. B., Talubo, J. P. P., & Hostallero, C. D. V. (2014). Sustainable agricultural production systems for food security in a changing climate in Batanes, Philippines. *Journal of Developments in Sustainable Agriculture*, 9(2), 111–119.

Fisher, M. 2013. This map shows why the Philippines is so vulnerable to climate change. *The Washington Post*, November 12, 2013. Retrieved from https://ww

w.washingtonpost.com/news/worldviews/wp/2013/11/12/this-map-shows-why-the- philippines-is-so-vulnerable-to-climate-change/?utm_term=.759af2d8451c.

Haines, A., Kovats, R. S., Campbell-Lendrum, D., & Corvalán, C. (2006). Climate change and human health: Impacts, vulnerability and public health. *Public Health*, 120(7), 585–596.

Horowitz, A. D. (2016). Planning before disaster strikes: An introduction to adaptation strategies. Issue on climate change and preservation technology. *The Journal of Preservation Technology: Association for Preservation Technology International*, 40–48. Retrieved from https://jstor.org.stable/43799262

IPCC (eds) 2012. *Managing the Risks of Extreme Events and Disasters to Advance Climate Change Adaptation*. A special report of Working Groups I and II of the Intergovernmental Panel on Climate Change, Cambridge: Cambridge University Press.

Jonkman, S. N. (2005). Global perspectives on loss of human life caused by floods. *Natural Hazards*, 34(2), 151–175.

Jonkman, S. N., & Kelman, I. (2005). An analysis of the causes and circumstances of flood disaster deaths. *Disasters*, 29(1), 75–97.

Kalkstein, L. S. (1991). A new approach to evaluate the impact of climate on human mortality. *Environmental Health Perspectives*, 96, 145.

Kunkel, K. E., Pielke Jr, R. A., & Changnon, S. A. (1999). Temporal fluctuations in weather and climate extremes that cause economic and human health impacts: A review. *Bulletin of the American Meteorological Society*, 80(6), 1077–1098.

Lavell, A., Mansilla, E., & others (2003). *Local Level Risk Management: Concept and Practices*. CEPREDENAC-UNDP, Quito, Ecuador.

Louis, M. E., Porter, J. D., Helal, A., Drame, K., Hargrett-Bean, N. A. N. C. Y., Wells, J. G., & Tauxe, R. V. (1990). Epidemic cholera in West Africa: The role of food handling and high-risk foods. *American Journal of Epidemiology*, 131(4), 719–728.

Luber, G., & McGeehin, M. (2008). Climate change and extreme heat events. *American Journal of Preventive Medicine*, 35(5), 429–435.

McMichael, A. J. (2003). *Climate Change and Human Health: Risks and Responses*. World Health Organization.

Meehl, G. A., Washington, W. M., Collins, W. D., Arblaster, J. M., Hu, A., Buja, L. E., . . . & Teng, H. (2005). How much more global warming and sea level rise? *Science*, 307(5716), 1769–1772.

Mercer, J., Dominey-Howes, D., Kelman, I., & Lloyd, K. (2007). The potential for combining indigenous and western knowledge in reducing vulnerability to environmental hazards in small island developing states. *Environmental Hazards*, 7(4), 245–256.

Nicholls, R. J., & Mimura, N. (1998). Regional issues raised by sea-level rise and their policy implications. *Climate Research*, 11(1), 5–18.

Osti, R. & K. Miyake (2011). *Forms of Community Participation in Disaster Risk Management Practices*. Nova Science Publishers, Inc. New York.

Paringit, E. C., & Abucay, E. R. (Eds.) (2017). LiDAR surveys and flood mapping of Babuyan River. In Enrico C. Paringit (Ed.), *Flood Hazard Mapping of the Philippines using LIDAR*. Quezon City: University of the Philippines Training Center for Applied Geodesy and Photogrammetry-194pp. Retrieved from0 https://lipad.dream.upd.edu.ph/documents/287203/download

Patz, J. A., Campbell-Lendrum, D., Holloway, T., & Foley, J. A. (2005). Impact of regional climate change on human health. *Nature*, 438(7066), 310–317.

Pezeshki, S. R., DeLaune, R. D., & Patrick, W. H. (1990). Flooding and saltwater intrusion: Potential effects on survival and productivity of wetland forests along the US Gulf Coast. *Forest Ecology and Management*, 33, 287–301.

Piñol, J., Terradas, J., & Lloret, F. (1998). Climate warming, wildfire hazard and wildfire occurrence in coastal eastern Spain. *Climatic Change*, 38(3), 345–357.

Quarantelli, E. L. (2000). Disaster planning, emergency management and civil protection. The historical development of organized efforts to plan for and to respond to disasters. Newark, Delaware (Preliminary Paper Nr. #301).

Quine, C. P. (1995). Assessing the risk of wind damage to forests: Practice and pitfalls. In M. P. Coutts, & J. Grace (Eds.), *Wind and Trees* (pp. 379–403). Cambridge: Cambridge University Press. doi:10.1017/CBO9780511600425.022.

Rosenzweig, C., Tubiello, F. N., Goldberg, R., Mills, E., & Bloomfield, J. (2002). Increased crop damage in the US from excess precipitation under climate change. *Global Environmental Change*, 12(3), 197–202.

Shyam, K. C. (2013). *Cost Benefit Studies on Disaster Risk Reduction in Developing Countries*. Washington, DC (Eap Drm Knowledge NOTES. Disaster Risk Management in East Asia And The Pacific Nr. 27).

Smith, K. (2013). *Environmental Hazards: Assessing Risk and Reducing Disaster*. Routledge.

Solomon, S., Plattner, G. K., Knutti, R., & Friedlingstein, P. (2009). Irreversible climate change due to carbon dioxide emissions. *Proceedings of the National Academy of Sciences*, PNAS-0812721106.

Sorensen, R. M., Weisman, R. N., & Lennon, G. P. (1984). Control of erosion, inundation, and salinity intrusion caused by sea level rise. In Barth, M. C., & Titus, J. G. (eds), *Greenhouse Effect and Sea Level Rise. A Challenge for this Generation*. Van Nostran Reinhold Company Inc, New York, pp. 179, 214.

Titus, J. G., Park, R. A., Leatherman, S. P., Weggel, J. R., Greene, M. S., Mausel, P. W., . . . & Yohe, G. (1991). Greenhouse effect and sea level rise: The cost of holding back the sea. *Coastal Management*, 19(2), 171–204.

Turvey, R. (2007). Vulnerability assessment of developing countries: The case of small-island developing states. *Development Policy Review*, 25(2), 243–264.

UNFCCC. (2007). *Investment and Financial Flows to Address Climate Change*. Bonn: U.N. Framework Convention on Climate Change.

Vanzi, S. J. (1998). Palawan, Puerto Princess in State of Calamity. Newsflash Philippine Headline News Online http://www.newsflash.org/199812/ht/ht000617.htm

World Bank. (2009). *The Costs to Developing Countries of Adapting to Climate Change: New Methods and Estimates. Global Report of the Economics of Adaptation to Climate Change Study*. Consultation Draft. Washington, DC.

Wu, S. Y., Yarnal, B., & Fisher, A. (2002). Vulnerability of coastal communities to sea-level rise: a case study of Cape May County, New Jersey, USA. *Climate Research*, 22(3), 255–270.

Yodmani, S. (2001). *Disaster Risk Management and Vulnerability Reduction: Protecting the Poor*. Paper Presented at The Asia Pacific Forum on Poverty.

Conclusion

Reframing "Disaster"

Noah Theriault

What is a disaster? Close your eyes and concentrate on the term. What do you see? If you're like me, your mind will cycle through a stream of demolished buildings, devastated landscapes, mangled infrastructure, and battered bodies. An online image search for "disaster" yields the same—a montage of what one encounters in the news in the wake of typhoons, fires, floods, earthquakes, tsunamis, volcanic eruptions, and other acute, large-scale events. If you dig a bit deeper, you may also turn up images of major industrial "accidents," perhaps the devastating gas leak at Union Carbide's pesticide plant in Bhopal, India (in 1984), or the catastrophic failure of a tailings dam at BHP Billiton's iron mine in Bento Rodrigues, Brazil (in 2015). Or perhaps you or your loved ones have lived through one of these events, leaving you with a personal stream of images to recall. If so, please forgive me for calling up those memories. But I would like to invite you, too, to join me in thinking about this question: what *is* a disaster?

Whether we know them firsthand or only through the media, disasters shape all of our lives. Preventing, preparing for, and responding to disasters have become primary functions of our governments—and a key indicator of a government's (in)competence, as both George W. Bush and Noynoy Aquino learned the hard way. Indeed, disasters are a ubiquitous part of our everyday lives not just because of their iconic place in the news and popular culture, but also because of how they motivate, test, and at times thwart so many of the institutions and infrastructures we interact with and depend on.

We can see, then, that disasters are more than catastrophic events. As critical theorists have argued, managing the risk of disaster constitutes a central organizing principle of contemporary governance (Beck, 2010; Dean, 2010; Giddens, 1999; Oels, 2013). And this principle is only reinforced by the fact that, despite all of the institutions and infrastructures arrayed against them, disasters continue to occur and continue to cause immense suffering. If, as some argue, the planet has entered a geologic epoch characterized by the cumulative impacts of (post)industrialism (Steffen et al., 2007; Zalasiewicz et al., 2015), then it should be no surprise that we also appear to be living in an age of disaster risk management. The same dynamics that have driven the global expansion of (post)industrial capitalism have impelled efforts to manage, securitize, and indeed profit from risk (Fletcher, 2012; Gunewardena & Schuller, 2008; Johnson, 2014).

Have we, then, gotten to the bottom of our question? Not yet. Disasters are catastrophic events that constitute an organizing principle of modern governance, to be sure. But even this broad view of disasters, I contend, is insufficient—or, rather, even this broad view of disasters points us toward too narrow a set of questions about what makes a disaster in a "disaster-prone" country like the Philippines.

What I hope to offer in this brief afterword is a provocation about the discursive work that the term "disaster" performs as a category for enframing lived experiences, ordering social relations, and interpreting the world. I draw the concept of enframing from political theorist Timothy Mitchell (2002), who has shown how certain concepts and categories come to "enframe" our reality—that is, how they are encoded in dominant epistemologies, codified in governing institutions, and ultimately imposed onto the material world. Mitchell has shown how the concept of "the economy" has come to enframe reality for a majority of the world's governments and societies, and I would argue (but here can only assert) that the same is true of "disaster" (ibid.). Echoing anthropologist Clifford Geertz's (1973) theory of religion, we can see how enframing concepts work not just as models of the world, but also as models *for* it.

So if you will allow me to stipulate that "disaster" is an enframing concept, then let us proceed with the provocation about its effects. What work does the concept of "disaster" do? Among the possible answers to this question, the most crucial, in my mind, concerns the patterns of ontogenesis, temporality, and spatiality that the concept of disaster enframes. Robert Barrios (2017, p. 153) reminds us that "disaster" comes from the old Italian *diastro*, which "was used to convey the idea that the positions of stars and planets could have destructive effects on human beings." Citing Anthony Oliver-Smith (1999), Roberto Barrios adds that "this particular view of disasters remained in use into the twentieth century, when the calamitous effects of floods, earthquakes, and technological malfunctions continued to be seen as unavoidable events that societies could only respond to, but not prevent" (p. 153–154). This generalization would seem to overlook the tendency on the part of many past (and present) societies to see disasters as a form of divine punishment (Bankoff, 2018). Still, though, the point remains that the term disaster enframes a world in which there are exceptional, destructive, potentially cosmogenic events that exceed human control.

As Barrios (2017, p. 54) also notes, mainstream Western perspectives on disasters have evolved as the physical and natural sciences have observed and sought to explain their ontogenesis and as the social sciences have sought to account for their uneven socio-spatial effects. Drawing on Verchik's concept of "disaster justice," Bankoff observes that scientific explanations of disasters have coincided with changing modes of governance, such that "the state is regarded as having a mandatory duty to shield people from physical harm through its laws and institutions" (2018, p. 364). Disasters are today one of the sources of harm that states are supposed to manage or even prevent. And even if states cannot always control the geophysical force of, say, an earthquake, the disaster-justice framework holds that societies (and states, in particular) should organize things in such a way as to mitigate the effects of such hazards on the population. That societies do this in systematically uneven ways has become the object of extensive research on vulnerability (Bankoff et al., 2004; Wisner et al., 2004).

I will have more to say on the social production of disasters below. For now, I want to draw our attention to what connects "modern" conceptions of disaster with earlier ones: disasters are above all framed as self-contained, exceptional, locatable *events* (see also Hewitt, 1983). They may intersect with gradually unfolding processes, they may have multiplex, diffuse, even global causality, and they may have far-reaching impacts. But they are, by definition, temporally and spatially circumscribed. Even as climate change and the prospect of the Anthropocene bring humans increasingly into the center of disaster causality narratives, we retain the concept of disasters as catastrophic *events* that exceed whatever measures are in place to prevent or control them. The entire cross-disciplinary field of disasters studies is organized around this concept, and as noted above it is one of the organizing principles of modern, technocratic governance.

So why does this matter? Why does this ontological, temporal, and spatial enframing of disaster concern me? The problem, I believe, lies in how this enframing undermines efforts to denaturalize disasters and pursue accountability for the systematic forms of violence and injustice they expose. As I hope to show below, the chapters in this volume offer an important but ambivalent set of insights with which we can think about these effects.

DENATURALIZING DISASTERS

In response to Hurricane Katrina, Marxist geographer Neil Smith famously wrote that "there's no such thing as a natural disaster" (Smith, 2006). This statement was and is something of a truism, but it is worth pausing to reflect on what it means in relation to the people and places addressed in this volume. Invoking a well-established principle in critical disaster studies, Smith reminded us that what makes an event disastrous with respect to human lives and livelihoods is not just the physical force of the event in itself, but also how that force interacts with the infrastructures that mediate our interactions with our surroundings and produce our exposures to hazards therein. Katrina would not have been so devastating if the levees had been stronger and the neighborhoods beneath them better served by governing institutions. This is how many critical scholars of disaster understand vulnerability—as a sociopolitical artifact rather than an inevitable effect of geography or "nature."

But if disasters cannot be said to be natural, what about the hazards that co-produce them? Hazard here refers to the force or source of harm and risk to the capacity or likelihood of a hazard to cause harm in a particular context. When critical scholars like Smith say that there is no such thing as a natural disaster, part of what they are saying is that risk is socially produced. Many scholars of risk, including Anthony Giddens (1999) and Ulrich Beck (2009), have long made a conceptual distinction between "manufactured" and "external" risks. External risks exist in the space where "forces of nature" collide with our infrastructures, while manufactured risks originate from the social, technological, and infrastructural (dis)order of society itself. Think earthquakes, on the one hand, and chemical spills on the other. In his highly influential work on the "risk society," Beck (1992) called attention to how manufactured risks have become so systemic and trans-scalar that they pose a threat to the very social orders that produced them. But to the extent that "modern" societies also manufacture their systemic vulnerability to certain putatively external hazards (e.g., drug-resistant pathogens), it becomes difficult if not impossible to sustain any meaningful sense of risks that are external to the infrastructures, institutions, and social orders in which we live.

But it's not just that risks are socially and relationally produced. It's that so too are many of the hazards that we have often imagined as "natural" or "external." Industrial activities are causative factors in extreme weather (exacerbated by anthropogenic climate change), earthquake swarms (induced by the underground disposal of wastewater from hydraulic fracturing), catastrophic wildfires (in the wake of fire suppression), and so on. In a time of anthropogenic disruption at the planetary scale, it now seems obsolete at best to distinguish risks that originate without human society from those that originate within. Risks are neither external nor internal to human society—they are systemic, and the systems that produce them are hybrid assemblages that include humans and our technologies along with all of the organisms, substances, and forces with which we co-produce the world.

What of disasters, then, if we accept that the risks they unleash are always hybrid, systemic, and more-than-human? As noted above, critical scholars have long since dispatched with the concept of "natural" disasters, but we cannot simply then conclude that all disasters are manufactured. Grappling with this puzzle, historian Sara Pritchard (2012) has described the interlocking earthquake, tsunami, and nuclear meltdown that struck Japan in March 2011 as an "envirotechnical disaster." "It is precisely," she writes, "the complex, dynamic, porous, and inextricable configuration of nature, technology, and politics that together helps us understand all that the single word 'Fukushima' now signifies" (p. 233). Security theorist Simon Dalby (Dalby, 2017) has gone a step further, arguing that "social formations are very much geological formations too, and understanding geopolitics in these terms is now unavoidable" (p. 238). This leads him to conclude that "the disaster at present loose in the biosphere is industrial humanity wreaking havoc directly and indirectly on most other species" (p. 247). Dalby's problematic choice of words erases the varying degrees of responsibility and exposure within so-called "industrial humanity." Nevertheless, his work is a clear example of how changing (perceptions of) geopolitical and geophysical conditions are shaping the evolution of critical thought on the ontogenesis, temporality, and spatiality of disasters.

To the extent that anthropology provides a disciplinary common denominator for this volume, it is worth noting that anthropologists are also playing an important role in rethinking hazards, risks, and disasters. In his recent literature review, Barrios (2017) asserts that many anthropologists define disasters as "the diachronic processes in which human practices enhance the destructive and disruptive capacities of geophysical phenomena, technological malfunctions, and communicable diseases" (p. 155). In light of the concerns I raised about (about the spatially, temporally, and ontologically circumscribed conception of disasters that enframes our reality), I should perhaps be heartened to see fellow anthropologists defining disasters in this way. And, in a sense, I am. Then, however, I scan the headlines, and I see how entrenched the older, more circumscribed notion of disaster remains in society at large. I read about multibillion-dollar efforts to shore up Lower Manhattan from future storm surges even as millions across the United States lack adequate shelter. Worse still is the fact that an academic volume on the Philippines is viable for international publication in large part because of its focus on disasters, as if matters of inequality, governance, and environmental change in the Philippines are not significant enough in their own right. All of this suggests the extent to which disasters remain a hegemonic enframing of our reality and a category immensely generative of thought, policy, and action.

Implying his own discomfort with this reality, Barrios also uses his review takes on the common framing of disasters as "revelatory crises" that lay bare the problems of (global) society. "Rather than being revelatory crises," he writes, "disasters are perhaps better described as contested arenas where hegemonic visions of societal advancement are challenged by the voices and experiences of those most impacted by catastrophes" (p. 157). Pivoting this point, I will in what follows endeavor to consider how this volume does (and does not) trouble the ontological, temporal, and spatial assumptions that underpin disaster as a hegemonic unit of analysis, governance, and experience.

INEQUALITY AND DISPOSSESSION
IN AN AGE OF SYSTEMIC RISK

If any one theme unites critical scholarship on disasters, it has to be inequality—and for good reason. In a transnational capitalist system structured around inequalities of class, race, gender, nationality, ability, etc., risks of all kinds are distributed unevenly: as Beck succinctly put it, "wealth accumulates at the top, risks at the bottom" (1992, p. 35). This is more than a correlation. At the root of this reality are historical and ongoing processes of what David Harvey (2004) calls accumulation by dispossession. Recent work in critical disaster studies has helped to reveal how long-standing forms of colonialism, institutionalized racism, and capitalist accumulation systematically extract labor and value from the same bodies and lands that are then treated as disposable repositories for risk (Giroux, 2006; Pulido, 2016).

But this dynamic shapes more than the outcomes of disastrous events—it is an integral part of the systems that carry out disaster preparation and recovery. In their study of disaster risk management in Manila, Maria Khristine Alvarez and Kenneth Cardenas (2019) show how the forced relocation of informal settlements constitutes a form of "resiliency revanchism" that is deeply entangled with the broader spatial politics of class struggle. Similarly, for Hurricane Katrina and the 2010 Haiti earthquake respective, Vincanne Adams (2013) and Mark Schuller (2016) uncover the complex, often unintended ways in which recovery efforts create exceptional moments for the accumulation of wealth and power at the expense of marginalized survivors. Such studies speak to what journalist Naomi Klein (2007) famously called "disaster capitalism."

Crucially, though, it's not just that disaster recovery provides rent-seeking opportunities for the most powerful capitalists and humanitarian-aid agencies. Disaster recovery can actually serve to *increase* the wealth and power of relatively privileged survivors. In a longitudinal, quantitative study of disaster recovery in the United States, James Elliott and Junia Howell (2017) find that "populations that are privileged in terms of education, race or homeownership *gain wealth* in the aftermath of natural disasters" (emphasis added; quote from Howell, 2018). While these findings do not speak directly to the specifics of post-disaster recovery in the Philippines, we can see similar dynamics at work in many of the chapters in this volume. Riosa and colleagues, for example, point to the inadequacy of international NGO services that target specific survivor groups, such as children, effectively commodifying them as objects of aid delivery. Cajilig likewise shows how Haiyan survivors' decisions not to evacuate are not "irrational," but rather based on detailed local knowledge and experience, including the reality that evacuation increases the likelihood of displacement and dispossession.

Some scholars of risk have proposed that conventional ways of analyzing difference—namely class, race, ethnicity, and gender—are insufficient for thinking about inequality in an age of global climate change and ecological crisis. Beck went so far as to suggest that such concepts were too "soft" to capture the "explosiveness of inequality" we face in the twenty-first century (Beck, 2010). As part of a broader critical conversation, this volume leaves no doubt about the central role of 'explosive' global inequality in producing disasters in the contemporary Philippines. And particularly in light of the neoliberal policies that have reshaped governance in the Philippines over the past generation, it is safe to say that the insights of Neil Smith, Naomi Klein, and Henry Giroux find traction here. But the contributors do more than reinforce established theories of global risk, accumulation by dispossession, and disaster capitalism. They also nuance and complicate our understanding of these phenomena.

DIFFERENCE AND AGENCY AMID THE DISASTERS OF EVERYDAY LIFE

Against this a backdrop of explosive global inequality, the contributors to this volume never lose sight of the highly localized material and cultural contexts in which people live out their daily lives and come to terms with the risks they face. This is significant, in part, because it reminds that class, gender, race, ethnicity, age, ability, and other intersecting structures of difference remain central to the production and experience of risk. More important still, the volume reminds us that experiences of risk are uneven not just across social groups but also within them. Across the chapters, we encounter varying experiences *within* communities of indigenous farmers (as seen in the chapters by Webb and Smith), ethnically diverse fishers (Regionel et al. and Membrebe et al.), displaced survivors (Cajilig, Luna et al., and Riosa), and urban slum residents (Alejandria and Ancheta et al.). We encounter these communities as they actually exist: internally differentiated and dynamic collections of actors with uneven access to resources, conflicting knowledges, and divergent desires.

Disasters in particular tend to efface such complexity—they help to reveal inequality but they are also, we are told, moments in which people unite, work together, and transcend difference. What we learn from the accounts in this volume is that, even and perhaps especially in the midst of disaster, differences matter. Not only are social differences at the core of what produce uneven levels of risk, differences powerfully influence how people respond to risks when they are realized. Disasters may demand cooperation, but they do not produce solidarity or altruism from thin air. The form of *bayanihan* cooperation described, for example, by Luna and colleagues occurs within not despite local, class-based solidarities and patronage networks.

This attention to context helps us see that, just as there is no such thing as a natural disaster, there is likewise no such thing as a disaster in the singular. Any event officially deemed a disaster, such as a typhoon, drought, or flood, is constituted by its relation with other hazardous forces—forces that are routinized despite the widespread harms they inflict. What made Typhoon Haiyan so disastrous was not just the storm's strength, but its collision with the social and environmental depredations of a disastrously unequal political-economic system. Cajilig's analysis suggests that many of those who refused to evacuate did so because typhoons are only one of the hazards they must negotiate at any given time, and these include the very institutions ordering them to evacuate.

The same can be said for slum communities in Manila, where recurrent floods are a harmful but by no means uncomplicated obstacle in residents' constant search for food and money. Manila's slum communities live with the everyday disaster of extreme inequality and precarity. But the accounts in this volume aim to break the mold of victimhood, which too often serves as the only template for representing the lives of marginalized communities. In the complementary chapters by Alejandria and Ancheta and colleagues, we learn how both elders and children perform vital, but frequently overlooked forms of labor that both ensure their survival and expose them to risk. We are reminded of their agency and *"diskarte"* (skill, resourcefulness, attraction of good fortune) as they develop ways to subsist and endure. These acts should not console us—the structural violence these people experience every day is an unconscionable tragedy. Rather, what these chapters offer is a concrete illustration of lives that endure *in spite of* that violence. Such insights are vital to challenging the erasure of groups usually imagined to be dependent or otherwise passive participants in social reproduction.

But these accounts show us the flipside of disaster capitalism: just as capital seeks "investment" opportunities in the wake of acute disasters, those who live most precariously in the aftermath of dispossession may look to floods as an "opportunity" to gather saleable or edible items in the runoff. Alejandria recounts the story of Aling Mary, an elder who died not in a flood but from heat stroke after years of struggling to feed herself and her disabled son. After Aling Mary was "buried in an unmarked grave in the city cemetery," her son was taken by state and her home "demolished by the neighbors who proceeded in claiming the land as an extension of their undocumented property."

The multiplicity of disaster also comes through clearly in the chapters by Smith and Webb, who explore how indigenous farmers in Pala'wan experience food insecurity amid rapid deforestation, dispossession, and frenzied commodification of the landscape. In Webb's account, indigenous Tagbanua honey gatherers attribute the ebbs and flows of wild forest honey to the intermittent blossoming of certain trees, which in turn reflects events like distant volcanic eruptions. But there is a more immediate disaster at work in Webb's analysis, that of honey's gradual decline—a phenomenon remarked upon by elder Tagbanua but difficult to independently quantify. Like honey, rice is symbolically ubiquitous in the lives of indigenous communities in Pala'wan even though materially it is quite often absent. Smith relates how rice, although long central to Pala'wan cosmology, has only recently become central to their diets. As rice has displaced other starches throughout island Southeast Asia, Pala'wan too have come to experience its scarcity as a manifestation of hunger and hardship. By using these key foods as ciphers for indigenous loss and persistence amid large-scale, often disastrous forces of change, these accounts show that disasters are produced not just socially but also culturally—that they ramify not just through social structures and class struggles, but also through collective memories and cosmologies.

Reflecting on the highly localized, co-constitution of disaster, several chapters suggest concrete changes in how the Philippine state and other institutions seek to prepare for and respond to hazards. Both Regionel et al. and Membrebe et al. indicate the need for democratic governance at the local level so that communities can address their needs in light of micro-level histories and conditions. This may mean taking specific technical or engineering measures to prepare for disasters, but it may also mean resisting land grabbing by developers, fostering alternative livelihoods, expanding education access, and providing better sanitation. Theirs is a vital reminder that basic principles of sustainable human development and political empowerment are often the best protection that communities have against hazards, whether those come from a spiraling global climate or a predatory global elite. And no less vital is Mangada et al.'s caution against uncritical visions of community "resilience." Examining the many systemic failures of accountability in the state's response to Haiyan, they suggest that focusing on local capacities for resilience is willfully naïve at best. Corrupt, unaccountable governance in the hands of predatory elites is, in some ways, the greatest hazard that the world faces today.

CONFRONTING RESURGENT AUTHORITARIANISM

What are the valences of disaster research in an age of resurgent right-wing authoritarianism? I have suggested that all of us—whether in the Philippines, the United States, or elsewhere—live amid multiple, overlapping disasters unfolding at different temporal and spatial scales and that our experiences of these disasters reflect structural inequalities and, in some cases, differing ontologies. When we organize our institutions—and our research—around conventional concepts of "disaster," we enframe reality in a way that obscures the temporal and spatial continuity of the multiple, overlapping disasters that characterize life on earth.

In seeing "disasters" everywhere I look, I risk sounding as if I have taken a page from the January 2017 inauguration speech of a certain aspiring authoritarian. That resonance is not a coincidence, but it's not because I agree with Trump's white-nationalist agenda. My aim is to amplify this volume's attention to the disasters of creative destruction, dispossession, and structural violence that surround us but that many of us are privileged enough not to notice. The mystification of these disasters is what makes it possible for demagogues to emerge and consolidate power. And these are the disasters that scholarship on disaster too often overlooks. As the contributions to this volume suggest, disaster research has the potential to contribute to the (re) making of worlds that are more conducive to what Anna Tsing calls "collaborative survival" (Tsing, 2015). But as long as we continue to treat "disasters" as discrete objects of governance and scholarly inquiry, we may unintentionally undermine parallel efforts to address uneven exposure to risk as part of larger historical processes and structures of inequality.

REFERENCES

Adams, V. (2013). *Markets of Sorrow, Labors of Faith: New Orleans in the Wake of Katrina*. Duke University Press.

Alvarez, M. K., & Cardenas, K. (2019). Evicting slums, 'Building Back Better': Resiliency revanchism and disaster risk management in Manila. *International Journal of Urban and Regional Research, 43*(2), 227–249.

Bankoff, G. (2018). Blame, responsibility and agency: 'Disaster justice'and the state in the Philippines. *Environment and Planning E: Nature and Space, 1*(3), 363–381.

Bankoff, G., Frerks, G., & Hilhorst, D. (2004). *Mapping Vulnerability: Disasters, Development and People*. New York: Earthscan.

Barrios, R. E. (2017). What does catastrophe reveal for whom? The anthropology of crises and disasters at the onset of the anthropocene. *Annual Review of Anthropology, 46*, 151–166.

Beck, U. (1992). *Risk Society: Towards a New Modernity*. London: Sage.

Beck, U. (2009). *World Risk Society and Manufactured Uncertainties*. Paper presented at the Iris.

Beck, U. (2010). Remapping social inequalities in an age of climate change: For a cosmopolitan renewal of sociology. *Global Networks, 10*(2), 165–181.

Dalby, S. (2017). Anthropocene formations: Environmental security, geopolitics and disaster. *Theory, Culture & Society, 34*(2–3), 233–252.

Dean, M. (2010). *Governmentality: Power and Rule in Modern Society*. Sage Publications.

Elliott, J. R., & Howell, J. (2017). Beyond disasters: A longitudinal analysis of natural hazards' unequal impacts on residential instability. *Social Forces, 95*(3), 1181–1207.

Fletcher, R. (2012). Capitalizing on Chaos: Climate change and disaster capitalism. *Ephemera: Theory & Politics in Organization, 12*.

Geertz, C. (1973). *The Interpretation of Cultures*. New York: Basic Books.

Giddens, A. (1999). Risk and responsibility. *The Modern Law Review, 62*(1), 1–10.

Giroux, H. A. (2006). *Stormy Weather: Katrina and the Politics of Disposability*. Routledge.

Gunewardena, N., & Schuller, M. (2008). *Capitalizing on Catastrophe: Neoliberal Strategies in Disaster Reconstruction*. Rowman Altamira.

Harvey, D. (2004). The "New Imperialism": Accumulation by dispossession. *Actuel Marx*, (1), 71–90.

Hewitt, K. (1983). The idea of calamity in a technocratic age. In K. Hewitt (Ed.), *Interpretation of Calamity: From the Viewpoint of Human Ecology* (pp. 3–32). Boston: Allen & Unwin.

Howell, J. (2018). Hurricane season not only brings destruction and death but rising inequality too. *The Conversation*. Retrieved from https://theconversation.com/hurricane-season-not-only-brings-destruction-and-death-but-rising-inequality-too-1 02085

Johnson, L. (2014). Geographies of securitized catastrophe risk and the implications of climate change. *Economic Geography, 90*(2), 155–185.

Klein, N. (2007). *The Shock Doctrine: The Rise of Disaster Capitalism*. Macmillan.

Mitchell, T. (2002). *Rule of Experts*. Berkeley: University of California Press.

Oels, A. (2013). Rendering climate change governable by risk: From probability to contingency. *Geoforum, 45*, 17–29.

Oliver-Smith, A. (1999). What is a disaster? Anthropological perspectives on a persistent question. In A. Oliver-Smith & S. Hoffman (Eds.), *The Angry Earth: Disaster in Anthropological Perspective* (pp. 18–34). Routledge.

Pritchard, S. B. (2012). An envirotechnical disaster: Nature, technology, and politics at Fukushima. *Environmental History, 17*(2), 219–243.

Pulido, L. (2016). Flint, environmental racism, and racial capitalism. *Capitalism Nature Socialism, 27*(3), 1–16.

Schuller, M. (2016). *Humanitarian Aftershocks in Haiti*. Rutgers University Press.

Smith, N. (2006). There's no such thing as a natural disaster. Retrieved from http: //forums.ssrc.org/understandingkatrina/theres-no-such-thing-as-a-natural-disaster/

Steffen, W., Crutzen, P. J., & McNeill, J. R. (2007). The Anthropocene: Are humans now overwhelming the great forces of nature. *AMBIO: A Journal of the Human Environment, 36*(8), 614–622.

Tsing, A. L. (2015). *The Mushroom at the End of the World: On the Possibility of Life in Capitalist Ruins.* Princeton University Press.

Wisner, B., Blaikie, P. M., Blaikie, P., Cannon, T., & Davis, I. (2004). *At Risk: Natural Hazards, People's Vulnerability and Disasters.* New York: Routledge.

Zalasiewicz, J., Waters, C. N., Williams, M., Barnosky, A. D., Cearreta, A., Crutzen, P., . . . Grinevald, J. (2015). When did the Anthropocene begin? A mid-twentieth century boundary level is stratigraphically optimal. *Quaternary International, 383*, 196–203.

Index

About the Editors

Will Smith is Associate Research Fellow in the Alfred Deakin Institute at Deakin University. He is an anthropologist and human geographer whose research is focused on human-forest interfaces, the social dimensions of agricultural production, the politics of indigenous knowledge and critical approaches to disaster management in both Australia and upland Southeast Asia. His research has explored indigenous Pala'wan experiences with climate change in the Philippines and the governance of swidden cultivation in forested landscapes. This work has been published in journals such as Annals of the American Association of Geographers, Political Geography and The Australian Journal of Anthropology. He is currently a member of a project exploring collaborations between indigenous people and the natural hazard sector across southern Australia.

Maria Carinnes Alejandria is an anthropologist who researches on issues relating to health inequalities in the Global South. Dr. Alejandria is the lead of the Social Health Studies of the University of Santo Tomas where is also an assistant professor in the Department of Sociology. She currently serves as the Editor in Chief of the Journal of Social Health. Her most current publications include an edited volume entitled *Aging in the Global South: Challenges and Opportunities* and journal articles that explored issues on food security, pediatric tuberculosis, mental health, and older adult health among informal settlers in Metro Manila. She has led projects related to social health, disaster resilience, and food security that were funded by Brown University, WHO, UNDP, UNAIDS, the Philippine's Department of Science and Technology, Department of Health, and the National Research Council of the Philippines. She also serves as a member of the international advisory board of the Philippine Studies Group of the Association of Asian Studies.

About the Contributors

Noah Theriault is Assistant Professor of Anthropology in the Department of History at Carnegie Mellon University, where he offers courses on Southeast Asia, environmental justice, and social change. His research uses ethnographic methods to trace how global-scale forces of social and environmental change shape the lives of rural and urban communities in the Philippines, with particular attention to the everyday practices through which those forces are enacted, contested, and potentially transformed. This includes a long-term study of indigeneity and biodiversity conservation in Palawan and more recently a political ecology of transportation infrastructure in Manila. Dr. Theriault's other primary interests include anti-authoritarian theory/practice and de-colonial approaches to global ecological crisis.

Sarah Webb is an Honorary Lecturer in anthropology at the University of Queensland. Her ethnographic work in the Philippines is based on central Palawan Island. Her research focuses on the intersections of environmental anthropology, material culture studies and the anthropology of development, with areas of specialization including the anthropology of value, sustainable consumption, tropical livelihoods and ecotourism. Her recent publications include 'Greening honey: Producing the underground origins of a forest wonder' (Journal of Material Culture), 'Some dilemmas of political consumerism: Class and ecotourism practices in the Philippines' (with Anna Cristina Pertierra, in the Oxford Handbook of Political Consumerism) and 'Domestic ecotourism and the production of a wondrous nature in the Philippines' (Green Asia: Ecocultures, Sustainable Lifestyles and Ethical Consumption).

Patrick Regoniel served more than thirty-two years in Philippine government, twenty-four years at Palawan State University. He held several key positions in the university including as Vice President for Research and Extension and Chair of the Bids and Awards Committee. He finished his PhD in Environmental Science at the University of the Philippines Los Baños. His professional interests include coral reef assessment, restoration and management; ecosystem modeling; and economic valuation of environmental and natural resources. He has advanced knowledge and skills in the use of statistical software, systems modeling software like Vensim, Stella, and Socioecological Socio-Ecological App for Mental Model Elicitation (SESAMME), LaTeX typesetting system using LyX as interface, search engine optimization and data analytics, a working knowledge of Quantum Geographic Information System (QGIS), among others. Prof. Regoniel authored two books and three e-books, several project reports and refereed journal articles, and hundreds of online educational articles hosted in simplyeducate.me and other online writing platforms.

Nelly I. Mendoza is Associate Professor at the College of Business and Accountancy at Palawan State University teaching Business and Economics subjects. She finished her Bachelor of Science in Agriculture major in Agricultural Economics at the University of the Philippines at Los Banos. She finished her Master of Business Administration at the International Academy of Management and Economics and completed two post-graduate degrees: Doctor of Business Administration at the American Heritage University and Ph.D. in Management at Akamai University. She formerly worked as the director of Planning, Monitoring, and Evaluation, then the director of Budget and Finance. Currently, she is serving as the chief finance officer of the University. Her area of interest runs from agriculture, marine biodiversity, environmental economics and business economics particularly on the economic aspect. She has published some articles on these topics in local and international publications.

Melissa Theodora U. Macasaet works for the City Government of Puerto Princesa as City Government Department Head II with the designation of City Agriculturist II. She finished her Bachelor of Science in Agriculture degree from the University of the Philippines at Los Banos in 1988 and is a Registered Agriculturist with the Professional Regulatory Commission. She took up graduate courses in Public Administration and Environmental Management to supplement her knowledge in governance and management of agricultural resources including fisheries in Puerto Princesa. She headed the Internal Audit and Quality Management Representative. She has implemented agriculture and fisheries related projects for the City with funding from the Department of Agriculture and international organizations such as United States Agency for International Development Strengthening Urban

Resilience with Growth and Equity, United Nations Development Fund, United Nations Educational, Scientific and Cultural Organization, Asian Development Bank and World Bank.

Fred Precillas is Assistant Professor of Anthropology at the University of the Philippines Los Baños. He finished a bachelor's degree in fine arts major in studio arts painting cum laude at the College of Fine Arts and holds a master's degree in Anthropology at the College of Social Sciences and Philosophy, both received from the University of the Philippines-Diliman. His research interests are in the areas of Internet or Smartphone-Mediated Communication, Visual, Socio-Cultural and Biological Anthropology. He is using the smartphone ethnography in his researches which is an emerging methodology in social sciences. He is a former faculty of Fine Arts at the University of the Philippines-Baguio and a former faculty of the Department of Sociology at the University of Santo Tomas

Mark Anthony Alindogan is a program evaluation specialist with a background in health, international aid, and disaster response. He received his Master of Public Health degree from the University of the Philippines and is currently completing Master of Evaluation from the University of Melbourne. He has worked in various post-disaster recovery programs in the Philippines, not just in an evaluation capacity but also in disaster needs assessments, program design and implementation. Most notable is his involvement in the rapid assessment and response during Typhoon Haiyan where he was part of a small multinational team sent to Panay Island a few days after the typhoon's landfall. He was also part of an evaluation team for a post-disaster recovery program implemented by a consortium of local and international NGOs after the 2013 Bohol earthquake. Anthony participated in the Brown International Advanced Research Institutes as a fellow under the Human Security and Humanitarian Response institute in 2014. He also has several conference papers on the use of mobile data collection systems during disaster response and on the Philippine disaster management system. He currently works as a Research and Evaluation Officer for Latrobe Community Health Service which operates in Victoria and Western Australia. He is involved in programs related to health promotion, alcohol, and other drug services, and the National Disability Insurance Scheme.

Zbigniew Norbert Piepiora is a doctor of economic sciences and a Polish environmental economist. He is a graduate of Wroclaw University of Economics and currently serves as an adjunct professor at the Department of Spatial Economics in Wroclaw University of Environmental and Life Sciences. On the basis of his PhD thesis (2009), he published a book entitled the

'Economic aspects of the local natural disasters policy' (2012). He stated that the current natural disasters policy on the local level doesn't allow to counteract the negative consequences of natural disasters. In 2019, he published his post-doc book. It was entitled the "Economic efficiency of structural flood protection in Poland." He defined an economic efficiency of structural flood protection. In 2014, he participated in Brown University's the Brown International Advanced Research Institutes (BIARI). He was a speaker, facilitator, and session host during the 2018 BIARI Philippines: Community Resilience for Natural Disasters held in Holy Angel University. In 2015, he became a fellow of University of Hradec Králové and the Krkonoše Mountains National Park in Czechia. His current research focuses on economic aspects of natural disasters and emergency management such as economic efficiency of structural flood protection, financing of catastrophic damage removal, valuation of environment, safety and landscape. His research interests result from the fact that his town—Kowary in Poland—was affected by the great flood when he was fifteen years old.

Oliver Belarga is currently Associate Professor teaching social science courses at Kansai University, Japan. His research interests lie in disaster risk education, civil society participation, climate change adaptation focusing on community resilience, indigenous knowledge, and community involvement. Oliver was a BIARI (Brown University International Advanced Research Institute) Fellow on Human Security and Humanitarian Response Cluster in 2014. He also completed the University of Tokyo`s Global Leadership Program (2015) with a project focusing on disaster preparedness particularly on creating detailed warning signals during extreme weather events at the Republic of Palau's national emergency management office (Palau NEMO). He also made contributions to several fieldwork projects assessing the activities of several NGOs' disaster management programs for people with disabilities in Japan, Korea, and Taiwan. Oliver is presently spearheading a training project with the High Commission of Canada in the Micronesian Pacific: strengthening the ability of young people to participate in disaster risk reduction efforts through disaster preparedness training, workshops, and a simulated disaster drill specifically designed for school children. This continuing project is in collaboration with grass-root civil society organizations functioning in Palau (2017), Marshall Islands (2018), Nauru (2019), Solomon Islands (2019) and Kiribati (2020). He earned his doctoral degree from the Graduate School of Human Sciences, Osaka, University, Japan.

Emmanuel M. Luna is Professor of Community Development at the College of Social Work and Community Development, University of the Philippines Diliman and the Education Director of the UP Resilience Institute. He is a licensed environmental planner and a Fellow at the Philippine Institute of Environmental Planners. Dr. Luna is Co-Editor of the Disaster Prevention and Management International Journal, published by Emerald and indexed in Scopus. He finished BS Community Development in 1979 as cum laude, MA and PhD in Urban and Regional Planning in 1986 and 2000, respectively, all in UP Diliman. He was also a United Nations Fellow at the United Nations Center for Regional Development in Nagoya, Japan from November 1989 to May 1990. Dr. Luna has been in the field of disaster management and disaster risk reduction (DRR) and management since 1990 when the Central Luzon earthquake hit the communities he was working with in Nueva Ecija. His researches and publications are in the areas of community-based disaster risk reduction and management, disasters and education, local and indigenous knowledge in DRR, disaster accountability platforms and disaster recovery in infrastructures. He now sits in the Board of Trustees of the Center for Disaster Preparedness and Operation Compassion and represents the CSWCD as one of the conveners of the Disaster Risk Reduction Network Philippines (DRRNet).

Rosalie T. Quilicol is Assistant Professor and former Chairperson of the Department of Social Work, at the College of Social Work and Community Development, and a Junior Fellow at the UP-Resilience Institute of the University of the Philippines-Diliman. She finished her Bachelor of Science in Social Work (Cum Laude) and Master of Social Work degrees from the University of the Philippines-Diliman. She is a member of the Pi Gamma Mu International Social Science Honor Society. Currently, she is pursuing Doctor of Social Development at University of the Philippines-Diliman. Her engagement in disaster risk reduction and resilience work started with her active involvement in the Disaster Risk Reduction and Management Committee of the College of Social Work and Community Development and in the initiatives of UP Diliman Padayon Office on disaster risk reduction. In 2017, she was a full scholar of the Advanced Institute on Knowledge-Based Actions for Disaster Risk Reduction in Taiwan. She was a recipient of the 2018 BIARI Philippine Fellowship on Community Resilience for Natural Disaster.

Victor G. Obedicen has interests in disaster risk management study on both academic and personal context. Growing up in Central Luzon during the 1990s, he had personally experienced some of the worst disaster events in Philippine history such as the 1990 Luzon earthquake and the Mount Pinatubo Eruption. Mr. Obedicen is a graduate of BS Community Development and Masters in Community Development at the College of Social Work and Community Development, and is currently taking up Doctor in Social Development. At present he is teaching both undergraduate and graduate classes in the areas of Community Organizing, Community Planning and Community Based Disaster Risk Reduction Management. He has been involved in Disaster Risk Management in various capacities since 2004.

Pamela Gloria Cajilig is a cultural anthropologist, design researcher, and women's advocate with two decades of qualitative research experience at the intersection of fields such as disaster, urban design, community and maternal health, violence against women (VAW), and strategic communication. She is currently pursuing a postgraduate research degree under the Humanitarian Architecture Research Bureau of RMIT University's School of Architecture and Urban Design. Her doctoral research is oriented toward developing a more-than-human view of citizen design within post-disaster housing reconstruction in Philippine communities affected by Typhoon Yolanda (Haiyan). This was inspired by her work as a humanitarian shelter researcher in the immediate aftermath of the same catastrophe. Pamela is the founding President and Executive Research Director of Curiosity, a design strategy firm that draws upon local insight to work with the private sector, NGOs, and government agencies in developing more meaningful services. She also cofounded Manila Urban Design, a social media and events platform that gathers built environment practitioners, residents, students, academics, and artists to discuss how life in Metro Manila can become more livable. Pamela serves as Advisor to NGOs working in the fields of maternal health and women's livelihood and education, and regularly shares critical reflection of her work through local and international publications, public presentations, training, and teaching.

Kathryn Francis is Lecturer in Psychology in the Faculty of Management, Law and Social Sciences at the University of Bradford, United Kingdom. Kathryn's research in moral psychology examines the way in which people make moral decisions across different contexts. She is interested in the interplay between people's moral judgments and their actions and also the role of pro- and anti-social traits in driving moral behavior. Kathryn's research interests also extend to other areas of experimental philosophy including epistemology. Much of her research is interdisciplinary in nature, incorporating methods and approaches from the sciences (cognitive psychology, psychopharmacology, and neuroscience) and the arts and humanities (philosophy, art and design). Her work has been published in psychology-specific journals (British Journal of Psychology), general science journals (PLOSOne, Scientific Reports), and philosophy journals (Ergo, Episteme). Kathryn completed her PhD in a multiple disciplinary program, CogNovo, at the University of Plymouth, United Kingdom and she previously worked as a Postdoctoral Research Fellow in psychology and philosophy at the University of Reading,

United Kingdom. Kathryn is a member of several interdisciplinary research groups including The CogNovo Foundation, CINNergies, and iCog.

Diego S. Maranan is a transdisciplinary artist and researcher who investigates how technology can help us reimagine our relationship with the environment, with other people, and with ourselves. His work is eclectic, ranging from exploring how digital technologies are changing the way we move as well as perceive human movement, to co-creating socially engaged art installations that build symbiotic relationships between plants, computers, and people. He is Assistant Professor at the Faculty of Information and Communication Studies at the University of the Philippines Open University (fics.upou.edu.ph); cofounded Curiosity (www.curiosity.ph), a Manila-based design strategy firm that helps businesses, NGOs, and government design meaningful services; co-initiated the CogNovo research network for Cognitive Innovation (www.cognovo.org); and cofounded SEADS (www.sead.network), an international transdisciplinary network of artists, scientists, engineers, and activists who reimagine and reshape the future through critical inquiry and hands-on experimentation.

Fernanda Claudio is a medical anthropologist who works as Curriculum Lead, Postgraduate Medical Education at McGill University. In her current position, she provides educational support to residency programs within the McGill University Health Centers. Fernanda completed her PhD at the London School of Economics and has researched and worked in Canada, the United Kingdom, Zimbabwe, and Australia. Her areas of specialty include global health, international development, and educational design. Dr. Claudio formerly taught at the University of Queensland where she designed and developed courses in medical anthropology, global health, health research methods, development effectiveness, and impact assessment. She received a Highly Commended for Teaching Excellence Award, Faculty of Humanities and Social Science, The University of Queensland in 2016. Dr. Claudio has published on global health, vulnerable populations, international development, and ethnography. Her current focus is on translating ethnographic approaches to curriculum design in postgraduate medical education. Dr. Claudio has leadership experience as former President of the African Studies Association of Australasia and the Pacific, and Board Member of Hubbard's School in Brisbane, Australia. She is a member of the international editorial boards of the journals Diversite Urbaine (Montreal) and Journal of Social Health (Philippines).

M. Adil Khan is Honorary Professor of Development Practice at the School of Social Science, University of Queensland, Brisbane (Australia). He is also former Chief of Socio-Economic Governance and Management Branch of the Division for Public Administration and Development Management of the United Nations Department of Economic and Social Affairs (UNDESA), New York. Prof. Khan possesses more than forty years of experience in international development and public policy and held senior policy-level positions in a developing country government; at the United Nations (country offices and at the UN secretariat in New York) and in academia; and worked as a consultant for the World Bank, the Asian Development Bank, AusAid and the UNDP; a periodic visiting professor at the Kyung Hee University Seoul, Korea (2005–2008) where he introduced the Graduate Certificate Course, *Global Governance and UN Development Agenda: The Case of East Asia*; Harvard University, University of Pennsylvania (USA), Ottawa University (Canada), Canada School of Public Service, BRAC University (Bangladesh), KU Leuven (Belgium). Prof. Khan has published extensively on issues of poverty, social development, and participatory governance. He is on the editorial board of several international journals and the founding/editor-in-chief of the journal, *Sustainable Development*. He is the Principal Author of the 2008 UN World Public Sector Report, *"People Matter: Civic Engagement in Public Governance"*. Prof. Khan holds a Master's degree in Economics, a Master's Degree in Social Planning and Development and a PhD in Political Economy.

Liezl Riosa is a Policy Specialist for the World Wide Fund for Nature Philippines. She is currently working with various national agencies and local governments in the Philippines on crafting policies that promote sustainable food consumption and production. Riosa was a recipient of the Australia Awards scholarship. She has a Master's degree in Development Practice from the University of Queensland. Among her most memorable postgraduate tasks were profiling and visioning of Southeast Queensland's most culturally diverse suburb; creating a support group for international students in her master's program; and writing about heart-wrenching struggles of the developing world. She worked for the Philippine Congress for eight years. She handled internal and external communications for the Majority Leader from 2007 to 2010. From 2010 to 2015, she was part of the committee technical support where she published reports on the status and development of legislative measures; researched on and analyzed both pending and enacted bills; and co-drafted an editorial stylebook.

Ladylyn Lim Mangada is Associate Professor in Political Science at UP Visayas Tacloban College, Philippines. She was former Associate Dean of the College. Her researches and published works are on local politics, community-driven development, governance, and disaster risk reduction.

Irma Ranola Tan is Assistant Professor in Communication at UP Visayas Tacloban College. She is currently the College Secretary. As a communication specialist, she is being tapped by local educational institutions as trainer in English language and literacy courses. In 2011, she received a Special Citation from the Province of Leyte for the Literacy Training Program conducted for six months among the Manobos in Tacloban City.

John Christian Cabasal Valeroso is a licensed Senior High School teacher at the University of Santo Tomas where he teaches subjects on social sciences. He is a graduate of a double degree program, AB- BSE Major in Social Sciences and Social Studies from the University of Santo Tomas; MA in Development Studies with the thesis entitled *Reaching out the Unreached: A qualitative assessment of the quality and accessibility aspects of the project Applied Academic for Excellence* and was graded as Benemeritus by UST Graduate School. He's currently taking his post-graduate studies, PHD in Development Studies from the same university. He was part of the exchange student teacher's program of the University of Santo Tomas—Hanyang University (South Korea) from 2007–2008.

Alain Jomarie G. Santos is a Certified Public Accountant and is an assistant professor at the University of Santo Tomas Faculty of Arts and Letters where he teaches Accounting, Economics, Computer Applications, Business and Management subjects. He earned his MBA and Accounting Degree both from the University of Santo Tomas and is currently a PhD Economics Candidate from the UST Graduate School where he will be defending his dissertation titled "Economic Resiliency Model for Floating Communities: Disaster Mitigation in the Philippines."

Zosimo Membrebe is the Chair of the University of Santo Tomas Senior High School Accountancy, Business and Management Strand, where he is teaching Business Enterprise Simulation. He earned his Bachelor of Arts in Economics and Master of Arts in Economics from the University of Santo Tomas. He completed the academic units for PhD Economics program at UST Graduate School. He has also made presentations at different international conferences in the Philippines, Thailand, Indonesia and China. He served as a co-author in environmental related research in both local and international journals. He is also a member of the Philippine Society in the Study of Nature and an incoming President of the Rotary Club of Kamuning East—Rotary International District 3780.

Arlen Angelada Ancheta has a PhD in Environmental Science. She is Professor at the Faculty of Arts and Letters and the Graduate School of the University of Santo Tomas. She has been Director (2012–2015) of the Research Center on Culture, Education and Social Issues (RCCESI), UST; and current Vice President Internal of Mother Earth Foundation (MEF), an NGO advocating community-based solid waste management. Dr. Ancheta is very active in environmental organizations as Vice President (2015–2017) of the Philippine Network for Environmental Educators (PNEE) and President (2017–2019) of the Philippine Society for the Study of Nature (PSSN). Her area of specialization is community-based resource management. Researches and publications include climate change, solid waste management, zero waste, tidal stream management, urban forest park, and street children. She has researches on constructing disaster among the locals in urban coastal community along Manila Bay and resilience in Pamarawan, Bulacan.

Dan Angelo Balita is a licensed secondary high school teacher at Paete Science And Business College. He graduated with a bachelor's degree in Sociology from the University of Santo Tomas after completing his thesis on children's perspectives on flooding in an informal settlement in Manila. He served as a research assistant (2014–2015) to the Manila Bay project funded by the Philippine's Commission on Higher Education (CHED). He is currently completing a diploma in teaching at the Laguna State Polytechnic University.

Clarence M Batan, PhD is a Filipino sociologist, Professor at the Faculty of Arts and Letters, and Research Associate of the Research Center for Social Sciences and Education (RCSSED) at the University of Santo Tomas (UST), Manila, Philippines. He obtained his AB in Sociology from UST; MA in Sociology from the University of the Philippines-Diliman; and PhD in Sociology from Dalhousie University at Nova Scotia, Canada. His research interests are sociology of childhood and youth, sociology of work and employment, and qualitative and mixed methods. He was Vice President for Asia of the Research Committee 34—Sociology of Youth of the International Sociological Association (2014–2018); former President of the Philippine Sociological Society (2017–2018); and a member of the Technical Committee for Sociology of the Philippine Commission of Higher Education. His dissertation on "istambays" at Dalhousie University (PhD Sociology, 2010) in Halifax, Nova Scotia, Canada, and his further research trainings at Brown University (Research Fellow, 2012; Visiting Fellow for International Studies, 2013) at Providence, Rhode Island, United States, generated a novel conceptual and methodological approach to understanding the phenomenon of "waithood" among Filipinos caught and intertwined along education-employment structural difficulties. At present, Dr. Batan leads a multi-million grant, The National Catechetical Study 2021: Pastoral Action Research and

Intervention Project commissioned by the Catholic Bishops' Conference in the Philippines–Episcopal Commission on Catechesis and Catholic Education to understand the state and condition of catechetical ministry in the country.

Tara Zaksaite is a post-doctoral research associate at the University of Plymouth, United Kingdom. She is working on project ExSpaND (Exploring Spatial Navigational Differences), which is a three-year, ESRC-funded project looking at individual differences in everyday navigation. To examine the causes and correlates of strengths and difficulties with navigation, she is collecting data from both typical adults and a patient group which has been known to struggle with navigation—people with hydrocephalus. She completed her PhD at the University of Plymouth, as part of the CogNovo programme. Her research interests include attention, learning, memory, and how these are affected by individual differences (e.g., in anxiety). She is also interested in how we can apply insights from experimental laboratory experiments to impact real-life outcomes.

Ingram Content Group UK Ltd.
Milton Keynes UK
UKHW020710170423
420292UK00015B/731